Transforming Visions

Princeton Theological Monograph Series

K. C. Hanson, Charles M. Collier, and D. Christopher Spinks,
Series Editors

Recent volumes in the series:

Linda Hogan
Religion and the Politics of Peace and Conflict

Chris Budden
Following Jesus in Invaded Space: Doing Theology on Aboriginal Land

Jeff B. Pool
*God's Wounds: Hermeneutic of the Christian Symbol of
Divine Suffering, Volume One: Divine Vulnerability and Creation*

Lisa E. Dahill
*Reading from the Underside of Selfhood:
Bonhoeffer and Spiritual Formation*

Samuel A. Paul
*The Ubuntu God: Deconstructing a South African Narrative
of Oppression*

Jeanne M. Hoeft
*Agency, Culture, and Human Personhood: Pastoral Thelogy
and Intimate Partner Violence*

Ryan A. Neal
*Theology as Hope: On the Ground and Implications
of Jürgen Moltmann's Doctrine of Hope*

Scott A. Ellington
Risking Truth: Reshaping the World through Prayers of Lament

Transforming Visions

Transformations of Text, Tradition, and Theology in Ezekiel

Edited by
WILLIAM A. TOOMAN
and MICHAEL A. LYONS

Foreword by Marvin A. Sweeney

☙PICKWICK *Publications* · Eugene, Oregon

TRANSFORMING VISIONS
Transformations of Text, Tradition, and Theology in Ezekiel

Princeton Theological Monograph Series 127

Copyright © 2010 Wipf and Stock Publishers. All rights reserved. Except for brief quotations in critical publications or reviews, no part of this book may be reproduced in any manner without prior written permission from the publisher. Write: Permissions, Wipf and Stock Publishers, 199 W. 8th Ave., Suite 3, Eugene, OR 97401.

Pickwick Publications
An imprint of Wipf and Stock Publishers
199 W. 8th Ave., Suite 3
Eugene, OR 97401

www.wipfandstock.com

ISBN 13: 978-1-55635-285-0

Cataloging-in-Publication data

    Transforming visions : transformations of text, tradition, and theology in Ezekiel / edited by William A. Tooman and Michael A. Lyons, with a Foreword by Marvin A. Sweeney.

    Princeton Theological Monograph Series 127

    xxvi + 350 p. ; 23 cm. —Includes bibliographical references and index.

    ISBN 13: 978-1-55635-285-0

    1. Bible. O.T. Ezekiel—Criticism, interpretation, etc. I. Tooman, William A. II. Lyons, Michael A. III. Sweeney, Marvin A. (Marvin Alan), 1953-. IV. Title. V. Series.

BS1545.52 T65 2010

Manufactured in the U.S.A.

Contents

Contributors / vii

Acknowledgments / ix

Abbreviations / x

Foreword—Marvin A. Sweeney / *xv*

PART ONE: Transformation of Antecedent Texts in Ezekiel

1. Transformation of Law: Ezekiel's Use of the Holiness Code (Leviticus 17–26)—Michael A. Lyons / 1

2. Transformation of Pentateuchal Descriptions of Idolatry—Tova Ganzel / 33

3. Transformation of Israel's Hope: The Reuse of Scripture in the Gog Oracles—William A. Tooman / 50

PART TWO: Transformation of Tradition and Theology in Ezekiel

4. Transformation of the Image—Jill Middlemas / 113

5. Ezekiel and Moral Transformation—Paul M. Joyce / 139

6. Transformation of History in Ezekiel 20—Thomas Krüger / 159

7. Transforming the International *status quo:* Ezekiel's Oracles against the Nations—Paul R. Raabe / 187

8. Transformation of Royal Ideology in Ezekiel—Daniel I. Block / 208

PART THREE: **Transformation of Ezekiel in the Versions and New Testament**

9   Transformation in Ezekiel's Textual History: Ezekiel 7 in the Masoretic Text and the Septuagint
    —Timothy Mackie / 249

10 Transformation of Ezekiel in John's Revelation
    —Beate Kowalski / 279

Index of Scripture / 313

Index of Authors / 345

Contributors

Daniel I. Block
Wheaton College Graduate School

Tova Ganzel
Bar-Ilan University

Paul M. Joyce
St. Peter's College, Oxford University

Beate Kowalski
Institut für Katholische Theologie,
Technische Universität Dortmund

Thomas Krüger
University of Zurich

Michael A. Lyons
Simpson University

Timothy Mackie
University of Wisconsin—Madison

Jill Middlemas
Århus University

Paul R. Raabe
Concordia Seminary

William A. Tooman
University of St. Andrews

Acknowledgments

Thanks are due, first of all, to Prof. Michael V. Fox, who first introduced both of us to the book of Ezekiel. He is a model scholar, patient, meticulous, and wise. This volume is dedicated to him. All our contributors graciously gave of their time and energy to make this project possible. Many of them are scholars whom we read and studied when we were students and whom we will continue to read throughout our academic careers. It is a great privilege to be able to collaborate with them. The editors at Pickwick Publications were gracious, even when we ran past our deadlines. For their acceptance of the project and their care in bringing it to fruition, we are grateful.

William Tooman would also like to acknowledge the financial support provided by Edgewood College in the form of several research grants, and for the unflagging support of the chair of Religious Studies, John Leonard. John has always exceeded his duties to find ways to support my research and writing. I owe him a deep debt. My greatest debt, however, is to Tricia, my wife, companion, and friend. Without her I would be lost.

Michael Lyons would like to acknowledge the financial support provided by Simpson University in the form of the Dale Scholar Grant. I would also like to express my appreciation for my department chair David Strong for his encouragement and support. Finally, my deepest thanks go to my wife Diane and our daughter Rianne for their support of my research.

Michael A. Lyons
Simpson University

William A. Tooman
University of St. Andrews

Abbreviations

AB	Anchor Bible
AHW	*Akkadisches Handwörterbuch*. 3 vols. Wolfram von Soden, 1965–81
ANET	*Ancient Near Eastern Texts Relating to the Old Testament*. Edited by James B. Pritchard. 3rd ed. 1969
ARAB	*Ancient Records of the Assyrians and Babylonians*. 2 vols. Daniel David Luckenbill, 1926–27
ASTI	*Annual of the Swedish Theological Institute*
ATD	Das Alte Testamant Deutsch
AUSS	*Andrews University Seminary Studies*
BBB	Bonner biblische Beiträge
BETL	Bibliotheca Ephemerides theologicae lovanienses
BHTh	Beiträge zur historischen Theologie
Bib	*Biblica*
BibSac	*Bibliotheca Sacra*
BibIntSer	Biblical Interpretation Series
BiOr	Biblica et Orientalia
BJRL	*Bulletin of the John Rylands Library, Manchester*
BZ	*Biblische Zeitschrift*
BZAW	Beihefte zur Zeitschrift für die alttestamentliche Wissenschaft
BZAW	Beihefte zur Zeitschrift für die neutestamentliche Wissenschaft

CAD	*The Assyrian Dictionary of the Oriental Institute of the University of Chicago.* 1956–
CahRB	Cahiers de la Revue Biblique
CBQ	*Catholic Biblical Quarterly*
CBQMS	Catholic Biblical Quarterly Monograph Series
CBOT	Coniectanea biblica: Old Testament
COS	*The Context of Scripture.* 3 vols. Edited by William W. Hallo et al. 1997, 2000, 2002
CRBS	*Critical Reviews: Biblical Studies*
CTA	*Corpus des tablettes en cuneiforms alphabétiques découvertes à Ras Shamra-Ugarit de 1929 à 1939.* Edited by A. Herdner, 1963
DJD	Discoveries in the Judaean Desert
DSD	*Dead Sea Discoveries*
ETL	*Ephemerides theologicae lovanienses*
FAT	Forschungen zum Alten Testament
FOTL	The Forms of Old Testament Literature
FRLANT	Forschungen zur Religion und Literatur des Alten und Neuen Testaments
FzB	Forschung zur Bibel
HAR	*Hebrew Annual Review*
HAT	Handkommentar zum Alten Testament
HSM	Harvard Semitic Monographs
HSS	Harvard Semitic Studies
HTR	*Harvard Theological Review*
HUCA	*Hebrew Union College Annual*
IBS	*Irish Biblical Studies*
IBT	Interpreting Biblical Texts

ICC	International Critical Commentary
IEJ	*Israel Exploration Journal*
Int	*Interpretation*
JAOS	*Journal of the American Oriental Society*
JBL	*Journal of Biblical Literature*
JJS	*Journal of Jewish Studies*
JNES	*Journal of Near Eastern Studies*
JQR	*Jewish Quarterly Review*
JSNTSup	Journal for the Study of the New Testament Supplement Series
JSOT	*Journal for the Study of the Old Testament*
JSOTSup	Journal for the Study of the Old Testament Supplement Series
JSPSup	Journal for the Study of the Pseudepigrapha Supplement Series
KAT	Kommentar zum Alten Testament
KHC	Kurzer Hand-Commentar zum Alten Testament
LHBOTS	Library of Hebrew Bible/Old Testament Studies
LXX	Septuagint
MT	Masoretic text
NCBC	New Century Bible Commentary
Neot	*Neotestamentica*
NICOT	New International Commentary on the Old Testament
NTS	*New Testament Studies*
OBO	Orbis biblicus et orientalis
OBT	Overtures to Biblical Theology
OTL	Old Testament Library
OTM	Oxford Theological Monographs

OtSt	Oudtestamentische Studiën
PEQ	*Palestine Exploration Quarterly*
PittsTMS	Pittsburgh Theological Monograph Series
RevQ	*Revue de Qumran*
SBB	Stuttgarter biblische Beiträge
SBFLA	*Studii biblici Franciscani liber annus*
SBLDS	Society of Biblical Literature Dissertation Series
SBLMS	Society of Biblical Literature Monograph Series
SBLSymS	Society of Biblical Literature Symposium Series
SBT	Studies in Biblical Theology
SDSSRL	Studies in the Dead Sea Scrolls and Related Literature
SHBC	Smyth & Helwys Bible Commentary
StBibLit	Studies in Biblical Literature
STDJ	Studies on the Texts of the Desert of Judah
TSAJ	Texte und Studien zum antiken Judentum
TWNT	*Theologische Wörterbuch zum Neuen Testament*
TWAT	*Theologische Wörterbuch zum Alten Testament*
UF	*Ugarit-Forschungen*
VT	*Vetus Testamentum*
VTSup	Vetus Testamentum Supplements
WBC	Word Biblical Commentary
WMANT	Wissenschaftliche Monographien zum Alten und Neuen Testament
WUNT	Wissenschaftliche Untersuchungen zum New Testament
YOS	Yale Oriental Series
ZAW	*Zeitschrift für die alttestamentliche Wissenschaft*
ZThK	*Zeitschrift für Theologie und Kirche*
ZNW	*Zeitschrift für die neutestamentliche Wissenschaft und die Kunde der älteren Kirche*

Foreword

Marvin A. Sweeney

EZEKIEL IS HARDLY A NORMAL PROPHET NOR IS THE BOOK OF EZEKIEL a normal prophetic book. The book is filled with bizarre imagery, language, and concepts, such as the inaugural vision of YHWH's throne chariot borne through the heavens by four "creatures" in Ezekiel 1–3 later identified as Cherubim in Ezekiel 10; the portrayal of Ezekiel's supernatural journey to witness the destruction of Jerusalem and the Temple in Ezekiel 8–11 by the command of YHWH; or the enigmatic Gog from Magog oracles from Ezekiel 38–39 with their imagery of burning corpses. Such imagery presupposes a priestly mythological worldview that often confounds modern interpreters. Working especially under the influence of Julius Wellhausen's antagonism to priestly theology, practice, and literature, early scholars attempted to deny Ezekiel's priestly identity or to declare the entire book to be a late forgery designed to serve priestly interests. Thus, Gustav Hölscher argued that the work of the ecstatic prophet, Ezekiel ben Buzi, had been heavily edited by priestly circles, and stripped away more than eighty percent of the book in an effort to recover what he considered to be the authentic oracles of the true prophet.[1] Charles Cutler Torrey took the argument a step further by declaring that the entire book was a forgery written by priestly circles during the Hellenistic period in an effort to condemn the Seleucid monarchy by establishing an analogy with the purportedly sinful monarch, King Manasseh ben Hezekiah of Judah.[2] Even today, interpreters struggle with Ezekiel's language, concepts, and imagery, sometimes prompting a rekindling of earlier charges that Ezekiel suffered from mental illness or drug use.[3]

---

1. Gustav Hölscher, *Hesekiel, der Dichter und das Buch: Eine literarkritische Untersuchung*, BZAW 39 (Giessen: Töpelmann, 1924).

2. Charles Cutler Torrey, *Pseudo-Ezekiel and the Original Prophecy*, YOS 18 (1930; reprint, New York: Ktav, 1970).

3. E.g., David J. Halperin, *Seeking Ezekiel: Text and Psychology* (University Park: Pennsylvania State University, 1993) esp. 7–38.

But modern critical scholarship has come a long way since the early twentieth century. Scholarly interpretation of the book of Ezekiel began to change in the years following World War II as scholars began to probe the book and to develop reading strategies for engaging the complexities of its distinctive forms of expression, literary development, and theological worldview. Georg Fohrer employed tradition-historical tools to argue that Ezekiel was indeed an exilic prophet who spoke to Jews in exile, but that later tradents shaped the book into a priestly work that addressed the people of Jerusalem and Judah.[4] Walter Zimmerli employed a combination of form- and tradition-critical tools to demonstrate the unique speech forms employed by the prophet and to trace the process of later interpretation in the book by the prophet's disciples who were themselves steeped in the priestly traditions of the Pentateuch.[5] Moshe Greenberg set aside tradition-historical research to focus on a holistic reading of the book that would demand the apprehension of the book as a whole—as well as its theological worldview—as a basis for understanding its presentation of the prophet and his message.[6] Ellen Davis emphasizes the impact of the textualization of the prophet's words as an essential aspect of the process by which Ezekiel's tradents interpreted the master's words.[7] Katheryn Pfisterer Darr employs literary tools to engage Ezekiel's message and to raise questions concerning the theological message of the book in the aftermath of the Shoah.[8] And my own work emphasizes the priestly character of Ezekiel's visionary experience and worldview as a basis for attempting to apprehend the holiness of G-d and creation and to grapple with the theological questions posed by the destruction of Jerusalem.[9] Today,

---

4. Georg Fohrer, *Die Hauptprobleme des Buches Ezechiel*, BZAW 72 (Berlin: Töpelmann, 1952); Fohrer, with Kurt Galling, *Ezechiel*, HAT 13 (Tübingen: Mohr/Siebeck, 1955).

5. Walther Zimmerli, *Ezekiel*, 2 vols., Hermeneia (Philadelphia: Fortress, 1979–83; German original, 1969).

6. Moshe Greenberg, *Ezekiel 1–20*, AB 22 (Garden City, NY: Doubleday, 1983); Greenberg, *Ezekiel 21–37*, AB 22A (Garden City, NY: Doubleday, 1997).

7. Ellen F. Davis, *Swallowing the Scroll: Textuality and the Dynamics of Discourse in Ezekiel*, JSOTSup 144 (Sheffield: JSOT Press, 1989).

8. Katheryn Pfisterer Darr, "The Book of Ezekiel," in L. E. Keck et al., eds., *The New Interpreter's Bible* (Nashville: Abingdon, 2001) 6:1073–1607.

9. Marvin A. Sweeney, "Ezekiel: Zadokite Priest and Visionary Prophet of the Exile," in *Form and Intertextuality in the Prophetic and Apocalyptic Literature*, FAT

scholars take Ezekiel quite seriously, and a host of commentaries and studies—and even a thriving program unit in the Society of Biblical Literature—demonstrate the importance of the book of Ezekiel in contemporary biblical scholarship.[10]

The present volume, edited by two rising Ezekiel scholars, Michael A. Lyons and William A. Tooman, makes a substantive contribution to the burgeoning discussion of the book of Ezekiel by emphasizing the theme of transformation, understood in relation to the text of Ezekiel, the traditions on which it draws and by which it developed, and its theological perspectives. Each essay engages a different aspect of the study of the book, and thereby opens and advances scholarly dialog in its own right.

Michael A. Lyons, "Transformation of Law: Ezekiel's Use of the Holiness Code (Leviticus 17–26)," examines the continuing problem of Ezekiel's intertextual relationship with the so-called Holiness Code of Leviticus 17–26. Based on observations of shared terminology between Ezekiel and the Holiness Code, scholars have long agreed that some interrelationship exists, although they have disagreed as to the nature of the interrelationship. Does Ezekiel make use of H? Does H make use of Ezekiel? Or do the two works simply share terminology? Lyons examines the shared locutions and argues that Ezekiel makes use of a preexisting body of material in the Holiness Code. Such an argument has important implications for recognizing—against Wellhausen and his followers—that priestly literature had already been composed at the outset of the exilic period and that it was therefore possible for a priest like Ezekiel to develop his prophetic self-consciousness on the basis of

---

45 (Tübingen: Mohr Siebeck, 2005) 125–43; Sweeney, *The Prophetic Literature*, IBT (Nashville: Abingdon, 2005) 127–64; Sweeney, "Ezekiel's Debate with Isaiah," in *Congress Volume: Ljubljana 2007*, ed. André Lemaire, VTSup (Leiden: Brill, forthcoming).

10. E.g., Daniel I. Block, *Ezekiel*, NICOT (Grand Rapids: Eerdmans, 1997–98); Julie Galambush, *Jerusalem in the Book of Ezekiel: The City as YHWH's Wife*, SBLDS 130 (Atlanta: Scholars, 1992); Paul Joyce, *Ezekiel* (London: T. & T. Clark, 2008); Andrew Mein, *Ezekiel and the Ethics of Exile* (Oxford: Oxford University Press, 2001); Margaret S. Odell, *Ezekiel*, SHBC (Macon, GA: Smyth & Helwys, 2005); Karl-Friedrich Pohlmann, *Der Prophet Hesekiel/Ezechiel*, ATD 22, 1–2 (Göttingen: Vandenhoeck & Ruprecht, 1996–2001). For publications of the SBL program unit on Ezekiel, see Stephen L. Cook and Corrine L. Patton, eds., *Ezekiel's Hierarchical World*, SBLSymS 31 (Atlanta: Society of Biblical Literature, 2004); Margaret S. Odell and John T. Strong, eds., *The Book of Ezekiel: Theological and Anthropological Perspectives*, SBLSyms 9 (Atlanta: Society of Biblical Literature, 2000).

his own engagement with priestly literature. The Jerusalem Temple—and before that Shiloh and other temples—had stood for centuries as the major religious establishments of ancient Israel and Judah, and it would be shortsighted to assume that the priests who served in these temples developed no body of teachings prior to the exilic and post-exilic periods. Lyons' argument attempts to demonstrate that Ezekiel was doing what he was trained to do, viz., interact with, interpret, and teach a body of priestly tradition in relation to the needs and circumstances of his time (see Lev 10:10–11). But one must also ask, to what degree is Ezekiel's envisioned restoration not simply a restoration of Israel/Judah, but a restoration of creation at large? Temples, after all, were the holy centers of creation in the ancient world, and H's preoccupation with land and blood would have implications for a defiled creation that must be purified and restored.

Tova Ganzel, "Transformation of Pentateuchal Descriptions of Idolatry," likewise points to Ezekiel's interrelationship with Pentateuchal literature by arguing that the portrayals of idolatry in the book of Ezekiel are drawn from the portrayal of idolatry in the book of Deuteronomy. Scholars have long argued that the laws of Deuteronomy predate the exilic and post-exilic periods; perhaps they originated in the northern kingdom of Israel or in King Josiah's court. But Ganzel's argument raises an important insight, i.e., the role that Deuteronomic law plays in relation to the Jerusalemite priesthood. D and P are often viewed in modern scholarship as distinct spheres of legal literature. But Ganzel's model maintains that a figure like Ezekiel, identified as a priest originally from the Jerusalem Temple, would have access to the Deuteronomic law code and make use of it in formulating his own prophetic perspectives while in exile. Whatever its origins, the Deuteronomic law code would have been promulgated from the Jerusalem Temple itself. Would it then have been viewed as antagonistic to priestly law? Or does it point to the dynamism of ancient Israelite/Judean legal literature, in which new understandings of law are developed during the course of Israel's and Judah's history and applied to the needs of a dynamic living society? For a priest like Ezekiel, the various law codes available in ancient Jerusalem prior to the exile would have constituted another portion of the basis for his own reflection, interpretation, and teaching, especially since the reality of exile would have prompted reflection on the issue of idolatry or apostasy, which is such a concern in Deuteronomy.

William A. Tooman, "Transformation of Israel's Hope: The Reuse of Scripture in the Gog Oracles," argues that Ezekiel 38–39 display extensive interaction with other biblical literature, including the book of Ezekiel itself, which indicates that these chapters are a later addition to the book. Important *Vorbilder*, literary models or templates for the Gog oracles, appear in Ezek 28:25–26; Ezek 6:1–14; and Ps 79:1–4. A host of other texts also play important roles in the Gog oracles, e.g., the Balaam oracles of Numbers 22–24; the portrayal of the downfall of the Babylonian king (itself based on an Assyrian model!) in Isaiah 14; the portrayal of judgment against Hazor in Jeremiah 49; the presentation of world-wide destruction in Zephaniah 1, and others. Again, the intertextual elements of the book of Ezekiel come to the forefront demonstrating that the book is well informed by earlier tradition and literature. At this point, Ezekiel and his tradents emerge as interpreters not only of legal literature, but of a variety of genres, such as the Psalms (which play such an important role in the Temple liturgy) and even the book of Ezekiel itself. Such a study indicates a potential window into the origins of the phenomenon of inner-biblical interpretation, i.e., does it begin with the priesthood, which acts as the fundamental interpreter of tradition in ancient Israelite/Judean society? And does such a phenomenon not then identify the priesthood as the major creative and potentially progressive theologians of ancient Israel/Judah, not as a body interested in self-preservation as Wellhausen and his followers would have it? As for Tooman's contention that Ezekiel 38–39 is a later addition to Ezekiel, one must also observe that the Gog oracle plays an important role in the book, i.e., the burning and consumption of the corpses of Gog's army purifies the land and thereby makes it possible for the Temple to be restored in Ezekiel 40–48. Does the later character of Ezekiel 38–39 then point to a post-Ezekielian composition of the book? Or does Ezekiel 38–39 elaborate on the imagery of purification from corpse contamination evident in Ezekiel 37? Or perhaps it is the later work of the prophet/priest himself?

Jill Middlemas, "Transformation of the Image," focuses on the images of idolatry envisioned by Ezekiel, including such dimensions as the various images portrayed in his tour of the Jerusalem Temple at the time of its destruction; the personification of the city of Jerusalem as woman; and the image of YHWH presented throughout the book. Presupposing

Davis's argument concerning the textualization of Ezekiel,[11] she argues that the book displays a rhetorical strategy designed to create distance between divinity and forms. Indeed, she discusses Ezekiel's use of simile, with terms such as "as," "like," "image of," etc., as means to describe elements of divine presence while simultaneously protecting the sanctity of G-d by refusing to identity the Deity with any tangible imagery. Of course, such a strategy corresponds well with the symbolic character of the Jerusalem Temple itself, the features of which would symbolize creation, the Garden of Eden, the passage through the Red Sea, etc., and would well inform the theological worldview of a priest like Ezekiel who would have been raised and educated in the Jerusalem Temple. Her comments on the emergence of the divine word as representation of the Deity therefore are particularly important, i.e., words and the teachings and concepts that they convey then become the representations of divine presence in the world. In her view, Ezekiel's understanding of divine Torah presupposes that Torah serves as an image of YHWH or YHWH's word to Israel, and such an understanding informs the presentation of the laws of the Temple in the final vision of Ezekiel 40–48. But then we must ask, does the book of Ezekiel itself not then become divine Torah? And would not the same apply to any other prophetic book?[12] Or even the totality of sacred literature in the Bible? Such a contention has tremendous possibilities for opening up our understanding of the formation of sacred literature in ancient Israel/Judah.

Paul Joyce, "Ezekiel and Moral Transformation," rightly notes the problems in the common assertion that Ezekiel focuses especially on the moral responsibility of the individual in the presentation of ethical perspective in the book. Indeed, Ezekiel 18 points to the roles of the various generations represented by individuals in its articulation of moral responsibility for righteousness and wrong-doing. Modern interpreters have been especially influenced by the role that individualism plays in modern western philosophy and theology, but Ezekiel's theological worldview presupposes a far more corporate understanding of reality and moral action. But does this not entail a sense of corporate responsibility on the part of individuals to the whole? Joyce correctly

---

11. Davis, *Swallowing the Scroll*.

12. See my essay, "The Book of Isaiah as Prophetic Torah," in *New Visions of Isaiah*, ed. R. F. Melugin and M. A. Sweeney, JSOTSup 214 (Sheffield: Sheffield Academic, 1996) 50–67; reprinted in *Form and Intertextuality*, 13–27.

portrays Ezekiel's presentation of a theocentric view of creation, history, and ethics in which the dimensions of the holy emerge as fundamental reality in the book of Ezekiel. Recognition of the holiness of YHWH and of the divine name then becomes the means by which creation and Israel itself relate to YHWH in the midst of national or world-wide crisis and develop moral perspective in an effort to sanctify corporate and individual self as well as creation at large. But such a contention points to the multifaceted character of human moral responsibility within a larger web of relationships in Ezekiel that includes the human individual, the human nation, and creation at large as well as G-d. Human responsibility in Ezekiel must then be directed not simply from the human to G-d, but from the individual to the nation at large and from the nation to creation at large. When such relationships are realized, then one recognizes the import of the Self-Recognition formula in Ezekiel, "and they shall know that I am YHWH."

Thomas Krüger, "Transformation of History in Ezekiel 20," eschews redaction-critical analysis of the text of Ezekiel to focus instead on the conceptual development of the understanding of history evident in Ezekiel 20. The chapter recounts the history of Israel from the time of the Exodus from Egypt to the present, with a particular focus on Israel's idolatry in the wilderness and YHWH's intentions to scatter Israel among the nations. YHWH emerges as an ambiguous figure in Krüger's analysis insofar as YHWH punishes Israel by misleading them with bad statutes and laws that prevent people from changing their attitudes or their behavior. Krüger attempts to justify YHWH's actions by arguing that YHWH misleads and punishes people who are already guilty. He argues that, according to Ezekiel 20, not everything that YHWH has said or done remains valid for perpetuity. Ultimately, YHWH will triumph. But, what kind of a triumph is achieved? One must ask whether such a position actually sidesteps the question of theodicy that emerges in the book of Ezekiel as well as in other prophetic literature, such as YHWH's command that Isaiah should make sure that the people of his time do not see, hear, understand, or repent, so that the divine purpose might be realized (see Isaiah 6).[13] Krüger nevertheless places his finger squarely on the theological problem of the book of Ezekiel, viz., does the destruction of Jerusalem and the exile of its people demonstrate

---

13. See my *Reading the Bible after the Shoah: Engaging Holocaust Theology* (Minneapolis: Fortress, 2008).

that the people have sinned against YHWH? Or does the charge of sin against YHWH become a means to explain the destruction of the city and the fate of its people?

Paul R. Raabe, "Transforming the International *status quo*: Ezekiel's Oracles against the Nations," reexamines the oracles concerning the nations in the book of Ezekiel as an essential element in the overall vision of the book. He argues that the chronological correlation of the oracles against the nations with the downfall of Jerusalem indicates a tight interlocking, viz., if Jerusalem is to suffer strict judgment from G-d, so must the other nations of the Levant. Why? So that "they will know that I am YHWH" emerges as the fundamental explanation for such judgment throughout. In looking at the issue of causation of punishment, Raabe distinguishes between efficient cause and final cause. The efficient causes include the principle of *lex talionis*, i.e., the principle that the nations will suffer the punishment that they have inflicted on Jerusalem or that they wished for Jerusalem as well as their own human pride. But such punishment also serves other purposes, viz., to direct attention away from the nations of the world and toward YHWH, to elicit Israel's exclusive loyalty to YHWH, and to give Israel hope. One must also ask of Ezekiel the question why YHWH demands such recognition and loyalty? Perhaps YHWH's role as creator must also come into play? The book of Ezekiel, after all, portrays the desecration of the Jerusalem Temple in Ezekiel 8–11 as the fundamental cause of the destruction of Jerusalem. Insofar as the Jerusalem Temple is the holy center of creation, its desecration has an impact upon all Judah/Israel and all creation at large, requiring the resanctification of the Temple, Israel, the nations, and creation itself throughout the book culminating in Ezekiel 40–48. Indeed, the sequence of nations included in Ezekiel's oracles is also significant, viz., Ammon, Moab, Edom, Philistia, Tyre, Sidon, and Egypt, the very nations that would have been the targets of Babylon's westward expansion in the late-sixth century B.C.E., which suggests that the oracles concerning the nations are included as a means to interpret Babylonia's intentions at expanding its empire as an act of YHWH that is designed to resanctify the world.[14]

---

14. See my *Isaiah 1–39, with an Introduction to Prophetic Literature*, FOTL 16 (Grand Rapids: Eerdmans, 1996) 212–17, which argues that the sequence of nations in Isaiah 13–23 reflects a similar interest in interpreting the rise of the Persian empire as an act of YHWH.

Daniel I. Block, "Transformation of Royal Ideology in Ezekiel," examines the means by which the book of Ezekiel adapts and transforms traditional texts and viewpoints concerning the monarchy in Israel. Block points out that Ezekiel rarely uses the title *melek*, "King," for the kings of Israel and Judah, but refers to them instead as *nāśîʾ*, "Prince." Such a designation points to the kings' subordination to YHWH who must be recognized as the true king throughout the book. His survey of Ezekiel's treatment of the kings of his own day points to Ezekiel's negative understanding of those kings. Josiah was the model for a pious and just king, but figures such as Jehoahaz, Jehoiakim, Jehoiachin, and Zedekiah failed to live up to the ideals set by their ancestor in Ezekiel's estimation. Looking to the future, Block observes that judgment cannot be the last word, especially when one considers the promises that YHWH has made cannot be revocable. Texts such as Ezek 17:22–24; 34:22–24; 37:22–25; and 40–48 point to Ezekiel's understanding of YHWH's commitment to the promise of a Davidic dynasty, although the role of the dynasty is to point to the presence of YHWH in the world. Such a role for the house of David nevertheless entails a measure of irony, insofar as the Babylonian royal house of Nebuchadnezzar plays the key role in ensuring the future of the dynasty. Such an interest in the transformation of the royal promise would provide interesting correlations with other prophetic books, such as Isaiah which grants the Davidic promise to the people of Israel (Isaiah 55) or MT-Jeremiah which grants the Davidic promise to the city of Jerusalem and the Levitical priesthood (Jeremiah 33). But one must also consider another dimension of the royal promise in Ezekiel. According to Ezek 1:1–3, the inauguration of Ezekiel's prophetic (and priestly) career commences in his thirtieth year, which is identified with the fifth year of Jehoiachin's exile in 592 BCE. This date indicates that Ezekiel's birth took place in 622 BCE, the eighteenth year of King Josiah's reign, which is the year that the Torah scroll that informed Josiah's reform program was discovered during the course of Temple renovations (2 Kgs 22:3; 2 Chr 34:8). Such a correlation indicates that Ezekiel's view of the monarchy was influenced by the ideals of Josiah's reform, but the failure of the reforms following Josiah's untimely death in 609 BCE would have prompted Ezekiel to reconsider his evaluation of the monarchy, pointing to a view that YHWH was the true king whereas the Davidic monarchs could only be regarded as *nĕśî'îm*, "princes."¹⁵

Timothy Mackie, "Transformation in Ezekiel's Textual History: Ezekiel 7 in the Masoretic Text and the Septuagint," presents a comparative study of the Masoretic Hebrew and the Septuagint Greek (and its presumed Hebrew *Vorlage*) texts of Ezekiel 7, which announce Ezekiel's oracles of judgment against the land. He observes the intertextual relationships between this chapter and the portrayal of the king of the north in Daniel 7–12 as well as the shorter text of the Septuagint version of Ezekiel 7 in an effort to argue that the Hebrew *Vorlage* of LXX-Ezekiel 7 must represent an earlier edition of this text when compared with MT Ezekiel 7. The term *ṣĕpîrâ*, "crown," plays a particularly important role in this text, especially since the term is employed as a metaphorical designation for the agent that will bring about disaster against the land in Ezekiel 7. Mackie's analysis attempts to demonstrate that the supposed expansions of MT-Ezekiel 7 are motivated by an interest in reading this term in relation to the insolent king of the north mentioned in Daniel 7–12. But one must also consider that Daniel 7–12 builds on Ezekiel as well as on other prophets, and that there would be ample reason to shorten the LXX text of Ezekiel 7, especially since Jews in Ptolemaic Egypt were living under the rule of a foreign dynasty that had granted them relatively high status—at least until the Romans came. Nevertheless, Mackie addresses a key issue in his comparative textual study of Ezekiel 7, i.e., how do we read LXX texts as literature with their own literary constructions and hermeneutical perspectives? This issue promises to be a key concern in future scholarship. Indeed, consideration of the literary characters and hermeneutical perspectives of all of the textual versions of Ezekiel, including the Masoretic text, the Septuagint text forms, Targum Jonathan, the Peshitta, the Vulgate, and the other versions remains a desideratum for biblical scholarship.¹⁶

---

15. See my essay, "The Royal Oracle in Ezekiel 37:15–28: Ezekiel's Reflection on Josiah's Reform," in *Israel's Prophets and Israel's Past: Essays on the Relationship of Prophetic Texts and Israelite History in Honor of John H. Hayes*, ed. B. E. Kelle and M. B. Moore, LHBOTS 446 (London: T. & T. Clark, 2006) 239–53.

16. See the forthcoming Claremont dissertation by Tyler Mayfield, who is examining the different literary constructions of the oracles concerning the nations in the MT and LXX versions of the book of Ezekiel.

Beate Kowalski, "Transformations of Ezekiel in John's Revelation," actually focuses on the use of Ezekiel in the book of Revelation, which refers to Ezekiel more than the other writings of the New Testament. Insofar as Revelation is an apocalyptic book, Ezekiel's visionary experience of the divine and his supernatural journeys from Babylon to Jerusalem make the book a natural resource on which Revelation would draw. Kowalski presents a series of signals that direct the reader to Hebrew Bible citations and allusions in the book of Revelation, such as the Song of Moses (Exodus 15; Deuteronomy 32); the so-called *Dreizeitenformel* based on the revelation of the divine Name in Exod 3:14; various institutions and characters from the Hebrew Bible; and other Hebrew Bible references. In discussing the transformation of Ezekiel in Revelation, she notes that Revelation does not constitute an interpretation of the Hebrew Bible, but instead constitutes a revelation of Jesus Christ. But she limits her understanding of Hebrew Bible interpretation to Midrashic forms. Does not the use of Ezekiel in Revelation constitute a form of scriptural interpretation even when it is employed for some other purpose, particularly when she rightly points out the influence that the structure of Ezekiel 37–48 has had on the structure of Revelation 18–22? Kowalski's study, growing out of her earlier monograph, *Die Rezeption des Propheten Ezechiel in der Offenbarung des Johannes*,[17] offers a very useful model for understanding how Ezekiel was read and interpreted at least in some circles of early Christianity. Her research will stimulate more interest in Revelation's intertextual relationships with the Hebrew Bible and other Jewish literature. But it also points to the need for consideration of the role that Ezekiel played in Jewish circles, especially the *Heikhalot* texts of the Rabbinic period and their development of Jewish mysticism.[18]

The essays in this volume open the doors to a wide-ranging discussion of the various dimensions of the book of Ezekiel, its transformation of text, traditions, and theology, and indeed its transformation of its readers. The seeds of transformation planted here have the potential to see much fruit in the future as scholarly discussion continues to advance.

17. Beate Kowalski, *Die Rezeption des Propheten Ezechiel in der Offenbarung des Johannes*, SBB 52 (Stuttgart: Katholisches Bibelwerk, 2004).

18. For an example of such work, see Gottfried Schimanowski, *Die himmlische Liturgie in der Apokalypse des Johannes*, WUNT 2/154 (Tübingen: Mohr/Siebeck, 2002).

PART ONE

Transformation of Antecedent Texts in Ezekiel

1

Transformation of Law
Ezekiel's Use of the Holiness Code
(Leviticus 17–26)

Michael A. Lyons

EZEKIEL LIVED IN A TIME OF CRISIS.[1] HIS COUNTRY HAD BEEN SUBJUgated by a superior power, and its elites captured and resettled in a foreign land. Ezekiel and the exilic community in which he lived were marginalized by the citizens of Jerusalem—until they too were conquered and subjected to exile, their city and temple in ruins. What was a prophet-priest to say to such a situation? How could Ezekiel make sense of the exile for his contemporaries and offer them hope for the future?[2]

---

1. For social and historical conditions in this period, see John H. Hayes and J. Maxwell Miller, eds, *Israelite and Judean History* (London: SCM, 1977) 469–88; Daniel L. Smith-Christopher, *The Religion of the Landless: The Social Context of the Babylonian Exile* (Bloomington, IN: Meyer-Stone, 1989) 17–47, 93–126; Smith-Christopher, *A Biblical Theology of Exile*, OBT (Minneapolis: Fortress, 2002) 34–73; Oded Lipschits and Joseph Blenkinsopp, eds., *Judah and the Judeans in the Neo-Babylonian Period* (Winona Lake, IN: Eisenbrauns, 2003); Lipschits, *The Rise and Fall of Jerusalem: Jerusalem under Babylonian Rule* (Winona Lake, IN: Eisenbrauns, 2005); Jill Middlemas, *The Troubles of Templeless Judah* (Oxford: Oxford University Press, 2005). On the religious crisis caused by the exile, see Rainer Albertz, *A History of Israelite Religion in the Old Testament Period*, Volume II: *From the Exile to the Maccabees*, trans. John Bowden, OTL (Louisville: Westminster John Knox, 1994) 369–436.

2. On the role of biblical texts as products of and responses to the exile, see in particular Rainer Albertz, *Israel in Exile: The History and Literature of the Sixth Century B.C.E.* (Atlanta: Society of Biblical Literature, 2003). See also Peter R. Ackroyd, *Exile and Restoration: A Study of Hebrew Thought of the Sixth Century B.C.*, OTL (Philadelphia: Westminster, 1968) 43–48, 218–56; Albertz, *Israelite Religion*, 2:370; Michael Fishbane, *Biblical Interpretation in Ancient Israel* (Oxford: Clarendon, 1985) 263–65, 408–19;

Ezekiel responded to the crisis of exile by his strategic use of earlier texts—in particular, the Holiness Code (Lev 17–26). Ezekiel reads the Holiness Code as Scripture: he treats its laws as authoritative instruction for his day. He uses it to explain the present, transforming its laws into accusations and its conditional covenant punishments into descriptions of imminent and actual devastation. But he also uses it to create hope for the future by radically transforming its conditional covenant blessings into descriptions of guaranteed blessing in a future restoration.

The Relationship between Ezekiel and H

It has long been recognized that Ezekiel and Lev 17–26 share a remarkable number of locutions—that is, not just individual words, but multiple words in combination and in syntactic relationship. Starting in the late 1800s, those who observed this phenomenon compiled lists of these shared locutions,[3] and there has been a broad consensus that they are due to literary dependence.[4] Unfortunately, few of these lists

---

Joseph Blenkinsopp, *A History of Prophecy in Israel* (Louisville: Westminster John Knox, 1996) 148–60, 173; Thomas M. Raitt, *A Theology of Exile: Judgment/Deliverance in Jeremiah and Ezekiel* (Philadelphia: Fortress, 1977) 83. For biblical texts containing direct responses to the crisis of the Babylonian invasion and exile, see e.g. attempts to explain the disaster (2 Kgs 23:26–27; 24:20; Isa 42:23–25; 50:1; Jer 44:20–23); questions about God's apparent rejection of the monarchy, temple, and covenant (Ps 89; Lamentations); attempts to locate hope in the exilic community rather than in Jerusalem (Ezek 11:14–17; 33:24).

3. For lists of locutions shared by H and Ezekiel, see Michael A. Lyons, *From Law to Prophecy: Ezekiel's Use of the Holiness Code*, LHBOTS 507 (New York: T. & T. Clark, 2009); Karl Graf, *Die geschichtlichen Bücher des Alten Testaments. Zwei historisch-kritische Untersuchungen* (Leipzig: Weigel, 1866) 81–82; August Klostermann, "Ezechiel und das Heiligkeitsgesetz," in *Der Pentateuch: Beiträge zu seinem Verständis und seiner Entstehungsgeschichte* (Leipzig: Böhme, 1893) 386–401 [368–418]; Rudolf Smend, *Der Prophet Ezechiel*, 2nd ed., KeH (Leipzig: Hirzel, 1880) xxv–xxvii; L. Horst, *Leviticus XVII–XXVI und Hezekiel: Ein Beitrag zur Pentateuchkritik* (Colmar: Barth, 1881) 72–83; Bruno Baentsch, *Das Heiligkeits-Gesetz Lev. XVII–XXVI: Eine historisch-kritische Untersuchung* (Erfurt: Güther, 1893) 81–88, 108–9, 121–24; L. B. Paton, "The Holiness Code and Ezekiel," *The Presbyterian and Reformed Review* 26 (1896) 98–101; Millar Burrows, *The Literary Relations of Ezekiel* (New York: Jewish Publication Society, 1925) 30–34; S. R. Driver, *An Introduction to the Literature of the Old Testament* (reprinted, Gloucester, MA: Smith, 1972) 146–51; Risa Levitt Kohn, *A New Heart and a New Soul: Ezekiel, the Exile and the Torah*, JSOTSup 358 (Sheffield: Sheffield Academic, 2002) 30–85.

4. See for example G. A. Cooke, *A Critical and Exegetical Commentary on the Book of Ezekiel*, ICC (Edinburgh: T. & T. Clark, 1936) 63; Driver, *Introduction*, 49; Rudolf Kilian,

were accompanied by criteria that could be used to determine whether the shared locutions were due to purposeful or non-purposeful borrowing.⁵

More startling has been the lack of curiosity about the reasons for these shared locutions: why would an author use an earlier text, and to what use is he putting the borrowed locutions? Most early studies of the relationship between Lev 17–26 and Ezekiel were undertaken in order to reconstruct the compositional history of the Pentateuch or its parts (Graf, Wellhausen, Baentsch, Kilian) or of Ezekiel (Burrows), or the history of the development of Israelite religion (Wellhausen).⁶ Even those who wrote commentaries did not consistently pursue the question of why an author would use an earlier text.⁷ Richard Schultz argues that the lack of interest in explaining the phenomenon of quotation and allusion was characteristic of older studies:

> The study of prophetic quotation consistently has been treated as a means to an end. The primary concern of scholars never has been the phenomenon of verbal parallels but the bearing it

---

Literarkritische und Formgeschichtliche Untersuchung des Heiligkeitsgesetzes, BBB 19 (Bonn: Hanstein, 1963) 185; Walther Zimmerli, *Ezekiel 1: A Commentary on the Book of the Prophet Ezekiel, Chapters 1–24*, trans. Ronald E. Clements, Hermeneia (Philadelphia: Fortress, 1979) 47–52; Levitt Kohn, *A New Heart*, 111–12; Christophe Nihan, "The Holiness Code between D and P: Some Comments on the Function and Significance of Leviticus 17–26 in the Composition of the Torah," in *Das Deuteronomium zwischen Pentateuch und Deuteronomistischem Geschichtswerk*. Edited by Eckart Otto and Reinhard Achenbach, 81–122, FRLANT 206 (Göttingen: Vandenhoeck & Ruprecht, 2004) 108–110.

5. This is not to say that all authors of these early studies were unaware of the problem; see e.g. Burrows, *Literary Relations*, 14: "Equally often, however, by the briefest quotations or by mere phraseological echoes he [Ezekiel] recalls utterances of his predecessors, though in such cases it is sometimes difficult to determine whether the reminiscence is intended or unconscious."

6. Note that Julius Wellhausen called Lev 17–26 "a perfect compendium of the literary history of the Pentateuch"; see *Prolegomena to the History of Ancient Israel*, trans. J. S. Black and A. Menzies (1885; reprinted, New York: Meridian, 1957) 376. For his evaluation of H and Ezekiel as evidence for reconstructing the development of Israelite religion, see 377–79.

7. That is, commentaries written by authors who explained the shared locutions by a model of literary dependence. For example, Zimmerli provides a partial list of locutions common to H and Ezekiel (*Ezekiel 1*, 46–51), but in the commentary proper he does not discuss the way in which borrowed locutions contribute to Ezekiel's argument; see e.g. his discussion of Ezek 5:1–2, 11–13 (172–73, 176); Ezek 6:3–7 (186–87); Ezek 24:21 (507); Ezek 24:23 (508).

might have on a particular theory of dating, authorship or inter-relationship. As a result, subjectivity tended to play a significant role: methodological problems were downplayed, superficial comparisons were made, the relevant data were investigated only in as much detail as was necessary to serve a particular scholar's purpose.[8]

Fortunately, this is no longer the case. Recent monographs and commentaries on Ezekiel show that authors are increasingly willing to investigate the rationale for and effects of the shared locutions in H and Ezekiel.[9] This willingness can be linked to a surge of interest in innerbiblical quotation, allusion, and interpretation.[10]

Disputed Issues

Perhaps the most vexing problem relating to the relationship between the Holiness Code (H) and Ezekiel is the issue of the direction of literary dependence and criteria that one could use to determine the direction

---

8. Richard L. Schultz, *The Search for Quotation: Verbal Parallels in the Prophets*, JSOTSup 180 (Sheffield: Sheffield Academic, 1999) 56; see also 113, particularly n. 142. Note also Burrows, *Literary Relations*, 29: "With the single exception of Hölscher, scholars seem to have approached the problem in the interest of the dating of H, assuming the traditional date of Ez."

9. In particular, see Levitt Kohn, *New Heart*, 76–85, 107–110; Ka Leung Wong, *The Idea of Retribution in the Book of Ezekiel*, VTSupp 87 (Leiden: Brill, 2001) 80–119. Henning Graf Reventlow studied Ezekiel's use of H, but rejected any model of literary dependence; see *Wächter über Israel: Ezechiel und seine Tradition*, BZAW 82 (Berlin: Töpelmann, 1962) 42–43. For treatment in commentaries, see Leslie Allen, *Ezekiel 1–19*, WBC 28 (Dallas: Word, 1994) 78, 92–96; parallels with Leviticus are discussed in his comments on Ezek 4:16–17; 5:1–2; 14:12–13; 18:8–9. Moshe Greenberg, *Ezekiel 1–20: A New Translation with Introduction and Commentary*, AB 22 (New York: Doubleday, 1983), claimed that he would treat the "genetic-historic relation of this book to others" (25) in a following volume, but see already his comments on the use of Lev 17–26 in 124–25, 127, 132, 262. Daniel Block, *The Book of Ezekiel, Chapters 1–24*, NICOT (Grand Rapids: Eerdmans, 1997) claims that Ezekiel is "heavily influenced" by H (40), and in several places discusses the argument created by his use of H; see his comments on Ezek 5:2 (194); 6:1–7 (218–19); 7:12–13 (259); 14:1–11 (423–24); 22:3 (704); 22:6 (708).

10. Michael Fishbane's work *Biblical Interpretation in Ancient Israel* is responsible for this interest, though I. L. Seeligmann's seminal essay "Voraussetzungen der Midraschexegese," in *Congress Volume. Copenhagen 1953*, ed. G. W. Anderson et al., VTSup 1 (Leiden: Brill, 1953) 150–81, has also been highly influential.

of dependence.¹¹ Some have argued that Ezekiel was using H;¹² others, that H and Ezekiel exhibit mutual literary dependence;¹³ still others that H used Ezekiel.¹⁴ Complicating this is the thorny issue of the compositional history and dating of H: was it an independent document, either pre-exilic (Driver) or post-exilic (Wellhausen), that was at some point incorporated into P?¹⁵ Or was H the product of compositional activity, either pre-exilic (Knohl, Milgrom) or post-exilic (Otto, Nihan), that was written to supplement and interact with P?¹⁶

For the purposes of this essay, it is unnecessary to determine whether H ever existed independently of its present context or not. However,

---

11. Determining the direction of literary dependence is acknowledged as a methodological problem in Wellhausen, *Prolegomena*, 379–84; Paton, "Holiness Code," 102–6, 109–15; Burrows, *Literary Relations*, ix–xi; Driver, *Introduction*, 150; Jacob Milgrom, *Leviticus 23–27*, AB 3B (New York: Doubleday, 2001) 2348–63.

12. See Klostermann, "Ezechiel und das Heiligkeitsgesetz," 386–402; Paton, "Holiness Code," 110–14; Burrows, *Literary Relations*, 28–36; Driver, *Introduction*, 145–51; Milgrom, *Leviticus 23–27*, 2348–62; Levitt Kohn, *A New Heart*, 84–85.

13. See e.g., Kilian, *Untersuchung*, 164–79, 185; Zimmerli, *Ezekiel 1*, 47, 52.

14. See Wellhausen, *Prolegomena*, 378–84; Baruch Levine, "The Epilogue to the Holiness Code: A Priestly Statement on the Destiny of Israel," in *Judaic Perspectives on Ancient Israel*, ed. Jacob Neusner et al., 9–34 (Philadelphia: Fortress, 1987) 24–30; Eckart Otto, "Innerbiblische Exegese im Heiligkeitsgesetz Levitikus 17–26," in *Levitikus als Buch*, ed. Heinz-Josef Fabry and Hans-Winfried Jüngling, BBB 119 (Berlin: Philo, 1999) 180–82 [125–96]; Nihan, "Holiness Code," 108–110, though these authors have very different ideas regarding the formation of H and its role in the development of the Pentateuch. Their belief that H uses Ezekiel is based solely on investigations of H, and do not include a comprehensive investigation of the locutions shared by H and Ezekiel.

15. Driver, *Introduction*, 47–48, 149–51; Wellhausen, *Prolegomena*, 379–84.

16. For Milgrom, H was a pre-exilic priestly author who created the book of Leviticus by editing earlier P material and adding his own legal material to it; see Milgrom, "HR in Leviticus and Elsewhere in the Torah," in *The Book of Leviticus: Composition and Reception*, ed. Rolf Rendtorff and Robert A. Kugler, VTSup 93 (Leiden: Brill, 2003) 24–25 [24–40]; see also Israel Knohl, *The Sanctuary of Silence: The Priestly Torah and the Holiness School* (Minneapolis: Fortress, 1995) 199–204, 225–30. For Otto and Nihan, H was a post-exilic composition; see Otto, "Innerbiblische Exegese"; Nihan, "Holiness Code"; Nihan, *From Priestly Torah to Pentateuch: A Study in the Composition of the Book of Leviticus*, FAT 2/25 (Tübingen: Mohr/Siebeck, 2007) 545–75. Both Otto and Nihan claim that H combined and reworked legal material from the Covenant Code, D, and P (for some plausible examples, see esp. Nihan, "Holiness Code," 85–88, 95–96, 98–100). They have argued that H contributed to the redaction of the Pentateuch (so Otto, "Innerbiblische Exegese," 180–81) or was a redactor of a "first edition" of the Pentateuch (see Nihan, "Holiness Code," 116; *From Priestly Torah*, 562–63, 616–19).

both Milgrom and Nihan provide convincing reasons for believing that H was interacting with earlier Priestly laws, which suggests that H was a supplement rather than an independent document.[17] Moreover, it seems most likely to me that H was composed in the pre-exilic period. This is suggested by its relationship to Ezekiel (see below), its warnings against emulating Egyptian and Canaanite practices (Lev 18:3), its reference to multiple (evidently legitimate!) sanctuaries in Lev 21:23; 26:31, and its laws regulating land tenure and resident aliens (which seem more likely to have been created and enforced during the freedom of the pre-exilic period rather than under Persian authority).[18]

Criteria for Determining Direction of Dependence and Purposeful Use

When two texts share enough significant locutions that literary dependence is likely, it is necessary to determine the direction of dependence. Three criteria are useful here. First, one of the texts containing shared locutions must also contain differences in the parallel material that can be interpreted as *modifications towards the author's distinctive language, ideas, and arguments*. In this case one must be able to offer plausible arguments that an author has made adjustments in the borrowed material that move it linguistically or conceptually away from the source text towards the target text, or has presented an interpretation of the source text. One should be able to show that the differences are *motivated* in one text (the borrowing text) but not the other (the source text). Here are two examples of this kind of modification:

---

17. Milgrom, *Leviticus 17–23*, 1349–55; Nihan, "Holiness Code," 100–105.

18. On H's reference to multiple Yahwistic sanctuaries, see Milgrom, *Leviticus 17–22*, AB 3A (New York: Doubleday, 2001) 1363. For a plausible reconstruction of a pre-exilic setting for H, see in particular Jan Joosten, *People and Land in the Holiness Code: An Exegetical Study of the Ideational Framework of the Law in Leviticus 17–26*, VTSup 67 (Leiden: Brill, 1996) 89–90, 165–68, 204–7. He remarks (89–90): "The functions attributed to the collective addressed in H largely exceed those of a cultic or religious community. The fact that they encompass such matters as the administration of justice and the organization of economic life does not accord well with the conditions of Israel in the Babylonian and Persian periods, when large parts of public life were directed by a foreign power. The rules concerning the treatment of the resident alien show with particular clarity that the Israelite people, as presented by H, are free to impose laws on non-Israelites living among them . . . we are led to the conclusion that the historical conditions addressed by H are those of the pre-exilic period."

> You shall not *rule* over him *with harshness*, but you shall fear your God. (Lev 25:43)

> You have not strengthened the weak, you have not healed the sick, you have not bound up the broken, you have not brought back the banished, you have not sought the lost; but with strength you *ruled* them, and *with harshness*! (Ezek 34:4)

The locution "rule with harshness" (רדה בפרך) occurs only in Lev 25:43, 46, 53; Ezek 34:4. Leviticus 25:35ff regulates slavery and indentured service, making careful distinctions between Israelites (אחיך "your brother," vv. 35, 39) and non-Israelites (הגוים, v. 44; הגרים, v. 45). It prohibits the enslaving of Israelites, which it regards as "ruling with harshness."[19] Ezekiel borrows H's locution and turns H's regulation into an accusation. What is significant is that he finds it necessary to gloss the rare word "harshness" with the more common word "strength." The fact that Ezekiel glosses the word indicates that Ezek 34:4 is the borrowing text, not the source text.[20]

> And those who are left over among you will *rot in their iniquity* in the lands of your enemies, and also in the iniquities of their fathers with them they will rot! (Lev 26:39)

> In order that, lacking bread and water, they will be appalled, each one and his brother; and they will *rot in their iniquity*. (Ezek 4:17)

The locution "rot in iniquity" (מקק בעון) is found only in Lev 26:39; Ezek 4:17; 24:23; 33:10. Is H borrowing Ezekiel's statement and expanding it by adding the reference to the "iniquities of their fathers"? Or is Ezekiel borrowing only part of H's locution? It seems to me that Ezekiel has a motive for selecting only part of the locution: in chap. 18 he rigorously argues against the idea of vertical retribution. Ezekiel attempts to convince his contemporaries that they are being punished for their own sins, not those of their ancestors (Ezek 18:2–3, 20). This

---

19. H may be borrowing from and reworking material from the Covenant Code (Exod 21:2–6) here; see Bernard M. Levinson, "The Birth of the Lemma: The Restrictive Reinterpretation of the Covenant Code's Manumission Law by the Holiness Code (Leviticus 25:44–46)," *JBL* 124 (2005) 617–39.

20. See Milgrom, *Leviticus 21–27*, 2356. Outside of H and Ezekiel, the word פרך "harshness" is found only in Exod 1:13, 14.

extended argument is congruent with other arguments in the book.²¹ Ezekiel's insistence that his contemporaries are being punished for their own misdeeds explains his reluctance to borrow a locution claiming that people *do* suffer for the misdeeds of their ancestors. In contrast, H does not contain any sustained argument that depends on the idea of vertical retribution. There is no contextual reason to explain why H would borrow the phrase from Ezekiel and expand it. It is more likely, then, that Ezekiel is borrowing from H because it is possible to demonstrate polemical intent in Ezekiel.²²

The second criterion for determining the direction of dependence is that the parallel material may be only partially integrated in one text, and therefore display indications of its original context that are incongruous within its new context, thus pointing to its derivative and secondary nature. Here are two examples of this incongruity:

> And I will destroy *your high places*, and I will cut off your *incense stands, and I will put* your *corpses* upon the *corpses of your idols*, and my soul will loathe you. And I will make your *cities* a *waste*, and I will make *desolate* your sanctuaries, and I will not smell your pleasing smells. (Lev 26:30–31)

---

21. While some of Ezekiel's accusations and judgments are general and reflect (or are condensations of) broad historical periods, others are provided with details specific to Ezekiel's own generation (e.g., Ezek 8:7–12; 11:1–13, 15; 12:1–16, 17–20). This juxtaposition of accusation and judgment against people in Ezekiel's own time creates linkages between behavior and consequences, underlining the guilt of his contemporaries. Note also the differences between H's and Ezekiel's descriptions of cannibalism during siege: "you will eat the flesh of your sons and the flesh of your daughters" (Lev 26:29); "fathers will eat sons among you, and sons will eat their fathers" (Ezek 5:10). Greenberg (*Ezekiel 1–20*, 113–14) explains Ezekiel's statement as a conflation of Lev 26:29 and Deut 24:16 ("a gem of literary adaptation and combination"). By using Deut 24:16 as a template and creating an "equal opportunity punishment," Ezekiel is also reinforcing his argument in chap. 18 that his contemporaries are being punished for their own sins.

22. Milgrom, *Leviticus 21–27*, 2328. Note that Targum Onkelos also modifies Lev 26:39, arguing that children are only punished for the parents' sins *when they sin in the same way*: "and also on account of the sins of their fathers—the bad deeds which are held in their hands—will they be faint." Of course, any argument about individual responsibility in Ezekiel must be balanced by a recognition of passages dealing with collective punishment, e.g., Ezek 21:8–9. For a careful treatment of individual and collective responsibility in Ezekiel, see Paul Joyce, *Divine Initiative and Human Response in Ezekiel*, JSOTSup 51 (Sheffield: Sheffield Academic, 1989), and the chapter by Joyce in this volume.

And your altars will *be desolate*, and *your incense stands* will be broken, and I will cause your slain to fall before your *idols*. *And I will put the corpses of* the sons of Israel before their *idols*, and I will scatter your bones around your altars. In all your dwelling places, the *cities* will be *waste* and *the high places* will be *desolate*, in order that your altars may *be waste* and incur guilt, and that *your idols* may be broken and come to an end, and your *incense stands* will be hewn down, and your works wiped out. And your slain will fall in your midst, and you will know that I am YHWH. (Ezek 6:4–7)

The words "idols" (גלולים), "incense stands" (חמנים), "high places" (במות), "cities will be waste" (ערים + חרב), and "desolate" (שמם) are used together only in Lev 26:30–31 and Ezek 6:4–7. However, the appearance of these locutions in Ezekiel contains an incongruity: the addressee in Ezekiel is "the mountains of Israel" (v. 3), yet v. 5b mentions "your bones," and v. 6 "your dwelling places," words that presuppose the *human* addressees of Leviticus 26. This incongruity suggests that Ezekiel is borrowing from Lev 17–26 and not fully integrating the borrowed material into its new context. This incongruity was noticed and "repaired" by a scribe: MT Ezek 6:5a, which is absent in LXX, introduces a reference to people ("and I will place the corpses of the sons of Israel before their idols").[23]

Ezekiel 34 contains another example of incongruity:

> And I will give your *rains in their time, and the land will give its produce, and the tree of the field will give its fruit.* (Lev 26:4)

> And I will make them and the regions around my hill a blessing, and I will bring down *rain in its time*; they will be *rains* of blessing. *And the tree of the field will give its fruit, and the land will give its produce.* (Ezek 34:26–27a)

Here Ezek 34:26 refers to "rain" (singular; "I will send rain in *its* time"), but continues with the comment "*They will be rains of blessing.*"

---

23. Greenberg (*Ezekiel 1–20*, 132) notes, "The first half of the verse, with its third-person formulation breaking the connection between vs. 4b and vs. 5b, its absence in G, and its similarity to Lev 26:30, may have originated as an explanation of a difficulty in vs. 4b: since it is a strain to understand the pronoun of 'your slain' in vs. 4b as still referring to the mountains, vs. 5a refers the pronoun to the inhabitants of the (mountainous) land in language inspired by Lev 26:30—a verse which doubtless is echoed in vs. 4b."

The incongruous slip into plural indicates Ezekiel's dependence on Lev 26:4 ("I will give your *rains* in *their* time").

The third criterion for determining the direction of dependence is that one of the texts must be capable of being described as *conceptually dependent* on the other in such a way that the reader is forced to supply information from the second text (the source text) in order to understand the first. The following example illustrates this conceptual dependence:

> If your brother becomes impoverished and he *sells* some of his property, then his next-of-kin shall come to him and redeem the *sold thing* of his brother. And if a man does not have a redeemer, but is able and finds sufficient means for his redemption, then he shall reckon the years since his sale, and he shall return the surplus to the man to whom he *sold*, then he shall *return* to his property. But if he is not able to find sufficient means to return it to him, then his *sold item* shall remain with the *one who acquired* it until the year of jubilee; and in the year of jubilee it will revert, and he shall *return* to his property. (Lev 25:25–28)

> Let not the *acquirer* rejoice, nor the *seller* mourn—for wrath is upon her entire multitude—because the *seller* will not *return* to the *thing sold* while they are still alive. (Ezek 7:12b–13a)

The words קנה, מכר, ממכר, and שוב ("acquire," "sell," "thing sold," and "return") are found together only in Lev 25:25–28 and Ezek 7:12–13. In the middle of an oracle of judgment, Ezekiel employs these words to create an obscure statement: the seller should not mourn, and the buyer should not rejoice, for the seller will not return to the thing sold. This unexplained reference to some kind of commercial transaction *presumes* a knowledge of Lev 25, Ezekiel's source text, which discusses the reversion of land sold by a person in financial difficulty. Ezekiel borrows these words from H to describe the imminence of the coming disaster: exile will occur before either party has a chance to rejoice or mourn at the sale of land. But there is no plausible way to describe why Lev 25 might be borrowing from Ezekiel's oracle of judgment to create laws about land tenure and redemption.

The examples listed above provide evidence that Ezekiel was using the Holiness Code. I do not rule out of hand the possibility that there could be mutual literary dependence. After all, both texts bear indications of redactional activity.²⁴ It could be the case that additions were made to H under the influence of Ezekiel.²⁵ Moreover, not all the shared locutions display the features listed above. However, even when redactional activity is taken into account, I cannot see any features in the shared locutions that would indicate H was using Ezekiel.

How can we determine whether the locutions common to H and Ezekiel are the result of purposeful borrowing? It is possible that the presence of verbal parallels in two texts could be attributed to other factors as well—coincidence, unconscious dependence, or the use of language that is fixed due to the genre or social setting in which it is used. To eliminate instances of shared locutions that are not due to purposeful borrowing, I use three criteria.²⁶ First, I isolate shared combinations of two or more words in close proximity or in the same syntactic construction, examining the frequency and distribution of these locutions in the entire biblical corpus. Second, I look for the presence of modification,²⁷ interpretation,²⁸ or the creation of arguments based

---

24. In H, see e.g., Lev 26:33b-35, 43-44, which contains *Wiederaufnahme* (cf. vv. 31-32 // 33b), introduces a new topic, and signals its retrospective exilic standpoint by a change in verb forms (v. 44). On this example, see Milgrom, *Leviticus 23-27*, 2322-23, 2337; for other examples, see *Leviticus 17-22*, 1332-33, 1346-47, 1439. In Ezekiel, see e.g., Ezek 28:25-26, or Ezek 38-39. On the latter, see the chapter by William Tooman in this volume. Locutions from H are employed in a substantially similar manner at both the compositional and redactional levels of Ezekiel.

25. This phenomenon has occurred in textual transmission; compare Lev 19:26 in the MT (לא תאכלו על־הדם, "you shall not eat with the blood") and LXX (Μὴ ἔσθετε ἐπὶ τῶν ὀρέων, "You shall not eat on the mountains"). The *Vorlage* of the LXX is a harmonization to Ezek 18:11, 15; 22:9 (אכל על ההרים [לא], "[not] eat on the mountains").

26. Here I am heavily indebted to the work of Richard Schultz; see *Search for Quotation*, 211, 222-27.

27. Note how Ezek 24:7, 8 uses the locution from Lev 17:13 ("spill blood, cover with dirt") in a completely different way than H; whereas H is discussing procedure for animal sacrifice, Ezekiel turns the words into an accusation of human murder. Similarly, see the use of locutions from Lev 21:7 + 14 in Ezek 44:22, where H's two laws directed to different priestly audiences are conflated and directed at all priests.

28. See the use of רדה בפרך "rule with harshness" from Lev 25:46 in Ezek 34:4, where Ezekiel glosses the rare word "harshness" with the common word "strength"; see the use of locutions from Lev 26:22 in Ezek 14:15, where the ambiguity of H (are desolate roads a consequence of wild animals, or the next punishment?) is clarified in Ezekiel (מפני החיה, "*because of* wild animals").

on H.[29] This eliminates instances of coincidental parallels and unconscious dependence. Third, I look for evidence that Ezekiel was aware of the larger context from which he borrowed the locutions. This includes instances where Ezekiel has juxtaposed, combined, or conflated two or more separate locutions, eliminating the possibility that he was simply using fixed language.[30]

Ezekiel's Use and Transformation of H

An examination of Ezekiel's use of H reveals the presence of regularly occurring formal patterns, which allow us to speak of Ezekiel's *techniques* of modification. These techniques include the inversion of word order,[31] the creation of word pairs,[32] the split-up and recombination of locutions into new forms,[33] the creation of word clusters,[34] the com-

---

29. See the use of locutions from Lev 26:5–6 in Ezek 34:25, 28. Here Ezekiel turns H's conditional covenant blessings into guaranteed future blessings; he changes person, number and gender; he creates reversals and inversions; he exaggerates the motif of "security"; and he makes "peace" relational.

30. See the combination of locutions from Lev 21:1–3 + 11 in Ezek 44:25, or from Lev 18:7–9+15+17+19 in Ezek 22:10–11.

31. Compare Lev 26:4b // Ezek 34:27a; Lev 26:5–6 // Ezek 34:25; Lev 26:9 // Ezek 36:11; Lev 18:19–20 // Ezek 18:6. On the technique of inversion, see Pancratius C. Beentjes, "Discovering a New Path of Intertextuality: Inverted Quotations and their Dynamics," in *Literary Structure and Rhetorical Strategy in the Hebrew Bible*, ed. L. J. de Regt, J. de Waard and J. P. Fokkelman, 31–49 (Assen: Van Gorcum, 1996).

32. The locution "cut off livestock" (Lev 26:22) is expanded into "cut off humans and livestock" in Ezek 14:13, 17, 19, 21; 25:13; 29:8.

33. Note the modification of locutions from Lev 26:33 in Ezek 22:15 (also Ezek 12:15; 20:23; 29:12; 30:23, 26; 36:19, and note the same pattern with variations in word choice in Ezek 6:8; 11:16); Lev 25:36 in Ezek 18:8, 13; Lev 18:5 in Ezek 20:11, 13, 21. See Lyons, "Marking Innerbiblical Allusion in the Book of Ezekiel," *Biblica* 88 (2007) 245–50.

34. The words "wild animals" (Lev 26:22) + "sword, plague" (Lev 26:25), and famine (Lev 26:26) are combined into "sword, famine, wild animals, and plague" (Ezek 5:17; 14:13+15+17+19, 21); "sword + famine + plague" (Ezek 5:12; 6:11, 12; 7:15; 12:16); "sword + wild animals + plague" (Ezek 33:27).

bination and conflation of locutions,[35] and the use of wordplay[36] and reversals.[37]

But why does Ezekiel use this material at all, and how does he employ it to solve the problems that he and his contemporaries were facing? Ezekiel's use of Leviticus was fundamentally rhetorical—that is, he used its images for persuasive effect, he appealed to the authoritative nature of its laws, and he used and transformed its arguments in order to develop his own arguments.

The ways in which Ezekiel employs locutions borrowed from the Holiness Code fall into five categories.[38] First, Ezekiel turns H's positive and negative instructions into accusations. Second, Ezekiel turns the conditional covenant punishments of Lev 26 into descriptions of present or imminent judgment on Jerusalem. Third, Ezekiel takes H's laws and appeals to them as authoritative standards for behavior. Fourth, Ezekiel turns the reference to the display of God's power in the Exodus (Lev 26:45) into an argument that the motivation for God's actions is concern for his reputation. Fifth, Ezekiel turns the conditional covenant blessings in Lev 26 into guaranteed covenant blessings in the future.

Accusation

First, Ezekiel turns the positive and negative instructions of Lev 17–26 into accusations:

> You shall *do my ordinances* and keep *my statutes* so as to *walk in* them; I am YHWH your God. And you shall keep *my statutes* and *my ordinances, by which a man will live if he does them*; I am YHWH. (Lev 18:4–5)

---

35. Lev 10:10 + 20:25 in Ezek 22:26; Lev 21:5+10 in Ezek 44:20; Lev 21:7+14 in Ezek 44:22; Lev 10:10 + 20:2 in Ezek 44:23; Lev 21:1–3 + 11 in Ezek 44:25; Lev 19:34 + 25:45–46 in Ezek 47:22.

36. Note the use of פנה שים / נתן "set the face" in Lev 20:3, 5, 6 // Ezek 14:3–8 and 15:6–8. See S. Talmon and M. Fishbane, "The Structuring of Biblical Books: Studies in the Book of Ezekiel," *ASTI* 10 (1976) 129–53, esp. 137–38.

37. Punishment ("send wild animals," Lev 26:22 in Ezek 5:17; 14:15, 21; "set my face against you," Lev 20:3; 26:17 in Ezek 14:8; 15:7; "scatter you among the nations," Lev 26:33 in Ezek 12:15; 20:23; 22:15; 29:12; 30:23, 26; 36:19; etc.) is reversed into blessing ("finish off wild animals," Lev 26:6 in Ezek 34:25; "I will turn to you," Lev 26:9 in Ezek 36:9; 37:26; "gather you from the peoples," Ezek 11:17; see also 20:34, 41; 34:13; 36:24; 37:21).

38. For a detailed description of how H's locutions are used by Ezekiel, see Lyons, *From Law to Prophecy*.

> But the house of Israel rebelled against me in the wilderness; they did not *walk in my statutes*, and they rejected *my ordinances, by which a man will live if he does them*. (Ezek 20:13)

The locution "my statutes ... my ordinances, by which a man will live if he does them" occurs only in Lev 18:5; Ezek 20:11, 13, 21; Neh 9:29, though only H and Ezekiel use the apocopated form וָחַי "will live." Unique variations on this locution occur in Ezek 20:25; 33:15. In chap. 20, Ezekiel surveys Israel's history and turns H's locution into a repeated accusation that the people did not obey. This chapter is designed to convince the reader that Ezekiel's contemporaries are incorrigible transgressors, displaying the same pattern of behavior as their forefathers.

Ezekiel also uses H's locutions to accuse his audience in Ezek 22:

> They *treat father and mother with contempt* among you; they act with extortion towards the alien in your midst; they oppress orphan and widow among you. You despise *my sacred contributions*, and you profane *my sabbaths*. *Slanderous* men are among you in order to shed *blood*, and they eat on the mountains among you; they commit *lewdness* in your midst. *The nakedness of a father one uncovers* among you; the *woman impure in her menstrual period* they rape among you. And one *commits abomination* with *the wife of his neighbor*, and in *lewdness* another defiles *his daughter-in-law*; and another among you rapes *his sister, the daughter of his father*. They take bribes among you in order to shed blood; you *take interest and accrued interest*; and you violently profit from *your neighbor* by *extortion*. And you forgot me!—utterance of Lord YHWH. (Ezek 22:7–12)

Ezekiel 22 contains a litany of accusations, most of them taken from laws regarding social justice and prohibited sexual relations in Lev 18–20. These accusations form the grounds for the judgment promised in Ezek 22:2, 4–5, 14–15. Some of the shared words are rare in the corpus of biblical Hebrew; other shared words are common individually, but occur in proximity with other shared words only in H and Ezekiel:

- "treat father and mother with contempt" (קִלֵּל אָת־אָב וְאֵת־אֵם): Exod 21:17; Lev 20:9; Ezek 22:7; Prov 20:20; 30:11 (see also "revere mother and father," Lev 19:3)
- "sacred contribution" (קֹדֶשׁ): The word קֹדֶשׁ is common, even when used in the specific sense of the "sacred contributions" that constitute priestly meals. Abuses of these contributions are de-

scribed with the verb חלל "to profane" in Lev 19:8; 22:2, 15; Num 18:32; Ezek 22:26 // Zeph 3:4, and with the verb בזה "to despise" in Ezek 22:8.

- "my sabbaths" (שבתותי): Exod 31:13; Lev 19:3, 30; 26:2; Isa 56:4; Ezek 20:12, 13, 16, 20, 21, 24; 22:8, 26; 23:38; 44:24. While some occurrences of "sabbaths" in Ezekiel cannot be traced to a definite context in H, the presence of other locutions occurring in the same context indicates that Ezek 22:8 draws from Lev 19:13 and Ezek 23:38 draws from Lev 19:30. Ezekiel has reversed H's locution "keep my sabbaths, reverence my sanctuary" (Lev 19:30; 26:2) to "they defiled my sanctuary, they profaned my sabbaths" (Ezek 23:38). The shorter locution "keep my sabbaths" (Lev 19:3) is reversed to "they profaned my sabbaths" in Ezek 22:8. It is likely that the use of "treat father and mother with contempt" (Lev 20:9) in Ezek 22:7 brought to mind the occurrence of its opposite, "revere mother and father" in Lev 19:3; the use of "my sabbaths" with "father and mother" occurs only in Lev 19:3; Ezek 22:7–8.

- "slander" (רכיל) + "blood" (דם): The word "slander" occurs six times (Lev 19:16; Jer 6:28; 9:3; Ezek 22:9; Prov 11:13; 20:19). The only place it occurs in proximity to the word "blood" is in Lev 19:16 and Ezek 22:9.

- "lewdness" (זמה): This word occurs twenty-nine times. Used with the sense "depravity, lewdness," it occurs four times in Leviticus (Lev 18:17; 19:29; 20:14 [2x]) and fourteen times in Ezekiel (Ezek 16:27, 43, 58; 22:9, 11; 23:21, 27, 29, 35, 44, 48 [2x], 49; 24:13). It is found elsewhere with this meaning only in Judg 20:6; Jer 13:27.[39]

- "uncover the nakedness of a father (גלה ערות אב): Lev 18:7; 20:11; Ezek 22:10

- "a woman impure in her menstrual period" (טְמֵאָה / טְמָאָה + נִדָּה, in construct): Ezek 18:6 uses Lev 18:19 לא קרב אל־אשה + נדה ("do not draw near to a woman in her period"). The phrase "a woman impure in her menstrual period" (טמאת הנדה) in Ezek 22:10 is probably a modification of אשה בנדת טמאתה

---

39. Used with the meaning "evil plan," it occurs eight times (Isa 32:7; Hos 6:9; Psa 26:10; 119:150; Job 31:11; Prov 10:23; 21:27; 24:9), though it can refer to a "plan" with no negative sense (Job 17:11).

"a woman in her menstrual impurity" in Lev 18:19, though it also resembles טמאת נדתה, "the uncleanness of her menstrual impurity" (Lev 15:26).

- "commit abomination" (עשה תועבה): Lev 18:26, 27, 29, 30; 20:13; Ezek 8:6, 9, 13, 17; 9:4; 16:50, 51; 18:12, 13, 24; 22:11; 33:26, 29; 43:8; 44:13 (but also in Deut 12:31; 13:15; 18:9; 20:18; 1 Kgs 14:24; 2 Kgs 21:2, 11; Jer 6:15; 7:10; 32:35; 44:22; Mal 2:11; 2 Chron 33:2; 36:8; etc.)
- "wife of a neighbor": אשת עמית, Lev 18:20; אשת רע, Exod 20:17; Lev 20:10; Deut 5:21; 22:24; Jer 5:8; 29:23; Ezek 18:6, 11, 15; 22:11; 33:26; Prov 6:29 (always with other words referring to impropriety)
- "daughter-in-law" (כלה): This word is found throughout the Hebrew Bible, but in H and Ezekiel it only occurs in contexts dealing with sexual impropriety (Lev 18:15; 20:12; Ezek 22:11; it also occurs in Gen 38, the story of Judah and Tamar). Ezekiel has modified H's locution "uncover the nakedness of a daughter-in-law" to "defile a daughter-in-law."
- "a sister, the daughter of a father" (אחות בת אב): Gen 20:12; Lev 18:9; 20:17; Deut 27:22; Ezek 22:11 (all in contexts of sexual impropriety)
- "take interest and accrued interest" (לקח נשך ותרבית): Lev 25:36; Ezek 18:8, 13, 17; 22:12
- "extortion/extort" (עשק) + "neighbor" (רע): Lev 19:13 (לא־תעשק את־רעך); Ezek 22:12 (תבצעי רעך בעשק)

In these passages and others, Ezekiel has borrowed locutions from positively and negatively phrased legal material in H in order to create accusations. He directs these accusations against his fellow-exiles in order to explain their condition as the result of God's just punishment for breach of covenant obligations.

Judgment

The second way Ezekiel uses H's locutions is to turn the conditional covenant punishments of Lev 26 into descriptions of present or imminent judgment on Jerusalem (though to some extent also on Edom,

Sidon, and Egypt). Ezekiel's descriptions of judgment depend heavily on the threats of invasion, siege, starvation, and ruin listed as punishments for covenant violation in Lev 26. Ezekiel claims that these disasters are about to fall, or have already fallen, upon the citizens of Jerusalem for their offenses against God and fellow humans:

> And I will send *wild animals* into you, *and they will bereave* you, and they *will cut off* your *cattle* and diminish you, and your roads will be desolate ... And *I will bring against* you *the sword* which avenges the covenant, and when you gather yourselves into your cities, then *I will send a plague into* your midst, and you will be given into the hand of the enemy. When *I break for you the staff of bread*, ten women will bake your bread in a single oven, and they will return your bread by weight; and you will eat, but you will not be satisfied.... And I will scatter you among the nations, and I will unsheathe a sword after you; and your *land will become a desolation*, and your cities will be a waste. (Lev 26:22, 25–26, 33)

> Son of man, if a land sins against me, so as to commit treachery, and I stretch out my hand against it and *break for it the staff of bread*, and I send famine into it, and *cut off* from it humans and *cattle*, and these three men were in its midst—Noah, Daniel, and Job—they would deliver themselves by their righteousness—utterance of Lord YHWH. If I cause *wild animals* to pass through the *land, and they bereave* it, and it *becomes a desolation*, without passerby because of the wild animals, if these three men were in its midst, as I live—utterance of Lord YHWH—they could deliver neither sons nor daughters; they alone would be delivered, *and the land would become a desolation*. Or if *I bring a sword against* that land, and I say, "A *sword* shall pass through the land," and I *cut off* from it humans and *cattle*, and these three men were in its midst, as I live—utterance of Lord YHWH—they could deliver neither sons nor daughters, but they alone would be delivered. Or if *I send a plague into* that land, and I pour out my wrath upon it in blood, in order to *cut off* from it humans and *cattle*, and Noah, Daniel, and Job were in its midst, as I live—utterance of Lord YHWH—they could deliver neither son nor daughter; they would deliver themselves by their righteousness. For thus says Lord YHWH: How much more when *I send* my four deadly judgments—*sword* and famine and *wild animals* and *plague*—against Jerusalem, in order to *cut off* from it humans and *cattle*! (Ezek 14:13–21)

Ezekiel borrows the following words and phrases from H:

- "break the staff of bread" (שבר מטה־לחם): Lev 26:26; Ezek 4:16; 5:16; 14:13; Psa 105:16. An even closer match exists between Lev 26:26 and Ezek 5:16, both of which use a suffixed preposition ("when I break *for you* the staff of bread"); Ezek 14:13 contains a similar construction ("break *for it* the staff of bread").

- "cut off cattle" (הכרית בהמה): Lev 26:22; Ezek 14:13, 17, 19, 21; 25:13; 29:8 (1 Kgs 18:5 uses the Nifal of כרת)

- "wild animals will bereave" (חיה שכלה): Lev 26:22; Ezek 5:17; 14:15. See also the wordplay on שכל "bereave" / כשל "stumble" in Ezek 36:12–15 (referring to the "mountains of Israel").

- "land" + "desolation," where the latter is describing the former (ארץ + שממה): Exod 23:29; Lev 26:33; Isa 1:7 (see also 62:4); Jer 4:27 (see also 6:8; 12:11); 32:43; Ezek 6:14; 12:20; 14:15, 16; 15:8; 29:9, 10, 12; 32:15; 33:28, 29; 36:34; Joel 2:20 (see also 2:3; 4:19); Mic 7:13. The word "desolation" (from the root שמם) occurs in other nominal forms as well; the locution ארץ + משמה "land" + "desolation" is attested in Ezek 6:14; 33:28, 29. A similar locution occurs in Jeremiah using the related noun form שמה (Jer 2:15; 4:7; 18:16; 25:11, 38; 44:22; 50:3; 51:29).

- "I will bring a sword against" (הבאתי חרב על): Lev 26:25; Ezek 5:17; 6:3; 11:8; 29:8 (all "against you"); Ezek 14:17; 33:2 ("against a land")

- "send a plague" (שלח דבר): Lev 26:25; Jer 24:10; 29:17; Ezek 14:19, 21; 28:23; Amos 4:10; 2 Chron 7:13.

In Lev 26, the punishments for breach of covenant are presented as God's instruments to induce repentance. This is accomplished by listing them in order of increasing intensity, and by separating them into groups with refrains that clearly state their restorative purpose: v. 18 "*if despite this* you will not obey ..."; v. 21 "*if you continue* hostile to me, and are not willing to listen ..."; v. 23 "*if in spite of these* you are not disciplined back to me ..."

However, when Ezekiel uses these threats, he argues that the judgment against Jerusalem is final and total. Here the punishments are *not* restorative, and there is *no* room for appeal.⁴⁰ But Ezekiel does not just modify the modality of the punishments, changing them from conditional threats into descriptions of actual devastation. He also modifies H's punishments by structuring them in order to make an argument about the *totality* of judgment: in Ezek 5:12, one third will die by pestilence and famine, one third by sword, and another third by scattering. In Ezek 6:12, the same threats are applied to those who are far off, those who are close by, and those who are left over. In Ezek 33:27 the threats are applied to those in the waste places, those in the field, and those in strongholds and caves. By using H's covenant punishments as descriptions of the actual or imminent state of affairs, Ezekiel interprets the fall of Jerusalem as punishment for covenant violation and implicates his contemporaries as covenant violators. By structuring H's locutions in different ways, Ezekiel is applying H's punishments to different groups that are representative of the totality of the people.

Instruction

Third, Ezekiel takes instructions from the Holiness Code and appeals to them as authoritative standards for behavior:

> *My ordinances* you shall do and *my statutes you shall keep* so as to *walk in* them; I am YHWH your God. And you shall *keep my statutes* and *my ordinances*, by which a man *will live* if he does them; I am YHWH. . . . *And you shall not come near to a woman in her menstrual* impurity in order to uncover her nakedness. And you shall not have sexual relations with *the wife of your neighbor* [עֲמִיתְךָ] *so as to become defiled* with her. (Lev 18:4, 5, 19–20)

> And if a man commits adultery with another man's wife—any one who commits adultery with *the wife of his neighbor* [רֵעַ]— the adulterer and the adulteress shall surely be put to death. (Lev 20:10)

> *Do not take interest or accrued interest* from him, but fear your God, so that the life of your brother shall be with you. *You shall not give* your money to him *at interest*, and you shall not give your food at a profit. (Lev 25:36–37)

---

40. See "my eye will not show pity, and I will not have compassion" (6x: Ezek 5:11; 7:4, 9; 8:18; 9:5, 10).

> [If] he does not eat on the mountains, and does not lift up his eyes to the idols of the house of Israel, and does not *defile the wife of his neighbor* [רע], *and does not come near a woman in her menstrual period*, . . . He does not give at interest, and does not take accrued interest; he withholds his hand from iniquity. He does true justice between one man and another. *He walks in my statutes, he has kept my ordinances* so as to act faithfully. He is righteous; he will surely *live*—utterance of Lord YHWH. (Ezek 18:6, 8–9)

In this passage, Ezekiel uses the following words and phrases from H:

- "neighbor's wife" + "defile" (אשת עמית / אשת רע + טמה): Lev 18:20; Ezek 18:6, 11, 15; 33:26 (cf. 22:11). While עמית "neighbor" occurs elsewhere in H, Lev 18:20 is the sole occurrence of אשת עמית "neighbor's wife." Ezekiel never uses the word עמית as the word for "neighbor," but prefers the word רע from Lev 20:10 for use in this locution.

- "come near a woman in her menstrual period" (קרב אל־אשה ... נדה): Lev 18:19; Ezek 18:6.

- "take interest and accrued interest" (לקח נשך ותרבית): Lev 25:36; Ezek 18:8, 13, 17; 22:12. Following Lev 25:37 (נתן בנשך, "give at interest"), Ezek 18:8, 13 introduce the verb נתן into the locution.

- "walk" (הלך) + "keep" (שמר) + "my statutes" (fem. חקתי) + "my ordinances" (משפטי) + "to live" (חיה), where "statutes" and "ordinances" are the object of the verbs "walk" and "keep": Lev 18:5; Deut 30:16 (variation: uses the three-element list "commands, statutes, and ordinances"); Ezek 18:9; 20:21.[41] The fact that Ezekiel is aware of Lev 18:5 is evident from his use of the longer locution "my statutes . . . my ordinances, by which a man will live if he does them" (which occurs only in Lev 18:5; Ezek 20:11, 13, 21;

---

41. The combination of "my statutes" (fem. חקתי) + "my ordinances" + "to live" occurs in Lev 18:5; Deut 30:16 (variation: uses the three-element list "commands, statutes, and ordinances"); Ezek 18:9, 21 (variation: "keeps all my statutes, and does righteousness and justice"); 20:11, 13, 21. A similar combination using the masculine form of "statute" (חק) occurs in Deut 4:1; Ezek 20:25.

Neh 9:29, though only H and Ezekiel use the apocopated form יְחִ֑י "will live").

In 33:10, 15, Ezekiel answers the people's question "How can we live?" with the response "walk in the statutes of life." Ezekiel has created this unique locution "walk in statutes of life" by condensing the phrasing of Lev 18:4–5 ("you shall *walk* in my *statutes* . . . by which if a man does them, then he will *live*"). For Ezekiel, these legal regulations are indeed "statutes of life." In fact, he fills chap. 18 with instructions from the Holiness Code and argues that God evaluates the exiles on the basis of how they—not their parents—do or do not keep these statutes. Those who obey God's instructions will live; those who do not will die.

Ezekiel also uses H's legal material as the basis for laws accompanying his vision of the restored temple and land in chaps. 40–48. Here Ezekiel is addressing the problem of past abuses to sanctity.[42] In response to these abuses, Ezekiel crafts laws that are based on older priestly legal traditions, yet which go beyond these in significant ways to create stricter safeguards for the holiness of the sanctuary, levitical and priestly service, offerings, and the land itself.[43]

For example, Lev 21 gives two sets of laws for priests: one for common priests (Lev 21:1–8), and the other for priests of a higher status (Lev 21:10–15). The rules for the latter are more strict: Lev 21:14 prohibits marriage to a widow, a divorced woman, or a "promiscuous or profaned woman." There are no restrictions, however, on a marriage between a common priest and a widow (Lev 21:7). In Ezek 44:22, Ezekiel takes the

---

42. While I do not wish to minimize the complexities of these chapters, I think much of the material can be plausibly attributed to the prophet Ezekiel. For various attempts to explain the compositional history of these chapters, see e.g. Cooke, *Ezekiel*, 425–29; Hartmut Gese, *Der Verfassungsentwurf des Ezechiel (Kap. 40–48) traditionsgeschichtlich untersucht*, BHTh 25 (Tübingen: Mohr/Siebeck, 1957); Jon Douglas Levenson, *Theology of the Program of Restoration of Ezekiel 40–48*, HSM 10 (Missoula, MT: Scholars, 1976); Menahem Haran, "The Law-Code of Ezekiel XL–XLVIII and its Relation to the Priestly School," *HUCA* 50 (1979) 45–71; Moshe Greenberg, "The Design and Themes of Ezekiel's Program of Restoration," *Int* 38 (1984) 181–208; Walther Zimmerli, *Ezekiel 2: A Commentary on the Book of the Prophet Ezekiel, Chapters 25–48*, trans. James D. Martin, Hermeneia (Philadelphia: Fortress, 1983) 328, 329, 409; Steven Shawn Tuell, *The Law of the Temple in Ezekiel 40–48*, HSM 49 (Atlanta: Scholars, 1992).

43. Most references to the legal material in H occur in Ezek 44 (cf. Ezek 44:7–8 and Lev 22:9–10; Ezek 44:20 and Lev 21:5+10; Ezek 44:22 and Lev 21:7+14; Ezek 44:23 and Lev 10:10 + 20:25; Ezek 44:25 and Lev 21:1–3+11; Ezek 44:31 and Lev 22:8).

locutions of Lev 21:14 and applies H's rules for the priest of high status to *all* priests.[44] Unlike H, Ezekiel needs no distinction between common priests and priests of higher status; he has already made a strong distinction between Levites and Zadokite priests (Ezek 44:10–14, 15–16) and is increasing priestly sanctity with new legislation (cf. Ezek 44:18b). He does, however, modify H's clause about priestly marriage to a widow, permitting it in the case of a woman who had previously been married to a priest.

Concern for God's Reputation

Fourth, Ezekiel turns the reference to the display of God's power in the Exodus into an argument that the motivation for God's actions is concern for his reputation:

> And I will remember for them the covenant of the former ones whom *I brought out from the land of Egypt in the eyes of the nations*, to be God for them; I am YHWH. (Lev 26:45)

> But they rebelled against me, and they were not willing to listen to me. Not one threw away the detestable things of their eyes, and they did not forsake the idols of Egypt. And I thought to pour out my wrath upon them, to finish off my anger on them in the midst of the land of Egypt. But I acted for the sake of my name, so as not to be profaned *in the eyes of the nations* in whose midst they were, in whose eyes I made myself known, to *bring them out from the land of Egypt*. (Ezek 20:8–9)

> When they entered the nations, wherever they entered, they profaned my holy name, in that it was said about them: "They are the people of YHWH, but they went out from his land!" ... Therefore, say to the house of Israel: Thus says Lord YHWH, "Not for your sake am I acting, O house of Israel, but for my holy name which you profaned among the nations into which you entered. And I will sanctify my great name which was profaned among the nations, which you profaned in their midst; and the *nations* will know that I am YHWH—utterance of YHWH—when I show myself holy among them *in their eyes*. (Ezek 36:20, 22–23)

---

44. **אלמנה וגרושה... לא לקח... כי אם־בתולה** "A widow or divorced woman ... he/they shall not take ... rather, a virgin." Note that Ezekiel changes H's singular verb form to a plural verb form.

Ezekiel uses the following locution from H:

- "bring them out" + "in the eyes of the nations" (הוֹצִיא אֹתָם + לְעֵינֵי הַגּוֹיִם): Lev 26:45; Ezek 20:9, 14, 22, 41. In each case the subject of the verb refers to God and the object to Israel.[45] A shorter form of this locution appears as לְעֵינֵי הַגּוֹיִם "in the eyes of the nations" (not attested with prepositions other than לְ); excluding the references above, it occurs in Isa 52:10; Ezek 5:8; 22:16; 28:25; 36:23 (the locution is split apart); 38:16 (the locution is split apart), 23; 39:27; Psa 98:2; 2 Chron 32:23.

Leviticus 26:45 refers to the Exodus as a public event, occurring "in the eyes of the nations." Ezekiel refers to this event in the same way. In chap. 20, Ezekiel states that God was ready to destroy the people because of their idolatry (vv. 8, 13, 21). However, after having publicly brought the people out of Egypt, God's reputation "in the eyes of the nations" would be damaged if he were to kill his people (Ezek 20:9, 14, 22). So God exiles the people instead of killing them (Ezek 20:23). But this solution is not satisfactory either. As we see in Ezek 36:20ff, Ezekiel argues that the condition of exile is publicly damaging God's reputation. In response, God will act to protect his name, publicly displaying his holiness "in the eyes of the nations" by bringing Israel out of captivity and into their own land.

Hope

Fifth, Ezekiel turns the conditional covenant blessings of Lev 26 into guaranteed covenant blessings in the future:

> And I will give your *rains in their time, and the land will give its produce, and the tree of the field will give its fruit.* And your threshing will overtake the grape harvest, and the grape harvest will overtake the sowing, and you will eat your bread to the full, *and you will live securely* in your land. And I will put *peace* in the

---

45. In Lev 26:45; Ezek 20:9 the people are brought out מֵאֶרֶץ מִצְרַיִם "from Egypt"; in Ezek 20:14, 22 the word "Egypt" is not used, though the verses clearly refer to the Exodus from Egypt. However, in Ezek 20:41, Israel is brought "from the peoples." References to the Exodus from Egypt can be phrased in a number of ways: e.g., הֶעֱלֵיתִי ... מִמִּצְרַיִם (Exod 3:17; Lev 11:45; Num 21:5; Deut 20:1; Josh 24:17; Judg 2:1; 1 Sam 8:8; 2 Kgs 17:7; Jer 16:14; Amos 2:10; Mic 6:4), or הוֹצִיא ... מֵאֶרֶץ מִצְרַיִם (common; e.g., Exod 7:4; 12:17; 13:9; Lev 19:36; 22:33; 26:13; Num 15:41; Deut 1:27; 4:37; Josh 24:6; 1 Sam 12:8; 1 Kgs 8:16; Jer 7:22; Ezek 20:6, 10; 2 Chron 7:22; etc).

land, and you will lie down *and there will be no one who terrifies. And I will finish off wild animals from the land,* and the sword will not pass through your land ... I am YHWH your God who brought you out from the land of Egypt, from being *slaves* to them; *and I broke the bars of your yoke,* and I made you walk upright. (Lev 26:4–6, 13)

And I will make a covenant of *peace* for them, *and I will finish off wild animals from the land, and they will live securely* in the wilderness, and they will sleep in the forests. And I will make them and the regions around my hill a blessing, and I will bring down *rain in its time*; they will be *rains* of blessing. *And the tree of the field will give its fruit, and the land will give its produce,* and they will be on their land *securely,* and they will know that I am YHWH, *when I break the bars of their yoke.* And I will deliver them from the hand of *those who used them as slaves.* And they will no longer be plunder for the nations, and *wild animals* will not devour them; *and they will live securely, and there will be no one who terrifies.* (Ezek 34:25–28)

In this passage, Ezekiel uses the following words and phrases from H:

- "rain in its time" (גשם בעתו): Lev 26:4; Jer 5:24 (adds יורה ומלקוש); Ezek 34:26.
- "and the land will give its produce" (והארץ תתן יבולה): Lev 26:4, 20; Ezek 34:27; Zech 8:12; Psalms 67:7; 85:13.
- "and the tree of the field will give its fruit" (ונתן עץ השדה את־פריו): Lev 26:4, 20 ("tree of the land"); Ezek 34:27. Note the variation "and I will multiply the fruit of the tree and the produce of the field" (Ezek 36:30).
- "live securely" (ישב לבטח): Lev 25:18, 19; 26:5; Deut 12:10; Judg 18:7; 1 Sam 12:11; 1 Kings 5:5; Isa 47:8; Jer 32:37; 49:31; Ezek 28:26 [2x]; 34:25, 27 (replaces ישב with היה), 28; 38:8, 11, 14; 39:6, 26; Zeph 2:15; Zech 14:11; Psa 4:9; Prov 3:29.
- "peace" (שלום): Lev 26:6 ("I will put peace in the land") and Ezek 34:25 ("covenant of peace") share this common word; it is only the presence of other shared locutions that suggests Ezekiel may be borrowing this from H.

- "there is no one who terrifies" (אֵין מַחֲרִיד): Lev 26:6; Deut 28:26; Isaiah 17:2; Jer 7:33; 30:10; 46:27; Ezek 34:28 (also includes חיה from Lev 26:6); 39:26; Micah 4:4; Nahum 2:12; Zeph 3:13; Job 11:19. The expression "terrify secure Cush" (MT Ezek 30:9) contains an expression in which יָשַׁב לָבֶטַח (Lev 26:5) and אֵין מַחֲרִיד (Lev 26:6) have been conflated.
- "I will finish off wild animals from the land" (וְהִשְׁבַּתִּי חַיָּה רָעָה מִן־הָאָרֶץ): Lev 26:6; Ezek 34:25.
- "slave/to enslave" (עבד): This common root occurs in Lev 26:13 and Ezek 34:27 in descriptions of liberation; in both cases it occurs in proximity to other shared locutions.
- "break the bars of the yoke" (שָׁבַר מֹטוֹת עַל): Lev 26:13; Ezek 34:27; both verses also include words from the root עבד (see also Lev 25:46).[46]

In Ezek 34:25–28, Ezekiel has used and transformed the covenant language of Lev 26 into a new blueprint for restoration. He has omitted H's covenant punishments (Lev 26:14–39) because—as is clear in Ezek 11:20; 36:27; 37:24—the people will be enabled to obey, thus rendering threats superfluous. He has also removed the conditional elements from H's blessings ("*If* you walk in my statutes," Lev 26:3) and turned them into unqualified guarantees.

Ezekiel does not simply take over H's locutions, but modifies them in order to make his model of restoration more extravagant than the description of the covenant relationship in H. Not only will Israel "live securely in the land" (Lev 26:5), but they will "live securely in the wilderness and sleep in the forests" (Ezek 34:25). The word "securely" is repeated three times (Ezek 34:25, 27, 28) to underscore its importance as a solution to the problem of the harassed flock described in vv. 1–6. Not only will there be "rain in its season" (Lev 26:4; Ezek 34:26b), but these will be "rains of blessing" (Ezek 34:26c). Ezekiel not only repeats H's blessing about the elimination of wild animals (Lev 26:6; Ezek 34:25), but he also reverses H's punishment of destructive wild animals (Lev 26:22; Ezek 34:28). Finally, Ezekiel reverses the punishment of famine

---

46. The shorter locution שָׁבַר מֹטוֹת "break (yoke) bars" occurs in Nah 1:13; Jer 28:10, 12,13; Ezek 30:18. The locution שָׁבַר עַל "break a yoke" occurs in Jer 2:20; 5:5; 28:2, 4,11; 30:8; "yoke will be broken" (חֶבֶל עַל) appears in Isa 10:27.

described in H (Lev 26:26; Ezek 34:29b). By juxtaposing this reversal with the statement "I will establish for them a planting of renown (מטע לשם, Ezek 34:29a)," he plays on the literal and figurative meanings of the word "planting" to argue for the fertility of both land and people.[47]

Ezekiel's Model of Restoration

The idea that the "house of Israel"—that is, Ezekiel's fellow-exiles (Ezek 11:15)—might come to an end is intolerable for the prophet. He had to contend with the dangers of marginalization (Ezek 11:15ff), religious assimilation (20:32ff), and fatalistic despondency (37:11ff). Ezekiel responds to these dangers by using the language of the Holiness Code to argue that there is a hopeful future in store for Israel.

One might ask: why doesn't Ezekiel simply use the model of restoration presented in Lev 26:40–42? According to H, if the people confess (Hitp. ידה), humble (כנע) their heart, and make amends (רצה) for their iniquity, God will remember the land and the covenant with the patriarchs. However, this program is based on the idea that restoration is contingent upon human repentance—an idea that Ezekiel cannot accept.

Ezekiel believes that the people are incorrigible.[48] He repeatedly calls them "the rebellious house" (Ezek 2:5, 6, 7, 8; 3:9, 26, 27; 12:2, 3, 9, 25; 17:12; 24:3; 44:6). God warns Ezekiel at the beginning of his ministry that they will not listen to what he says (Ezek 3:7). Ezekiel describes the history of the people in purely negative terms, showing that they are unable and unwilling to depart from the evil practices of their ancestors (Ezek 16, esp. vv. 44–45; chap. 20, esp. v. 30). There are only three references to repentance in the entire book (Ezek 14:6; 18:30–32; 33:11)—and there is no indication in any of these contexts that Ezekiel expects a positive response.[49] Even more significant is the fact that Ezekiel never

---

47. See Greenberg, *Ezekiel 21–37: A New Translation with Introduction and Commentary*, AB 22A 5(New York: Doubleday, 1997) 703–4; see also Isa 60:21; 61:3.

48. See Baruch Schwartz, "Ezekiel's Dim View of Israel's Restoration," in *The Book of Ezekiel: Theological and Anthropological Perspectives*, ed. Margaret S. Odell and John T. Strong, SBLSymS 9 (Atlanta: SBL, 2000) 46 [43–67].

49. Other commentators have noted this rarity; see Schwartz, "Ezekiel's Dim View," 46–47. Paul Joyce (*Divine Initiative*, 57–58) argues that the function of these appeals is to underscore Israel's responsibility and God's yearning for obedience, not to pro-

ties his descriptions of restoration to these appeals to repent. The idea that the people are incorrigible is brought out most clearly in Ezekiel's statement of their need for a "new heart": the people are spiritually abnormal, and must therefore undergo some kind of ontological change in order to follow God's commands (Ezek 11:19–20).

Not only does Ezekiel reject the possibility that the people might take the initiative to repent, but he depicts restoration as the result of God's initiative. In every description of restoration (Ezek 11:14–21; 16:60–63; 20:33–44; 28:25–26; 34:11–16, 23–31; 36:8–15, 22–38; 37), the blessings described are not contingent on any action by the people, but on God's action alone.[50] This is argued quite clearly in Ezek 36:22, 32, where God announces that he is not restoring Israel because of any action they take, but for the sake of his reputation alone.

Ezekiel's departure from the model of restoration in H is reflected in his vocabulary. Of H's three words for restoration (Lev 26:40–41), Ezekiel never uses "confess" (Hitp. ידה) or "humble" (כנע), and only uses רצה with God as the subject in the sense "to accept." Ezekiel's alternative program for the future is expressed by a different constellation of words he uses to describe the people's response to God's unilateral action: the people will "remember (זכר) their wicked ways" (Ezek 16:61, 63; 20:43; 36:31; 39:26); they will "feel shame" (בוש, כלם) for what they have done (16:54, 61, 63; 36:32; cf. 39:26, כלמה), and they will "loathe themselves (קוט)" (20:43; 36:31). These actions are not the preconditions for restoration; they are the results of it. The function of

---

duce a response that would result in restoration; see also Joyce, *Ezekiel: A Commentary*, LHBOTS 482 (New York: T. & T. Clark, 2007) 20–23, 26–27. Even Andrew Mein, who wonders whether "perhaps the calls for repentance are to be understood straightforwardly," agrees that "no direct connection is made between repentance and YHWH's action in restoration"; see Mein, *Ezekiel and the Ethics of Exile* (Oxford: Oxford University Press, 2001) 211–12.

50. On the unilateral action of God in Ezekiel's model of restoration, see Joyce, *Divine Initiative*, 126: "Israel's obedience will be the result rather than the cause of deliverance, part and parcel of the restoration and certainly not a condition upon which it depends"; Milgrom, *Leviticus 23–27*, 2330: "Interestingly, Ezekiel denies any role to Israel in the redemptive process. God will restore Israel to its land unconditionally . . . Ezekiel, like Jeremiah before him, despairs of Israel's ability to change its ways and, as a consequence, predicts that God will perform a "heart transplant," which will guarantee that Israel will sin no more . . ."; and Baruch Schwartz, "Ezekiel's Dim View," 49: "Ezekiel severs the nexus between the two elements [viz., between repentance and mercy], asserting that YHWH remembers his covenant with Israel irrespective of the latter's return to him and not as an act of reconciliation."

these responses is to testify to the fact of spiritual transformation: for the first time the people will be capable of grasping the enormity of their offenses against God.[51]

Ezekiel's problem with the model of restoration found in Lev 26 is that it does not address the possibility that the people might not repent. Nor does it address the possibility that a repentant people might someday apostatize again. Ezekiel solves these problems in a very radical way. Instead of simply copying the covenant of Lev 26 and projecting it into the future, Ezekiel removes the punishments from the covenant and envisions a change that guarantees the covenant stipulations will always be kept. This change is one that God will perform in the hearts of the people.

This radical reconceptualization of the covenant can be seen in passages where Ezekiel transforms the commands of Leviticus into guarantees of future behavior. Whereas H *commanded* the people to walk in God's statutes (Lev 18:4–5), Ezekiel argues that God will *make* the people walk in his statutes (Ezek 36:27). Whereas H commanded the people to keep God's ordinances, Ezekiel argues that God will give them a new heart *so that they will* keep his ordinances (Ezek 11:19–20).

Leviticus 26, then, does not provide the full model behind Ezekiel's outlook; it only provides part of the conceptual imagery. When Ezekiel envisions the physical aspects of restoration in Ezek 34:25–28—a return to the land, the rebuilding of waste places, fertility of the ground, living in security—he uses the blessings of Lev 26 for his descriptions. When he envisions the spiritual aspects of restoration—a covenant relationship, the divine presence, an obedient people—he again uses locutions from Lev 26, but carefully omits all of its threats, because he believes these will no longer be necessary in the future.

Conclusion

Thomas Renz argues that the book of Ezekiel represents an attempt to convince the reader of four things:

---

51. See Jacqueline E. Lapsley, "Shame and Self-Knowledge: The Positive Role of Shame in Ezekiel's View of the Moral Self," in *The Book of Ezekiel: Theological and Anthropological Perspectives*, ed. Margaret S. Odell and John T. Strong, SBLSymS 9 (Atlanta: SBL, 2000) 143–73.

At first, the readers were only asked to see the end of Jerusalem as the result of her sin, then they were asked to "judge" Jerusalem, and with Jerusalem their own rebellious behavior. In the oracles against the nations the readers were invited to see the same pattern of rebellion against Yahweh at work which had brought Jerusalem to its end. The readers are encouraged to see that rebellion against Yahweh reduces Israel to the level of other nations and does not have a future, since Yahweh will destroy pride against him everywhere. Thus they will realise that assimilation into other nations will only continue the rebellious history of the past and consequently will not open up a future for their community. Chaps. 33–48 then show that the beginning and end of New Israel is the acknowledgement of Yahweh's kingship which has the promise of transformation.[52]

The analysis of Ezekiel's use of H laid out in this essay supports Renz's conclusions. Ezekiel's transformation of H's laws into accusations and H's conditional covenant punishments into descriptions of imminent or actual punishment form the basis for the first three arguments noted by Renz. The Holiness Code is the authoritative standard by which Ezekiel finds his contemporaries guilty, and it contains the punishments with which he targets the Jerusalemites and the nations. The fourth argument that Renz notes deals with Ezekiel's outlook for restoration, and it is here that Ezekiel uses the description of the conditional covenant blessings in H as a paradigm for the future, transforming them into guaranteed blessings of a new relationship.

Ezekiel's recontextualization of H's locutions necessitated the transformation of their literary form, addressees, scope, temporal frame, and modality. By transforming earlier legal material into accusations and conditional covenant punishments into descriptions of actual devastation, Ezekiel could account for the exile by creating a causal connection between the people's behavior and the disaster they experienced. By selectively and paradigmatically using imagery from H's description of covenant blessings, Ezekiel described a future involving both physical and spiritual restoration. In this description, however, Ezekiel radically

---

52. Renz, *The Rhetorical Function of the Book of Ezekiel*, VTSup 76 (Leiden: Brill, 1999) 230–31. However, Renz's remark that "acknowledgement of Yahweh's kingship . . . has the promise of transformation" does not entirely bring out the nuances of Ezekiel's concept of restoration. For Ezekiel, YHWH *forcibly assumes* kingship over the people (Ezek 20:33), and the people's acknowledgment *follows* transformation rather than preceding it (Ezek 37:13–14).

redefines the very notion of covenant by omitting all of H's punishments in his description of the future relationship between God and Israel. His use of H was therefore primarily rhetorical in nature: he appealed to its authority and used its arguments and imagery to create his own arguments.

Bibliography

Ackroyd, Peter R. *Exile and Restoration: A Study of Hebrew Thought of the Sixth Century B.C.* OTL. Philadelphia: Westminster, 1968.

Albertz, Rainer. *A History of Israelite Religion in the Old Testament Period. Volume II: From the Exile to the Maccabees*. Translated by John Bowden. OTL. Louisville: Westminster John Knox, 1994.

———. *Israel in Exile: The History and Literature of the Sixth Century B.C.E.* Translated by David Green. StBibLit 3. Atlanta: Society of Biblical Literature, 2003.

Allen, Leslie. *Ezekiel 1–19*. WBC 28. Dallas: Word, 1994.

Baentsch, Bruno. *Das Heiligkeits-Gesetz Lev. XVII–XXVI: Eine historisch-kritische Untersuchung*. Erfurt: Güther, 1893.

Beentjes, Pancratius C. "Discovering a New Path of Intertextuality: Inverted Quotations and their Dynamics." In *Literary Structure and Rhetorical Strategy in the Hebrew Bible*, edited by L. J. de Regt, J. de Waard and J. P. Fokkelman, 31–49. Assen: Van Gorcum, 1996.

Blenkinsopp, Joseph. *A History of Prophecy in Israel*. Rev. ed. Louisville: Westminster John Knox, 1996.

Block, Daniel I. *The Book of Ezekiel, Chapters 1–24*. NICOT. Grand Rapids: Eerdmans, 1997.

Burrows, Millar. *The Literary Relations of Ezekiel*. New York: Jewish Publication Society, 1925.

Cooke, G. A. *A Critical and Exegetical Commentary on the Book of Ezekiel*. ICC. Edinburgh: T. & T. Clark, 1936.

Driver, Samuel Rolles. *An Introduction to the Literature of the Old Testament*. Edinburgh: T. & T. Clark, 1891. Reprinted, Gloucester, MA: Peter Smith, 1972.

Fishbane, Michael. *Biblical Interpretation in Ancient Israel*. Oxford: Clarendon, 1985.

Gese, Hartmut. *Der Verfassungsentwurf des Ezechiel (Kap. 40–48) traditionsgeschichtlich untersucht*. BHTh 25. Tübingen: Mohr/Siebeck, 1957.

Graf, Karl Heinrich. *Die geschichtlichen Bücher des Alten Testaments: Zwei historisch-kritische Untersuchungen*. Leipzig: Weigel, 1866.

Greenberg, Moshe. *Ezekiel 1–20: A New Translation with Introduction and Commentary*. AB 22. New York: Doubleday, 1983.

———. *Ezekiel 21–37: A New Translation with Introduction and Commentary*. AB 22A. New York: Doubleday, 1997.

———. "The Design and Themes of Ezekiel's Program of Restoration." *Int* 38 (1984) 181–208.

Haran, Menahem. "The Law-Code of Ezekiel XL–XLVIII and its Relation to the Priestly School." *HUCA* 50 (1979) 45–71.

Hayes, John H., and J. Maxwell Miller, editors. *Israelite and Judaean History*. London: SCM Press, 1977.
Horst, L. *Leviticus XVII–XXVI und Hezekiel: Ein Beitrag zur Pentateuchkritik*. Colmar: Barth, 1881.
Joosten, Jan. *People and Land in the Holiness Code: An Exegetical Study of the Ideational Framework of the Law in Leviticus 17–26*. VTSup 67. Leiden: Brill, 1996.
Joyce, Paul. *Divine Initiative and Human Response in Ezekiel*. JSOTSup 51. Sheffield: Sheffield Academic, 1989.
———. *Ezekiel: A Commentary*. LHBOTS 482. New York: T. & T. Clark, 2007.
Kilian, Rudolf. *Literarkritische und Formgeschichtliche Untersuchung des Heiligkeitsgesetzes*. BBB 19. Bonn: Hanstein, 1963.
Klostermann, August. "Ezechiel und das Heiligkeitsgesetz." In *Der Pentateuch: Beiträge zu seinem Verständis und seiner Entstehungsgeschichte*, 368–418. Leipzig: Böhme, 1893. Originally published as "Beiträge zur Entstehungsgeschichte des Pentateuchs." *ZLThK* 38 (1877) 401–45.
Knohl, Israel. *The Sanctuary of Silence: The Priestly Torah and the Holiness School*. Minneapolis: Fortress, 1995.
Lapsley, Jacqueline E. "Shame and Self-Knowledge: The Positive Role of Shame in Ezekiel's View of the Moral Self." In *The Book of Ezekiel: Theological and Anthropological Perspectives*, edited by Margaret S. Odell and John T. Strong, 143–73. SBLSymS 9. Atlanta: Society of Biblical Literature, 2000.
Levenson, Jon Douglas. *Theology of the Program of Restoration of Ezekiel 40–48*. HSM 10. Missoula: Scholars, 1976.
Levine, Baruch. "The Epilogue to the Holiness Code: A Priestly Statement on the Destiny of Israel." In *Judaic Perspectives on Ancient Israel*, edited by Jacob Neusner et al., 9–34. Philadelphia: Fortress, 1987.
Levinson, Bernard M. "The Birth of the Lemma: The Restrictive Reinterpretation of the Covenant Code's Manumission Law by the Holiness Code (Leviticus 25:44–46)." *JBL* 124 (2005) 617–39.
Levitt Kohn, Risa. *A New Heart and a New Soul: Ezekiel, the Exile and the Torah*. JSOTSup 358. Sheffield: Sheffield Academic, 2002.
Lipschits, Oded. *The Rise and Fall of Jerusalem: Jerusalem under Babylonian Rule*. Winona Lake, IN: Eisenbrauns, 2005.
Lipschits, Oded, and Joseph Blenkinsopp, editors. *Judah and the Judeans in the Neo-Babylonian Period*. Winona Lake, IN: Eisenbrauns, 2003.
Lyons, Michael A. *From Law to Prophecy: Ezekiel's Use of the Holiness Code*. LHBOTS 507. New York: T. & T. Clark, 2009.
———. "Marking Innerbiblical Allusion in the Book of Ezekiel." *Bib* 88 (2007) 245–50.
Mein, Andrew. *Ezekiel and the Ethics of Exile*. Oxford: Oxford University Press, 2001.
Middlemas, Jill. *The Troubles of Templeless Judah*. Oxford: Oxford University Press, 2005.
Milgrom, Jacob. "HR in Leviticus and Elsewhere in the Torah." In *The Book of Leviticus: Composition and Reception*, edited by Rolf Rendtorff and Robert A. Kugler, 24–40. VTSup 93. Leiden: Brill, 2003.
———. *Leviticus 17–22*. AB 3A. New York: Doubleday, 2001.
———. *Leviticus 23–27*. AB 3B. New York: Doubleday, 2001.

Nihan, Christophe. *From Priestly Torah to Pentateuch: A Study in the Composition of the Book of Leviticus.* FAT 2/25. Tübingen: Mohr/Siebeck, 2007.

———. "The Holiness Code between D and P: Some Comments on the Function and Significance of Leviticus 17–26 in the Composition of the Torah." In *Das Deuteronomium zwischen Pentateuch und Deuteronomistischem Geschichtswerk*, edited by Eckart Otto and Reinhard Achenbach, 81–122. FRLANT 206. Göttingen: Vandenhoeck & Ruprecht, 2004.

Otto, Eckart. "Innerbiblische Exegese im Heiligkeitsgesetz Levitikus 17–26." In *Levitikus als Buch*, edited by Heinz-Josef Fabry and Hans-Winfried Jüngling, 125–196. BBB 119. Berlin: Philo, 1999.

Paton, Lewis Bayles. "The Holiness Code and Ezekiel." *Presbyterian and Reformed Review* 26 (1896) 98–115.

Raitt, Thomas M. *A Theology of Exile: Judgment/Deliverance in Jeremiah and Ezekiel.* Philadelphia: Fortress, 1977.

Renz, Thomas. *The Rhetorical Function of the Book of Ezekiel.* VTSup 76. Leiden: Brill, 1999.

Reventlow, Henning Graf. *Wächter über Israel. Ezechiel und seine Tradition.* BZAW 82. Berlin: Töpelmann, 1962.

Schultz, Richard L. *The Search for Quotation: Verbal Parallels in the Prophets.* JSOTSup 180. Sheffield: Sheffield Academic, 1999.

Schwartz, Baruch. "Ezekiel's Dim View of Israel's Restoration." In *The Book of Ezekiel: Theological and Anthropological Perspectives*, edited by Margaret S. Odell and John T. Strong, 43–67. SBLSymS 9. Atlanta: Society of Biblical Literature, 2000.

Seeligmann, I. L. "Voraussetzungen der Midraschexegese." In *Congress Volume. Copenhagen 1953*, edited by G. W. Anderson et al., 150–81. VTSup 1. Leiden: Brill, 1953.

Smend, Rudolf. *Der Prophet Ezechiel.* 2nd ed. KeH. Leipzig: Hirzel, 1880.

Smith-Christopher, Daniel L. *A Biblical Theology of Exile.* OBT. Minneapolis: Fortress, 2002.

———. *The Religion of the Landless: The Social Context of the Babylonian Exile.* Bloomington, IN: Meyer-Stone, 1989.

Talmon, S., and M. Fishbane. "The Structuring of Biblical Books: Studies in the Book of Ezekiel." *ASTI* 10 (1976) 129–53.

Tuell, Steven Shawn. *The Law of the Temple in Ezekiel 40–48.* HSM 49. Atlanta: Scholars, 1992.

Wellhausen, Julius. *Prolegomena to the History of Ancient Israel.* Translated by J. S. Black and A. Menzies. 1885. Reprinted, New York: Meridian, 1957.

Wong, Ka Leung. *The Idea of Retribution in the Book of Ezekiel.* VTSup 87. Leiden: Brill, 2001.

Zimmerli, Walther. *Ezekiel 1: A Commentary on the Book of the Prophet Ezekiel, Chapters 1–24.* Translated by Ronald E. Clements. Hermeneia. Philadelphia: Fortress, 1979.

———. *Ezekiel 2: A Commentary on the Book of the Prophet Ezekiel, Chapters 25–48.* Translated by James D. Martin. Hermeneia. Philadelphia: Fortress, 1983.

2

Transformation of Pentateuchal Descriptions of Idolatry

Tova Ganzel

A FOCAL ISSUE IN THE STUDY OF EZEKIEL IS THE EXTENT TO WHICH he depends on and continues existing conceptions, or presents an independent, innovative development. Through an examination of how Ezekiel relates to pentateuchal pericopae concerning idolatry, this chapter utilizes Ezekiel's depiction of idolatry as a test case for comprehending Ezekiel's literary-conceptual path.

Several prevailing assumptions are widely accepted in Ezekiel scholarship. The first assigns Ezekiel's activity to the period preceding and following the destruction of the First Temple. Another assumes Ezekiel's familiarity with the Priestly literature and identifies stylistic-contextual links between his oracles and this literature.[1] Although

---

1. *I thank Dr. Baruch J. Schwartz for his generosity in reading this and earlier versions of this article and for his insightful, pertinent comments. I also thank Dena Ordan both for translating and editing the article and for her help in bringing this article to its present form.

The dating of the Priestly sources is a matter of scholarly debate. From Wellhausen's day P was identified as the latest source in the Torah and dated to the exilic or the Persian period. Other scholars have since questioned this determination and argue that P is pre-exilic. See the survey by Ernest W. Nicholson, *The Pentateuch in the Twentieth Century: The Legacy of Julius Wellhausen* (Oxford: Clarendon, 1998) 20–21, 218–21. Some distinguish between two priestly strata, one pre-exilic and one exilic. See Richard E. Friedman, *The Exile and Biblical Narrative: The Formation of the Deuteronomistic and Priestly Works*, HSM 22 (Chico, CA: Scholars, 1981) 132–44. Avi Hurvitz's linguistic study set the scholarly foundation, since followed by many, for dating Ezekiel later than the Priestly literature (*A Linguistic Study of the Relationship between the Priestly Source and the Book of Ezekiel*, CahRB 20 [Paris: Gabalda, 1982]). The underlying assumption of this study is that the prophet Ezekiel lived and prophesied during the period of the

I concur with both of these assumptions, we cannot overlook recent studies that have raised and reexamined a possible literary-conceptual connection between the book of Ezekiel and the book of Deuteronomy (D) and the Deuteronomistic School (Dtr).[2] Unlike the scholarly consensus regarding the links between the book of Ezekiel and the Priestly literature, the connection between Ezekiel, Deuteronomy, and the Deuteronomistic History is still a matter of debate.[3] Ezekiel's oracles depicting Israelite idolatry serve as a vehicle for exploring the relationship between Ezekiel and D/Dtr.

Notwithstanding their ties to priestly conceptions of idolatrous practices and their result, Ezekiel's descriptions of these practices, surprisingly, reflect a far more notable connection to D and to Dtr than to the Priestly literature.[4] Although, as noted, recent studies have broadly addressed a possible connection between D, Dtr, and Ezekiel, to date none have fully investigated the influence of D/Dtr on Ezekiel's portrayal of idolatry and how this fundamentally Deuteronomistic influence on Ezekiel's teaching is integrated into the prophet's essentially priestly worldview.[5] This will therefore be the aim of the present study. I begin with the detailed visions of idolatrous practices in Ezekiel 8, in the depic-

---

destruction and that his oracles can be dated to this period. See Moshe Greenberg, *Ezekiel 1–20,* AB 22 (Garden City, NY: Doubleday, 1983) 12–17.

2. Risa L. Kohn, *A New Heart and a New Soul: Ezekiel, the Exile and the Torah,* JSOTSup 358 (London: Sheffield Academic, 2002); Rimon Kasher, *Ezekiel: Introduction and Commentary,* vol. 1: *Chapters 1–24,* Mikra Leyisra'el (Tel Aviv: Am Oved, 2004) 62–64 (Hebrew).

3. The determination of the direction of the allusions is grounded in the widely accepted assumption, following Noth, that Deuteronomy and the Early Prophets constitute a single planned work: the Deuteronomistic History or Work, composed shortly before the destruction of the First Temple. See Martin Noth, *The Deuteronomistic History,* 2d ed., JSOTSS 15 (Sheffield: JSOT, 1991 [German original, 1943]); Enzo Cortese, *Deuteronomistic Work,* trans. Silas Musholt, SBFA 47 (Jerusalem: Franciscan Printing Press, 1999); C. L. Patton, "Pan-Deuteronomism and the Book of Ezekiel," in *Those Elusive Deuteronomists: The Phenomenon of Pan-Deuteronomism,* ed. L. S. Schearing and S. L. McKenzie, JSOTSup 268 (London: Sheffield, 1999) 200–215, and the bibliography on 200–201.

4. The phrase "Priestly literature" is used here in its broad sense, as inclusive of the Holiness Code and the Holiness School. For a valuable consideration of the question of the sources with which Ezekiel was familiar, see Kohn's recent study, *New Heart.* Kohn notes, among other things, that Ezekiel makes equal use of all of the Priestly literature (p. 85).

5. Kohn, *New Heart.*

tion of which I shall point out the literary relations with Deuteronomy 4. I then examine additional Deuteronomic terms employed by Ezekiel in reference to the Israelites' idolatrous practices.[6] This article concludes with a consideration of Ezekiel's use of the Priestly literature in oracles depicting idolatry as causing impurity and how this contributes to clarification of the relationship between Ezekiel and D/Dtr.

The Depiction of Idolatry: Ezekiel and Deuteronomy

A key theme throughout the book of Ezekiel is the unbridled, sinful idolatry of the Israelite people from earliest times until the present. According to Ezekiel, this sin carries a number of consequences: the desecration of the divine name in the eyes of the nations, the destruction of the Temple, and the exile of the people from their land. For Ezekiel, the Israelites' longstanding failure to comply with YHWH's commands on the one hand and its unceasing practice of idolatry on the other, extend from the formative period of the Israelite nation in Egypt to the time of Ezekiel's own deportation from Jerusalem. Consequently, the people, the land, and the temple are impure. Moreover, in Ezekiel's eyes, their idolatrous practices have not only desecrated (חלל) but also defiled (טמא) the Israelites.[7]

In his oracles, Ezekiel assigns a variety of terms to the idolatrous practices of the Israelite people. At times, he merely notes the existence of these practices; in other instances, he goes into greater detail.[8] The rarity of the terms used by Ezekiel and their concentration in a single

6. Not to say that Ezekiel was influenced by Dtr, but only that the Dtr writings assist the identification of these phrases and concepts.

7. No prophecy by Ezekiel describes a time or situation in which the Israelites preserved their sanctity or purity; this despite the fact that Ezekiel is more concerned with holiness than any other prophet, as seen from his far more frequent use of the roots קדש (holy), חלל (profane), טמא (defile), and טהר (purge). Moreover, Ezekiel's survey of the condition of the Israelite people from its formative days in Egypt until its arrival and behavior in the land of Canaan in chapter 20 repeatedly stresses that, from the time of the Exodus, the Israelites did not abandon the idolatry practiced in Egypt; neither did they abandon idolatry from their arrival in the land until their scattering among the nations. See Tova Ganzel, "The Concept of Holiness in the Book of Ezekiel" (PhD diss., Bar-Ilan University, 2004) 186 (Hebrew).

8. Jacob Milgrom enumerates eighty-two (!) instances in which Ezekiel protests against the Israelites' idolatry ("The Nature and Extent of Idolatry in Eighth-Seventh Century Judah," *HUCA* 69 [1998] 1). The present discussion is limited to those verses in which Ezekiel specifies a particular kind of idolatry.

chapter, as found in Ezekiel 8, requires close examination of these terms. Arriving at an understanding of these references and their exact meaning calls for a historically contextualized literary analysis of Ezekiel and of other biblical books.[9] This terminological discussion also impacts the question of the sources available to Ezekiel and may contribute to the longstanding debate regarding textual links between various biblical books and determination of the direction of influence. The relevant criteria include shared, especially rare and distinctive, language, and similar contexts. In conjunction, these provide added weight to the evidence for, and direction of, literary-conceptual influence, in this case of Deuteronomy on Ezekiel.

In the majority of contexts where Ezekiel treats idolatrous practices, we find almost exclusive use of terminology and descriptions from Deuteronomy.[10] Consideration of these terms not only demonstrates Ezekiel's deliberate use of this terminology and content; it sheds light on what may have motivated Ezekiel's preference for Deuteronomic terms in his descriptions of idol worship. A list of these terms encompasses:[11]

a) סמל—*statue* (Deut 4:16; Ezek 8:3, 5);

b) תבנית—*likeness* (Deut 4:16, 17, 18; Ezek 8:10);

c) the prohibition against sun worship (Deut 4:19; 17:3; Ezek 8:16);

d) שקוצים—*detestable things* (Deut 29:16; Ezek 5:11; 7:20; 11:8, 21; 20: 7, 8, 30; 37:23);

e) עץ ואבן—*worshiping wood and stone* (Deut 4:28; 28:36, 64; 29:17; Ezek 20:32);

f) העברת הבנים באש—*pass sons through fire* (Deut 18:10; Ezek 20:31);

---

9. S. Tamar Kamionkowski proposes this type of analysis as the key to unlocking Ezekiel 16: "By historically contextualized, I mean an analysis of the meanings of words and phrases within their original textual and cultural contexts. While the typical historical critic seeks to find a single meaning in a text, the literary critic relishes in multiple meanings and ambiguities" (*Gender Reversal and Cosmic Chaos: A Study on the Book of Ezekiel*, JSOTSup 368 [London: Sheffield, 2003] 114).

10. This phenomenon may also apply to other contexts in Ezekiel. See Kohn, *New Heart*, 86–95. She also treats Ezekiel's deliberate choice of D/Dtr terminology (ibid., 96–118).

11. Biblical verses translated by author. In the translations an attempt was made to reflect, and distinguish between, the many, varied terms for idolatry used by Ezekiel.

g) ‏בכל גבעה רמה / בכל ראשי ההרים ותחת כל־עץ רענן‎
on every hill/every mountain height and under every leafy tree (Deut 12:2; Ezek 6:13);

h) ‏גדע‎—*cut down idols or pillars* (Deut 7:5, 12:3; Ezek 6:6).[12]

Ezekiel's most comprehensive description of idolatrous practices is found in chapter 8. There he mentions ‏סמל הקנאה‎ (*statue of outrage*), ‏תבנית רמש ובהמה שקץ‎ (*likeness of creeping thing and beasts, detestations*), ‏גלולים‎ (*idols*), bewailing Tammuz, and sun worship. Ezekiel 8, with its dense depiction of a variety of idolatrous practices, demonstrates Ezekiel's penchant for applying Deuteronomic terms to the Israelites' idolatrous practices. In the first of its four visions (8:5–6), Ezekiel sees a manifestation of idolatry ‏סמל‎ (*statue*), which appears twice in this chapter as part of the combination ‏סמל הקנאה‎ (8:3, 5). Evidently, like ‏צלם‎ (*figure*), this word connotes *graven image* (‏פסל‎), and, in this context, means *statue of outrage*.[13] The word ‏סמל‎ appears only once in the Pentateuch, in Deuteronomy 4: "not to act destructively and make yourselves a graven image (‏פסל‎), the form of any statue (‏תמונת כל סמל‎), the likeness of a male or female" (‏תַּבְנִית זָכָר אוֹ נְקֵבָה‎; v. 16).[14]

Like the first, the second vision (8: 7–12) also exhibits direct links to Deuteronomy 4. There, Ezekiel uses the phrase ‏תבנית כל רמש‎ (*likeness of any creeping thing*; v. 10)[15] with reference to an additional

---

12. For a list of Deuteronomic and Priestly terms found in Ezekiel divided according to source, see Kohn, *New Heart*, 139–46. I supplement the idolatry-related terms cited in Kohn's list with the following additional ones from D: the prohibition against sun worship, ‏סמל‎, and ‏גדע‎. From the Priestly literature I add: ‏חמן‎ and ‏צלם‎.

13. The distinction between ‏צלם‎ and ‏סמל‎ is not unequivocal, as seen from the LXX's use of the same word, εἰκών, in its translations of the root ‏צלם:צלמי כשדים,צלמי זכר,צלמי תועבותם‎, and ‏סמל הקנאה‎. For a discussion of the connotation of ‏סמל‎, see Susan Ackerman, *Under Every Green Tree*, HSM 46 (Atlanta: Scholars, 2004) 55–57; and Kasher, *Ezekiel*, 246.

14. ‏סמל‎ appears in the Bible five times: once in Deuteronomy 4, twice in Ezekiel 8, and twice more in 2 Chronicles (33:7, 15) in the context of the description of the idolatry introduced to the temple by Manasseh. Based on this linguistic link, some scholars submit that Ezekiel 8 reflects Manasseh's day (see, for example, Moshe Greenberg, *Ezekiel 1-20*, AB 22 [Garden City, NY: Doubleday & Company, 1983] 202).

15. Note that the terms ‏תבנית‎ (*likeness*) and ‏רמש‎ (*creeping thing*) also appear separately in the Priestly literature, where ‏תבנית‎ refers to the plan of the Tabernacle (Exod 25:9, 40) and ‏רמש‎ is a collective noun for all creeping things (Lev 11:44). See

form of idolatry.¹⁶ The second vision's portrayal of the idolatrous images on the temple walls: "Likeness of any creeping thing and beasts (תבנית כל רמש), detestations and all the idols of the House of Israel engraved on the wall all around" echoes Deuteronomy's warning against making various 'forms' or 'likenesses': "Be strictly on your guard ... not to act destructively and make yourselves a graven image, the form of any statue ... likeness of any creeping thing on the ground" (תבנית כל רמש באדמה; Deut 4:15–18).¹⁷

The third vision (8:13–14), in which Ezekiel sees women bewailing Tammuz, has no biblical parallels.¹⁸ But the fourth vision (8:15–16) mirrors yet another admonition exclusive to Deuteronomy. Ezekiel 8:16 describes a group of men engaging in sun worship: "There, at the entrance of YHWH's Temple, between the portico and the altar, were about twenty-five men, whose backs were to YHWH's Temple and whose faces were turned east and they were prostrating themselves eastward to the sun." This reflects Deuteronomy's warning against worshiping heavenly bodies: "And when you look up to the sky and behold the sun and the moon and the stars, the whole heavenly host, you must not be lured into bowing down to them or serving them" (Deut 4:19). An additional link between Ezekiel 8 and Deuteronomy 4 is the conjugation of the verb כעס following the fourth vision: the expression להכעיסני found in Ezek 8:17 is singular to D/Dtr and matches the suffixed *hiphil* pattern להכעיסו in reference to God's anger in Deut 4:25.

Thus, in three of the four visions found in chapter eight's description of the Israelites' behavior in the temple, Ezekiel makes what appears to be intentional use of terms from Deuteronomy 4. Up to this point, this consideration clearly demonstrates that Ezekiel knew and was linguistically influenced by Deuteronomy as an independent source and,

---

also Menahem Zevi Kaddari, *A Dictionary of Biblical Hebrew (Alef—Taw)* (Ramat Gan: Bar-Ilan Press, 2006), s.v. רמש (Hebrew).

16. See Kasher's comment on this verse: "The language of the verse is influenced by Deut 4:17–18 ... but whereas Deuteronomy relates to idols, here the reference is to figures carved or engraved on a wall" (*Ezekiel,* 250). See also Andrew Mein, *Ezekiel and the Ethics of Exile,* OTM (Oxford: Oxford University Press, 2001) 124–27.

17. See also John F. Kutsko, *Between Heaven and Earth: Divine Presence and Absence in the Book of Ezekiel,* Biblical and Judaic Studies 7 (Winona Lake, IN: Eisenbrauns, 2000) 42–46.

18. Consequently, the discussion of this vision calls upon extrabiblical sources. See, for example, Ackerman, *Under Every Green Tree,* 79–92.

as we shall see, by its unique ideology.[19] Nevertheless, it is difficult to determine precisely with which parts of D or Dtr Ezekiel was familiar.[20]

Contextual examination of this terminology, based on the supposition that Ezekiel was familiar, at least, with Deuteronomy 4, sheds further light on Ezekiel's dependence on Deuteronomy. Deuteronomy's warnings against idolatry appear in the framework of the directive to adhere to the divine commandments, repeated several times in the opening of chapter four: "You shall not add anything to what I command or take anything away from it" (Deut 4:2); "See, I have imparted to you laws and rules...Observe them faithfully" (Deut 4:5–6); "But take utmost care and watch yourselves scrupulously, so that you do not forget the things you saw with your own eyes and so that they do not fade from your mind . . ." (Deut 4:9); "Be strictly on your guard, therefore, because you saw no form on the day that YHWH spoke to you at Horeb out of the fire" (4:15). The explicit contrast between these warnings and the description of the nation's deeds (מעשי) in Ezekiel underscores and heightens the Israelites' sinfulness.

Following its expostulations against idolatry, Deuteronomy 4 recalls the divine covenant with Israel established at Horeb, and spells out the consequences of abandoning this covenant once the Israelite people are well established in their land:

> . . . should you . . . act destructively and make for yourselves a graven image in any likeness, causing YHWH displeasure and vexation. I call heaven and earth this day to witness against you that you shall soon perish from the land that you are crossing the Jordan to possess . . . YHWH will scatter you among the nations, and only a scant few of you shall be left among the nations to which the Lord will drive you. There you will serve man-made gods of wood and stone, which cannot see or hear or eat or smell. (vv. 25–28)[21]

19. As opposed to Patton who suggests that although the texts in Ezekiel evincing Deuteronomistic influence may testify to Ezekiel's incorporation of Deuteronomistic conceptions into his message one can also cite influence in the opposite direction, of Ezekiel on Jeremiah and Deuteronomy ("Pan-Deuteronomism," 209–15).

20. For the link between the books of Ezekiel and Jeremiah, see, for example, K. W. Carley, *Ezekiel among the Prophets* (London: SCM, 1975) 51–57.

21. Through the use of terms typical to D Ezekiel refers indirectly to additional aspects of Deut 4:1–40 in other of his oracles. Consequently, the importance of a comparison between this passage and Ezekiel goes beyond the latter's descriptions of idolatry. Other points of contact include (a) the scattering of the Israelites among the

By echoing Deuteronomy's admonitions against idolatry and its enumeration of its consequences, and by drawing implied parallels between these admonitions and the actions of the Israelite people that were carried out in spite of repeated warnings to the contrary, Ezekiel intensifies his prophetic message, outlining the causes for the destruction of Jerusalem and the exile.[22] I ascribe Ezekiel's greater reliance on Deuteronomic, as opposed to Priestly, terminology in his depiction of idolatry to his perception of the religious and cultic practices he identifies as leading to Israel's destruction and to its effectiveness in reifying these causes. This lends added strength to his criticism of the people and their behavior.

In addition to the direct relationship posited here between Ezekiel 8 and Deuteronomy 4, the book of Ezekiel shares with Deuteronomy additional terms describing idolatry unique to these two books. Examination of these terms, and their contexts, sheds further light on Ezekiel's treatment of idolatry as a cause for the destruction.

The first of these terms is שִׁקּוּצִים (*detestable things*).[23] שִׁקּוּץ appears in D, Ezekiel, and other books, but it never appears in the Priestly literature. In Ezekiel, שִׁקּוּץ appears eight times (5:11; 7:20; 11:18, 21; 20:7, 8, 30; 37:23). If in the Priestly literature the noun שֶׁקֶץ describes various creatures unfit for human consumption, its single occurrence in Ezekiel, as in Deuteronomy, refers to idolatry. In the Pentateuch, Deut 29:16 alone reflects this connotation: "the detestable things (שִׁקּוּצֵיהֶם) and the idols of wood and stone, silver and gold, which they keep."[24]

---

nations (Deut 4:27; Ezek 11:17; 12:15; 20:23, 34, 41; 22:15; 29:12; 30:23, 26; 36:19); (b) the combination בְּיָד חֲזָקָה וּבִזְרוֹעַ נְטוּיָה (Deut 4:34; Ezek 20:33); and (c) God's choosing of the Israelites: וַיִּבְחַר בְּזַרְעוֹ (Deut 4:37), בָּחֲרִי בְיִשְׂרָאֵל (Ezek 20:5).

22. For the view that chapters 1–4 belong to the book of Deuteronomy and are not, as Noth and other submit, Deuteronomistic, see the recent study by Menahem Haran, *The Biblical Collection: Its Consolidation to the End of the Second Temple Times and Changes of Form to the End of the Middle Ages*, vol. 2 (Jerusalem: Bialik and Magnes, 2003), 195–200 (Hebrew).

23. For discussions of the signification of the word שקץ in Ezekiel, see Jacob Milgrom, "Two Priestly Terms *Šeqeṣ* and *Ṭāmē*," *Tarbiz* 60 (1991) 423–28 (Hebrew); Kohn, *New Heart*, 89–90 and Ganzel, "Concept of Holiness," 26.

24. We may possibly add to the list of terms the designation תּוֹעֵבָה found in Deut 7:26. For a discussion of the meaning of this term in Ezekiel in particular, see Paul Humbert, "Le substantive *toʿēbā* et le verbe *tʿb* dans l'Ancien Testament," *ZAW* 72 (1960) 227–31; Winston H. Pickett, "The Meaning and Function of 'T'B/TOʿEVAH' in the Hebrew Bible" (PhD diss., Hebrew Union College–Jewish Institute of Religion, 1985)

The context of this verse is the covenant in the land of Moab, including its conditions and punishments, for future generations. By alluding to Deuteronomy, Ezekiel creates a cause-and-effect relationship between the current sins of the people and the punishments of destruction and exile cited in the Deuteronomic covenant. These additional connections between the books of Ezekiel and Deuteronomy strengthen the premise that Ezekiel was directly familiar with D/Dtr in addition to the Priestly literature and indicate that this influence was not simply rhetorical, but conceptual as well.

Another shared phrase is עץ ואבן (*worshiping wood and stone*), found four times in Deuteronomy (4:28, 28:36, 64; and 29:16) and once in Ezekiel (20:32), but which is absent from the Priestly literature.²⁵ Similarly, Ezekiel's choice of the expression העברת הבנים באש (*pass sons through fire*) shows a clear preference for Deuteronomic terminology over the Priestly literature's נתן למלך (*gives to Molech*).²⁶ The sole pentateuchal warning against consigning children to the fire appears in Deut 18:10, part of an injunction not to imitate the ways of the nations: "Let no one be found among you who *passes his son or daughter through fire* (מעביר בנו ובתו באש), or who is an augur, a soothsayer, a diviner, a sorcerer." Two verses later, Deuteronomy stresses the objectionable nature of such acts and their results: "For anyone who does such things is abhorrent to YHWH, and it is because of these abhorrent things that YHWH your God is dispossessing them before you" (18:12). In line with this Deuteronomic notion, Ezekiel grasps the dire consequences of the people's actions as inevitable: "you defile yourselves

---

233–70. Nonetheless, I suggest that the sins or immoral acts referred to as תועבה in Ezekiel cannot be enumerated or categorized, and that they encompass both the restricted meaning of the root תעב in the Priestly literature and its varied uses in Deuteronomy. Ezekiel aimed to include the broad expanse of intolerable acts by the people under this rubric and therefore, any attempt to apply this term to specific acts reduces and distorts its meaning. תועבה appears 45 times in Ezekiel, almost always as a plural noun (out of 117 occurrences in the Bible). See mainly Ezek 7:3, 4, 8, 9; 8:2, 6, 9, 13, 15, 17; and 16:22, 25, 36, 43, 47, 50, 51, 52, 58. This also explains the unique combinations found in Ezekiel: צלמי תועבותם, תועבות גדולות, תועבות רעות. See Ganzel, "Concept of Holiness," 32–33.

25. See Kohn, *New Heart*, 92.

26. See Ganzel, "Concept of Holiness," 26–30, and Kohn's conclusions (*New Heart*, 89). For a different view, which sees no distinction between the terms נתן למלך and להעביר באש, see Baruch J. Schwartz, *The Holiness Legislation: Studies in the Priestly Code* (Jerusalem: Magnes, 1999) 187–203 (Hebrew).

by the offer of your gifts and by passing your sons through the fire (בהעביר בניכם באש), your idolatries of all sorts—to this day; shall I then respond to your inquiry, O House of Israel?" (Ezek 20:31).

Both Deuteronomy and Ezekiel make a single mention of the existence of במות: על כל הר / גבוהה ותחת כל עץ רענן ("On every mountain height / hill and under every leafy tree"). Deuteronomy supplies a directive to destroy such places of worship: "You must destroy all the sites at which the nations you are to dispossess worshiped their gods, whether on mountain height or hill and under every leafy tree" (12:2). In Ezekiel these places become the sites where God carries out his judgment on all those who not only failed to destroy these places as Deuteronomy commands, but also worshiped there: "And you shall know that I am YHWH, when their slain lie amidst their idols around their altars, on every high hill, on every mountaintop, and under every leafy tree, and every luxuriant oak, the place where they offered a pleasing odor to all their idols" (6:13).

Finally, another shared term is to "cut down idols," to which both Ezekiel and Deuteronomy assign the root גדע. Ezekiel uses this root in his description of the future destruction which will include the uprooting of idolatry:

> Wherever you live, cities shall be ruined and shrines desolated; So that your altars shall be ruined and desolate, your idols shall be broken and banished, Your incense stands cut down (ונגדעו חמניכם) and what you have made wiped out. (Ezek 6:6)

By employing the root גדע to depict the punishment, Ezekiel implies that it could have been averted had the people adhered to the ideology expressed by the Deuteronomic injunction: "tear down their altars, smash their pillars, cut down their sacred posts (תגדעון), and consign their graven images to the fire" (Deut 7:5); and "tear down their altars, smash their pillars, put their sacred posts to the fire, and cut down (תגדעון) the graven images of their gods, obliterating their name from that site" (Deut 12:3).

On this basis, I argue that, as a means of reinforcing his message concerning the sins of the people and underscoring the harsh nature of the impending divine punishment, Ezekiel intentionally applied to the wide-ranging idolatrous practices of the people terminology grounded in the familiar Deuteronomic injunctions against imitating the ways of the nations and worshiping their gods, preferring them over the Priestly literature's less apposite terminology for his description of the Israelites' sins. Ezekiel patterns his depiction of the exile of the people from their land and their scattering among the nations as a direct result of their actions, which, divine admonitions notwithstanding, are precisely the activities against which they were so starkly warned. By incorporating many forms of idol worship in chapter 8, Ezekiel compounds the people's sinfulness and conveys his message that their intense practice of idolatry clearly justifies the imminent destruction and exile.[27] Thus, not only does Ezekiel consistently rely almost exclusively on D/Dtr for textual-rhetorical devices, he also draws upon them for his conceptual framework.

The Depiction of Idolatry: Ezekiel and the Priestly Literature

For this analysis to be complete, we must compare Ezekiel's descriptions of idolatry to those found only in the Priestly literature, and examine the contexts in which Ezekiel combines Deuteronomic and Priestly terminology. Ezekiel's descriptions of idolatry and the Priestly literature share three terms: (a) משכית—carved image, found in Lev 26:1, Num 33:52,[28] and Ezek 8:12;[29] (b) חמן—another form of idolatry,[30] found in

---

27. Schwartz proposes a different explanation for Ezekiel's use of Deuteronomic terms: "because the terms provided by P were anachronistic and unconnected with the historical reality as it had transpired, a natural outgrowth of the same feature of P . . . it is cast in the distant past." Baruch J. Schwartz, "Ezekiel, P, and the Other Pentateuchal Sources" (paper presented at the annual meeting of the SBL, Washington, DC, November 19, 2006) 1–10.

28. For a consideration of this passage's source, which is disputed, see the recent treatment by Baruch J. Schwartz, "Reexamining the Fate of the 'Canaanites' in the Torah Traditions," in *Sefer Moshe: The Moshe Weinfeld Jubilee Volume*, ed. C. Cohen, A. Hurwitz, and S. M. Paul (Winona Lake, Ind.: Eisenbrauns, 2004) 151–70, where he submits that it should be attributed neither to P nor to H but is rather redactional. This differs from Itamar Kislev who concludes that this verse is part of the Priestly source ("Sources and Traditions, Structure and Redaction in the Pentateuch: The Description of the Preparations for Entering the Land" [PhD diss., Hebrew University, 2007] 216–38 [Hebrew]).

29. See Kohn, *New Heart*, 54.

30. In his commentary, Kasher notes: "It is possible that חמן designated a cultic building, at whose center there was a large quadrangular stone, at times with niches, or a room for displaying idols. Surrounding the stone were columns supporting a flat roof,

Lev 26:30 and Ezek 6:4, 6; and (c) צלם—found in Num 33:52, which mandates the destruction of images: "You shall dispossess all the inhabitants of the land; you shall destroy all their carved images (משכיתם); you shall destroy all their molten images (צלמי מסכתם), and you shall demolish all their cult places." For his part, Ezekiel notes three types of images in use by the people: צלמי זכר (7:20), צלמי תועבותם (16:17), and צלמי כשדים (23:14).³¹

Ezekiel's familiarity with Priestly literature and terminology is not surprising, as he was himself a member of the priestly caste. More unexpected was his acquaintance with the book of Deuteronomy, at least with the unit of chapters 1–4 in written form, and his marked preference for Deuteronomic terms and notions to depict the Israelites' idolatry in his oracles.³² By and large, this terminology is unique to Deuteronomy and is not found in the Priestly literature. Indeed, even in those cases where a Priestly alternative exists, Ezekiel shows a predilection for the Deuteronomic terminology (passing sons through fire, שקץ). But this tendency is not absolute. On a few occasions, Ezekiel makes use of terms defined as Priestly in his oracles against idolatry.³³

Significantly, Ezekiel makes no distinction between Priestly and Deuteronomic terminology, but combines terms from these sources in his oracles. Thus the Priestly literature's word משכית appears in Ezekiel 8, which, as we have seen, displays the strong influence of Deuteronomic style. Moreover, Ezekiel juxtaposes the Priestly combination צלמי תועבותם to the Deuteronomic term וצלמי תועבתם שקוציהם עשו בו: שיקוצים (7:20).³⁴ This tendency is also recognizable in Ezekiel's use of terminology shared by the Priestly literature and Deuteronomy, which includes: תועבות,³⁵

---

and an altar was set up in front of the stone" (*Ezekiel*, 217). See also Kaddari, *Dictionary*, s.v. חמנים.

31. צלם always describes idolatry, but its precise denotation changes according to specific combinations. Thus, צלמי מסכותם are "molten images" (see Baruch A. Levine, *Numbers 21–36*, AB 4A [New York: Doubleday, 2000] 523); from the context צלמי תועבותם evidently refer to decorative elements. צלמי זכר are probably phallic images; and צלמי כשדים most likely Babylonian images.

32. See note 1 above.

33. See also Kohn, *New Heart*, 94–95.

34. Kohn as well concludes that Ezekiel makes combined use of the sources, as she demonstrates for Ezekiel 20 (*New Heart*, 96–104).

35. For a discussion of the denotation of תועבות in Ezekiel, see Ganzel, "Concept of Holiness," 32–33, and appendix 3.

גִּילוּלִים,³⁶ the root נתץ,³⁷ and the prohibition against eating "with the blood."³⁸

Although, for Ezekiel, as for Deuteronomy, the people's practice of idolatry results in exile, Ezekiel takes the Deuteronomic dynamic of divine abandonment and finally Israel's destruction and exile further to encompass the defilement of the people, the land, and the Temple. Thus, even though Ezekiel relies almost exclusively on Deuteronomic terminology to describe the idolatry of his day—as a means of demonstrating that the people's actions adhere to the model against which they were warned—his treatment of the outcome of the people's actions incorporates other categories, such as impurity, from the Priestly literature. Although in the Priestly literature impurity relates mainly to bodily defilement,³⁹ two exceptional contexts explicitly link the Israelites' defilement to idolatry.⁴⁰ The first, which defiles the *people*, appears in Lev 19:31: "Do not turn to ghosts and do not search for wizard-spirits, to be defiled by them: I am YHWH your God." The second, which defiles the sanctuary, is found in Lev 20:3: "And I will set my face against that man and cut him off from among his people, because he gave of his offspring to Molech and so defiled my sanctuary and profaned my holy name."

Like the above-cited verses, Ezekiel ascribes impurity to the people and to the Temple because of the people's idolatrous practices; Ezekiel also submits that these practices defile the land. But, in contrast to the Priestly literature, whose treatment of the defiling characteristics of idolatry vis-à-vis the people and the Temple—as opposed to scores of verses treating bodily defilement—is very limited in scope, Ezekiel re-

---

36. גלולים appears only twice in the Pentateuch (as opposed to thirty-nine times in Ezekiel): once in Lev 26:30 and once in Deut 29:16. For a discussion of the etymology of this word and its use by Ezekiel, see Ganzel, "Concept of Holiness," 25–26, and appendix 1.

37. The root נתץ appears in Lev 11:35, 14:45, and in Deut 7:5, 12:3, as well as in Ezek 16:39, where he relates to Jerusalem as an adulterous woman (but also in the prophecy on Tyre, 26:9, 12).

38. The commandment not to eat with the blood appears several times in the Priestly Sources and in Deuteronomy. Ezekiel 33:25 stresses that the people sinned in this regard.

39. Including birth, physical defects, genital fluxes (male and female), a menstruant, ṣara'at, sotah, a nazirite, the red heifer, and corpse impurity, among others.

40. To this we can add the defilement of the land as a result of trespassing the prohibition in Leviticus 18 against incest and that of Numbers 35 against murder.

turns to this topic on *thirty* occasions.[41] This impurity, so prominently singled out by Ezekiel, requires a process of purification (36:21–30) cast metaphorically in the terms of the Priestly literature: "I will throw purifying water on you and you will be purged: of all your impurities and of all your idols I will purge you . . . I will deliver you from all your impurities . . ." (v. 25).[42] Thus Ezekiel issues a promise of the future purging of the people from their impurities, caused mainly by indulging in idolatry in its various forms. Ezekiel's link with the Priestly literature is well known; this word-picture constitutes an outstanding example of Ezekiel's rhetorical adaptation of existing pentateuchal terminology and concepts to his unique message.

Conclusion

I have demonstrated here Ezekiel's reliance on Deuteronomic terminology and notions, with which he was familiar as an independent source, for his depiction of idolatry and how he creates a new synthesis by combining them with concepts of impurity from the Priestly literature.[43] By relying primarily on Deuteronomy, as in chapter 8, Ezekiel concretizes for his audience the causes of the destruction of the Temple, throwing the sins of the people into high relief. He also incorporates Deuteronomic ideology in his message, such as the Deuteronomic warnings regarding the exile and scattering of the people among the nations. Moreover, the

---

41. On the verses treating the types of idolatry that, according to Ezekiel, defiled the people, the land, the Temple, and the divine name, see Ganzel, "Concept of Holiness."

42. The nature of this impurity has been the subject of much discussion. See Tikva Frymer-Kensky, "Pollution, Purification, and Purgation in Biblical Israel," in *The Word of the Lord Shall Go Forth: Essays in Honor of David Noel Freedman*, ed. C. L. Meyers and M. O'Connor (Winona Lake, Ind.: Eisenbrauns, 1983) 399–414; David P. Wright, *The Disposal of Impurity*, SBLDS 101 (Atlanta: Scholars, 1987); and Jonathan Klawans, *Impurity and Sin in Ancient Judaism* (Oxford: Oxford University Press, 2000). This is not the place for an extended discussion.

43. Kohn notes Ezekiel's use of the different sources. See her conclusions based on the historical survey in Ezekiel 20: "Ezekiel expected his contemporaries to live by laws in both P and D that were still relevant. When it came to formulating a plan for the future, however, neither P nor D provided the ideal. The exclusivity evinced by each school was appraised by Ezekiel and deemed an unrealistic goal . . . The prophet's portrayal of Yahweh's hand in Israelite history is an odd combination of the God of the Priestly tradition and that of the Deuteronomic tradition" (*New Heart*, 113–14). It is not possible, in my opinion, to determine precisely how Ezekiel made his synthesis but only to point to his use of Deuteronomic terminology.

Priestly view of defilement undergoes a partial shift here from mainly physical causes to Ezekiel's unique conclusion, conceptually grounded in Deuteronomic notions, that the people's overwhelming engagement in idolatry was responsible for their defilement. Ezekiel deliberately chose this emphatic means to single out the severity, and consequences, of the people's idolatrous actions, perhaps motivated to create a new, unique viewpoint grounded in the combination of familiar ideas by the need to confront the traumatic events in the land of Israel from exile, as the medieval commentator Rabbi Eliezer of Beaugency proposes in the introduction to his commentary to Ezekiel:

> For you will find no other prophet who takes his generation to task according to Torah and the commandments except for Ezekiel ... and as the Torah was revealed to them in his day, and he was in exile, where there were no priests or prophets as in the land of Israel, he berated them according to the Torah in his possession, as one who renews the Torah's teachings, because they were suppressed in Manasseh's day.[44]

This study demonstrates the fallacy of viewing Ezekiel as most influenced by the Priestly literature and of assuming that he was not familiar with the present version of Deuteronomy. Notably, Moses' warnings to the Israelites on the eve of their entry to the land of Israel as found in Deuteronomy are what underlie Ezekiel's depiction of idolatry. Forced to confront an unprecedented crisis, postexilic prophetic literature drafted the existing rhetorical means at its disposal and also created new models, in order to strengthen its message that the Babylonians implemented the divine will. Ultimately, despite prophetic warnings, it was the Israelites' sins, and their sins alone, that brought the destruction of the Temple and exile.

---

44. "Introduction by Rabbi Eliezer of Beaugency," in *Mikra'ot Gedolot 'Haketer'*: *Ezekiel*, ed. Menachem Cohen (Ramat Gan: Bar-Ilan University Press, 2000) xvii (Hebrew).

Bibliography

Ackerman, Susan. *Under Every Green Tree*. HSM 46. Atlanta: Scholars, 2004.
Carley, K. W. *Ezekiel among the Prophets*. London: SCM, 1975.
Cortese, Enzo. *Deuteronomistic Work*. Translated by Silas Musholt. Studium Biblicum Franciscanum Analecta 47. Jerusalem: Franciscan Printing, 1999.
Friedman, Richard E. *The Exile and Biblical Narrative: The Formation of the Deuteronomistic and Priestly Works*. HSM 22. Chico, CA: Scholars, 1981.
Frymer-Kensky, Tikva. "Pollution, Purification, and Purgation in Biblical Israel." In *The Word of the Lord Shall Go Forth: Essays in Honor of David Noel Freedman*, edited by Carol L. Meyers and Michael O'Connor, 399–414. Winona Lake, IN: Eisenbrauns, 1983.
Ganzel, Tova. "The Concept of Holiness in the Book of Ezekiel." PhD diss., Bar-Ilan University, 2004 (Hebrew).
Greenberg, Moshe. *Ezekiel 1–20*. AB 22. Garden City, NY: Doubleday, 1983.
Haran, Menahem. *The Biblical Collection: Its Consolidation to the End of the Second Temple Times and Changes of Form to the End of the Middle Ages*. Vol. 2. Jerusalem: Bialik & Magnes, 2003 (Hebrew).
Humbert, Paul. "Le substantive *toʿēbā* et le verbe *tʿb* dans l'Ancien Testament." *ZAW* 72 (1960) 227–31.
Hurvitz, Avi. *A Linguistic Study of the Relationship between the Priestly Source and the Book of Ezekiel*. CahRB 20. Paris: Gabalda, 1982.
"Introduction by Rabbi Eliezer of Beaugency." In *Mikra'ot Gedolot 'Haketer': Ezekiel*. Edited by Menachem Cohen. Ramat Gan: Bar-Ilan University Press, 2000 (Hebrew).
Kaddari, Menahem Zevi. *A Dictionary of Biblical Hebrew (Alef—Taw)*. Ramat Gan: Bar-Ilan University Press, 2006 (Hebrew).
Kamionkowski, S. Tamar. *Gender Reversal and Cosmic Chaos: A Study on the Book of Ezekiel*. JSOTSup 368. London: Sheffield, 2003.
Kasher, Rimon. *Ezekiel: Introduction and Commentary*. Vol. 1: *Chapters 1–24*. Mikra Leyisra'el. Tel Aviv: Am Oved, 2004 (Hebrew).
Kislev, Itamar. "Sources and Traditions, Structure and Redaction in the Pentateuch: The Description of the Preparations for Entering the Land." PhD diss., Hebrew University, 2007 (Hebrew).
Klawans, Jonathan. *Impurity and Sin in Ancient Judaism*. Oxford: Oxford University Press, 2000.
Kohn, Risa L. *A New Heart and a New Soul: Ezekiel, the Exile and the Torah*. JSOTSup 358. London: Sheffield, 2002.
Kutsko, John F. *Between Heaven and Earth: Divine Presence and Absence in the Book of Ezekiel*. Biblical and Judaic Studies 7. Winona Lake, IN: Eisenbrauns, 2000.
Levine, Baruch A. *Numbers 21–36*. AB 4A. New York: Doubleday, 2000.
Mein, Andrew. *Ezekiel and the Ethics of Exile*. OTM. Oxford: Oxford University Press, 2001.
Milgrom, Jacob. "The Nature and Extent of Idolatry in Eighth-Seventh Century Judah." *HUCA* 69 (1998) 1–13.
———. "Two Priestly Terms *Seqeṣ* and *Ṭāmēʾ*." *Tarbiz* 60 (1991) 423–28 (Hebrew).
Nicholson, Ernest W. *The Pentateuch in the Twentieth Century: The Legacy of Julius Wellhausen*. Oxford: Clarendon, 1998.

Noth, Martin. *The Deuteronomistic History*. 2nd ed. JSOTSup 15. Sheffield: JSOT, 1991.
Patton, C. L. "Pan-Deuteronomism and the Book of Ezekiel." In *Those Elusive Deuteronomists: The Phenomenon of Pan-Deuteronomism*, edited by L. S. Schearing and S. L. McKenzie, 200–215. JSOTSup 268. London: Sheffield, 1999.
Pickett, Winston H. "The Meaning and Function of 'T'B/TO'EVAH' in the Hebrew Bible." PhD diss., Hebrew Union College–Jewish Institute of Religion, 1985.
Schwartz, Baruch J. "Ezekiel, P, and the Other Pentateuchal Sources." Paper presented at the annual meeting of the SBL. Washington, DC, November 19, 2006.
———. "Reexamining the Fate of the 'Canaanites' in The Torah Traditions." In *Sefer Moshe: The Moshe Weinfeld Jubilee Volume*, ed. C. Cohen, A. Hurwitz, and S. M. Paul, 151–70. Winona Lake, Ind.: Eisenbrauns, 2004.
———. *The Holiness Legislation: Studies in the Priestly Code*. Jerusalem: Magnes, 1999 (Hebrew).
Wright, David P. *The Disposal of Impurity*. SBLDS 101. Atlanta: Scholars, 1987.

3

Transformation of Israel's Hope

The Reuse of Scripture in the Gog Oracles

William A. Tooman

NEARLY THREE DECADES AGO, IN A METICULOUS STUDY OF COMPOsitional techniques used by the author of the Temple Scroll, Stephen Kaufman identified portions of the scroll as *mosaics*, "composed of tiny fragments from a large number of biblical sources." According to Kaufman, the author used a technique, which he called "fine conflation," to produce a new composition in the biblical style. Reflecting on the relationship of this technique to biblical compositions, Kaufman wrote:

> The existence of this type of construction raises an interesting question. Has any literary critic ever been bold enough to suggest that in a biblical text several verses long each and every phrase comes from a different source? Doubtful indeed. Yet the presence of this kind of conflation in the Temple Scroll, albeit rare, suggests that there could well be biblical texts composed in a similar fashion.[1]

This chapter suggests this very thing. That is, I argue that the Gog Oracles (GO), Ezekiel 38–39, are an addition to the book of Ezekiel, created by conflating locutions from many scriptural sources, including Ezekiel itself.[2] The author of GO mined not only locutions but topics, *topoi* and images from select texts from across the scriptures. What

---

1. Stephen Kaufman, "The Temple Scroll and Higher Criticism," *HUCA* 53 (1982) 39.

2. In the discussion below, I will use the term "Ezekiel" to refer to the book of Ezekiel, excepting the Gog Oracles. I will use "the prophet" to refer to the historical character Ezekiel, to whom the book is attributed.

motivated the expansion was a desire to settle certain unresolved topics in Ezekiel and to coordinate the book with other scriptural texts.³ Along the way, I will note many parallels in compositional style and inter-textual technique between GO and Qumran literature, which help place GO within the stream of Second Temple literature.

The Form of the Gog Oracles

That GO borrows extensively from antecedent scripture has long been recognized. Scholars have not always agreed, however, upon who is responsible for this borrowing. Some have argued that GO is original to Ezekiel or his immediate "school," others that it is, in its totality, an addition to the book. Still others have argued that GO evolved, bit-by-bit, under the hands of many writers.⁴ A reexamination of the language shared by Ezekiel and GO, will, I believe, reveal that it is unlikely Ezekiel or one of his disciples is responsible for GO.⁵

---

3. I will use the terms "scripture" and "scriptural" for GO's literary sources rather than "Bible" or "biblical." The term "Bible" suggests a canon, a fixed body of supremely authoritative books. It is difficult to know what constituted "Bible" for a Second Temple author. "Scripture" acknowledges that the author of GO viewed his sources as having authority without suggesting the existence of a canon. See the helpful discussions by J. E. Sanderson, *An Exodus Scroll from Qumran: 4Qpaleo-Exod^m and the Samaritan Tradition*, HSS 30 [Atlanta: Scholars, 1986] 261–306) and Peter Flint, "Scriptures in the Dead Sea Scrolls: The Evidence from Qumran" in *Emanuel: Studies in Hebrew Bible, Septuagint, and Dead Sea Scrolls in Honor of Emanuel Tov*, edited by Shalom Paul et al., VTSup 94 [Leiden: Brill, 2003] 269–304.)

4. The history of the historical-critical investigation of GO has been mapped by Margaret Odell ("Are You He of Whom I Spoke by My Servants the Prophets? Ezekiel 38-39 and the Problem of History in the Neobabylonian Context" [PhD diss., University of Pittsburgh, 1988] 1–42) and Paul Fitzpatrick (*The Disarmament of God: Ezekiel 38-39 in its Mythic Context*, CBQMS 37 [Washington, DC: Catholic Biblical Association of America: 2004] 1–48).

5. One point should be clarified at the outset. It has been suggested, on occasion, that GO may be dependant upon oral materials and traditions rather than written sources (see Fitzpatrick, *Disarmament*; cf. M. Greenberg, *Ezekiel 1-20*, AB 22 [New York: Doubleday, 1983] 29). The following discussion will show that the locutions recycled by GO often match their source-texts word-for-word, without adaptation. This is true not just for common or stereotypical locutions but for rare locutions as well, making it difficult to avoid the conclusion that the author of GO is utilizing written sources that he knows well.

Reuse of Ezekielian Language and "Style"

GO makes use of a great deal of Ezekiel's formulaic language, locutions like "son of man" (95x in Ezek), "set your face against" (6:2; 13:17; 21:2, 7; 25:2; 28:21; 29:2; 35:2; 38:2; 40:4; 44:5), "prophesy against" (6:2; 13:17; 21:2, 7; 25:2; 28:21; 29:2; 35:2; 38:2), "thus says Adonai YHWH" (121x in Ezek), "an utterance of YHWH" (83x in Ezek), "behold I am against" (5:8; 13:8 [pl.]; 21:8; 26:3; 28:22; 29:3, 10; 35:3; 36:9 [pl.]; 38:3; 39:1), "prophecy and say" (21:14, 33; 30:2; 34:2; 36:1, 3, 6; 37:9, 12; 38:14; 39:1), the recognition formula (58x in Ezek), and so on. These formulae, found extensively throughout Ezekiel, are either unique to the book, or they are staples of its idiolect.[6]

GO also makes use of many locutions that are entirely unique to the book of Ezekiel. Among these Ezekielian locutions are: "hook in the jaw" (29:4; 38:4), "clothed perfectly" (23:12; 38:4 [cf. 16:14; 27:3]), "grasping swords" (21:16; 30:21; 38:4), "mantlet and shield" (27:10; 38:5); "all his/your horde" (12:14; 17:21; 38:6, 9, 22; 39:4), "mountains of Israel" (6:2, 3; 19:9; 33:28; 34:13, 14; 35:12; 36:1, 4, 8; 37:22; 38:8; 39:4, 17), "inhabited ruin" (33:23 [27]; 38:12); "merchants of Tarshish" (27:12; 38:13), "come against the land (אדמה) of Israel" (20:42; 38:18; 19 [cf. 33:24; 36:6]), "speak in jealousy" (5:13; 36:5-6; 38:19), "fire of fury" (21:36; 22:21, 31; 38:19), "bleeding pestilence" (5:17; 14:19; 28:23; 38:22 [cf. 33:27]), "overflowing rain" (13:11, 13; 38:22), "stones of hail" (13:11, 13; 38:22), and "nations will know that . . ." (22:16; 36:23; 37:28; 38:23; 39:7, 23). Many more examples like these could be cited. This list serves merely to illustrate the Ezekielian stamp that has been given to GO.[7]

---

6. GO does not share any locutions with Ezek 40-48 that do not appear elsewhere in Ezekiel. Though suggestive that GO was added to a version of Ezekiel that did not yet include chs. 40–48, this same phenomena occurs with 4QPseudo-Ezekiel. It too lacks any reference to Ezek 40–48. Devorah Dimant has suggested, correctly I think, that this is simply due to the great difference in the themes and character of the two works ("Apocalyptic Interpretation of Ezekiel at Qumran," in *Messiah and Christos: Studies in the Jewish Origins of Christianity Presented to David Flusser on the Occasion of His Seventy-Fifth Birthday*, edited by I. Gruenwald et al. [Tübingen: Mohr/Siebeck, 1992] 50).

7. It has been common for critics to use these Ezekielian locutions to identify a core within GO that is original to Ezekiel (e.g., Walther Zimmerli, *Ezekiel 2*, Hermeneia [Philadelphia: Fortress, 1983] 302–4; Ronald M. Hals, Ezekiel, FOTL 19 [Grand Rapids: Eerdmans, 1989] 361; Frank L. Hossfeld, *Untersuchungen zu Komposition und Theologie des Esechielbuches*, FB 20 [Würzburg: Echter, 1977] 466).

Moving beyond phrases and clauses, it is also plain that the literary style of GO is similar to Ezekiel's. Two literary conventions that are common in Ezekiel resurface in GO. The first is the so-called "halving technique", by which individual oracles are divided into two discursive units that overlap in subject, theme, and argument (e.g., chs. 6, 7, 13, 16, 18, 20, 38–39).[8] The second is the Ezekielian habit of quoting the errant notions of those to be rebuked or judged (8:12; 11:3, 15; 12:22, 27; 18:2, 25, 29; 20:32, 49; 25:8; 26:2; 28:2, 9; 29:2, 9; 33:20, 24; 35:10; 36:2; 38:10–12).

In the face of all this evidence, it is tempting to conclude that the author of GO is the same person or school responsible for the majority of the book of Ezekiel.[9] This was, in fact, the consensus opinion until the beginning of the twentieth century and has been, again, since the middle of the twentieth century.[10] Before taking this step, however, the points of similarity between GO and Ezekiel must be closely examined. In particular, the language of Ezekiel and GO must be compared in terms of vocabulary choice and usage.

Vocabulary Choices

Ezekiel is fond of certain words and phrases. He often prefers to use and reuse a select expression when another could be used with similar effect. The author of GO, on occasion, fails to note one of these preferences,

---

8. On "halving" see Greenberg, *Ezekiel 1–20*, 25–26; D. I. Block, *The Book of Ezekiel 1–24*, NICOT (Grand Rapids: Word, 1997) 23, 218.

9. Most notable here is Stephen L. Cook, *Prophecy and Apocalypticism: The Postexilic Social Setting* (Minneapolis: Fortress, 1995) 98–103. Cook compiled a list of forty-two locutions shared by Ezekiel and GO from which he concluded that GO was composed by Ezekiel or his immediate Zadokite circle.

10. For example, S. R. Driver, at the end of the nineteenth century, and Paul M. Joyce, at the end of the twentieth, expressed comparable opinions regarding the unified authorship of the book as a whole. "No critical question arises in connection with the authorship of the book, the whole from beginning to end bearing unmistakably the stamp of a single mind" (S. R. Driver, *Introduction to the Literature of the Old Testament*, 2d ed. [Edinburgh: T. & T. Clark, 1891] 261). Ezekiel "has proved notoriously resistant to any straightforward division into primary and secondary material," because "secondary material (even where it can be identified) bears an unusually close 'family resemblance' to primary" (P. Joyce, "Synchronic and Diachronic Perspectives on Ezekiel," in *Synchronic or Diachronic? A Debate on Method in Old Testament Exegesis*, edited by J. C. de Moor, OtSt 34 [Leiden: Brill, 1995] 115–28).

and uses a different word or phrase than Ezekiel, one found nowhere else in the book. The following examples illustrate this point.

Ezekiel 39:23 and 28 use the verb גלה to refer to the exile: "the house of Israel was exiled because of their iniquity," גלו בית־ישראל כי בעונם (39:23); "when I exiled them among the nations," בהגלותי אתם אל־הגוים (39:28). This is not the expression for the exile found elsewhere in Ezekiel. Ezekiel always describes Israel being scattered (זרה or פוץ) to the winds (רוח or כל־רוח), among the lands (ארצות), or among the nations (עמים / גוים).[11] When a finite verb of גלה appears in Ezekiel it usually does so with the meaning "uncover, expose," rather than with the meaning "to go into exile."[12]

A similar discontinuity appears in 39:21. God says "all the nations will see my judgment, which I delivered, and my hand which I set upon them." The locution "my hand, which I set upon them" (שׂים + יד + ב-) is unique to 39:21.[13] Though the exact expression is unique, the notion is quite common in the book, occurring eleven times. But it is always expressed by the alternative designation "I will stretch out my hand against them" (נטה + ידי + על).[14]

At the close of GO, God promises to "restore the fortunes of Jacob" and to "have compassion (רחמתי) on all the house of Israel." The lexeme רחם is common in the HB, but this is the only occurrence of the word in the book. To express compassion, Ezekiel prefers חוס or חמל, and in all but one case, Ezekiel uses them with negative connotations (i.e., "I will not have compassion").[15]

---

11. The combination רוח + זרה is found in 5:2, 10, 12, and 12:14. The expression זרה + (ב)ארצות appears in 6:8 (5), 12:15; 20:23; 22:15; 29:12; 30:23; 30:26; 36:19. In 11:16, 17; 20:34, 41, we find פוץ + (ב)ארצות, and in 12:15; 20:23; 22:15; 29:12; 30:23, 26; 36:19 we find פוץ + (ב)גוים. Finally, פוץ + (ב)עמים appears in 28:25, and 29:13. On three occasions פוץ occurs without an accompanying prepositional phrase (34:5, 6; 46:18). On one occasion it occurs with שׁם (34:12), and on another with אל־החוצה (34:21).

12. See 13:14 (uncover foundations); 16:36, 37; 22:10; 23:10, 29 (uncover nakedness); and 16:57; 21:29; 23:18 (expose sin). However, see the imperative and perfect in 12:3 ("go into exile"). See also the nouns גּוֹלָה and/or גָּלוּת in 1:1, 2; 3:11, 15; 11:24, 25; 12:3, 4, 7, 11; 25:3; 33:21; 40:1.

13. This may be a conflation of the common expressions "set the face" and "stretch the hand." The closest examples to Ezek 39:21 are Gen 48:12 and 18, Ps 89:26 (of another's hand), and 2 Kgs 11:16 (= 2 Chr 23:15).

14. Ezekiel 6:14; 14:9, 13; 16:27; 20:33, 34; 25:7, 13, 16; 30:25; 35:3.

15. Ezek 20:17, "nevertheless my eye spared them," is the one use of חוס in Ezekiel with a positive sense. חוס and חמל appear together in 5:11; 7:4, 9; 8:18; 9:5, 10; 16:5.

Finally, when describing the regathering of the scattered people of Israel, 39:27 and 28 use the following language: "when I return them from the peoples and I gather them from the lands," בְּשׁוֹבְבִי אוֹתָם מִן־הָעַמִּים וְקִבַּצְתִּי אֹתָם מֵאַרְצוֹת, and "I will gather them to their land," כְנַסְתִּים עַל־אַדְמָתָם. Neither שׁוב nor כנס is used in Ezekiel for return from exile.[16] Ezekiel has fixed ways of describing the return from exile.

קבץ (Piel) + מן + עמים...אסף (Qal) + מן + ארצות   11:17

יצא (Hiphil) + מן + עמים...קבץ (Piel) + מן + ארצות   20:34

יצא (Hiphil) + מן + עמים...קבץ (Piel) + מן + ארצות   20:41

קבץ (Piel) + מן + עמים   28:25

קבץ (Piel) + מן + עמים   29:13

יצא (Hiphil) + מן + עמים...קבץ (Piel) + מן + ארצות   34:13

קבץ (Pual) + מן + עמים...יצא (Hophal) + מן + עמים[17]   38:8

Neither expression, either 39:27 or 39:28, matches the stereotypical ways that Ezekiel describes the regathering. The result is a pair of unique clauses, which are unremarkable unless one is familiar with Ezekiel's idiolect.

These unique vocabulary choices are highly revealing. They show us an author who is familiar with the style of Ezekiel and who is attempting to mimic that style. But the author does so, on occasion, imperfectly.

רחם appears by itself in 20:17 and 24:14. נחם occurs by itself, with the meaning "feel compassion," in 24:14.

16. The lexeme שׁוב, though never used for return from exile, is common in Ezekiel (1:14; 3:19, 20; 7:13; 8:6, 13, 15, 17; 9:11; 13:22; 14:6; 18:8, 12, 17, 21, 23, 24, 26, 27, 28, 30, 32; 20:22; 21:10, 35; 27:15; 29:14; 33:9, 11, 12, 14, 15, 18, 19; 34:4, 26; 35:7, 9; 38:4, 8, 12; 39:2; 44:1; 46:9, 17; 47:1, 6, 7 [cases of the phrase שׁוב שְׁבוּת are omitted]). כנס, conversely, is uncommon in the Hebrew Bible, occurring in only eight instances, all of them examples of LBH (Ezek 39:28; Ps 3:7; 147:2; Qoh 2:8; 3:5; Esth 4:16; Neh 12:44; I Chr 22:2).

17. Excluded from this list is 36:24, קבץ מִן־אֲרָצוֹת (Piel)...לקח מִן־גוים (Qal). As Papyrus 967 and Codex Wirceburgensis show, Ezek 36:23c–38 is an expansion in MT (A. C. Johnson et al., *The John H. Scheide Biblical Papyri: Ezekiel* [Princeton, New Jersey: Princeton University Press, 1938]; E. Tov, "Recensional Differences Between the MT and LXX of Ezekiel," *ETL* 62 (1986) 99–101.

These imperfections arise not only in the selection of vocabulary, but also in the way Ezekiel's vocabulary is used.

Use of Ezekielian Locutions

GO makes use of twenty-nine locutions that are found, in HB, only in the book of Ezekiel (excluding those which are found only in GO). A close look at these locutions reveals differences in the ways that they are used in Ezekiel and in GO.

In GO, God conscripts Gog, chief prince of Meshek and Tubal, to assail his land. He says to the prince "I will put hooks in your jaw" and "bring you and all your army" against the mountains of Israel. The expression, "put hooks in your jaw" (חח + ל חיי) is striking and immediately calls to mind its original context, the oracle against Pharaoh in Ezek 29. In that text, Pharaoh is likened to a crocodile who "stretches out in the midst of his rivers" (29:3), content in his supremacy. YHWH promises to catch him with a hook in the jaw, to drag him onto dry ground, and to allow lesser creatures, the birds and beasts, to feed on his carcass (29:4–5). The term "hook" (חח) reappears in the parable of the young lions in Ezek 19. In that context, two lions of Israel are captured with hooks and dragged into exile in Babylon. The metaphor in 19:4, 9 is similar to that in 29:4. Both use the image of a "hook" in their description of capturing wild animals and dragging them about against their will. In contrast, the expression "put hooks in your jaw" is utilized in 38:4 as an image of subtle coercion, so subtle that Gog is not even conscious of it. Though the reader has no difficulty navigating this semantic shift, it seems clear that the use in 29:4 is the original one. There is a stronger logical relation between a "hook in the jaw" and capture than there is with inconspicuous coercion.

Another example of unique usage appears in Ezek 38:22. In Ezekiel's prophecies against Jerusalem and Sidon, he discloses several disasters which will befall those cities for their sins. Jerusalem will endure "famine, wild beasts, bleeding pestilence (דֶּבֶר וָדָם), and warfare" (5:17).[18] Sidon will suffer bleeding pestilence (דֶּבֶר וָדָם) and military defeat (28:23). The phrase "bleeding pestilence" is distinctive of Ezekiel's

---

18. There is good reason to think that דֶּבֶר וָדָם, "plague and blood" should be understood as a hendiadys, "bleeding pestilence." It is used to refer to a single judgment in 5:17 (where it will kill one third of the people), and in 14:12–19 God suggests four judgments: famine, beast, sword, and "pestilence and blood."

language, occurring in 5:17; 14:19; 28:23; 38:22 (cf. 33:27). In GO, the author has included it in a list of weapons that God will hurl against Gog when he ascends the mountains of Israel. "I will contend with him with bleeding pestilence, and flooding rain, and hail stones. Fire and brimstone I will rain upon him" (38:22). The inclusion of pestilence in this list stands out. With the exception of "bleeding pestilence," the list of images depicts a sudden, supernatural, cataclysmic destruction. The author of GO, in his effort to sound like Ezekiel, appears to have compiled an indiscriminate inventory of disasters culled from other oracles in the book.[19]

Also appearing in the list of disasters in 38:22 are two images borrowed from Ezek 13. In that passage, Ezekiel announces judgment against false prophets who comfort the exiles with messages of peace (13:10). He likens them to workmen who plaster over a damaged wall, attempting to disguise the peril of their situation. Ezekiel announces that God will break the plaster, wiping it from the wall with "hailstones" (אבני אלגביש) and "flooding rain" (שוטף + גשם; 13:11, 13), and cause the wall to fall (13:12, 14). In other words, God's judgments against his people will reveal the falsehood of comforting prophecies (13:14–15). The author of GO borrowed the expressions "hailstones" (אבני אלגביש) and "flooding rain" (שוטף + גשם), but he did not use them as *metaphors* for judgment. In 38:22, they appear as literal, supernatural manifestations of YHWH's power. YHWH will destroy Gog with earthquake, flood, hail, and brimstone.

The author of GO appropriated many locutions from the book of Ezekiel, including many expressions that are unique to the book. As these three examples illustrate, however, the author sometimes utilized locutions in ways that are discordant with the rest of the book. This suggests that the author of GO is not to be identified with the person (or persons) responsible for most of the book.

---

19. GO depicts events in sets of seven. Gog has seven allies. The weapons they leave behind provide fuel for seven years (39:9). It takes seven months to bury the dead (39:12, 14). The dead are designated as food for the wild animals with seven appellatives (39:18). On two occasions, seven terms are used to designate the enemy's military gear (38:4-5; 39:9). There are seven variations on the recognition formula (38:13, 23; 39:6, 7 [2x], 22, 28), and so on. The list of judgments in 38:21–22 also equals seven, if the author expects us to understand דֶּבֶר וָדָם as two judgments, "blood and pestilence." Though not conclusive, this raises the possibility that the author did not recognize "bleeding pestilence" as a hendiadys.

Reuse of Elements from the Torah, Prophets, and Psalms

When it came to borrowing literary material, the author of GO in no way limited the borrowing to the book of Ezekiel. If we isolate those locutions in GO that are signatures of a particular scriptural book or corpus, the rich variety of texts that the author mined for images and language becomes apparent.[20] Images, motifs, and locutions from all five books of the Torah and from many of the Prophets, including DtrH, Isaiah, Jeremiah, Joel, Amos, and Zephaniah, resurface in GO. Among the most well-known of these allusions are the motif of the foe from the "remote places of the north" (38:6, 15; 39:2 // Isa 14:13; Jer 6:22–23), the names of Gog's confederate nations (38:2–3, 6 // Gen 10:2–3), and the sacral feast of the animals (39:17–20 // Isa 34:6–7 [Jer 46:10; 50:25–27]). When we highlight all the borrowed locutions in GO, as we have done in the Appendix below, it becomes clear that GO is pastiche. To speak just of these locutions, excluding implicit allusions to images or *topoi*, there are two hundred three clauses that make up GO (including participial and infinitive clauses). All or part of one hundred sixty-six of these clauses occur, verbatim or nearly so, in some other scriptural text. To borrow the words of Stephen Kaufman, GO is "composed of tiny fragments from a large number of biblical sources."

To be sure, I have not yet demonstrated that GO is deliberately alluding to these texts, nor have I demonstrated that the direction of dependence runs from Jeremiah, for example, to GO and not vice versa. These issues will be discussed in the next section, "Content and Method," to which we now turn.

Content and Method[21]

GO's reuse of antecedent scripture is key to its purpose and meaning. The pattern of continuous allusion in GO reflects something more than

---

20. There are a range of ways to define what a "signature" or "distinctive" expression might be. I use these terms to refer to locutions that are: (1) unique to a particular book or corpus, (2) original to a particular book or corpus, though they might be taken up by other authors (e.g., distinctive H locutions reused by Ezekiel), or (3) characteristic of a particular book or corpus. That is, the preponderance of occurrences of the locution are in one book or corpus. For example, the expression "hide the face" is characteristic of Deut (e.g., 31:17, 18; 32:20), but also appears in Isaiah, GO, and the Psalms.

21. In this essay, I make a simple dichotomy between "quotation" and "allusion." A quotation is explicit in that it includes not only a verbatim repetition of elements

a writer saturated with scriptural idiom. It is a practice of disciplined and deliberate reference to select texts on select themes. The author of GO made liberal use of many types of material, including specific written sources, literary *topoi*, traditions, and genre conventions. Recognizing the volume and density of scriptural reuse in GO is indispensible for understanding its role in the book, its composition, and its place within the phylogeny of Second Temple literature.[22]

Examining the Reuse

Borrowed locutions, particularly if they are rare and distinctive, can effectively direct readers to their source text. Recognizing *how much* of an evoked text is in view, however, is not always as clear. A locution may be borrowed simply because it is a particularly well-turned or evocative phrase, in which case the locution does not point to a context at all. A borrowed locution may have been chosen to appeal to an idea or concept in a source text, for which the borrowed locution is a distinguishing expression. Or, a locution may be borrowed to draw attention to a larger text: an entire verse or passage. In this last case, the parameters of the source text can be indicated in more than one way. An author

---

from the source text but also a citation formula of some sort. Allusions, which are implicit, lack a citation formula. By this definition, GO contains no quotations. On the hermeneutical theory and poetics involved see Ziva Ben-Porat, "The Poetics of Literary Allusion," *PTL: A Journal of Descriptive Poetics and Theory of Literature* 1 (1976): 105–28; Heinrich Plett, ed., *Intertextuality* (Berlin and New York: Walther de Gruyter, 1991); Gary Iseminger, ed., *Intention and Interpretation* (Philadelphia: Temple University Press, 1992). On this phenomena in Jewish Second Temple and early Christian literature see, for example, Richard B. Hays, *Echoes of Scripture in the Letters of Paul* (New Haven: Yale University Press, 1989) 18–21, 29–32; Michael Fishbane, "Types of Biblical Intertextuality," in *Congress Volume. Oslo, 1998*, edited by A. Lemaire and M. Saebø (Leiden: Brill, 2000) 39–44; B. N. Fisk, *Do You Not Remember? Scripture, Story and Exegesis in the Rewritten Bible of Pseudo-Philo*, JSPSup 37; Sheffield: Sheffield Academic, 2001) 68–89, 114–15.

22. Most studies of GO have focused largely on allusions to *topoi* and traditions rather than reused phrases and clauses as such. See, for example, Ruben Ahroni, "The Gog Prophecy and the Book of Ezekiel," *HAR* 1 (1977) 1–27; Cook, *Prophecy and Apocalypticism*, 84–121; Gillis Gerleman, "Hesekielbokens Gog," *Svensk exegetisk Årsbok* 12 (1947) 132–46; Fitzpatrick, *The Disarmament of God*, 49–73; John L. Myres, "Gog and the Danger from the North in Ezekiel," *PEQ* 64 (1932) 213–19. One notable exception is Marvin A. Sweeney, "The Priesthood and the Protoapocalyptic Reading of Prophetic and Pentateuchal Texts," in *Knowing the End from the Beginning*, edited by L. L. Grabbe and R. D. Haak, JSPSup 46 (London: Continuum, 2003) 167–78.

can, for example, reuse several locutions from across the source text, enabling the reader to map its boundaries with some specificity. Less precisely, the author can use just one or two distinctive locutions to allude to an entire context, trusting the reader to recognize that the two texts, the alluding text and the evoked text, conform in their themes, topics, arguments, or images.[23] The author of GO, used a wide variety of techniques to evoke dozens of antecedent texts, ranging in size from an individual phrase to a whole chapter.

Vorbilder

We begin with three texts that the author of GO used as *Vorbilder*, literary models or templates, for his composition: Ezek 28:25–26; Ezek 6:1–14; and Ps 79:1–4. The author employed different techniques to evoke the three texts, but within them we can find virtually every scene and motif that makes up GO. To evoke Ezek 28:25–26, the author reused most of its phrases and clauses in his own composition (locutions that are identical in 28:25–26 and GO are underlined).

Ezekiel 28:25–26	GO
25. Thus says Lord YHWH, "<u>When I gather the house of Israel from the peoples</u> among whom they were scattered, <u>then I will be sanctified among them in the sight of the nations. And they dwell upon their land that</u> I gave to my servant <u>Jacob</u>. 26. <u>And they will dwell upon it securely</u>. And they will build houses, and they will plant vineyards, <u>and they will dwell securely. When I have executed judgments</u> upon all those despising them round about, then they will know that <u>I am YHWH their God</u>."	38:8 // בקבצי את־בית ישראל 38:8 // מן־העמים 38:23, 39:27 // ונקדשתי בם לעיני הגוים 39:26 // וישבו על־אדמתם 39:25 // יעקב 39:26 // וישבו עליה לבטח 39:26 // וישבו לבטח 39:21 // עשה + שפטים 39:22, 28 // אני יהוה אלהיהם

---

23. See note 20.

The author of GO not only drew attention to 28:25–26 by repeating most of its locutions verbatim but also by distributing them widely and, in some cases, repeatedly across the new composition.[24] The connection between the two texts is established by the fact that some of the borrowed locutions ("I will be sanctified before the eyes of the nations," for example) occur only in 28:25–26 and GO. That 28:25–26 served as a template for GO is further indicated by the remarkable correspondence between the two texts not only in language but topics. Ezek 28:25–26 speaks of peaceful resettlement of the land, manifestation of YHWH's holiness, judgment upon the nations, and acknowledgment of YHWH by Israel and the nations. These are, broadly speaking, the main topics of GO as well. Still more remarkable, these topics are introduced in GO in nearly the same order that they appear in 28:25–26. This corroborates Daniel Block's argument that "the Gog pericope may be interpreted as a full-blown commentary on xxviii 25–6."[25]

The second text that inspired much of the content and substance of GO is the oracle against the mountains of Israel in Ezek 6:1–14. In 6:1–10 the prophet announced judgments against the mountains of Israel, because they had been defiled by idolatry. The land will not be purified by efforts at reform (2 Kgs 23:4–20) but by the sword of God, which will cleanse the land by making it a waste. Verses 11–14 go on to translate the metaphor "God's sword" into terms from the covenant curses of Lev 26: God will kill pagan Judahites with sword and pestilence; he will destroy the high places and defile the sites with the corpses of the worshipers; he will surrender Israel to invaders, and her cities will destroyed.

The author of GO evoked 6:1–14, principally, by repeating its dominant catch-phrase: הרי ישראל, "mountains of Israel." This locution is most distinctive of Ezek 6 (vv. 2, 3, cf. 13), 36 (vv. 1, 4, 8), and GO (38:8; 39:4, 17).[26] The reappearance of "mountains of Israel" in GO

---

24. A similar phenomena occurs in 11Q13 (Melchizedek), for example, where key locutions from a source text are replicated in several places in an effort to expose the originating text (see Timothy Lim, "Biblical Quotations in the Pesharim and the Text of the Bible—Methodological Considerations," in *The Bible as Book: The Hebrew Bible and the Judean Desert Discoveries*, edited by Edward Herbert and Emanuel Tov [London: British Library, 2002] 73–79).

25. Daniel I. Block, "Gog in Prophetic Tradition: A New Look at Ezekiel XXXVIII 17," *VT* 42 (1992) 155.

26. Ezekiel's standard locutions for the land are אדמה, אדמת־ישראל, and ארץ. All three are far more common in Ezekiel than הרי ישראל. The locution

suggests a connection to chapter 6. What confirms the connection is the remarkable correspondence between YHWH's judgments against Judah in 6:1–14 and those against Gog and his allies in Ezek 38–39. In both texts, God summons a foreign invader to the mountains of Israel (6:3; 38:4, 39:2) for the purpose of executing his judgments (38:22). In 6:1–14, the Judahites are slain when God brings his "sword" (Babylon) against them, because they sacrificed on the mountains. In the Gog oracles, God wields his "sword" (supernatural actions) against the invaders, making a sacrifice of them on the mountains (39:17–20). In the aftermath of the judgment in 6:1–14, the slain are scattered on the mountains, their bones left exposed, and the survivors—the "fugitives of the sword"—are exiled. In the aftermath of the battle between God and Gog, the dead are scattered on the mountains, their bones exposed, and the exiles—"returnees from the sword"—return to a land where they can dwell securely (39:28). The goal in both cases is also the same. God smites his people in 6:1–14 and sends them into exile so they might "know that I am YHWH" (6:7, 10). God smites Gog, so that both the house of Israel and the nations will "know that I am YHWH" (39:22, 28). In other words, the author of GO reapplied the judgments on Judah from ch. 6 to Gog and his host in an act of reversal that inverted the position and power of Israel with that of her foreign oppressors.[27]

The third and final text that the author used as a *Vorbild* is Ps 79:1–4. A number of dominant images in GO—unprovoked invasion, defiled land, uninterred corpses, and carrion-eaters—clearly mirror Ps 79:1–4:

אדמת־ישראל appears in 7:2; 11:17; 12:19; 22; 13:9; 18:2; 20:38, 42; 21:7, 8; 25:3, 6; 33:24; 36:6; 37:12; 38:18, 19. The locution אדמה occurs as a designation for Israel in 28:25; 34:13, 27; 36:17, 24; 37:14, 21; 38:20; 39:26, 28 The locution ארץ is extremely common in Ezekiel, occurring one-hundred seventy-three times. It is used to refer to the land of Israel on seventy of those occasions (6:14; 7:2, 7, 23, 27; 8:12, 17; 9:9; 11:15, 17; 12:12, 19, 20; 14:13, 15, 16, 17, 19; 15:8; 16:3; 17:5, 13; 20:6, 15, 28, 38, 40, 42; 22:24, 29, 30; 23:48; 27:17; 33:2, 3, 24, 25, 26, 28, 29; 34:13, 25, 27, 28, 29; 35:10; 36:5, 18, 24, 28, 34, 35; 37:22, 25; 40:2; 45:1, 4, 8, 16, 22; 46:3, 9; 47:13, 14, 15, 18, 21; 48:12, 14, 29.)

27. The only significant elements in the plot of GO that have no parallel in Ezek 6 are the identification and description of Gog's allies (38:3–9), God's cosmic actions against Gog (38:18–23), the plundering of dead (39:9–10), the cleansing of the land (39:11–16), and the wild animals feasting on the dead (39:17–20). Each of these elements, with the exception of 39:11–16, as we shall see, is borrowed from another text.

> O God, the nations have come into your inheritance;
> they have defiled your holy temple;
> they have laid Jerusalem in ruins.
> They have given the bodies of your servants to the birds of the air for food,
> the flesh of your faithful to the wild animals of the earth.
> They have poured out their blood like water all around Jerusalem,
> and there was no one to bury them.
> We have become a taunt to our neighbors,
> mocked and derided by those around us.

Unlike the Psalmist, the author of GO studiously avoided any inkling of Zion theology in his composition.[28] Despite this one difference, the array of images found in Ps 79:1-4 appear as a group nowhere else in HB except in GO. The images from Ps 79:1-4 exerted their greatest influence on chapter 39, where the combined themes of defilement, unburied dead, and wild animals feasting on human carcasses reappear.[29]

The substance of GO, its *topoi*, topics, and plot, is derived, by in large, from Ezek 28:25-26, Ezek 6:1-14, and Ps 79:1-4. But these texts do not determine all its contents, nor do they accommodate the totality of its message. For instance, although Ezek 6 inspired many of the individual plot-points in GO, these points are often articulated using the language of a different legal or prophetic text. To identify these allusions, which, though less determinative of GO's shape and message as a whole, dot its literary landscape, we must look more closely at the individual oracles.[30]

Ezekiel 38:1–6

Ezekiel 38:1-6 introduces the principle characters in the oracle: YHWH, Gog, and Gog's confederates. YHWH and Gog are the main characters.

---

28. For more on Ezekiel's rejection of the notion of Zion's inviolability see W. A. Tooman, "Ezekiel's Radical Challenge to Inviolability" *ZAW* 121/3 (2009): in press.

29. Despite suggestions that Psalm 79 is Maccabean it appears to be older than GO. Psalm 79 is alluded to by Ps 102, Zeph 3:8-10 and 1 Macc 7:17. Zephaniah 3, at least, is known to the author of GO (see below under "Ezekiel 38:18-23"). See the discussion in F.-L. Hossfeld and E. Zenger, *Psalms 2*, trans. L. M. Maloney, Hermeneia (Philadelphia: Fortress, 2005) 303-7.

30. The discussion below is by no means exhaustive. There are many allusions in GO to texts from the Torah, Prophets, and Psalms, which are not discussed here.

The allies of Gog are an extension of Gog himself, never acting on their own initiative but miming his behavior. The Israelites, who have returned to the land, are minor characters throughout GO. They have no role in the drama apart from cleaning up the battlefield after the action has concluded. None of these characters are constructs of the author's creativity. Gog and his confederates, excepting one of them, are derived from texts in the Torah.

The central character, Gog, is almost certainly taken from the Balaam Oracles. In Num 23–24 Balaam anticipates a "star" who will rise out of Jacob. This star, who is a king, is predicted to be higher "than Agag" (מֵאֲגַג) in the MT of Num 24:7. A wide variety of witnesses however, including Septuagint, Samaritan Pentateuch, Theodotian, and Vetus Latina, have Balaam predicting that the coming king will be higher "than Gog" (מִגּוֹג).[31] The name "Gog" is most common in the tradition of the LXX. It appears in 1 Chr 5:4 (MT and LXX), in Deut 3:1, 13, and 4:47 (LXX[B]), in Esth 3:1 and 9:24 (LXX[93]), in Sir 48:17 (LXX[B]), and in Amos 7:1 (LXX). Despite this wide attestation, there are several good reasons to identify Num 24:7 as the original source for the character in GO. First, the appearance of Gog son of Shemaiah in 1 Chr 5:4 is, by all accounts, a coincidence, bearing no relation to the character in GO.[32] Second, the other appearances of "Gog" in the LXX appear to be scribal variants inspired, secondarily, by GO.[33] Third, GO and Num 24 have a common temporal reference. According to Num 23:14, Balaam's Oracles are about "the end of days," אחרית הימים. Regardless of how one chooses to translate אחרית הימים, the author of GO used the phrase to refer to a new historical age, an age predicted by Israel's prophets (38:17) and inaugurated by Gog's invasion (38:8,

---

31. Though damaged at precisely this point, it has been suggested that 4QNum[b] read "Gog" as well (see Nathan Jastram, "The Book of Numbers from Qumran, Cave VI [4QNumb]" [PhD dissertation, Harvard University, 1990] 45; E. C. Ulrich and F. M. Cross, *Qumran Cave 4.VII: Genesis to Numbers*, DJD 12 [Oxford: Clarendon, 1994] 235–36).

32. See the discussion in Sverre Bøe, *Gog and Magog: Ezekiel 39–39 as Pre-text for Revelation 19,17–21 and 20,7–10*, WUNT 135 (Tübingen: Mohr/Siebeck, 2001) 49–50.

33. On the variant "Gog" in the LXX of Deut 3:1, 13; 4:47; Esth 3:1, 9:24; Sir 48:17 see the bibliography and discussion in Bøe, *Gog and Magog*, 50–75. It is possible that the author of GO was influenced by the reference to Gog the locust-king in the *Vorlage* of LXX-Amos 7:1, but we do not have room to explore the issue here.

16).³⁴ In crafting his picture of the "end of days," the author's attention was drawn, understandably, to texts which he understood to be about the same time and events, including the Balaam oracles.

Gog's allies, with one exception, were taken from the Torah as well. The list of nations that make up Gog's horde (38:2-6) was adapted from the Table of Nations in Gen 10. Meshek, Tubal, Cush, Put, Gomer, Togarmah, and even Magog itself appear in Gen 10:2-8.³⁵ Most of these nations appear elsewhere in Ezekiel as well (32:26; 27:10, 14). Gomer, however, does not appear in Ezekiel, and Persia does not appear in Gen 10 (Gen 10:2-3; Ezek 27:10; 38:5-6). The composer of the Gog oracles created his list of confederates by combining nations in Gen 10 with Tyre's trading partners in Ezek 27.³⁶ These particular nations were selected because they are nation-descendants of Japhet and Ham from the primeval past.³⁷ With the exception of Persia, they are not well-known historical enemies of Israel but far-flung nations of rumor. Taken together, they represent widely distributed stations on the compass.³⁸ GO depicts a global gathering of peoples, from remote provinces and di-

---

34. On the proper translation of this phrase see, especially, H. Seebass, "אחר," in *TDOT* I:211-12; A Steudel, "אחרית הימים in the Texts from Qumran," *RevQ* 16 (1993-94) 225-46; S. Talmon, "The Signification of אחרית and אחרית הימים in the Hebrew Bible," in *Studies in Hebrew Bible, Septuagint, and Dead Sea Scrolls in Honor of Emmanuel Tov*, ed. Shalom Paul et al., VTSup 94 (Leiden: Brill, 2003) 795-810.

35. It is entirely possible that the appearance of "Magog" in Gen 10 drew the author's attention to "Gog" in Num 24, since most of Gog's allies were derived from Gen 10. He chose then to make "Gog" his main character and interpreted "Magog" as a *mem*-preformative noun of location. See the lengthy discussion in Bøe, *Gog and Magog*, 50-75.

36. In 38:13 three more nations appear as witnesses of Gog's invasion: Sheba, Dedan, and Tarshish. All three appear in Ezekiel (27:12, 15, 22-23) and Genesis (10:4, 7, 28; 25:3). They appear to be removed from the confederates in 38:2-6 to restrict the number of allies there to seven (see n. 19).

37. See the discussion in C. Westermann, *Genesis 1-11*, trans. J. J. Scullion, CC (Minneapolis: Augsburg, 1984) 504-8, 528-30; Bøe, *Gog and Magog*, 99-107.

38. A. Lauha, *Zaphon, der Norden und die Nordvölker im Alten Testament*, AASF B49 (Helsinki: Der Finnischen Literaturgesellschaft, 1943) 70; Block, *Ezekiel 25-48*, 439-42; Odell, "Are You He," 101-3, 107-8; Bøe, *Gog and Magog*, 106-7. This is reinforced by the depiction of Israel as the center of the world (טבור הארץ "navel of the earth," 38:12) surrounded by foes, which may have been inspired by Ezek 5:5 ("This is Jerusalem. I have set her in the midst of the nations, and countries are round about her").

verse directions, who converge on the mountains of Israel. In effect, the whole world will be against Israel.[39]

Ezekiel 38:7–16

The muster of Israel's foes is followed by a lengthy description of their arrival in the land. The pericope begins and ends with a picture of the vastness of the invading host, as viewed from a high vantage (38:8–9, 16). In the intervening verses, the author of GO provides an intimate glimpse into Gog's heart, revealing his impulses, thoughts, and motives and a description of conditions in the land just before he arrives. The shape of this section, which seems unfocused and wandering, is actually dictated by two prophetic texts: Isaiah 10 and Jeremiah 49. The pieces and parts of 38:7–13 follow the order of elements in those two texts:

---

[39]. 4QPseudo-Ezekiel interprets GO in the same way, as a universal judgment against the nations of the earth. "A day of doom for *the gentiles* is coming […] and anguish shall be in Put, and a sword shall be in […] will shake, and Ethiopia and […] and the mighty of Arabia and also some of the […]" (4Q385b, lines 2–4; italics mine).

Transformation of Israel's Hope 67

Isaiah 10:3–6	Jeremiah 49:30–33	Ezek 38:7–13
(3) יום + פקדה the day of visitation		(8) מימים רבים תפקד after many days you will be visited
(3) לשואה...תבוא the devastation will come		(9) כשאה תבוא like a devastation, you will come
	(30) חשב עליהם מחשבה consider a plan against them	(10) וחשבת מחשבת רעה you will consider an evil plan
	(31) קומו עלו אל־גוי שליו arise, go up against a nation at ease	(11) אעלה על־ארץ...השקטים I will go up against a land...at rest
	(31) יושב לבטח dwelling securely	(11) ישבי לבטח dwelling securely
	(31) לא־דלתים ולא־בריח לו they have no gates and no bar	(11) ובריח ודלתים אין להם they have neither bar nor gates
(5–6) ולבז בז לשלל שלל to take spoil and to seize plunder	(32) לבז...לשלל to spoil and to plunder	(12–13) לשלל שלל ולבז בז to take spoil and to seize plunder
	(32) גמליהם...מקניהם camels...cattle	(12–13) מקנה cattle
	(33) שממה עד־עולם perpetual waste (33) לא־ישב שם without an inhabitant	(12) על־חרבות נושבת against inhabited ruins

The text of Ezek 38:7–13 does not slavishly mimic Isaiah and Jeremiah. On occasion, the verbiage of Isaiah and Jeremiah has been adapted, but it does follow them closely enough that its reliance upon them is evident. Nor does 38:7–13 draw exclusively upon these two texts. Scattered around and among the phrases and clauses inspired by

Isa 10 and Jer 49 are a potpourri of locutions borrowed from elsewhere in the Torah and Prophets.[40] One side effect of this rich mix of scriptural language and *topoi* is the disjointed quality of the pericope, its shifting point of view and redundancy. The ungainliness of the pericope notwithstanding, the author of GO saw in Isa 10 and Jer 49 texts well-suited to his purposes.

Isaiah 10 is a cautionary exhortation to the inhabitants of Judah, warning them of God's impending judgment in the form of an Assyrian invasion. Jeremiah 49 is also an invasion warning, in this case about military action by Babylonian against Judah. The author of GO uses them not as *prophecies* about Israel's future *per se*, but paradigmatically, as if future events will be patterned on events from the past. Ezekiel 38–39 relates past events to future events so closely that they correspond in many of their details. This technique, sometimes referred to as "typology," is widely attested in late scriptural texts like Daniel 11–12 and in scriptural interpretation throughout the Second Temple and beyond.[41] This technique is also apparent, as we have seen, in the author's reuse of Ezek 6 as a template for the future judgment of the nations.

---

40. Ezekiel 38:7–16 is filled out with numerous locutions adapted from the Exodus tradition (Exod 3:10, 12; 7:4; 11:8; 12:31; Num 14:3, 8, 24), the Holiness Code (Lev 25:18, 19; 26:5), Deuteronomy (3:5; 30:3), Judges (9:37), Isaiah (14:13); Joel (2:16, 20, 25, 27) and Zechariah (10:5).

41. For principles and examples see especially I. L. Seeligmann, "Voraussetzungen der Midraschexegese," in *Gesammelte Studien zur Hebräischen Bibel, mit einem Beitrag von Rudolf Smend* (Tübingen: Mohr/Siebeck, 2004) 1–30; M. Fishbane, *Biblical Interpretation in Ancient Israel* (Oxford: Clarendon, 1985) 350–79. So-called "typological interpretation" at Qumran, for example, often depicted Israel's past as paradigmatic of her future (D. Flusser, "פרושים צדוקים, ואסיים בפשר נחום," in *Essays in Jewish History and Philology in Memory of Gedaliah Alon* [Tel Aviv: Hakibbutz Hameuchad, 1970] 133–68; M. Horgan, *Pesharim: Qumran Interpretations of Biblical Books*, CBQMS 8 [Washington, DC: Catholic Biblical Association of America, 1979] 245–47; Johann Maier, "Early Jewish Biblical Interpretation in the Qumran Literature," in *Hebrew Bible/ Old Testament: The History of Its Interpretation, I/1. Antiquity*, edited by Magne Sæbø et al. [Göttingen: Vandenhoeck & Ruprecht, 1996] 125, 127), whereas certain streams of Christian interpretation depicted the past a supplanted by the present (see O. Betz, "Past Events and Last Events in the Qumran Interpretation of History," *WCJS* 6 [1977] 27–34). See also D. Daube, "Typology in Josephus," *JJS* 31 (1980) 18–36; George Brooke, "The Thematic Content of 4Q252," *JQR* 85 (1994) 33–59; Shanni Berrin, "Qumran Pesharim," in *Biblical Interpretation at Qumran*, edited by M. Henze (Grand Rapids: Eerdmans, 2005) 110–33.

Ezekiel 38:18–23

The destruction of Gog begins in 38:18-23. The pericope describes an enraged deity waging war on Gog with weapons only God can wield: earthquakes, landslides, pestilence, rain, hail, fire and brimstone. In a triumphant declaration, YHWH proclaims his reasons for inciting the invasion and destroying the invaders: "I will magnify myself, and cause myself to be hallowed, and I will be known in the eyes of many nations. And they will know that I am YHWH" (38:23). There is no concern for Israel evident in the announcement; she is merely the catalyst. God acts for the sake of his reputation.

The story has been told before. The scene, YHWH acting to destroy invaders before they can harm his people, is reminiscent of 2 Kgs 19:35-37 (= Isa 37:36-38), to cite just one example. But the language of Ezek 38:18-23 closely mirrors that of Ezekiel. Most of the judgment images in verses 19-22 are characteristic of the book (see Appendix). God's motives in verse 23, though expressed in terms reminiscent of the Exodus tradition, also exhibit an Ezekielian flavor. Most elements of God's declaration can be found in passages like 20:5-9, 28:25 and 36:23. There are three elements of 38:18-23, though, which cannot be found in Ezekiel.[42]

God's rage with Gog is dramatically, and redundantly, expressed in 38:18b-19a: "My wrath will be aroused with my anger (בְאַפִּי). For in my jealousy, in the fire of my fury I have spoken."[43] The utterance "in my jealousy, in the fire of my fury" is a formulation from Zephaniah's idiolect. Only Zephaniah combines the words "jealousy" (קִנְאָה), "fire" (אֵשׁ), and "fury" (עֶבְרָה) as an expression of God's anger (Zeph 1:18; 3:8). This locution is significant mainly because it points to the original inspiration for the entire pericope. In Zeph 1:2-3, God swears to sweep the earth clean as a consequence of his wrath.

---

42. There are many thematic parallels between 38:18-23 and other portions of the HB. For example, Gog's allies turning their weapons on one another is a familiar motif from DtrH (Judg 7:22; 1 Sam 14:20). This discussion is restricted to allusions revealed by precise locutions that have been adopted from other sources.

43. The announcement seems overstuffed because the phrase "with my anger" is an addition in MT. A scribe, possibly influenced by the turn of phrase in Isa 66:15, added בְאַפִּי, as attested by its absence in LXX. Ezekiel prefers the expression "pour out (שְׁפָךְ) my wrath" (20:8, 13, 33, 34; 22:22).

> I will utterly sweep away everything
> > from the face of the earth—an utterance of YHWH
> I will sweep away humans and animals
> I will sweep away the birds of the air
> > and the fish of the sea
> I will make the wicked stumble[44]
> I will cut off humanity
> > from the face of the earth—an utterance of YHWH.

This same motif—YHWH overturning creation—appears in Ezek 38:19b–20a. "Surely in that day there will be a great shaking against the land of Israel, and they will quake before me: the fishes of the sea, the birds of the air, the beasts of the field, and all creepers that creep upon the earth, and all the people who are upon the face of the earth." The author of GO, though inspired by Zephaniah, chose to express the motif with a different set of vocabulary. The announcement in 38:20a, "they will quake before me: the fishes (דָּג) of the sea, the flying things (עוֹף) of the sky, the beasts of the field (חַיַּת־הַשָּׂדֶה), and all creepers (רֶמֶשׂ) that creep upon the earth, and all the humans (אָדָם) who are upon the face of the earth," follows the order of living creatures found in Gen 1:26–28. By evoking the creation story, the author cast God's rage against Gog in inflated terms. When unleashed against creation, God's wrath spills over all bounds and threatens cosmic collapse.

There is a second allusion to Genesis in 38:18–23 as well. In 38:22, at the tail-end of the inventory of judgments, we find three dyads: "pestilence and blood," "rain and hail," "fire and brimstone." All of the judgments that appear in 38:18–23, including "pestilence and blood" and "rain and hail" occur elsewhere in Ezekiel. Even so, the last judgment "fire and brimstone" cannot be found in Ezekiel. That expression, worded this way (מָטָר + גָּפְרִית + אֵשׁ), is from Genesis 19, the story of Sodom and Gomorrah (verse 24).[45] The author, by means of this association, suggests that Gog is deserving of God's wrath, even though Gog is never directly accused of any capital crime.

---

44. On this problematic line see Ehud Ben Zvi, *A Historical-Critical Study of the Book of Zephaniah*, BZAW 198 (Berlin: de Gruyter, 1991) 58–60.

45. The same locution appears in Ps 11:6, but it reflects a different development of the image. The psalmist envisions God testing the wicked, blending the images of raining fire and purifying metal. It reads: "Upon the wicked he will rain *coal* (read פֶּחָם with Symmachus), fire, and brimstone, and burning wind shall be the portion of their cup."

In this pericope, then, the author of GO constructed a new judgment oracle almost entirely from Ezekielian expressions. This is not to say that Ezekiel was the sole inspiration for the oracle. The author derived his central motif, the overthrow of creation, from Zephaniah and wove locutions from Genesis into the fabric of the oracle, elevating its cosmic qualities and condemning Gog by associating him with Sodom.

Ezekiel 39:1–8

The overthrow of Gog and his host is recited again in ch. 39, with greater detail and using different images and language. The first oracle, 39:1–8, begins by reintroducing Gog in language that is nearly identical to 38:2–4 (39:1–2). It goes on to describe the death of Gog on the mountains of Israel, adds an image of birds and beasts devouring the slain, and threatens Gog's homeland—Magog—with fire (39:3–6). Finally, the author reaffirms that Gog's destruction will force the nations to acknowledge YHWH (38:7–8 // 38:23). This passage, for the first time, asserts that the episode will have a beneficial effect on Israel as well: "and I will make known my holy name in the midst of my people Israel, and I will not let my holy name be polluted again." What polluted God's name was the Babylonian exile, which damaged YHWH's status and reputation (20:41, 44; 36:20–23 [cf. 20:9, 14, 22]).[46] The destruction of Gog will redeem YHWH's reputation with Israel and inaugurate a new age, an age in which exile will never again become necessary.

The pericope is replete with locutions from other scriptural texts. It draws many of its phrases and clauses from Ezekiel and the Holiness Code. More precisely, it draws language from the restoration oracles in Ezekiel (11:17–20; 16:53–63; 20:33–44), which have borrowed, in their own right, from the H corpus (see Appendix).[47] The dependence of GO on Ezekiel's restoration oracles becomes more pronounced as GO

---

46. The locution used to express this theme (variations on חלל + שׁם קדשׁי) is adopted from the Holiness Code (Lev 18:21; 19:12; 20:3; 21:6; 22:2, 32 // Amos 2:7; Jer 34:16). In H God's name is defiled when the Israelites violate his precepts, as they do, for example, in idol-worship.

47. It has long been recognized that Ezekiel borrowed many phrases and clauses from H. GO, not surprisingly, also contains many H locutions, but it does not contain a single H locution that is not also found in Ezekiel 1–37. In other words, there is no conclusive evidence that the author of GO used H as a *source*. The H language in GO may well have been obtained exclusively from Ezekiel 1–37.

winds to a finish and the status of Israel, following the invasion, comes into sharper focus (esp. 39:21–29).

The principal images in this oracle, though, were drawn from Psalm 79 (discussed above) and Isaiah 14. Isaiah 14:4b–21 describes a ruler, the king of Babylon, who oppresses the whole earth only to be slain and left unburied on the battlefield. This *topos* is clearly present in 39:3–6, as is the phrase "the remote parts of the north," ירכתי צפון, the seat of the enemy in Isa 14 and in GO (Isa 14:13; Ezek 38:6, 15; 39:2).[48] It is widely accepted that the oracle in Isa 14 originally announced judgment on Assyria.[49] Isaiah, deeming the king of Assyria and the king of Babylon to be typologically aligned, simply reapplied the oracle to the king of Babylon.[50] The author of GO, in turn, appropriated the oracle for his own purposes, using it to paint a picture of a future invading king: Gog of Magog.

Not content to rely solely upon Isa 14, the author of GO filled out the scene with locutions from two other texts describing the overthrow of powerful kings. The line "to the birds of prey, every flying thing, and beast of the field I will give you for food" (39:4b) was borrowed from the oracle against Pharaoh in Ezek 29: לחית הארץ ולעוף השמים נתתיך לאכלה (29:5).[51] The judgment against the land of Magog in 39:6, "I will send fire upon Magog" (שלחתי אש ב-), is borrowed from the idiolect of Amos. Amos used the same clause in his judgments on Damascus, Gaza, Tyre, Edom, Moab, and Judah (1:4, 7, 10, 12; 2:2, 5). No other prophet uses the locution. In other words, the author of GO is continuing a habit of reuse that became apparent in chapter 38. That is, the author draws upon one or two antecedent texts for the signature themes or images in the new oracle but articulates the prophecy using individual phrases and clauses drawn from many sources.

---

48. Apart from Isa 14:13 and GO, the phase only occurs in Ps 43:3.

49. As argued by H. L. Ginsberg, "Reflexes of Sargon in Isaiah after 715 B.C.E.," *JAOS* 88 (1968) 47–53.

50. Fishbane, *Biblical Interpretation*, 372–79.

51. Ezek 29:5 adapted the line from Deut 28:26,

והיתה נבלתך למאכל לכל־עוף השמים ולבהמת הארץ.

Ezekiel 39:9–16

Ezekiel 39:9–16 interrupts the plot of the chapter. In 39:1–8, the prophet foretells the death of Gog and his host, who will be devoured by a vast assembly of wild animals. In 39:17–24, God summons the wild animals to his table, an event that is described in some detail. In between these two scenes is an extended interlude, narrating the plunder of Gog's host by the Israelites (39:9–10) and the purification of the land. This purification can only be effected by the arduous process of locating and interring the stripped bones of the dead (39:11–16).

In the opening scene, the inhabitants of the land spill out of their towns to collect the war-gear of Gog's host for use as firewood (38:9–10). The motif of burning weapons, as a symbol of the end of warfare on earth, is well-known, especially from the messianic hymn in Isaiah 9 and the cosmic hymn in Psalm 46.

> For all the boots of the tramping warriors
> and all the garments rolled in blood
> will be burned as fuel for the fire. (Isa 9:5)

> Come, behold the works of YHWH,
> who made desolate places on the earth.
> He makes wars cease to the end of the earth;
> he breaks the bow, and shatters the spear;
> he burns the shields with fire. (Ps 46:9–10)

The author of GO chose to express this motif, for the first time, in his own language, not in the language of Isaiah or the psalm. This is a consistent feature of 39:9–16, which has the lowest density of borrowed locutions in all of GO. This is not to say that 39:9–10 is wholly devoid of reused language. The author supplemented verses 9–10 with two borrowed locutions. The word-pair "mantlet and shield" (צנה ומגן) is derived from Ezek 23:24, and the dyad "to take spoil" and "to seize plunder" (ולבז בז + לשל שלל) was taken from Isa 10:6 (= Ezek 29:19).[52] Since both have appeared previously, the first in 38:4 and the second in 38:12–13, they contribute nothing new to the composition. They do

---

52. Sweeney has suggested that the span of seven years (39:9) was drawn from the seven-year sabbatical cycle in Exod 23:10–11 and Lev 25:1–7 ("The Priesthood and Protoapocalyptic Reading," 171). This is certainly possible and accords with the author's habits of allusion. It is difficult to verify though, since the author of GO is fond of sets of seven and may have selected the number for reasons of symmetry (see n. 19 above).

serve, nonetheless, to create cohesion between this pericope and the broader composition.

In the next scene, the Israelites are given the task of interring the slain, a task that will take seven months to complete. The episode is unique, unknown outside of GO. Despite this, the author of GO again described the scene using language influenced by other scriptural texts. For example, the threat, "I will give to Gog a place there," אתן לגוג מקום־שם (39:11), sounds very much like a parody of deuteronomic land-allotment language (Josh 20:4; Judg 20:36; 1 Sam 9:22; 27:5). The "valley of Hamon-Gog" (39:11, 15) is a pun on "the valley of Hinnom," where Israelites sacrificed their children (2 Kgs 23:10; Jer 7:30–34).[53] Also, the obscure line "it will stop the travelers" (39:11) may very well be an allusion to Joel 4:17 (Eng 3:17), which says, regarding the restored Jerusalem, "strangers shall never again travel through it." Beyond the level of individual locutions, the whole passage (39:11–16) is predicated upon Priestly notions of the purity of the land, as expressed in texts like Lev 18:25–28 and the defiling effects of corpses on it, as expressed in texts like Lev 17:15–16 and 22:4.[54]

This pericope is the most unique of all the Gog oracles. In it, the author of GO maintained the practice of borrowing individual phrases and clauses as linguistic building blocks for the oracle, but more of the language is his own than in any other portion of GO. Likewise, he alluded to essential *topoi* from other scriptural texts (the end of war, the purity of the land) in keeping with his usual custom, but for the first time he introduced a wholly new motif into the story: the precise and lengthy description of the burial of Gog.

Ezekiel 39:17–20

The author of GO returned to the motif of animals devouring the slain in verses 17–20. The literary devices in the pericope are like those of a fable. The animals are anthropomorphized, eating and drinking at God's table in a great celebratory feast. Gog's host is zoomorphized, presented as sacrificial animals slaughtered for the feast. The direct inspiration for

---

53. So Zimmerli, *Ezekiel 2*, 316–17.

54. On the priestly qualities of the pericope see Zimmerli, *Ezekiel 2*, 318 and Hossfeld, *Untersuchungen*, 474.

the scene was most likely Isaiah 34:6–7, where the destruction of the Edomites is pictured in a strikingly similar fashion.[55]

> YHWH has a sword
>   it is sated with blood,
>   it is gorged with fat,
>   with the blood of lambs and goats,
>   with the fat of the kidneys of rams.
> For YHWH has a sacrifice in Bozrah,
>   a great slaughter in the land of Edom.
> Wild oxen shall fall with them,
>   and young steers with the mighty bulls.
> Their land shall be soaked with blood,
>   and their soil made rich with fat.

A number of motifs and tropes from Isa 34:6–7 reappear in GO, too many to be coincidental. The agent in both cases is God's sword. Humans are depicted as livestock. Their blood and fat satiates the devourer, and the slaughter is portrayed as a sacrifice.[56] The language of the oracle is also colored by Priestly instruction, in this case instructions prohibiting the eating of fat and blood. Leviticus 7:23–27 reads:

> Speak to the people of Israel, saying, "You will not eat the fat of an ox or a sheep or a goat. The fat of an animal that died or was torn by wild animals may be put to any other use, but you must not eat it. If any one of you eats the fat from an animal of which an offering by fire may be made to YHWH, you who eat it will be cut off from your kindred. You must not eat any blood at all, either of bird or of animal, in any of your settlements. Any of you who eats blood shall be cut off from your kindred."

---

55. The oracle begins in Isa 34:2 with an announcement of judgment upon all the nations, "YHWH is incensed with all the nations, his fury is directed against all their hosts, he has doomed them and destined them for slaughter." This dictum provided the author of GO with the opportunity to apply the oracle to Gog as well.

56. Isaiah 25:6–7; 56:9; Jer 46:10; 50:25–27, and Zeph 1:7–8 all contain similarities to Ezek 39:17–20, but none reflect the complex combination of motifs found in Isa 34:6–7 and Ezek 39:17–20. Isaiah 25:6–7 describes a feast ordained by God, but lacks wild animals or human slain. In Isa 56:9 God summons wild beasts to eat, but they eat the flock of Israel. Jeremiah 46:10 describes a battle between Babylon and Egypt as a divine sacrifice, but it too lacks animals who devour human corpses. In Jer 50:25–27 the Babylonians are described as bulls slaughtered by God, but the feast and carrion-animal images are absent. Finally, in Zeph 1:7–8 God consecrates a sacrifice of humans, but the humans are not described as animals, nor is the sacrifice presented as a feast for wild animals.

By means of these allusions, the author of GO introduced role-reversal into the story to highlight the extraordinary, unlikely fate of Gog and his allies. In the case of Isa 34, the ironic turning was already present in the evoked text. The humans became like animals, the warriors like the slaughtered. The author of GO merely stretched the reversal and made it into parody, imagining the wild animals who devour the slain as so many lords and ladies sitting down to table. Leviticus 7, though, contains no role-reversal. In this case, the author supplied it. Leviticus 7:23–27 is an injunction by YHWH, prohibiting the eating of certain fats and all blood on pain of death. In GO, YHWH himself consecrates the violation, overturning his own decree. But, when combined with the motifs from Isa 34, it is a violation in the reverse. We do not see humans eating animal fat and drinking animal blood but animals eating human fat and drinking human blood, and the animals violate sacrificial law at the behest of the deity who gave the law.

Ezekiel 39:17–20 maintains the pattern of richly textured layers of allusion that we have seen throughout GO, but here we also see the playful, mocking face of the author. In 39:9–16, the author of GO introduced pun and word-play into the story to mock the invaders and their fate. Here in 39:17–20 he takes greater creative license and recrafts prophetic images and legal stipulations into a full-blown parody of Gog. This is the last that the author of GO has to say about the invaders. His attention now turns to the fate of Israel.

Ezekiel 39:21–29

The last nine verses of GO describe the results of the entire episode. Once Gog is destroyed, both Israel and the nations will acknowledge YHWH. In particular, Gog's downfall will prove that the exile was due not to YHWH's inability to protect his people, but to his judgment, as a punishment for Israel's sins. Once YHWH's reputation is restored, he will relent and return his people. They will dwell again in safety and there will be no one left to oppress them. YHWH will restore them to his favor and pour out his spirit on them. The unit is replete with language and themes from Deuteronomy, Isaiah, Ezekiel and Joel (see Appendix). I will focus my attention on the allusions to Isaiah 40–66 at the beginning of the pericope and the allusion to Joel at its end.

The oracle opens with a verse composed almost entirely of locutions borrowed from Isaiah and Deuteronomy (identical locutions are underlined; locutions in Isa 66:19 that appear elsewhere in GO are underlined with dashes).

Ezek 39:21	And I will set <u>my glory upon the nations</u> (אֶת־כְּבוֹדִי בַּגּוֹיִם), <u>and all the nations will see</u> (וְרָאוּ כָל־הַגּוֹיִם) <u>my judgment that I have done</u> (מִשְׁפָּטִי אֲשֶׁר עָשִׂיתִי), and my hand, which I have laid upon them
Deuteronomy	<u>my judgment which I have done</u> (מִשְׁפָּטִי אֲשֶׁר עָשִׂיתִי). This is a common expression in Deuteronomy, appearing, for example, in 5:31, 12:1, and 17:11.
Isa 42:8b	I am YHWH, that is my name, <u>my glory</u> (כְּבוֹדִי) I give to no other
Isa 52:10	YHWH has bared his holy arm, before the eyes of <u>all the nations</u> (כָל־הַגּוֹיִם) And the ends of the earth <u>will see</u> (וְרָאוּ), the salvation of our God.
Isa 62:2	<u>The nations will see</u> (וְרָאוּ גוֹיִם) your vindication, and all the kings your glory (כְּבוֹדֵךְ)
Isa 66:19	I will send survivors to the nations, to Tarshish, Put, and Lud—which draw the bow— to Tubal and Javan, to the coast lands far away that have not heard of my fame or <u>seen my glory</u> (רָאוּ אֶת־כְּבוֹדִי); and they shall declare <u>my glory among the nations</u> (אֶת־כְּבוֹדִי בַּגּוֹיִם).

The similar combinations of motifs present in Ezek 39:21 and Isaiah is remarkable: glory, witness of the nations, and vindication of Israel. It has long been recognized that Isa 40–66 was composed after Ezekiel and borrowed from it.[57] In the case of GO, however, it is likely that the author of GO reused materials from Isaiah 40–66, as is indicated by the distinctive Isaianic language in 39:21. The locutions "set my glory," "glory among the nations," and "all nations will see" are distinctive expressions of Isaiah 40–66, largely unknown outside of the book.[58] More telling,

---

57. D. Baltzer, *Ezechiel und Deuterojesaja*, BZAW 121 (Berlin: Walther de Gruyter, 1971).

58. "Set my glory" (נתן כבוד with God as subject) occurs only in Isa 42:8, 48:11, Ezek 39:21, Ps 84:12, and 115:1. "Glory among the nations" (כבוד בגוים) occurs only in Isa 66:19 and Ezek 39:21. "All the nations will see" (ראה + כל־גוים) occurs in Exod 34:10, Isa 52:10, 62:2, and Lam 1:10. Finally, "judgment I have done" (1st per. עשה + משפט / שפט), though not distinctive of Isaiah, occurs both in Ezek 39:21 and Isa 58:2.

such language is completely unattested elsewhere in Ezekiel. Its sudden appearance here is due to literary dependence.[59] It seems likely that the author's attention fell upon Isa 66:19, in particular, because of its subject matter (eschatological judgment), and its reuse of foreign nations from Gen 10, which the author of GO also reused (compare 38:1–6). What differs between the two texts is the mechanism by which the nations acknowledge YHWH's glory. In Isaiah 66, survivors of YHWH's day of vindication (66:5–16) bring word of his glory to the nations. In GO, the unexpected, supernatural annihilation of Gog's host leads the nations to acknowledge YHWH's power.

The oracle concludes with an allusion to Joel 3:1–2.

Joel 3:1–2 (Eng 2:28–29)	Ezek 39:29
Then afterward, I will pour out my spirit on (אשפוך את־רוחי על) all flesh; your sons and your daughters shall prophesy, your old men shall dream dreams, and your young men shall see visions. Even on the male and female slaves, in those days, I will pour out my spirit.	Neither will I hide my face any more from them, because I will have poured out my spirit upon (שפכתי את־רוחי על) the house of Israel"—an utterance of Lord YHWH

At first glance, the expression "I will have poured out my spirit upon the house of Israel" (Ezek 39:29) may appear to be nothing more than a rewording of Ezek 37:14, "I will put my spirit within you." However, when the book of Ezekiel speaks of giving the spirit, it always uses נתן (Ezek 11:19; 36:26, 27; 37:14).[60] Ezekiel uses שפך exclusively for pouring out wrath.[61] In fact, שפך occurs sixty times in the prophetic corpus, and in every case it is used in a negative expression as part of an oracle of judgment (for blood, anger, fornication, and so on)—in every case, that is, except Ezek 39:29 and Joel 3:1–2.[62]

59. The dependence of GO on Isa 40–66 confirms evidence that GO is an addition to Ezekiel.

60. So also Num 11:25, 29; 1 Kgs 22:23; 2 Kgs 19:7; Isa 37:7; 42:1; Qoh 12:7; Neh 9:20; 2 Chr 18:22.

61. See Ezek 7:8; 9:8; 20:8, 13, 21, 33, 34; 30:15; 36:18 (cf. 21:36; 22:31).

62. There are two primary positions on the date of Joel. The most common position is to date the book, as a unity, to the fifth century (see, for example, Hans Walter Wolff, *Joel and Amos*, Hermeneia [Philadelphia: Fortress, 1977] 5; Siegfried Bergler, *Joel als Schriftinterpret*, BEATAJ 16 [Frankfurt: Peter Lang, 1988] 9–13). Other scholars identify

The author of GO alluded to Joel 3:1–2 to explain the gift of the spirit, which was promised in Ezek 11:19–20 and 37:14.[63] Ezekiel 11:19–20 promised the people "one heart" and a "new spirit." Ezekiel 37:14 promised the coming of "my spirit" as part of the revivification of the nation. The notion of a new heart was explained as God's transformation of the people, changing their constitution, so that they would be able to keep the covenant (11:19b–20a), but neither 11:19–20 nor 37:14 explained the "new spirit." Joel, though, described an outpouring of God's spirit following the *yôm YHWH*. For him, the spirit is the gift of prophetic inspiration poured out on all the people in the eschaton.[64] The author of GO filled the gap in Ezekiel's explanation of the transformation of the people by linking the book of Ezekiel to Joel. In his view, the whole people will be obedient (per Ezek 11:19–20), and all the people will be prophets (per Joel 3:1–2). Of all the allusions in GO, this is the only clear-cut case of GO reusing one text to interpret another.

CONCLUSIONS

What we observe from all these allusions is that the author of GO drew many locutions, images, and themes from other scriptural texts, especially texts regarding the judgment of the nations and the vindication of Israel. Some of these texts are set in the eschaton (e.g., Isa 66:19; Joel 3:1–2), while others speak of the imminent future (e.g., Isa 34:6–7 and Jer 49:30–33). Regardless of their time frame, all were viewed as relevant to the author's global, eschatological vision.[65] With this in mind, we can

---

two principal strata in the book: one attributed to Joel ben-Pethuel that was inspired by a locust plague (usually, 1:1–14, 16–20; 2:2b–11a, 12–27), and a second comprehensive redactional reworking of the collection (usually, 1:15; 2:1b–2a, 11b; 3:1–4:21) that recasts the whole as an eschatological prophecy (for example, B. Duhm, "Anmerkungen zu den Zwölf Propheten," *ZAW* 31 [1911] 184–87; E. Sellin, *Das Zwölfprophetenbuch. Übersetz und erklärt*. 3d ed., KAT 12 [Leipzig: Deichert, 1929]; T. H. Robinson and F. Horst, *Die Zwölf kleinen Propheten*, 3d ed., HAT 13 [Tübingen: Mohr/Siebeck, 1964]; J. Blenkinsopp, *History of Prophecy*, 258–59). In this case also the completed book is dated to the fifth century. As will be argued below, this is, by either estimation, earlier than the date of the Gog oracles.

63. I am excluding the similar text in Ezek 36:26–27 because the entire passage, 36:23c–38, which is absent in Papyrus 967, is, in my judgment, a late scribal addition to the book. See bibliography in n. 81.

64. Joel 3:1–2 is itself an allusion to Num 11:29, where Moses expresses a desire that all the people be endowed with the spirit of prophecy.

65. A. Steudel ("אחרית הימים," 225–46) has demonstrated that, in the Qumran documents, the phrase "end of days," אחרית הימים, encompasses past, present and

further refine our understanding of the literary form of GO. Not only is it is pastiche, as we have observed, but it might more accurately be called "thematic pastiche," pastiche constructed from texts that revolve, by in large, around select themes, in this case the vindication of Israel and the ultimate fate of the nations. Certainly, GO alludes to texts that are neither eschatological, nor about foreign nations, nor about Israel's vindication (e.g., Gen 1:26–28 and Lev 7:23–27), but the vast majority of the evoked texts either are about at least one of those themes, or, though reversal and reapplication, are reapplied to one of those themes (e.g., Ezek 6:1–14).

Methods and Techniques of Reuse

From this rich textual mosaic, we can observe much about the author's methods and techniques of scriptural reuse. Though easy to overlook, it is important to note that the author of GO never quoted his sources. That is, there are no citation formulae or verbatim duplications of locutions that are longer than a few words. There is only an oblique acknowledgment of literary dependence in 38:17. Instead, the author revealed his sources by borrowing from their more distinctive locutions, or by seeding a pericope with numerous locutions from an identifiable source text. Rather than crafting a commentary, then, the author of GO created a new text from a rich mosaic of allusions.

Exegesis of existing texts is clearly not at the forefront of the author's purposes.[66] Though borrowing extensively from other scriptural texts, the author of GO almost never interprets those texts and never

---

future events. Almost any event, regardless of chronology, could be understood as "eschatological" if it were pertinent to and part of the sequence of events leading to the "end of days." This kind of thinking could very well explain GO's affinity for reapplying antecedent prophecy to the end of days. See also G. L. Doudna, *4Q Pesher Nahum* (London: Sheffield Academic, 2001) 63–66.

66. Interpretation, for the author of GO, is implicit in the combination and recontextualizing of locutions and allusions. For similar examples see Menahem Kister, "A Common Heritage: Biblical Interpretation at Qumran and its Implications," in *Biblical Perspectives: Early Use and Interpretation of the Bible in Light of the Dead Sea Scrolls. Proceedings of the First International Symposium of the Orion Center for the Study of Dead Sea Scrolls and Associated Literature*, edited by M. E. Stone and E. G. Chazon, STDJ 28 (Leiden: Brill, 1998) 101–11; "Biblical Phrases and Hidden Biblical Interpretations and *Pesharim*," in *The Dead Sea Scrolls: Forty Years of Research*, edited by Devorah Dimant and Uriel Rappaport, STJD 10 (Leiden: Brill, 1992) 27–39.

overturns them. On only one occasion, the allusion to Joel 3:1–2 in Ezek 39:29, does GO use allusion to interpret a text (in this case interpreting Ezek 11:19–20 and 37:14). In several cases, antecedent judgment oracles are reapplied to Gog (Ezek 6:1–14; Isa 10 and 14; Zeph 1, for example), but there is no indication that the author intended to supplant these older oracles. Rather, the author of GO sought to amalgamate a variety of texts and ideas into a harmonious whole.

All this borrowing allowed GO's author to introduce new topics to the book of Ezekiel, integrating the book with a wider corpus of scriptures. The borrowing, though, is highly selective. Despite the fact that the author of GO is discussing the future of Israel, he shows little interest in many of its usual topics, including Jerusalem, the temple, the cult, and the regathering. Instead, he chose to borrow from texts which address the vindication of Israel and the ultimate fate of the nations, topics that are, apart from GO, almost entirely absent from Ezekiel's portrait of Israel's future. These topics were then articulated using language and motifs that were borrowed from prophets who *did* speak to these subjects.[67]

Perhaps most striking is the way that the author reused texts in grand ways and in minuscule ways to create a sophisticated scaffolding of allusions that permeate every level of his composition. At the highest level, that of the entire composition or a major portion of it, the author of GO used three texts as templates, *Vorbilder*, sketching GO's major themes and plot-points from them (Ezek 28:25–26; Ezek 6:1–14; Ps 79:1–4). It is telling that two of these texts are from Ezekiel. GO's author, in composing a supplement to the book, took his chief inspiration from Ezekiel and constructed his composition on Ezekiel's foundation. It is also telling that two of the three *Vorbilder*, Ezek 6:1–14 and Ps 79:1–4, speak of misfortunes for Israel, which, when appropriated by the author of GO, are inflicted upon Gog and his nation-confederates. This reveals one of the author's pressing concerns: the restoration of the proper world order. As he envisions it, this entails a peaceful, protected, pious Israel, who should not, and indeed, does not suffer greater judgments than do the gentile nations who have afflicted her.

---

67. See Fishbane *Biblical Interpretation*, 423–24; compare M. J. Bernstein, "Re-Arrangement, Anticipation and Harmonization as Exegetical Features in the Genesis Apocryphon," *DSD* 3 (1996) 37–57.

At the next level, that of the individual oracles, we see a similar technique at work. That is, the content of many of the individual oracles was also shaped by one or two antecedent texts. At this level, all the model texts are from outside of Ezekiel:

> Ezek 38:1–6 // Gen 10 and Num 23–24
>
> Ezek 38:7–16 // Isa 10:3–6 and Jer 49:30–33
>
> Ezek 38:18–23 // Zeph 1:2–3
>
> Ezek 39:1–8 // Isa 14:4–21
>
> Ezek 39:9–16 // ———
>
> Ezek 39:17–20 // Isa 34:6–7
>
> Ezek 39:21–29 // ———

In some cases, the author of GO revealed his sources through verbatim citation (e.g., Gen 10, Isa 10, Jer 49), in others he mined them for *topoi* and images but used language from other scriptural texts to articulate his oracles (e.g., Zeph 1; Isa 14). In the case of 39:9–16, the major motif, burial of the slain, is entirely the creation of GO's author. The last oracle, 39:21–19, does not draw upon a single source for its major inspiration, but it is dense with allusions nonetheless. The effect of these oracle-level allusions is the same: the coordination of Ezekiel with other prophetic visions of the future.

Finally, within the individual oracles the author of GO reused hundreds of locutions from all across the Torah, Prophets, and Psalms. The majority are from Ezekiel, stamping the composition in an Ezekielian mold. Others evoke passages from all across the scriptural landscape, creating a complex tapestry of biblical idioms and ideas unlike anything else in the book.

Effects of Textual Reuse

One unavoidable effect of intertwining all these borrowed phrases and clauses is that the new prophecy tends to be awkward and repetitious. This feature of GO has inspired numerous speculative theories on the redactional history of these two chapters.[68] Though resulting in a text

---

68. See, for example, K. von Rabenau, "Die Entstehung des Buches Ezechiel in forgeschichtlicher Sicht," *WZ* 4 (1955–56) 659–94; H-M. Lutz, *Jaweh, Jerusalem und die Völker*, WMANT 27 (Neukirchen: Nekirchner Verlag, 1968) 63–84, 125–30; J. Garscha,

that is difficult to scan, the technique had a beneficial effect as well, a benefit that is key to the author's purpose: integration. Employing phrases and key words from Ezekiel enabled the author of GO to create cohesion between his composition and the rest of the book. This cohesion disguised the addition, placing GO within the stream of accepted prophetic revelation.[69]

Thus, the author's concerns and approach resulted in a creative expansion of the prophetic tradition. Because the main topics of GO, the vindication of Israel and fate of the nations, are barely apparent in the book of Ezekiel, the author deems it necessary to expand it. Judgment is announced against neighboring countries in chs. 25–32 and 35, but several prominent nations from Ezekiel's day are conspicuously absent. The only statements in Ezekiel about the future of *all* nations use the phrase "in the sight of the nations," which reveals little beyond the fact that the nations will persevere after Israel's restoration.[70] The nations are also conspicuously absent from the vision of the future temple in chs. 40–48. Their place and role in the eschaton is cloudy at best. This omission is surely one of the principal factors that prompted the author of GO to craft his oracle.

The author of GO chose to fill this gap not by freely composing a new work with new ideas but by reusing extant themes and ideas, in effect harmonizing Ezekiel with other scriptural witnesses. This harmonization had the effect of making the book more deterministic and global. Within Ezekiel, Israel's history was already presented as having been predetermined in the past, present, and future (esp. chapter 20). The past and future of the nations, though, is less certain. Clearly YHWH acts, on occasion, to alter the fate of the nations through judgments, but

---

Studium zum Ezechielbuch: Eine redaktionskritische Untersuchung von 1–39 (Bern: Lang, 1974) 230–39; Hossfeld, *Untersuchungen*, 494–528; K-F. Pohlmann, *Ezechielstudien: Zur Redactiongeschichte des Buches und zur Frage nach den älteste Texten*, BZAW 202 (Berlin: de Gruyter, 1992) 77–87.

69. George Brooke has designated this technique "imitative allusion" and illustrated its wide use in poetic and liturgical commentaries from Qumran and in the NT (see "Biblical Interpretation in the Qumran Scrolls and in the New Testament," in *The Dead Sea Scrolls Fifty Years after their Discovery*, edited by Lawrence Schiffman et al. [Jerusalem: Israel Exploration Society, 2000] 67–69).

70. "In the eyes of the nations," לעיני הגוים, is a stock element in Ezekiel's idiolect. It does occur outside of the book (Lev 26:45; Isa 5:10; [cf.: Ps 66:7]; 98:2; 2 Chr 32:23), but two-thirds of all occurrences in HB are from the book of Ezekiel (5:8; 20:9, 14, 22, 41; 22:16; 28:25; 38:16 [as a broken phrase], 23; 39:27; cf. 26:3; 31:6).

whether or not he frequently or persistently intervenes in their history is not addressed. The author of GO contends that the future of the nations is also foreordained. They will be forced to invade Israel, and they will be humbled by God. This deterministic impulse places GO within the emerging intellectual stream of Jewish apocalypticism and elevates the theocentric qualities of the book. It is not just Israel's fate that has been foreordained for the purpose of revealing God's sanctity. The nations' fate, too, is fashioned to reveal the glory and majesty of the deity (39:7–8). The author's reuse of the nations from Gen 10 also widened its perspective to global proportions. The fate of the whole world is encompassed within YHWH's plan for Gog (see comments on 38:1–6 above). And this fate follows a pattern, one established by YHWH's treatment of nations in the past, nations like Assyria (Isa 10), Babylon (Jer 49), Edom, and Judah herself (Zeph 1; Ezek 6).

This is not to say that GO is merely a catalogue and combination of ideas from other scriptures. As Moshe Bernstein observes, "All rewriting is commentary, and the methodology of selection, rearrangement, supplementation, and omission in the process of rewriting is a form of commentary."[71] The author of GO contributes to existing prophecy in his specific delineation of the time and circumstances of Israel's vindication. First of all, the author set Israel's anticipated restoration in the eschaton. Most facets of the restoration are placed in the "end of days" (38:8, 16).[72] Those will be days of universal peace and harmony, uncorrupted fidelity to YHWH, and renewal of divine attention (39:21–29).

---

71. Bernstein, "Interpretation of Scriptures," in *EDSS* 1:379.

72. Considering that the author of Ezek 38–39 could have persistently referred to these future events with the generic temporal designation "in that day," ביום ההוא, as other oracles in the book do (20:6; 23:38, 39; 24:26, 27; 29:21; 30:9; 38:10, 14, 18, 19; 39:11; 45:22), the appearance of "in the last years," באחרית השנים, and "in the end of days," באחרית הימים, is conspicuous. Still, the translation of אחרית הימים is hotly disputed. Regarding the use of the phrase in GO, I agree with the assessment of Hans Wildberger in his comments on Isa 2:2, "Even if one does not find an apocalyptic sense for באחרית הימים ... the term is not intended as a description of a vague time period yet to come ... it refers to an altered future, resulting from God's entering into history, envisioning the coming time of salvation. As long as this intervention by YHWH in history is designated 'eschatological' and is clearly differentiated from 'apocalyptic,' one can say that באחרית הימים is used to introduce an eschatological prediction" (*Isaiah 1–12*, CC [Minneapolis: Fortress, 1991] 88; see also G. W. Buchanan, "Eschatology and the 'End of Days,'" *JNES* 20 (1961) 189–90; J. Klausner, *The Messianic Ideal in Israel* (London: Allen & Unwin, 1956), 30; and Seebass, "אחר," 211–12).

This specification, mirrored later in Daniel 11–12, may have been motivated by a desire to addresses the people's understandable disappointment with circumstances in and around Jerusalem during much of the Persian and Hellenistic periods. The return and restoration compared poorly with the vision of the restoration painted by the prophets. GO is explicit that the promised restoration is still to come and should not to be identified with the contemporary community or its circumstances. Second, the author of GO divided the restoration into stages. Return and resettlement are part of the restoration promises, but for the author of GO, the resettlement of Yehud was a past reality.[73] As a result, not every element of the restoration could be fixed in the eschaton. The author of GO was forced to divide the fulfillment of the restoration oracles into two parts. In the first stage, some exiles have returned and settled into an agrarian life (38:8, 11–13). This period will culminate in the invasion and destruction of Gog. In the second stage, the entire diaspora will return (39:28) and all the restoration promises will be poured out on the people (universal return, Davidic monarch, covenant of peace, transformation of the people, multiplication of the people, reunified nation, rebuilt temple, resurrected cult, and divine presence [37:21–28 and 39:21–29]).

GO in the Context of Post-Exilic Literature

GO is a type of literature widely attested in the Second Temple period. Its form and content correspond closely with many Second Temple texts, as do its techniques and effects of scriptural reuse.[74] These correspondences are especially evident when GO is compared with texts found among the DSS. There is not space in the present study to articulate the many parallels in hermeneutical and compositional technique and in subject matter between GO and DSS. Nor is there space to place GO

---

73. This will be argued more clearly below (see "Synthesis").

74. The Second Temple period is divided, roughly speaking, into the Persian period (539 BCE–332 BCE) and the Greco-Roman period (332 BCE—70 CE). The second part of the period, the Greco-Roman era, saw a flourishing of literacy and religious writing in general and of scriptural interpretation specifically. On certain dynamics that contributed to this circumstance see A. I. Baumgarten, "Literacy and the Polemics Surrounding Biblical Interpretation in the Second Temple Period," in *Studies in Ancient Midrash*, edited by J. Kugel (Cambridge: Harvard Center for Jewish Studies, 2001) 27–41.

within a trajectory of literary development from its scriptural precursors to Tannaitic and early Christian literature. What I want to suggest here is that thematic-pastiche, though rare in the HB, is well-known in Jewish literature of the Second Temple period, as is the phenomena of expanding the scriptural tradition though new composition in biblical style. To this end, I wish to turn again to the text with which this study began: the Temple Scroll.

Column 59 of the Temple Scroll (11QT) itemizes the curses that will fall upon the king and the people, if the king does not properly observe the Torah. The pericope is similar to GO in its composition, in that it was crafted by thematic pastiche. That is, the author conflated phrases and clauses drawn from scriptural texts on certain themes, particularly the king and covenant fidelity. Also like GO, the column has a principal base text, Deut 28, but it incorporates elements from many other sources as well, including Genesis, Leviticus, Judges, Kings, Jeremiah, Ezekiel, Hosea, and Zechariah. From these borrowed locutions, the author has fashioned a new text in the biblical style.[75]

The underlined elements in the 11QT column are borrowed locutions. A dotted underline indicates that the original locution was altered or adapted to fit the new context and readership.

---

75. On the composition of 11QT see, most notably, Gershon Brin, "המקרא במגלת המקדש," *Shnaton: An Annual for Biblical and Ancient Near Eastern Studies* 4 (1980) 182–225; "Concerning Some of the Uses of the Bible in the Temple Scroll," *RevQ* 12 (1987) 519–28; Phillip Calloway, "Extending Divine Revelation: Micro-Compositional Strategies in the Temple Scroll," 149–62 in *Temple Scroll Studies: Papers Presented at the International Symposium on the Temple Scroll, Manchester, December 1987,* edited by George J. Brooke, JSPSup 7 (Sheffield: JSOT Press, 1989); S. Kaufman, "Temple Scroll"; Hartmut Stegemann, "The Literary Composition of the Temple Scroll and Its Status at Qumran," in *Temple Scroll Studies: Papers Presented at the International Symposium on the Temple Scroll, Manchester, December 1987,* edited by George J. Brooke, JSPSup 7 (Sheffield: JSOT Press, 1989) 123–48; Dwight Swanson, *The Temple Scroll and the Bible: The Methodology of 11QT,* STJD 14 (Leiden: Brill, 1995); Andrew Wilson and Lawrence Wills, "Literary Sources of the Temple Scroll," *HTR* 75/3 (1982) 275–88.

Transformation of Israel's Hope 87

Sources	MT	11QT[76]
		2- ויבזרום בארצות רבות
Deut 28:37	והיית לשמה למשל ולשנינה	והיו לשמה למשל ולשנניה
1 Kgs 12:11	על כבד	ובעול כבד
Deut 28:48[77]	ובחסר כל	3- ובחסור כול
Deut 28:36[78]	ועבדת שם אלהים אחרים עץ ואבן	ועבדו שמה אלוהים מעשי ידי אדם עץ ואבן כסף
Lev 26:31–32	ונתתי את־עריכם חרבה	4- וזהב ובכול זה יהיו עריהמה
Jer 25:9–10	לשמה ולשרקה ולחרבות	לשומה ולשרקה ולחורבה והיו
Lev 26:32	ושממו עליה איביכם	5- אויביהמה שוממים במה והמה בארחות אויביהמה מתאנחים
Zech 7:13	יקראו ולא אשמע	6- ומזעיקים מפני עול כבד ויקראו
Jer 11:11	וזעקו אלי ולא אשמע אליהם	ולוא אשמע וזעקו ולוא אענה
Jer 21:12	מפני רע מעלליהם	7- אותמה מפני רוע מעלליהמה
Ezek 39:23	ואסתר פני מהם	ואסתיר פני מהמה
Ezek 34:8[79]	יען היות־צאני ... לאכלה	והיו לאוכלה

---

76. Text from Y. Yadin, *The Temple Scroll* (Jerusalem: Israel Exploration Society & Institute of Archaeology of the Hebrew University of Jerusalem, 1983) 2:266–68.

77. Lines 2–3 paraphrase Deut 28:48. "Therefore you shall serve (ועבדת) your enemies whom YHWH will send against you, in hunger and thirst, in nakedness and lack of everything (ובחסר כל). He will put an iron yoke (על ברזל) on your neck until he has destroyed you."

78. 11QT 59.3 is a conflation of Deut 28:48, 36 and 2:28 (Yadin, *Temple Scroll*, 2: 266).

79. The expression "hide my face" is common (see Deut 31:17–18); but the phrase represented here appears to be influenced by Ezek 34 where God's rejection of Israel resulted in the people becoming food (לאכל; cf. Jer 23:1–8).

8-	ולבז ולמשוסה	לבז ולמשסה	2 Kgs 21:14
	ואין מושיע מפני רעתמה	ואין מושיע:	Deut 28:29
	אשר הפרו בריתי	אשר־המה הפרו את־בריתי	Jer 31:32[80]
9-	ואת תורתי געלה נפשמה	ואת־חקתי געלה נפשם	Lev 26:43
	עד יאשמו כול שמה	עד אשר־יאשמו ובקשו פני	Hos 5:15
	אחר ישובו	אחר ישבו	Hos 3:5
10-	אלי בכול לבבמה ובכול נפשמה	בכל־לבבך ובכל־נפשך	Deut 4:29 (30:2)
	ככול דברי התורה הזואת	את־כל־דברי התורה הזאת	Deut 17:19
11-	והושעתים מיד אויביהמה	והושיעם מיד איביהם	Judg 2:18
	ופדיתי מכף שונאיהמה והביאותים	ופדתיך מכף ערצים	Jer 15:21
12-	לארץ אבותיהמה ופדיתים	אל־ארץ אבתיכם	Gen 48:21
	והרביתים וששתי עליהמה	פדיתים ורבו כמו רבו	Zech 10:8
		ישיש יהוה עליכם	Deut 28:63
13-	והייתי להמה לאלוהים	והייתי לכם לאלהים	Lev 26:12[81]
	והמה יהיו לי לעם	ואתם תהיו־לי לעם	

It is immediately clear, just from scanning the lines, that 11QT 59.2–13a is constructed almost entirely from locutions borrowed from the Torah and Prophets. By creatively recombining these locutions, the author has produced an original document. The author's skill is evident in the fact that he has accomplished this feat without creating tensions

---

80. The expression "break the covenant," פרר (*hiphil*) + ברית (as object), is not uncommon in the Torah (Lev 26:15, 44; Deut 31:16, 20; cf. Ezek 16:59), but the exact expression represented in 11QT 59.8 is found only in Jer 31:32.

81. The covenant formula is common in Hebrew Bible, but, in this case, 11QT likely derived it from Lev 26:12. This judgment is based on the number of locutions in col. 59 borrowed from Lev 26.

between his sources. The new text is not only original, it is cohesive and coherent.

Although virtually unknown in HB, examples like this are not as rare as scholars once imagined.[82] Within Second Temple Jewish literature, there are many examples of texts composed from fragments of pre-existing scriptures. Among the clearest examples are texts like 4QCatena (4Q177, 182) and 4QFlorilegium (4Q174), but portions of Damascus Document, Jubilees, Melchizedek, Pseudo-Ezekiel, Pseudo-Jeremiah, and the Songs of Sabbath Sacrifice, to name a few, also contain sections of pastiche.[83] Nor is the technique limited to Second Temple literature. It persists for centuries, as is evidenced by its continuing use in the versions. The expansions to Ezek 36 in the MT (36:23c–38), for example, are composed in a remarkably similar fashion.[84] The point here is that pastiche, though rare in HB, is a well-established literary form by the second half of the Second Temple period.[85]

The similarities between GO and Second Temple texts is not limited to GO's compositional style. GO shares many interpretive attributes with those texts that are commonly designated as "rewritten Bible" or "rewritten scripture." Identifying which texts can rightly be designated "rewritten scripture" has been a matter of some debate in recent schol-

---

82. One of the rare exceptions within the HB is the prayer of Daniel in Dan 9:4b–19.

83. This is not to suggest that all these texts are identical in genre or compositional style. There is a wide range of techniques for reusing scripture in all these texts. See, for example, the excellent survey by George Brooke, "Thematic Commentaries on Prophetic Scriptures," in *Biblical Interpretation at Qumran*, edited by M. Henze, SDSSRL (Grand Rapids: Eerdmans, 2005) 134–57.

84. See Johann Lust, "Ezekiel 36–40 in the Oldest Greek Manuscript," *CBQ* 43 (1981) 518–25; "Major Divergences Between LXX and MT in Ezekiel," in *The Earliest Text of the Hebrew Bible: The Relationship Between the Masoretic Text and the Hebrew Base of the Septuagint Reconsidered*, edited by Adrian Schenker, SCS 52 (Atlanta: Scholars, 2003) 89–90; E. Tov, "Recensional Differences," 99–101.

85. There are also many thematic compositions among the DSS, texts composed of or inspired by scriptural sources on a select theme or themes. Some of these contain portions of pastiche, others do not. See J. Carmignac, "Le document de Qumrân sur Melkisédeq," *RevQ* 7 (1969–1971) 360–61; Brooke, "Thematic Commentaries"; I. Frölich, "'Narrative Exegesis' in the Dead Sea Scrolls," in *Biblical Perspectives: Early Use and Interpretation of the Bible in Light of the Dead Sea Scrolls. Proceedings of the First International Symposium of the Orion Center for the Study of Dead Sea Scrolls and Associated Literature*, edited by M. E. Stone and E. G. Chazon, STDJ 28 (Leiden: Brill, 1998) 81–99.

arship.⁸⁶ For the sake of this argument and without wading too deeply into the debate, I would like to adopt the following list of characteristics, identified by George Brooke, as definitive of rewritten scripture:

1. The source is thoroughly embedded in its rewritten form not as explicit citation but as running text.

2. The dependence of a rewritten scriptural text on its source is also such that the order of the source is followed extensively.

3. The dependence of a rewritten scriptural text on its source is also such that the content of the source is followed relatively closely without very many major insertions or omissions.

4. The original genre or genres stays much the same.

5. And finally, the new texts are not composed to replace the authoritative sources which they rework.⁸⁷

Brooke has in mind here texts like the *Genesis Apocryphon*, which recraft a particular biblical book. If we replace the singular noun "source" in his list with the plural noun "sources," his definition, with only minor qualifications to the second and fourth items, applies equally well to GO. Regarding Brooke's second characteristic, GO tends to follow the order of locutions or topics in its sources, but only in those cases where it borrows several elements from a single context (e.g., Ezek 6:1–10; 28:25–26; Jer 49:30–33). Though, as we have seen, the author's style is to weave individual locutions from several sources together with the elements from its primary source. Regarding the fourth characteristic, GO draws upon many texts in many genres. In accord with its intended context, though, it retains not only the principal genre of Ezekiel, the

---

86. The title "rewritten Bible" was coined by Geza Vermes in 1961 (*Scripture and Tradition in Judaism*, StPB 4 [Leiden: Brill, 1961]). The title itself has been the subject of much discussion and debate. See especially P. R. Alexander, "Retelling the Old Testament," in *It Is Written: Scripture Citing Scripture*, edited by D. A. Carson and H. G. M. Williamson (Cambridge: Cambridge University Press, 1988) 99–121; George J. Brooke, "The Rewritten Law, Prophets, and Psalms: Issues for Understanding the Text of the Bible," in *The Bible as Book: The Hebrew Bible and the Judean Desert Discoveries*, edited by Edward D. Herbert and Emmanuel Tov (London: British Library, 2002) 31–40; and M. Bernstein, "'Rewritten Bible': A Generic Category which has Outlived its Usefulness?" *Textus* 22 (2005) 169–96. I use the term to include documents that are sometimes labeled "thematic commentaries" and/or "paraphrases."

87. Brooke, "The Rewritten Law, Prophets, and Psalms," 32–33.

oracular utterance, but it attempts to replicate Ezekiel's idiolect and style, as we have observed (see "Reuse of Ezekielian Language and "Style"" above). This simple comparison is not intended to suggest that GO is an exemplar of rewritten scripture. This comparison merely illustrates that GO is not only similar to Second Temple texts in its compositional style, pastiche; it is also similar in its techniques of scriptural reuse. GO can be compared with the spirit of Second Temple literature in its form, content, and methods.[88]

I have hesitated, to this point, in ascribing a specific date to GO. Many features of GO, as we have seen, can assist us in locating it within the stream of post-exilic literature. The author's use of Ezekielian language suggests that GO is an addition to the book of Ezekiel, crafted to mirror its style. The consistent character of the composition in its techniques of reuse and density of allusion suggests that GO is a unified composition, all of it composed by a single author in a single historical "moment." The literary form of GO, thematic pastiche, points to the Second Temple period, and accords with the dates of comparable texts. Still, despite these diverse streams of evidence, it remains difficult to be precise about the date of GO. The surest method of dating is from evidence of literary dependence. That is, if the author's sources could be dated with some certainty, they would establish a *terminus ad quo* for GO. Likewise, if texts that use GO as a source could be dated, they, in turn, would establish a *terminus ad quem* for GO. But scholars can seldom agree on the date of any scriptural text, which renders any judgment in this regard indeterminate. That point being granted, it is the allusions we have noted between GO and Joel, Isaiah 40–66, and Daniel that are most helpful for establishing its date. That GO alludes to Joel and Third Isaiah points to a date after the fifth century BCE, the most commonly acknowledged date for the completion of those two works. The reuse of GO in Dan 11:40–45, conversely, indicates that GO predates Daniel's 2nd century provenance.[89] By this judgment, it would appear

---

88. Bernstein has made a similar argument regarding the Temple Scroll, asserting that it too should be considered "rewritten scripture" ("Rewritten Bible," 169–96, esp. 194–95; followed, most recently, by Sidnie White Crawford, *Rewriting Scripture in Second Temple Times*, SDSSRL [Grand Rapids: Eerdmans, 2008] 84–104).

89. See James Montgomery, *A Critical and Exegetical Commentary on the Book of Daniel*, ICC (Edinburgh: T. & T. Clark, 1927) 464–68; Adam S. van der Woude, "Prophetic Prediction, Political Prognostication, and Firm Belief," in *The Quest for Context and Meaning: Studies in Biblical Intertextuality in Honor of James A. Sanders*,

that GO was composed between the 4th and 2nd centuries BCE, toward the latter part of the compositional history of the Hebrew Bible.[90]

Synthesis

Four related claims lie at the core of this study. First, the Gog Oracles are an addition to the book of Ezekiel. Its unique language choices and its use of recycled biblical idioms indicate that, although it was crafted to mirror the style of Ezekiel, its mimicry of Ezekiel's style is less than perfect. Second, the Gog Oracles are a pastiche. It was composed by combining bits and pieces of preexisting texts. The oracles' author mined texts from across the Torah, Prophets, and Psalms for the language, topics, themes and images to be used as the building blocks of the new composition. Third, the principal purposes of the Gog Oracles are to fill gaps in the book and to situate the restoration of Israel in the eschaton, the future utopian state of reality. Drawing upon many texts regarding the judgment of Israel and the nations, the author reapplied them to Gog and to the eschaton. In this way he identified the invasion of Gog as the historical event that would inaugurate the eschaton, assured readers of the nations' eventual judgment, and affirmed the future vindication of Israel. One major effect of this strategy was to harmonize the book of Ezekiel with other scriptural texts. Fourth, and finally, the content of the Gog Oracles and its use of antecedent texts show remarkable similarities to compositional techniques and ways of reading scripture that are found commonly in Jewish writings from the Second Temple period (539 BCE—70 CE). This evidence, when combined with evidence from literary dependency, points to a priestly author working in the Hellenistic period.

In this study I have argued that recognizing scriptural reuse is key to understanding the composition and purpose of GO. This does not, by any means, exhaust the potential of this type of study for advancing our understanding of Ezekiel or the dynamics of textual formation in Second Temple Judaism. But it does contribute to our understanding of

---

edited by Craig A. Evans, Shemaryahu Talmon, and James A. Sanders (Leiden: Brill, 1997) 63–73.

90. Other lines of inquiry that should be pursued to tighten the date of GO include issues of genre evolution and social setting.

the literary evolution of Ezekiel and the variety and dynamics of scriptural reuse in late Biblical compositions.

Appendix
Scriptural Reuse in Ezekiel 38–39

It should be carefully noted that this chart does not distinguish between deliberate reuse and simple sharing of language that might be common to a genre, social class, or school. It serves only to illustrate GO's linguistic overlapping with other scriptural texts. The citations are not exhaustive; many incidental similarities to other texts are not marked.

Locutions shared by Ezekiel and GO are underlined. Locutions shared by GO and the Torah or Prophets are outlined.

CHAPTER 38

1 ויהי דבר־יהוה אלי לאמר:	• word of YHWH came to me saying: 47x in Ezek
2 בן־אדם שים פניך אל־גוג	• son of man: 95x in Ezek.
ארץ המגוג	• set your face against: 6:2; 13:17; 21:2, 7; 25:2; 28:21; 29:2; 35:2 40:4; 44:5
נשיא ראש משך ותבל	
והנבא עליו:	• Gog: Num 24:7 (LXX); Amos 7:1 (LXX)
3 ואמרת כה אמר אדני יהוה	• Magog: Genesis 10:2
הנני אליך גוג	• chief + prince: Num 10:4; 36:1
נשיא ראש משך ותבל:	• Meshek and Tubal: 32:26; Gen 10:2
4 ושובבתיך ונתתי חחים בלחייך	• prophesy ... and say: 13:2, 17; 21:14, 33; 30:2; 34:2; 36:1, 3, 6; 37:4, 9, 12
והוצאתי אותך ואת־כל־חילך	
סוסים ופרשים לבשי מכלול כלם	• thus says Adonai YHWH: 121x in Ezek
קהל רב צנה ומגן	• behold I am against: 5:8; 13:8 (pl) 21:8; 26:3, 7; 28:22; 29:3, 10; 35:3; 36:9 (pl.); 38:3; 39:1
תפשי חרבות כלם:	
5 פרס כוש ופוט אתם	• hooks in jaws: 29:4
כלם מגן וכובע:	• horse (in battle list): 23:6, 12, 23; 26:7
6 גמר וכל־אגפיה	• horsemen: 26:7 (cf. 38:15)
בית תוגרמה	• perfectly clothed: 23:12
ירכתי צפון ואת־כל־אגפיו	• company: 16:14; 23:46, 47; 26:7; 38:4, 15
עמים רבים אתך:	• mantlet & shield: 23:24; 26:8
	• Persia: 27:10
	• Cush: 27:10, 30:4–5, 9; Gen 10:6–8
	• Put: 27:10; 30:5; Gen 10:6
	• shield & helmet: 27:10
	• Gomer: Gen 10:2–3
	• all ... hordes: 12:14; 17:21
	• Togarmah: 27:14; Gen 10:3
	• far reaches of the north: Isa 14:13 (Jer 6:22–23; Joel 2:20, 27)
	• all ... hordes: 12:14; 17:21
	• many peoples: 3:6; 17:9, 15; 26:7; 27:33; 32:3, 9, 10; 36:6, 8, 9, 15, 22

CHAPTER 38

7 הכן והכן לך אתה וכל־קהלך הנקהלים עליך והיית להם למשמר: 8 מימים רבים תפקד באחרית השנים תבוא אל־ארץ משובבת מחרב מקבצת מעמים רבים על הרי ישראל אשר־היו לחרבה תמיד והיא מעמים הוצאה וישבו לבטח כלם: 9 ועלית כשאה תבוא כענן לכסות הארץ תהיה אתה וכל־אגפיך ועמים רבים אותך: ס	• all your company: 27:27, 34; 32:33. • many days: 12:27 (21x in Torah and Prophets; see esp. Isa 10:3) • summoned: Isa 10:3 • end of years: Deut 1:12 (cf. 38:16) • come to land: Exod 6:8; 13:5, 11; Num 14:3, 8, 24; Deut 8:7; 9:28; 31:21 • brought back from the sword: reversal of 6:8 • gathered out of peoples: Deut 30:3 • mountains of Israel: 6:2, 3; 19:9; 33:28; 34:13, 14; 35:12; 36:1, 4, 8; 37:22 • ruin: 5:14; 13:4; 25:13; 26:2, 20; 29:9, 10, 12; 33:24, 27; 35:4; 36:4, 10; (verb appears in 6:6; 12:20; 19:7; 26:2, 19; 29:12; 30:7) • brought forth out of nations: Exod 3:10, 12; 7:4; 12:31 (11:8); Josh 5:5 • dwell securely: 28:26; 34:28; Lev 25:18, 19; 26:5 (Deut 12:10) • devestation: Isa 10:3 • cloud covering: 30:18; 32:7 (Jer 4:12–13) • all ... hordes: 12:14; 17:21 • many people: 3:6; 17:9, 15; 26:7; 27:33; 32:3, 9, 10; 36: 6, 8, 9, 15, 22

CHAPTER 38	
10 כה אמר אדני יהוה והיה ביום ההוא יעלו דברים על־לבבך וחשבת מחשבת רעה: 11 ואמרת אעלה על־ארץ פרזות אבוא השקטים ישבי לבטח כלם ישבים באין חומה ובריח ודלתים אין להם: 12 לשלל שלל ולבז בז להשיב ידך על־חרבות נושבת ואל־עם מאסף מגוים עשה מקנה וקנין ישבי על־טבור הארץ: 13 שבא ודדן וסחרי תרשיש וכל־כפריה יאמרו לך הלשלל שלל אתה בא הלבז בז הקהלת קהלך לשאת כסף וזהב לקחת מקנה וקנין לשלל שלל גדול: ס	• thus says Adonai YHWH: 121x in Ezek. • in that day: 20:6; 23:38, 39; 24:26, 27; 29:21; 30:9; 38:10, 14, 18, 19; 39:11; 45:22 • it will happen in that day: common in first Isaiah (7:18, 21, 23; 10:20, 27; 11:10, 11; 17:4; 22:20; 23:15; 24:21; 27:12, 13) and deutero-Zechariah (12:3, 9; 13:2, 4; 14:6, 7, 8, 13), unattested in Ezekiel.[91] • rise in mind: 14:4, 7; Isa 10:7 • consider a plan: Jer 49:30 • go up against a nation at rest: Jer 49:31 • unwalled villages: Deut 3:5 • secure (בטח) + dwell/inhabitant (ישׁב): 28:26; 34:25, 26, 28 (16:49); Lev 25:18, 19; 26:5 (Deut 12:10) • without a wall: Lev 25:31 • bar and gate: Deut 3:5 • spoil + plunder: Isa 10:2, 6; Jer 49:32; Ezek 7:21; 29:19 • spoil spoil: Isa 10:6; Ezek 29:19 • plunder plunder: Isa 10:6; Ezek 29:19 • inhabited ruins: 33:23 (27) • regathered from nations: cf. 11:17; 29:5 • cattle and goods: Gen 31:18; 34:23; 36:6 (Jer 9:32) • navel of the earth: Judg 9:37 • Sheba: 27:22, 23; 38:13; Gen 10:7, 28 • Dedan: 27:15, 20; Gen 25:3 • merchants of Tarshish: 27:12 (Isa 23:6; Jer 10:9)

---

91. Also, Jer 4:9; 30:8; Hos 1:5; 2:18, 23; Joel 4:18; Amos 8:9; Mic 5:9; Zeph 1:11.

CHAPTER 38

14 לכן הנבא בן־אדם ואמרת לגוג כה אמר אדני יהוה הלוא ביום ההוא בשבת עמי ישראל לבטח תדע: 15 ובאת ממקומך מירכתי צפון אתה ועמים רבים אתך רכבי סוסים כלם קהל גדול וחיל רב: 16 ועלית על־עמי ישראל כענן לכסות הארץ באחרית הימים תהיה והבאותיך על־ארצי למען דעת הגוים אתי בהקדשי בך לעיניהם גוג ס	• son of man: 95x in Ezek. • prophesy (impv.) … and say: 13:2, 17; 21:14, 33; 30:2; 34:2; 36:1, 3, 6; 37:4, 9, 12 • Gog: Num 24:7 (LXX); Amos 7:1 (LXX) • thus says Adonai YHWH: 121x in Ezek. • in that day: 20:6; 23:38, 39; 24:26, 27; 29:21; 30:9; 45:22 • my people Israel: 14:9; 25:14; 36:8, 12; 38:14, 16; 39:7 • dwell safely: 28:26; 34:28 (25); Lev 25:18, 19; 26:5 (Deut 12:10); Jer 49:30–31 • far reaches of the north: Isa 14:13 (Jer 6:22–23; Joel 2:20, 27) • many peoples: 3:6; 17:9, 15; 26:7; 27:33; 32:3, 9, 10; 36: 6, 8, 9, 15, 22 • horsemen (riders of horses): 23:6, 12, 23; Zech 10:5 • mighty army: 17:17; 37:10; Joel 2:25 • cloud covering: 30:18; 32:7 (Jer 4:12–13) • end of days: Gen 49:1; Num 24:14; Deut 4:30; 31:29; Isa 2:2; Jer 23:20; 30:24; 48:47; 49:39; Hos 3:5; Mic 4:1; Dan 10:14 • against my land: 36:5; Joel 1:6 • nations know: 36:23, 36; 37:28 • show myself holy + before eyes (of nations): only 28:25

CHAPTER 38

כֹּה־אָמַר אֲדֹנָי יְהוִה 17 הַאַתָּה־הוּא אֲשֶׁר־דִּבַּרְתִּי בְּיָמִים קַדְמוֹנִים בְּיַד עֲבָדַי נְבִיאֵי יִשְׂרָאֵל הַנִּבְּאִים בַּיָּמִים הָהֵם שָׁנִים לְהָבִיא אֹתְךָ עֲלֵיהֶם: ס	• thus says Lord YHWH: 121x in Ezek. • spoke by the hand of: common DtrH expression (Josh 20:2; 1 Sam 28:17; 1 Kgs 8:53, 56; 12:15; 14:18; 15:29; 16:12, 34; 17:16; 2 Kgs 9:36; 10:10; 14:25; 17:23; 21:10; 24:2) • servants the prophets: 2 Kgs 9:7; 17:13; Jer 7:25; 26:5; 29:19; 35:15; 44:4; Zech 1:6 • in those days: common in Torah and Prophets (Gen 6:4; Exod 2:11, 23; Deut 17:9; 19:17; 26:3; Josh 20:6; Judg 17:6; 18:1; 19:1; 20:27, 28; 21:25; 1 Sam 3:1; 28:1; 2 Sam 16:23; 1 Kgs 10:32; 15:37; 20:1; 2 Kgs 10:32; 15:37; 20:1; Isa 38:1; Jer 31:29; 33:15, 16; 50:20; Zech 8:6), but unattested in Ezekiel.

CHAPTER 38

וְהָיָה בַּיּוֹם הַהוּא 18	• it will happen in that day: see 38:10
בְּיוֹם בּוֹא גוֹג עַל־אַדְמַת יִשְׂרָאֵל	• Gog: Num 24:7 (LXX); Amos 7:1 (LXX)
נְאֻם אֲדֹנָי יְהוִה	• come against the land of Israel: 20:42 (against the land: 12:22; 18:2; 33:24; 36:6)
תַּעֲלֶה חֲמָתִי בְּאַפִּי:	
וּבְקִנְאָתִי בְאֵשׁ־עֶבְרָתִי דִבַּרְתִּי 19	• signatory formula: 83x in Ezekiel
אִם־לֹא בַּיּוֹם הַהוּא	• fury be aroused: 24:8 (cf. Isa 66:15)
יִהְיֶה רַעַשׁ גָּדוֹל עַל אַדְמַת יִשְׂרָאֵל	• jealousy + fire + fury: Zeph 1:18; 3:8
וְרָעֲשׁוּ מִפָּנַי דְּגֵי הַיָּם 20	• fire of fury: 21:26; 22:21, 31
וְעוֹף הַשָּׁמַיִם	• speak in jealousy: 5:13; 36:5–6
וְחַיַּת הַשָּׂדֶה	• great shaking: 3:12, 13; Jer 10:22
וְכָל־הָרֶמֶשׂ הָרֹמֵשׂ עַל־הָאֲדָמָה וְכָל הָאָדָם אֲשֶׁר עַל־פְּנֵי הָאֲדָמָה	• against the land of Israel: 20:42; 33:24; 36:6; 38:18; 19
וְנֶהֶרְסוּ הֶהָרִים	• fish + bird + beast + creeping thing (in order): only Gen 1 (esp. 25–26)
וְנָפְלוּ הַמַּדְרֵגוֹת	• people on face of earth: Gen 7:23 (1:26)
וְכָל־חוֹמָה לָאָרֶץ תִּפּוֹל:	• every wall will fall: 13:10–11 (12, 14, 15)
וְקָרָאתִי עָלָיו לְכָל־הָרַי חֶרֶב 21	• my mountain(s): Isa 14:25; 49:11; 65:9; Ezek 20:40; Zech 14:5
נְאֻם אֲדֹנָי יְהוִה	
חֶרֶב אִישׁ בְּאָחִיו תִּהְיֶה:	• call + sword: Jer 25:29
וְנִשְׁפַּטְתִּי אִתּוֹ בְּדֶבֶר וּבְדָם 22	• mountains + sword: 6:3; 35:8
וְגֶשֶׁם שׁוֹטֵף וְאַבְנֵי אֶלְגָּבִישׁ	• signatory formula: 83x in Ezekiel
אֵשׁ וְגָפְרִית אַמְטִיר עָלָיו וְעַל־אֲגַפָּיו	• enemy turns on one another: Zech 14:13; Enoch 56:7; 66:7; 100:1.
וְעַל־עַמִּים רַבִּים אֲשֶׁר אִתּוֹ:	• I will execute judgment against: 17:20; 20:35, 36
וְהִתְגַּדִּלְתִּי וְהִתְקַדִּשְׁתִּי 23	• bleeding pestilence: 5:17; 14:19; 28:23; (33:27)
וְנוֹדַעְתִּי לְעֵינֵי גּוֹיִם רַבִּים	• overflowing rain: 13:11, 13
וְיָדְעוּ כִּי־אֲנִי יְהוָה: ס	• hail stones: 13:11, 13
	• rain (*Hiphil*) + fire and brimstone: Gen 19:24
	• all...horde: 12:14; 17:21
	• many peoples: 3:6; 17:9, 15; 26:7; 27:33; 32:3, 9, 10; 36:6, 8, 9, 15, 22.
	• magnify myself: Is 10:15
	• show myself holy + before eyes (of nations): only 28:25
	• be known + in eyes of nations: only 20:9
	• in the eyes of nations: Lev 26:45; Ezek 5:8; 20:9, 14, 22, 41; 22:16; 28:25; 36:23
	• recognition formula: 58x in Ezekiel

CHAPTER 39	
1 ואתה בן־אדם הנבא על־גוג ואמרת כה אמר אדני יהוה הנני אליך גוג נשיא ראש משך ותבל: 2 ושבבתיך וששאתיך והעליתיך מירכתי צפון והבאותיך על־הרי ישראל: 3 והכיתי קשתך מיד שמאולך וחציך מיד ימינך אפיל: 4 על־הרי ישראל תפול אתה וכל־אגפיך ועמים אשר אתך לעיט צפור כל־כנף וחית השדה נתתיך לאכלה: 5 על־פני השדה תפול כי אני דברתי נאם אדני יהוה:	• son of man: 95x in Ezek. • Gog: Num 24:7 (LXX); Amos 7:1 (LXX) • prophesy (impv.) ... and say: 13:2, 17; 21:14, 33; 30:2; 34:2; 36:1, 3, 6; 37:4, 9, 12 • thus says the Lord YHWH: 121x in Ezek • behold I am against: 5:8; 13:8; 21:8; 26:3; 28:22; 29:3, 10; 35:3; 36:9 • chief + prince: Num 10:4; 36:1 • Meshek & Tubal: Gen 10:2; Ezek 32:26 • far-reaches of the north: Isa 14:13 (Jer 6:22–23; Joel 2:20, 27) • mountains of Israel: 6:2, 3; 19:9; 33:28; 34:13, 14; 35:12; 36:1, 4, 8; 37:22 • fall from hand: 30:22 • all ... hordes: 12:14; 17:21 • I will give ... for food: Gen 9:3 (covenant blessing; cf. Deut 28:26); Ezek 29:5; 35:12 (15:4, 6) • fall upon face of field: 29:5 (Deut 21:1) • (for) I have spoken: 5:15, 17 (12:25, 28); 17:21, 24; 21:22, 37; 22:14; 23:34; 24:14; 26:5, 14; 28:10; 30:12; 34:24; 36:36; 37:14 • signatory formula: 83x in Ezek

CHAPTER 39

Hebrew	v.	Notes
וְשִׁלַּחְתִּי־אֵשׁ בְּמָגוֹג וּבְיֹשְׁבֵי הָאִיִּים לָבֶטַח וְיָדְעוּ כִּי־אֲנִי יְהוָה׃	6	• send fire upon: Amos 1:4, 7, 10, 12; 2:2, 5 • Magog: Gen 10:2 • inhabitants of coastlands: 27:35 (cf. Isa 20:6; 23:2, 6) • dwell safely: 28:26; 34:28 (25); Lev 25:18, 19, etc.) • recognition formula: 58x in Ezek
וְאֶת־שֵׁם קָדְשִׁי אוֹדִיעַ בְּתוֹךְ עַמִּי יִשְׂרָאֵל וְלֹא־אַחֵל אֶת־שֵׁם־קָדְשִׁי עוֹד וְיָדְעוּ הַגּוֹיִם כִּי־אֲנִי יְהוָה קָדוֹשׁ בְּיִשְׂרָאֵל׃	7	• (nations) will know: 22:16; 36:23; 37:28 • my holy name: Lev 20:3; 22:2, 32; Ezek 20:39; 36:20, 21, 22; 43:7, 8; Amos 2:7 • I will make known: 20:11 • my people Israel: 14:9; 25:14; 36:8, 12 • name profaned: Lev 18:21; 19:12; 20:3; 21:6; 22:2, 32; Ezek 20:39; 36:20; Amos 2:7 • Holy One in Israel: Joel 2:27
הִנֵּה בָאָה וְנִהְיָתָה נְאֻם אֲדֹנָי יְהוִה הוּא הַיּוֹם אֲשֶׁר דִּבַּרְתִּי׃	8	• behold it is coming: 7:5, 6, 10; 30:9; 33:33 (24:24) • היה Niphal (God as subject): 21:12 • signatory formula: 83x in Ezek • (for) I have spoken: 5:15, 17 (12:25, 28); 17:21, 24; 21:22, 37; 22:14; 23:34; 24:14; 26:5, 14; 28:10; 30:12; 34:24; 36:36; 37:14
וְיָצְאוּ יֹשְׁבֵי עָרֵי יִשְׂרָאֵל וּבִעֲרוּ וְהִשִּׂיקוּ בְּנֶשֶׁק וּמָגֵן וְצִנָּה בְּקֶשֶׁת וּבְחִצִּים וּבְמַקֵּל יָד וּבְרֹמַח וּבִעֲרוּ בָהֶם אֵשׁ שֶׁבַע שָׁנִים׃	9	• inhabit + city: 36:10, 33 • mantlet & shield: 23:24; 26:8 • plundering slain: Isa 9:2–5; 10:6; 14:2; Joel 4:11 (of heavenly host)
וְלֹא־יִשְׂאוּ עֵצִים מִן־הַשָּׂדֶה וְלֹא יַחְטְבוּ מִן־הַיְּעָרִים כִּי בַנֶּשֶׁק יְבַעֲרוּ־אֵשׁ וְשָׁלְלוּ אֶת־שֹׁלְלֵיהֶם וּבָזְזוּ אֶת־בֹּזְזֵיהֶם נְאֻם אֲדֹנָי יְהוִה׃ ס	10	• spoil spoilers: Isa 10:6; Ezek 29:19 (cf. Jer 49:32) • plunder plunderers: Isa 10:6; Ezek 29:19 (cf. Jer 49:32) • spoil + plunder: Isa 10:2, 6; Jer 49:32; Ezek 7:21; 29:19 • signatory formula: 83x in Ezek

CHAPTER 39

וְהָיָה בַיּוֹם הַהוּא אֶתֵּן לְגוֹג מְקוֹם־שָׁם קֶבֶר בְּיִשְׂרָאֵל גֵּי הָעֹבְרִים קִדְמַת הַיָּם וְחֹסֶמֶת הִיא אֶת־הָעֹבְרִים וְקָבְרוּ שָׁם אֶת־גּוֹג וְאֶת־כָּל־הֲמוֹנֹה וְקָרְאוּ גֵּיא הֲמוֹן גּוֹג:	11	• it will happen in that day: see 38:10 • Gog: Num 24:7 (LXX); Amos 7:1 (LXX) • give a place: Josh 20:4; Judg 20:36; 1 Sam 9:22; 27:5 • grave: 32:22, 23, 25, 26; 37:12, 13 • travelers: 5:14; 16:15, 25; 33:28; 35:7; 36:34 • crowd: 5:7; 7 (4x); 23:42; 26:13; 29:19, 30 (3x); 31:2, 18; 32 (9x); 55x outside of Ezekiel.
וּקְבָרוּם בֵּית יִשְׂרָאֵל לְמַעַן טַהֵר אֶת־הָאָרֶץ שִׁבְעָה חֳדָשִׁים:	12	• Hamon-gog/Hamonah: 2 Kgs 23:10; Jer 7:30–34 (pun on Hinnom) • house of Israel: 78x in Ezekiel; 63x elsewhere.
וְקָבְרוּ כָּל־עַם הָאָרֶץ וְהָיָה לָהֶם לְשֵׁם יוֹם הִכָּבְדִי נְאֻם אֲדֹנָי יְהוִה:	13	• cleanse land: 22:24 (cf: 22:26; 36:17). • all people of land: 7:21; 12:19; 22:29; 33:2; 45:16, 22 • be their reputation: Neh 6:13 • glorification of God: Exod 14:18; Ezek 28:22 (cf. Exod 14:4, 17; Lev 10:3; Isa 26:15; Hag 1:8) • signatory formula: 83x in Ezek
וְאַנְשֵׁי תָמִיד יַבְדִּילוּ עֹבְרִים בָּאָרֶץ מְקַבְּרִים אֶת־הָעֹבְרִים אֶת־הַנּוֹתָרִים עַל־פְּנֵי הָאָרֶץ לְטַהֲרָהּ מִקְצֵה שִׁבְעָה־חֳדָשִׁים יַחְקֹרוּ:	14	• travelers/ones passing through: 5:14; 16:15, 25; 33:28; 35:7; 36:34 • undertakers/ones burying: Num 33:4; Jer 14:16 • cleanse land: 22:24 (cf: 22:26; 36:17)
וְעָבְרוּ הָעֹבְרִים בָּאָרֶץ וְרָאָה עֶצֶם אָדָם וּבָנָה אֶצְלוֹ צִיּוּן עַד קָבְרוּ אֹתוֹ הַמְקַבְּרִים אֶל־גֵּיא הֲמוֹן גּוֹג:	15	• human bone: Num 19:16; cf. Ezek 6:5; 24:4, 5, 10; 37:1–14 (10x) • sign-post: 2 Kgs 23:17; Jer 31:21 • Hamon-gog/Hamonah: 2 Kgs 23:10; Jer 7:30–34 (pun on Hinnom)
וְגַם שֶׁם־עִיר הֲמוֹנָה וְטִהֲרוּ הָאָרֶץ: ס	16	• cleanse land: 22:24 (cf: 22:26; 36:17)

CHAPTER 39		
וְאַתָּה בֶן־אָדָם כֹּה־אָמַר אֲדֹנָי יְהוִה	17	• son of man: 95x in Ezek.
אֱמֹר לְצִפּוֹר כָּל־כָּנָף		• thus says Adonai YHWH: 121x in Ezek.
וּלְכֹל חַיַּת הַשָּׂדֶה		• speak (impv. addressed to prophet): 24x in Ezek.
הִקָּבְצוּ וָבֹאוּ		• assemble & come: 34:13; 37;21
הֵאָסְפוּ מִסָּבִיב עַל־זִבְחִי		• slain as sacrificial banquet, fed to beasts: Isa 34:6–7 (cf. Isa 25:6–7; 56:9; Jer 46:10; 50:25–27; Zeph 1:7–8)
אֲשֶׁר אֲנִי זֹבֵחַ לָכֶם		
זֶבַח גָּדוֹל עַל הָרֵי יִשְׂרָאֵל		
וַאֲכַלְתֶּם בָּשָׂר וּשְׁתִיתֶם דָּם:		• sacrifice for you: reversal of common expression זבח + לְ + deity (esp. Exod and Deut)
בְּשַׂר גִּבּוֹרִים תֹּאכֵלוּ	18	
וְדַם־נְשִׂיאֵי הָאָרֶץ תִּשְׁתּוּ		• mountains of Israel: 6:2, 3; 19:9; 33:28; 34:13, 14; 35:12; 36:1, 4, 8; 37:22
אֵילִים כָּרִים וְעַתּוּדִים פָּרִים		
מְרִיאֵי בָשָׁן כֻּלָּם:		• eat flesh/fat + drink blood: reversal of Lev 7:23–27 (cf. Ps 50:13)
וַאֲכַלְתֶּם־חֵלֶב לְשָׂבְעָה	19	• rams, lambs, he-goats + fat and blood: Isa 34:6 (cf. Jer 51:40)
וּשְׁתִיתֶם דָּם לְשִׁכָּרוֹן		
מִזִּבְחִי אֲשֶׁר־זָבַחְתִּי לָכֶם:		• eat ... for satiety: 34:3
וּשְׂבַעְתֶּם עַל־שֻׁלְחָנִי סוּס וָרֶכֶב	20	• God's table: Ps 78:19
גִּבּוֹר וְכָל־אִישׁ מִלְחָמָה		• horse + horsemen: 26:7 (cf. 38:4)
נְאֻם אֲדֹנָי יְהוִה:		• signatory formula: 83x in Ezek

CHAPTER 39

ונתתי את־כבודי בגוים וראו כל־הגוים את־משפטי אשר עשיתי ואת־ידי אשר־שמתי בהם:	21	• glory (of God) upon/among nations: Isa 42:8; 48:11; 66:19 • all nations will see: Isa 52:10; 62:2 • judgment I executed: common in Deut (5:31; 12:1; 17:11; etc.)
וידעו בית ישראל כי אני יהוה אלהיהם מן־היום ההוא והלאה:	22	• house of Israel: 78x in Ezek; 63x elsewhere in HB • recognition formula: 58x in Ezek
וידעו הגוים כי בעונם גלו בית־ישראל על אשר מעלו־בי ואסתר פני מהם ואתנם ביד צריהם ויפלו בחרב כלם:	23	• YHWH their God: 28:26; 34:30 (24x elsewhere in HB) • nations will know: 22:16; 36:23; 37:28 • house of Israel: 78x in Ezek; 63x elsewhere in HB • unfaithful to me: Lev 26:40; Deut 32:51; Ezek 17:20; 20:27 • hide my face from them: Deut 31:17, 18; 32:20 (Isa 8:17; 54:8) • gave into hand of enemies: cf. Lev 26:25; Josh 21:44; Judg 16:24; 2 Kgs 21:14; Jer 20:5; 34:20, 21[92]
כטמאתם וכפשעיהם עשיתי אתם ואסתר פני מהם: ס	24	• fall by sword: 5:12; 6:12; 11:10; 17:21; 23:25; 24:21; 25:13; 30:5, 6, 17; 32:12, 20, 22, 23, 24; 33:27; 35:8

---

92. This is a common deuteronomic expression. The author of GO appears to recall it (inaccurately) from memory. Everywhere else in HB (except Neh 9:27) the locution is נתן ביד איב (not צר).

CHAPTER 39

לָכֵן כֹּה אָמַר אֲדֹנָי יְהוִה	25	• thus says Adonai YHWH: 121x in Ezek.
עַתָּה אָשִׁיב אֶת־שְׁבִית[93] יַעֲקֹב		• restore the fortunes: 16:53
וְרִחַמְתִּי כָּל־בֵּית יִשְׂרָאֵל		• Jacob: 28:25
וְקִנֵּאתִי לְשֵׁם קָדְשִׁי:		• have mercy on house of Israel: Hos 1:6 ("house of Israel" is distinctive of Ezek [8:10; 12:24; 13:9; 17:2; 20:40; 33:20; 43:7])
וְנָשׂוּ אֶת־כְּלִמָּתָם וְאֶת־כָּל־מַעֲלָם	26	
אֲשֶׁר מָעֲלוּ־בִי		• my holy name: Lev 20:3; 22:2, 32; Ezek 20:39; 36:20, 21, 22; Amos 2:7
בְּשִׁבְתָּם עַל־אַדְמָתָם לָבֶטַח		
וְאֵין מַחֲרִיד:		• bear shame: 16:52, 54 (61–63); 34:29; 36:6, 7 (31).
בְּשׁוֹבְבִי אוֹתָם מִן־הָעַמִּים	27	
וְקִבַּצְתִּי אֹתָם מֵאַרְצוֹת אֹיְבֵיהֶם		• unfaithful with me: Lev 26:40; Deut 32:51; Ezek 20:27
וְנִקְדַּשְׁתִּי בָם לְעֵינֵי הַגּוֹיִם רַבִּים:		
וְיָדְעוּ כִּי אֲנִי יְהוָה אֱלֹהֵיהֶם	28	• dwell securely: Lev 25:18, 19; 26:5; Ezek 28:25–26; 34:25, 28; 36:17 (Deut 12:10)
בְּהַגְלוֹתִי אֹתָם אֶל־הַגּוֹיִם		• dwell upon their land: 28:25; 36:17
וְכִנַּסְתִּים עַל־אַדְמָתָם		
וְלֹא־אוֹתִיר עוֹד מֵהֶם שָׁם:		• no one to cause fear: Lev 26:6; Isa 17:2; Jer 7:33; 30:10; 46:27; Mic 4:4; Nah 2:12; Zeph 3:3
וְלֹא־אַסְתִּיר עוֹד פָּנַי מֵהֶם	29	• return (שׁוּב) used for exile: 34:4, 16
אֲשֶׁר שָׁפַכְתִּי אֶת־רוּחִי		• gathered from lands: Isa 11:12; Jer 23:3; 31:8; 32:37; Ezek 20:34, 41; 34:13; Zech 10:10; Ps 107:3
עַל־בֵּית יִשְׂרָאֵל		
נְאֻם אֲדֹנָי יְהוִה: פ		• lands of enemies: Lev 26:34, 36, 38, 39, 41, 44; 1 Kgs 8:48; Jer 31:16 (cf. Ezek 36:2)
		• display holiness (reflexive): Lev 22:32; Ezek 20:41; 28:22, 25
		• in the eyes of nations: Lev 26:45; Ezek 5:8; 20:9, 14, 22, 41; 22:16; 28:25; 36:23
		• YHWH their God: 28:26; 34:30 (24x outside of Ezek)
		• hide my face: Deut 31:17, 18; 32:20 (Isa 8:17; 54:8; Jer 16:17; Pss 22:25; 38:10)
		• [my] spirit: 11:19; 37:1, 5, 6, 8, 9 (x3), 10 (x2), 14
		• pour out my spirit: Joel 3:1–2
		• signatory formula: 83x in Ezek

---

93. Qere שָׁבוּת.

Bibliography

Ahroni, Ruben. "The Gog Prophecy and the Book of Ezekiel." *HAR* 1 (1977) 1-27.

Alexander, P. R. "Retelling the Old Testament." In *It is Written: Scripture Citing Scripture*, edited by D. A. Carson and H. G. M. Williamson, 99-121. Cambridge: Cambridge University Press, 1988.

Baltzer, D. *Ezechiel und Deuterojesaja: Berührungen in der Heilswartung der beiden großen Exilspropheten*. BZAW 121. Berlin: de Gruyter, 1971.

Baumgarten, A. I. "Literacy and the Polemics Surrounding Biblical Interpretation in the Second Temple Period." In *Studies in Ancient Midrash*, edited by J. Kugel, 27-41. Cambridge: Harvard Center for Jewish Studies, 2001.

Ben-Porat, Ziva. "The Poetics of Literary Allusion." *PTL: A Journal of Descriptive Poetics and Theory of Literature* 1 (1976) 105-28.

Ben Zvi, Ehud. *A Historical-Critical Study of the Book of Zephaniah*. BZAW 198. Berlin: de Gruyter, 1991.

Bergler, Siegfried. *Joel als Schriftinterpret*. Beiträge zur Erforschung des Alten Testaments und des antiken Judentum 16. Frankfurt: Lang, 1988.

Bernstein, Moshe J. "Re-Arrangement, Anticipation and Harmonization as Exegetical Features in the Genesis Apocryphon." *DSD* 3 (1996) 37-57.

———. "'Rewritten Bible': A Generic Category which has Outlived its Usefulness?" *Textus* 22 (2005) 169-96.

———. "Interpretation of Scriptures." In *Encyclopedia of the Dead Sea Scrolls* 1:376-83.

Berrin, Shanni. "Qumran Pesharim." In *Biblical Interpretation at Qumran*, edited by Matthias Henze, 110-133. Studies in the Dead Sea Scrolls and Related Literature. Grand Rapids: Eerdmans, 2005.

Betz, O. "Past Events and Last Events in the Qumran Interpretation of History." In *Proceedings of the Sixth World Congress of Jewish Studies*, 27-34. Jerusalem: World Union of Jewish Studies, 1977.

Blenkinsopp, Joseph. *History of Prophecy in Israel: From the Settlement in the Land to the Hellenistic Period*. Philadelphia: Westminster, 1983.

Block, Daniel I. "Gog in Prophetic Tradition: A New Look at Ezekiel XXXVIII 17." *VT* 42 (1992) 154-71.

———. *The Book of Ezekiel 1-24*. NICOT. Grand Rapids: Eerdmans, 1997.

Bøe, Sverre. *Gog and Magog: Ezekiel 39-39 as Pre-text for Revelation 19,17-21 and 20,7-10*. WUNT 2/135. Tübingen: Mohr/Siebeck, 2001.

Brin, Gershon. "המקרא במגלת המקדש." *Shnaton: An Annual for Biblical and Ancient Near Eastern Studies* 4 (1980) 182-225.

———. "Concerning Some of the Uses of the Bible in the Temple Scroll." *RQ* 12 (1987) 519-28.

Brooke, George. "The Thematic Content of 4Q252." *JQR* 85 (1994) 33-59.

———. "Biblical Interpretation in the Qumran Scrolls and in the New Testament." In *The Dead Sea Scrolls Fifty Years after Their Discovery*, edited by Lawrence Schiffman et al., 60-73. Jerusalem: Israel Exploration Society, 2000.

———. "The Rewritten Law, Prophets, and Psalms: Issues for Understanding the Text of the Bible." In *The Bible as Book: The Hebrew Bible and the Judean Desert Discoveries*, edited by Edward D. Herbert and Emmanuel Tov, 31-40. London: British Library, 2002.

———. "Thematic Commentaries on Prophetic Scriptures." In *Biblical Interpretation at Qumran*, edited by Matthias Henze, 134–57. Studies on the Dead Sea Scrolls and Related Literature. Grand Rapids: Eerdmans, 2005.
Buchanan, George Wesley. "Eschatology and the 'End of Days.'" *JNES* 20 (1961) 188–93.
Calloway, Phillip. "Extending Divine Revelation: Micro-Compositional Strategies in the Temple Scroll." In *Temple Scroll Studies: Papers Presented at the International Symposium on the Temple Scroll, Manchester, December 1987*, edited by George J. Brooke, 149–62. JSPSup 7. Sheffield: JSOT Press, 1989.
Carmignac, J. "Le document de Qumrân sur Melkisédeq." *RQ* 7 (1969–71) 360–61.
Cook, Stephen L. *Prophecy and Apocalypticism: The Postexilic Social Setting*. Minneapolis: Fortress, 1995.
Crawford, Sidnie White. *Rewriting Scripture in Second Temple Times*. SDSSRL. Grand Rapids: Eerdmans, 2008.
Daube, D. "Typology in Josephus." *JJS* 31 (1980) 18–36.
Dimant, Devorah. "Apocalyptic Interpretation of Ezekiel at Qumran." In *Messiah and Christos: Studies in the Jewish Origins of Christianity Presented to David Flusser on the Occasion of His Seventy-Fifth Birthday*, edited by I. Gruenwald et al., 31–52. TSAJ 32. Tübingen: Mohr/Siebeck, 1992.
Doudna, Gregory L. *4Q Pesher Nahum: A Critical Edition*. JSPSup 35. London: Sheffield Academic, 2001.
Driver, S. R. *Introduction to the Literature of the Old Testament*. 2nd ed. Edinburgh: T. & T. Clark, 1891.
Duhm, Bernard. "Anmerkungen zu den Zwölf Propheten." *ZAW* 31 (1911) 184–87.
Fishbane, Michael. *Biblical Interpretation in Ancient Israel*. Oxford: Clarendon, 1985.
———. "Types of Biblical Intertextuality." In *Congress Volume: Oslo, 1998*, edited by A. Lemaire and M. Saebø, 39–44. VTSup 80. Leiden: Brill, 2000.
Fisk, B. N. *Do You Not Remember? Scripture, Story and Exegesis in the Rewritten Bible of Pseudo-Philo*. JSPSup 37. Sheffield: Sheffield Academic, 2001.
Fitzpatrick, Paul. *The Disarmament of God: Ezekiel 38–39 in its Mythic Context*. CBQMS 37. Washington, DC: Catholic Biblical Association of America: 2004.
Flint, Peter. "Scriptures in the Dead Sea Scrolls: The Evidence from Qumran." In *Emanuel: Studies in Hebrew Bible, Septuagint, and Dead Sea Scrolls in Honor of Emanuel Tov*, edited by Shalom Paul et al., 269–304. VTSup 94. Leiden: Brill, 2003.
Flusser, D. "פרושים צדוקים, ואסיים בפשר נחום." In *Essays in Jewish History and Philology in Memory of Gedaliah Alon*, edited by M. Dorman et al., 133–68. Tel Aviv: Hakibbutz Hameuchad, 1970.
Frölich, I. "'Narrative Exegesis' in the Dead Sea Scrolls." In *Biblical Perspectives: Early Use and Interpretation of the Bible in Light of the Dead Sea Scrolls. Proceedings of the First International Symposium of the Orion Center for the Study of Dead Sea Scrolls and Associated Literature*, edited by M. E. Stone and E. G. Chazon, 81–99. STDJ 28. Leiden: Brill, 1998.
Garscha, Jörg. *Studien zum Ezechielbuch: Eine redaktionskritische Untersuchung von 1–39*. Euroäische Hochschulschriften, Theologie 23. Bern: Lang, 1974.
Gerleman, Gillis. "Hesekielbokens Gog." *Svensk exegetisk Årsbok* 12 (1947) 132–146.
Ginsberg, H. L. "Reflexes of Sargon in Isaiah after 715 B.C.E." *JAOS* 88 (1968) 47–53.

Greenberg, Moshe. *Ezekiel 1–20*. AB 22. New York: Doubleday, 1983.
Hals, Ronald M. *Ezekiel*. FOTL 19. Grand Rapids: Eerdmans, 1989.
Hays, Richard B. *Echoes of Scripture in the Letters of Paul*. New Haven: Yale University Press, 1989.
Horgan, M. *Pesharim: Qumran Interpretations of Biblical Books*. CBQMS 8. Washington, DC: Catholic Biblical Association of America, 1979.
Hossfeld, Frank-Lothar. *Untersuchungen zu Komposition und Theologie des Esechielbuches*. Forschung zur Bibel 20; Würzburg: Echter, 1977.
Hossfeld, Frank-Lothar, and Erich Zenger. *Psalms 2*. Translated by Linda M. Maloney. Hermeneia. Philadelphia: Fortress, 2005.
Iseminger, Gary, editor. *Intention and Interpretation*. Philadelphia: Temple University Press, 1992.
Jastram, Nathan. "The Book of Numbers from Qumran, Cave VI (4QNumb)." Ph.D. diss., Harvard University, 1990.
Johnson, A. C., H. S. Gehman, E. H. Kase, Jr., editors. *The John H. Scheide Biblical Papyri: Ezekiel*. Princeton: Princeton University Press, 1938.
Joyce, Paul. "Synchronic and Diachronic Perspectives on Ezekiel." In *Synchronic or Diachronic? A Debate on Method in Old Testament Exegesis*, edited by J. C. de Moor, 115–28. OtSt 34. Leiden: Brill, 1995.
Kaufman, Stephen. "The Temple Scroll and Higher Criticism." *HUCA* 53 (1982): 29–43.
Kister, Menahem. "A Common Heritage: Biblical Interpretation at Qumran and its Implications." In *Biblical Perspectives: Early Use and Interpretation of the Bible in Light of the Dead Sea Scrolls. Proceedings of the First International Symposium of the Orion Center for the Study of Dead Sea Scrolls and Associated Literature*, edited by M. E. Stone and E. G. Chazon, 101–111. STDJ 28. Leiden: Brill, 1998.
———. "Biblical Phrases and Hidden Biblical Interpretations and *Pesharim*." In *The Dead Sea Scrolls: Forty Years of Research*, edited by Devorah Dimant and Uriel Rappaport, 27–39. STDJ 10. Leiden: Brill, 1992.
Klausner, J. *The Messianic Ideal in Israel*. London: Allen & Unwin, 1956.
Lauha, A. *Zaphon, der Norden und die Nordvölker im Alten Testament*. Annales Academiae scientiarum fennicae B49. Helsinki: Der Finnischen Literaturgesellschaft, 1943.
Lim, Timothy. "Biblical Quotations in the Pesharim and the Text of the Bible—Methodological Considerations." In *The Bible as Book: The Hebrew Bible and the Judean Desert Discoveries*, edited by Edward Herbert and Emanuel Tov, 73–79. London: British Library, 2002.
Lust, Johann. "Ezekiel 36–40 in the Oldest Greek Manuscript." *CBQ* 43 (1981) 517–33.
———. "Major Divergences Between LXX and MT in Ezekiel." In *The Earliest Text of the Hebrew Bible: The Relationship Between the Masoretic Text and the Hebrew Base of the Septuagint Reconsidered*, edited by Adrian Schenker, 83–92. Septuagint and Cognate Studies 52. Atlanta: Scholars, 2003.
Lutz, H.-M. *Jaweh, Jerusalem und die Völker*. WMANT 27. Neukirchen-Vluyn: Nekirchner, 1968.
Maier, Johann. "Early Jewish Biblical Interpretation in the Qumran Literature." In *Hebrew Bible/Old Testament: The History of Its Interpretation*, Vol. I/1, *Antiquity*,

edited by Magne Sæbø et al., 108-129. Göttingen: Vandenhoeck & Ruprecht, 1996.
Mandel, Paul. "Midrashic Exegesis and Its Precedents in the Dead Sea Scrolls." *DSD* 8 (2001) 149-68.
Montgomery, James. *A Critical and Exegetical Commentary on the Book of Daniel.* ICC. Edinburgh: T. & T. Clark, 1927.
Myres, John L. "Gog and the Danger from the North in Ezekiel" *PEQ* 64 (1932) 213-19.
Odell, Margaret. "Are You He of Whom I Spoke by My Servants the Prophets? Ezekiel 38-39 and the Problem of History in the Neobabylonian Context." Ph.D. diss., University of Pittsburgh, 1988.
Patte, Daniel. *Early Jewish Hermeneutic in Palestine.* SBLDS 22. Missoula: Scholars, 1975.
Plett, Heinrich, ed. *Intertextuality.* Research in Text Theory 15. Berlin: de Gruyter, 1991.
Pohlmann, K-F. *Ezechielstudien: Zur Redactiongeschichte des Buches und zur Frage nach den älteste Texten.* BZAW 202. Berlin: de Gruyter, 1992.
Rabenau, K. von. "Die Entstehung des Buches Ezechiel in forgeschichtlicher Sicht." *Wissenschaftliche Zeitschrift* 4 (1955-56) 659-94.
Robinson, T. H. and F. Horst. *Die zwölf kleinen Propheten.* 3rd ed. HAT 13. Tübingen: Mohr/Siebeck, 1964.
Sanderson, Judith E. *An Exodus Scroll from Qumran: 4Qpaleo-Exod^m and the Samaritan Tradition.* HSS 30. Atlanta: Scholars, 1986.
Seebass, Horst. "אחר." In *Theological Dictionary of the Old Testament* 1:211-12
Seeligmann, I. L. "Voraussetzungen der Midraschexegese." In *Gesammelte Studien zur Hebräischen Bibel, mit einem Beitrag von Rudolf Smend*, 1-30. FAT 41. Tübingen: Mohr/Siebeck, 2004.
Sellin, Ernst. *Das Zwölfprophetenbuch. Übersetzt und erklärt.* 3rd ed. KAT 12. Leipzig: A. Deichertsche Verlagsbuchhandlung, 1929-30.
Silbermann, L. "Unriddling the Riddle: A Study in the Structure and Language of the Habakkuk Pesher (1QpHab)." *RQ* 3 (1961-62) 323-64.
Stegemann, Hartmut. "The Literary Composition of the Temple Scroll and Its Status at Qumran." In *Temple Scroll Studies: Papers Presented at the International Symposium on the Temple Scroll, Manchester, December 1987*, edited by George J. Brooke, 123-148. JSPSup 7. Sheffield: JSOT Press, 1989.
Steudel, A. "אחרית הימים in the Texts from Qumran." *RQ* 16 (1993-94) 225-46.
Swanson, Dwight. *The Temple Scroll and the Bible: The Methodology of 11QT.* STJD 14. Leiden: Brill, 1995.
Sweeney, Marvin A. "The Priesthood and the Protoapocalyptic Reading of Prophetic and Pentateuchal Texts." In *Knowing the End from the Beginning*, edited by L. L. Grabbe and R. D. Haak, 167-78. JSPSup 46. London: Continuum, 2003.
Talmon, Shemaryahu. "The Signification of אחרית and אחרית הימים in the Hebrew Bible." In *Studies in Hebrew Bible, Septuagint, and Dead Sea Scrolls in Honor of Emmanuel Tov*, edited by S. Paul et al., 795-810. VTSup 94. Leiden: Brill, 2003.
Tooman, William A. "Ezekiel's Radical Challenge to Inviolability." *ZAW* 121/3 (2009) in press.

Tov, Emanuel. "Recensional Differences Between the MT and LXX of Ezekiel." *ETL* 62 (1986) 89–101.

Ulrich, Eugene C., and Frank Moore Cross. *Qumran Cave 4. VII: Genesis to Numbers.* DJD 12. Oxford: Clarendon, 1994.

Vermes, Geza. *Scripture and Tradition in Judaism.* Studia post-biblica 4. Leiden: Brill, 1961.

Westermann, Claus. *Genesis 1–11.* Translated by J. J. Scullion. Continental Commentaries. Minneapolis: Augsburg, 1984.

Wildberger, Hans. *Isaiah 1–12.* Translated by Thomas H. Trapp. Continental Commentaries. Minneapolis: Fortress, 1991.

Wilson, Andrew and Lawrence Wills. "Literary Sources of the Temple Scroll." *HTR* 75 (1982) 275–88.

Wolff, Hans-Walter. *Joel and Amos.* Translated by Waldemar Janzen et al. Hermeneia. Philadelphia: Fortress, 1977.

Woude, Adam S. van der. "Prophetic Prediction, Political Prognostication, and Firm Belief." In *The Quest for Context and Meaning: Studies in Biblical Intertextuality in Honor of James A. Sanders*, edited by Craig A. Evans, Shemaryahu Talmon, and James A. Sanders, 63–73. BibIntSer 28. Leiden: Brill, 1997.

Yadin, Yigel. *The Temple Scroll.* Jerusalem: Israel Exploration Society & Institute of Archaeology of the Hebrew University of Jerusalem, 1983.

Zimmerli, Walther. *Ezekiel 2.* Translated by R. E. Clements. Hermeneia. Philadelphia: Fortress, 1983.

PART TWO

Transformation of Tradition and Theology in Ezekiel

4

Transformation of the Image[1]

Jill Middlemas

Introduction

IT IS WELL RECOGNIZED THAT THE BOOK OF EZEKIEL IS DISTINGUISH-able from the other writing prophets by being more literary in character than oracular. In fact, this is one of the features of the book that has led to arguments for single authorship.[2] It is more generally accepted that the book of Ezekiel was composed in a prophetic circle and it is the understanding adopted here, such that mention of Ezekiel as author refers to this circle rather than a single man.[3] An important examination of the literality of the book has been conducted by Ellen Davis, who finds that the prophetic medium is actually the text itself. In light of a different style of presentation, Davis examines the distinctive mode of interpretation available through a written prophecy and how it requires

---

1. At the forefront, I would like to gratefully acknowledge that the funding for the research that forms the backdrop of this paper has been generously provided by the Leverhulme Trust in Great Britain.

2. For a review of the discussion, see Paul M. Joyce, *Ezekiel: A Commentary*, LHBOTS 482 (New York: T. & T. Clark, 2007) 7–16.

3. Walther Zimmerli, *Ezechiel 1–24*, BKAT 13/1 (Neukirchen-Vluyn: Neukirchener, 1979, original 1969); Keith W. Carley, *Ezekiel Among the Prophets: A Study of Ezekiel's Place in Prophetic Tradition*, SBT 31 (London: SCM, 1975); Ronald E. Clements, "The Ezekiel Tradition: Prophecy in a Time of Crisis," in *Israel's Prophetic Tradition: Essays in Honour of Peter R. Ackroyd*, ed. Richard J. Coggins et al. (Cambridge: Cambridge University Press, 1982) 119–36; Ellen F. Davis, *Swallowing the Scroll: Textuality and the Dynamics of Discourse in Ezekiel's Prophecy*, JSOTSup 78 (Sheffield: Almond, 1989).

more of the audience.[4] One of the important points for our purposes has to do with a clear recognition of the rhetorical power of the written word, somewhat akin to what John Kutsko notes as a feature particular to Ezekiel.[5] Through the written word, a writer can be more precise about the use of language. The ability of Ezekiel to manipulate words in order to convey meaning has been recognized quite rarely, but it is one of the singular most important features of the book as Davis and Kutsko have shown.

The book of Ezekiel evidences a literary artistry whereby the use of imagery conveys concepts important to the prophet or prophetic circle. The most obvious examples occur in the three visionary experiences of divine presence that function as the skeleton of the collection. The first appears in chaps. 1–3 where the call of the prophet is related via the vision of the deity's mobile chariot. Next, the downfall of Judah is recounted by the vision of the defiled temple and the movement of the deity's mobile chariot away from the temple and the city of Jerusalem in chaps. 8–11. The closing chapters of the book (Ezek 40–48) contain a vision that relates to the second, except that it portrays restoration made possible by the purified temple and reorganization of worship. In addition to these quite graphic scenes, the famous vision of the dry bones shows the very physical rebirth of a people metaphorically presented as long dead (chap. 37). In these four visionary sequences, there is an astonishing amount of detail. In fact, the depiction of the deity and the heavenly throne was so minute in chaps. 1–3 that the rabbis forbade the reading of these chapters to anyone under the age of 30. In addition to visual encounters, the prophet depicts the coming judgement of the nation and its people (chaps. 5–6; 12; 14; 21; 24) as well as the restoration of the united kingdom (37:15–28) in sign-acts, where the prophet was told to physically enact actual events as part of the divine message. The use of imagery in an intensely graphic way appears also in the allegories of the nations of Israel and Judah personified as sexually promiscuous and adulterous women (chaps. 16 and 23).

It is ironic, then, that while Ezekiel uses imagery to a large extent to emphasize his prophetic message, the singular most important reason for the downfall of Jerusalem and Judah according to the book is the

---

4. Davis, *Swallowing the Scroll*, 30–37, 73–104.

5. Kutsko, John F. *Between Heaven and Earth: Divine Presence and Absence in the Book of Ezekiel*, BJSUCSD 7 (Winona Lake, IN: Eisenbrauns, 2000).

breach of the covenant through the adherence to and worship of other gods figured as idols, images, and statues. Ezekiel's stance on the worship of other gods appears to follow the line of the Deuteronomic Code that forbids the worship of other deities and representations of deities; but with so much visual representation, does the book of Ezekiel send mixed messages about images after all?

Distancing the Image

There are three types of representation that form the basis of a study of how Ezekiel conceives of and uses imagery. It is through Ezekiel's depiction of the gods of other nations, the cities of Jerusalem and Samaria personified, and the God of ancient Israel, that a singular prophetic stance on images becomes clear.

Images of Idols

The most prevalent and pervasive type of image found in the book of Ezekiel is that of fashioned objects worshipped as deities. In his analysis of the presence and absence of Yahweh in Ezekiel, Kutsko notes a correlation between the divine presence and the issue of ritual practices employing images and notes, "more dramatically than either Jeremiah or Second Isaiah (indeed than any single book of the Hebrew Bible, including the Deuteronomic corpus), Ezekiel targets the sin of idolatry."[6] Certainly other social evils, such as adultery, robbery, and oppression of the poor, appear, but they are not cited as pervasively as grounds for judgement as the failure of Judah to worship Yahweh alone. The issue of idolatry appears in the context of kindling the wrath of the deity and as the rationale for the divine decision to destroy Jerusalem and the land of Judah. Even the return of the deity's presence to Jerusalem is predicated on the commitment of the people and leaders of the nation to refrain from the worship of images. In the vision of the purified temple, the deity states categorically, "Now let them put away their idolatry and the corpses of their kings far from me, and I will reside among them forever" (Ezek 43:9). The issue of idol worship remains consistently at

---

6. Kutsko, *Between Heaven and Earth*, 25; see also his "Ezekiel's Anthropology and Its Ethical Implications," in *The Book of Ezekiel: Theological and Anthropological Perspectives*, ed. Margaret S. Odell and John T. Strong (Atlanta: Society of Biblical Literature, 2000) 119–41.

the forefront in the prophet's rhetoric of judgement and functions (as Thomas Renz has argued) to transfer hope to the exiles in Babylon who fail to participate in the unorthodox ritual practices taking place in the homeland.[7]

As Kutsko has shown, two rhetorical strategies are employed in the book of Ezekiel in discussions of the worship of other deities that deny them efficacy or divinity.[8] In the first place, the term אלהים, "God/gods" is never used with reference to deities other than Yahweh. In spite of the fact that the Deuteronomic corpus speaks of "going after other gods" using the expression אלהים אחרים, Ezekiel shies away from this terminology preferring instead to use terms that connote things. The language used of other deities clearly designates them inanimate—even unattractive—objects. In the description of idols, Ezekiel typically speaks of "abominations" (42 times), "dung idols" (38 times), and "detestable things" (8 times). Other terms appear as well, including an "image" (Ezek 8:3, 5) and "statue" (7:20; 16:17; 23:14). The terms for "a male" (16:17) and "men" used of figures engraved on the walls that were the object of worship (23:14) should also be included among these types of expressions. Words that convey divinity never occur in conjunction with deities other than Yahweh in the book of Ezekiel. Through the careful use of language, Ezekiel denies divine status to objects venerated by human beings. As objects they have no independent existence.

Another strategy found in the book that accomplishes a similar aim is to refer to other deities without making exact references to them or their worship practices.[9] Except for the specific mention of Tammuz (Ezek 8:14) and the sun (8:16–17), the exact referents for the deities spoken of in conjunction with different ritual practices are difficult to determine. In addition, details about the rituals themselves remain vague. When Ezekiel condemns the practice of child sacrifice, for instance, he uses language like העביר, "to pass through (the fire)" (16:21; 20:26, 31; 23:37), that is ambiguous in meaning. Because of the lack of specificity—especially when compared to Jeremiah, who speaks of "burning with fire" (Jer 7:31; 19:5)—scholars continue to debate the

---

7. Thomas Renz, *The Rhetorical Function of the Book of Ezekiel* (Leiden: E. J. Brill, 1999).

8. Kutsko, *Between Heaven and Earth*; "Ezekiel's Anthropology," 120–25.

9. Ibid.; Jill Middlemas, *The Troubles of Templeless Judah*, OTM (Oxford: Oxford University Press, 2005) 91–93, 110–17.

actual practice underlying the words: did this practice really entail the immolation of children, for example?[10]

Again, a prominent feature of Ezekiel's vision at the defiled temple is the vague reference to the deities worshipped and to the actual ritual practices taking place. Three of the four scenes contain inexact referents. The first abominable worship practice encountered by the prophet is the mysterious "image of jealousy that causes jealousy" (8:3, 5).[11] Scholars continue to debate the exact identity of the figure,[12] although it appears that the biblical writers understood this image as an Asherah pole (tracing the appearance of an Asherah cultic object in 2 Kgs 21:7 through 2 Chr 33:7, 15). This interpretation finds support in the exegesis of those who take the verb as a variant spelling of קנא and translate "zeal" in the sense of lust or love, understanding a goddess to be implied[13] or who trace the root to קנה ("to acquire, create"), which yields a vague allusion to Asherah, the creatrix (procreator) of the gods in Ugaritic tradition.[14]

Recently, Margaret Odell has offered another interpretation that might be more fitting in the context of Ezekiel. She argues that the סמל erected is a votive statue rather than the image of a deity and that the sacrifices made are the problem, rather than the image itself. In support of her contention that the statue is not representative of an Asherah pole, Odell observes that a goddess is never the object of prophetic condemnation in the book of Ezekiel. Instead, the deities castigated by Ezekiel are all male. For example, the prophet condemns the worship of the male god Tammuz as well as idols, which are understood to be male because in the allegories of Samaria and Jerusalem, the personified cities

---

10. E.g., Moshe Weinfeld, "Burning Babies in Ancient Israel," *UF* 10 (1979) 411–13.

11. The full description of the figures occurs only in v. 3. There the image is called the סמל הקנה המקנה. The key word is המקנה, presumably the *hiphil* of a variant spelling of the root קנא 'to be jealous' (GKC §75*qq*), supported by the Syriac translation. Since there is no other attestation of such a case, it may be more attractive to favour taking the root from קנה "to acquire, (pro)create". In Ugaritic, the root קנה is most frequently used of Athirat—the consort of El and the etymological equivalent of the biblical Asherah. See, H. C. Lutzky, "On 'The Image of Jealousy,'" *VT* 46 (1996) 121–24.

12. See the discussion in Middlemas, *The Troubles of Templeless Judah*, 91–92; Margaret S. Odell, *Ezekiel* (Macon, GA: Smyth & Helwys, 2005) 104–8.

13. Walther Eichrodt, *Der Prophet Hesekiel Kapital 1–18*, ATD 22/1 (Göttingen: Vandenhoeck & Ruprecht, 1959).

14. Lutzky, "Image of Jealousy," 121–24.

figuratively violate their covenant with Yahweh through sexual liaisons with lovers. The idols are said to be male in the allegorical presentations of the waywardness of Jerusalem and Samaria (Ezek 16:17; 23:14). After establishing that male deities are consistently subject to prophetic rebuke, Odell raises the question of what feature of the statues of jealousy actually provokes the wrath of the deity in the scene at the defiled temple. She argues that it is the sacrifices that are made to the votive statue that are the problem. They represent those that would have been perceived as the most zealous and that functioned to ensure blessing. In her view, the most likely type of sacrifice that would spark such divine angst is child sacrifice.[15] If she is correct, the first abomination Ezekiel encounters has to with unorthodox ritual practice. It is a provocative suggestion that fits to some extent with Ezekiel's concerns about child sacrifice elsewhere in the text (16:20–36; 20:26, 31; 23:37). We will return to this argument later, but the important point is that the vague details present in the text avail themselves of multiple interpretations.

In another sequence, Ezekiel finds the elders of ancient Israel worshipping carved images set up in niches in the walls of a hidden room. Not only is the exact nature of the ritual practice not known with any degree of certainty, the identity of the deities symbolized remains debatable.[16] Three of Ezekiel's favourite terms for idols—"abominations" (Ezek 8:9), "detestable things" (8:10),[17] and "dung idols" (8:10)—appear in conjunction with worship directed at carved images (8:12).[18] The preponderance of words for idols and the description of the practice directed to carved figures highlight the use of images in worship, but little information appears to enable the identification of the actual ritual taking place. In the last vision at the impure temple, a group of men, arguably priests, bows down to the sun (8:16–18). A question remains

15. Odell, *Ezekiel*, 104–8.

16. See the מזרות debate in Middlemas, *The Troubles of Templeless Judah*, 112–14.

17. I regard שקץ as a variant spelling of שקוץ (supported by the Targum, שקוצין), which is frequently found elsewhere in Ezekiel with reference to idol worship (5:11; 7:20; 8:9, 13; 11:18, 21; 20:7, 8, 30–31; 37:23), see Middlemas, *The Troubles of Templeless Judah*, 110.

18. MT משכיתו has been taken to mean stone reliefs, but is more naturally a reference to carved idols (see Num 33:52 where it is parallel to "molten images" and the use of the term in the Aramaic inscription, Panammuwa II, in Herbert Donner and Wolfgang Röllig, *Kanaanäische und aramäische Inschriften*, vol. 1 [Wiesbaden: Harrassowitz, 1966] 39–49).

about the exact problem being condemned: are the men worshipping the sun as a god?; does the sun represent a natural idol?; or has the worship of the sun has been incorporated into Yahweh worship?[19] The description of the practice is similar to those found elsewhere in Ezekiel concerning other deities and in the defiled temple vision in particular, in that details remain resolutely unspecific. Vague references to the actual identities of other deities as well as the lack of clear details about worship practices in their honour function along with their objectification to dissuade veneration.

However, if this were the only reason for a lack of specificity with reference to other gods, one would expect this to be a consistent rhetorical strategy found throughout the book of Ezekiel, and especially in the vision of the abused sanctuary. Oddly enough, Ezekiel becomes remarkably specific when he encounters the third scene in his vision in 8:14–15. After meeting the jealousy inspiring statue and a series of carved images, but before the encounter with the worship of the sun, Ezekiel is presented with women wailing over Tammuz—a Mesopotamian dying and rising god.[20] Tammuz is the only deity other than Yahweh mentioned by name in the book of Ezekiel and his mention has long perplexed interpreters. It could be that Ezekiel is being remarkably pointed in his critique by specifying the Mesopotamian deity, Tammuz, to an exiled audience in Babylon, a deity whom he encounters in his vision at the temple in Jerusalem.[21] Again, if Ezekiel were noting a Mesopotamian deity for effect, it seems odd that Tammuz—a relatively minor deity in the pantheon—is cited instead of Ishtar or Marduk. Presumably there is another feature about the worship of Tammuz that concerns the prophet at this point. Arguably, the problem with the worship of Tammuz in the third vision may have to do with the fact that one consistent and well known ritual practice was the use of the deity's image or other representative images in worship. An image of the god or other representative symbols were paraded about, even from village

19. John Glen Taylor, *Yahweh and the Sun: Biblical and Archaeological Evidence for Sun Worship in Ancient Israel*, JSOTSup 111 (Sheffield: JSOT Press, 1993).

20. There is much written about this deity. A helpful overview is provided by Bendt Alster, "Tammuz" in Karel van der Toorn, et al (eds.), *Dictionary of Deities and Demons in the Bible* (2d ed.; Leiden: Brill, 1999) 828–34 and a short bibliography appears in Middlemas, *The Troubles of Templeless Judah*, 114–15.

21. I have Bill Tooman to thank for this provocative suggestion.

to village. The mention of this cult could relate to concerns about the use of images in worship. An additional rhetorical strategy, overlooked by attempts to clarify each of the unorthodox religious practices and the unnamed gods more precisely, may be in evidence.

Can a consideration of the other three visions at the temple support this interpretation? The first point to take into consideration is that there is a particular emphasis on what Ezekiel sees. That Ezekiel's experience at the defiled temple takes place within one of the three מראות אלהים (visions of God) (8:3, 4) suggests at the outset that there is an importance ascribed to the visual nature of the experience. Each of the scenes at the temple has four main components: Ezekiel is taken to a location, where he is instructed to or does see ritual practices taking place, the deity asks a question regarding whether Ezekiel has seen, followed by a divine statement that in the first three scenes declares that the prophet will see even greater abominations (the final scene concludes the cycle with a statement of divine judgement). The emphasis throughout is on what is seen by the prophet and by the deity. Even Yahweh's statement of incredulity that the elders think what they do is not seen by the deity in the second scene—"Yahweh does not see. Yahweh has forsaken the land"—stresses the important role ascribed to vision. What Ezekiel's (and thus the audience's) gaze is directed towards is of great importance in understanding the main thrust of the rhetoric in the visions of the defiled temple.

In the first scene, Ezekiel encounters the statue of jealousy that has traditionally been understood as an Asherah cultic object, but effectively challenged by Odell's argument for child sacrifices presented to a votive statue. Does the appearance of child sacrifice in this context make sense? Notably, with few exceptions child sacrifices in Ezekiel are made to idols (גלולים), rather than to Yahweh (16:20–36; 20:31; 23:37).[22] The one instance where the sacrifices are said to be made to Yahweh is part of the recitation of the failed history of the people and specifically associates the practice with the wilderness wanderings rather than the temple in Jerusalem (20:26). At the close of the recital, child sacrifices are said to be offered to idols, rather than to Yahweh (גלולים, 20:31)

---

22. The literature on child sacrifice is vast. For an entry to the discussion, see the references in Francesca Stavrakopoulou, *King Manasseh and Child Sacrifice*, BZAW 338 (Berlin: Gruyter, 2004) and Middlemas, *The Troubles of Templeless Judah*, 97–105.

upon entry in the land (20:28).²³ It is doubtful that the issue at stake in Ezekiel 8:3–6 is that of child sacrifice. Nevertheless, Odell's objections to the traditional interpretation of the statue as an Asherah pole, particularly her awareness that a goddess never appears castigated by the deity within the context of Ezekiel, are points well taken. In the immediate context of the temple vision and when considered alongside other passages about child sacrifice, it is more difficult to justify the shift to understanding the sacrifices themselves as the point of departure, however. It is conceivably not the type of sacrifice represented by the votive statue that spurs Yahweh's jealous rage, but the appearance of an image in worship. It is significant that the statue is mentioned twice (8:3, 5) in this vision.

Because the other visions at the temple (idols, and the sun, arguably also the image of Tammuz) represent objects being worshipped instead of or in addition to Yahweh, it raises the question of whether the issue at stake throughout is the object itself. The key word in exposition is the participle המקנה in v. 3. Without the masoretic pointing it would more naturally taken as a *hophal* and translated "the one created or fashioned". The Septuagint translation offers some measure of support for this view as it renders, "the statue of the buyer," obviously understanding the root from קנה "to acquire" (but also "to create") and suggesting a passive sense "the one that was bought." The image that sparks Yahweh's jealous rage has been fashioned by human hands. In the ancient world, votive statues often included or were fashioned in the image of the petitioner, although sometimes the type of sacrifice is illustrated. Rather than the activity, the passage points to the image itself.

The use of images in worship appears to be the thread that connects the four practices. The סמל in the first vision, however understood, is clearly an image as are the engraved or carved idols in the second vision. Tammuz worship included the use of representative symbols, and the sun in the fourth vision is also an image, even if a natural one as Glen Taylor has already suggested.²⁴ These examples show that a third rhetorical strategy appears with reference to other deities in the book

---

23. On the issue of whether child sacrifice was intrinsic to ancient Israelite practice, see Jon D. Levenson, *The Death and Resurrection of the Beloved Son* (New Haven, CT: Yale University Press, 1993); cf. John Day, *Molech: A God of Human Sacrifice in the Old Testament* (Cambridge: Cambridge University Press, 1989).

24. Taylor, *Yahweh and the Sun*.

of Ezekiel to highlight the illicit nature of the use of images in ritual observance. The prophet refrained from being precise about the exact identity of the gods involved and the nature of the ritual practices in their honour, not simply to dissuade the worship of deities other than Yahweh or even because his audience would have recognized the practices as Odell has argued, but, more importantly, to draw attention to the activity itself, namely, the use of an object in the context of worship.[25] Vague details serve as the backdrop of the scene, so Ezekiel's eyes and thus that of the audience are directed to the objects that stir divine consternation and wrath.

The above analysis has shown that three rhetorical strategies occur with respect to the presentation of idols in the prophetic discourse. The first functions effectively to deny divinity to deities other than Yahweh. It appears alongside another device whereby there are no overtly precise details about the worship of other deities. Together these two rhetorical devices strip divine status from deities other than Yahweh. The most obvious conclusion from this is that Ezekiel contributes in a significant way to the concept of exclusive monotheism as Kutsko has argued. Ezekiel admits of no divinity other than that of the god Yahweh. One of the first transformations of the image made in the book of Ezekiel is the transmutation of a divinity to a mere image. In this Kutsko, along with many other interpreters, is surely correct. That which is divine is not compatible with objects made by human hands, any natural object (like the sun), or even human beings themselves. By distancing divinity from things occurring in the natural order, Ezekiel also accomplishes an important preliminary step towards the creation of an aniconic ideal.

How the creation of deities in the forms of images takes on meaning in the book of Ezekiel becomes a more interesting question. When the two rhetorical strategies are considered in conjunction with the third—to direct attention to the (unorthodox) use of images in worship—these literary devices function on another level, as iconoclasm. A second important step in the establishment of aniconism has to do with clarifying what is considered proper worship. In Ezekiel, the definition of unorthodox ritual practice includes the use of images in worship. Ezekiel condemns the veneration of deities other than Yahweh figured

---

25. Odell, *Ezekiel*, 107.

as idols, but an equally important issue at stake in the prophetic book is the use of images in worship.

Images of Cities

Another effective prophetic rhetorical technique, closely related to the issue of idolatry in Ezekiel, is the use of allegory to recast the cities of Jerusalem and Samaria (representing their nation-states) as sexually promiscuous women who have transgressed their close relationship with, even marriage to, Yahweh. In chapters 16 and 23, the cities are portrayed graphically as women who engage in adulterous affairs with other nations. Ezekiel has turned a political scenario into an issue of false loyalty and false worship.[26] The latter argument is present because it was the treaties with other peoples, portrayed as sexual liaisons, that led Israel and Judah to stray from its covenant with Yahweh. In chapters 16 and 23 the issue of idol worship is discussed and depicted in terms of sexual promiscuity, using terms for harlotry.[27]

Julie Galambush has produced a careful analysis of the personification of Jerusalem and Samaria in Ezekiel 16 and 23, along with other texts where Jerusalem is portrayed as a female person who acts as a prostitute or is unclean (5:7–17; 6:8–10; 7:19–22; 22:1–5; 24:3–14, 15–24).[28] One of the striking insights afforded by her study is that the metaphorical depiction of Jerusalem as a woman fades from view after the announcement of the city's fall in Ezekiel 33:21. Even the sign-act of the death of Ezekiel's wife signifies the demise of the city.[29] Galambush notes further that in the final chapters where the vision of the restored temple appears, there is no redemption promised for the personified city; instead, only its walls and structures are to be rebuilt. In addition,

---

26. See Peggy L. Day, "Adulterous Jerusalem's Imagined Demise: Death of a Metaphor in Ezekiel XVI," *VT* 50 (2000) 285–309.

27. Kutsko, *Between Heaven and Earth*, 30–31; Sharon Moughtin-Mumby, *Sexual and Marital Metaphors in Hosea, Jeremiah, Isaiah, and Ezekiel*, OTM (Oxford: Oxford University Press, 2008). The monograph by Moughtin-Mumby has appeared too recently to be considered here, but it should be a valuable resource for anyone interested in the marriage metaphor as well as divine violence found in Ezekiel 16 and 23 and elsewhere.

28. Julie Galambush, *Jerusalem in the Book of Ezekiel: The City as Yahweh's Wife*, SBLDS 131 (Atlanta: Scholars, 1991).

29. Ibid, 129.

after the fall of Jerusalem the city as a woman fades from view. More startling still is that the city is never again called Jerusalem, even in the final chapters of the book. Instead, the city receives a new name, "Yahweh is there" (Ezek 48:35). In addition, personified Samaria also fades from view. In the sign act of the two sticks Ezekiel envisions a reunited kingdom where Samaria is the political entity, but not the woman (37:15–28).

Galambush rightly points out that Ezekiel employs another literary strategy to dissociate the personified city of Jerusalem from the divine purview. Language consistent with that used for the ritual impurity of Jerusalem is applied through a simile to indict the elites of the nation:

> Son of Man, when the house of Israel lived on their own soil, they defiled it with their ways and their deeds; their conduct in my sight was like the uncleanness of a woman in her menstrual period. So I poured out my wrath upon them for the blood they had shed upon the land, and for the idols with which they had defiled it . . . Therefore say to the House of Israel, Thus says Yahweh Elohim: it is not for your sake, O House of Israel, that I am about to act, but for the sake of my holy name. (Ezek 36:17, 22)

Here the nation's elites receive a promise of a future beyond disaster. By transferring the imagery associated with personified and guilty Jerusalem to the male leaders of the nation, the book of Ezekiel glosses over any hope for the personified city in the period of restoration predicted by the prophet. In this way the prophet clarifies the true identity of the condemned, in that it is not an indirect attack on women in general, but instead on the true perpetrators of the crime of idol worship, the leaders of Judah and Israel. Nevertheless, the lack of prophecies of return and renewal to the city as a woman suggests that she has no part in the future life of the nation. The language of prostitution appears in chapters 40–48 in spite of their focus on the nature of restoration, but indicts the house of Israel, rather than the city personified (43:7–9). The metaphorical presentation of Jerusalem as a woman is never redeemed in the book.

Personified Jerusalem functions as a literary strategy employed by priestly writers concerned with the issue of holiness.[30] In the final

---

30. Ibid., 147–57.

chapters the territory of Judah is envisioned as a territory of graded holiness—probably better understood as radiated holiness as Odell has argued—around a temple complex, not around the monarchical state of a king and country.[31] The geography of the former country in the final vision sequence in chapters 40–48 portrays the temple at the center of the province as the place where Yahweh alone reigns as king. The implication of Ezekiel's failure to redeem the image of Jerusalem is that when the city is depicted as a female, it threatens the maintenance of holiness or the ability of the new community to maintain holiness in order to safeguard the ongoing presence of Yahweh in its midst. The image of the city as a woman is considered to be a threat to the new community because of issues of ritual purity that become increasingly important in the Persian period. In particular, the femininity of Jerusalem—as a woman, ritually unclean once a month—must be distanced from the deity in order to safeguard Yahweh's holiness. As such, it evidences concerns about creating strategies to ensure the perpetual governance of Yahweh consistent with other literature reacting to the downfall of Jerusalem.[32]

Certainly one way to understand the loss of personified Jerusalem is as a literary effort to ensure holiness in the restored community by ejecting women, as do Galambush and Stevenson. However, within the context of Ezekiel, where there is an effort to distance divinity from images, the rhetorical strategy could be less a problem with the city as a woman and more with the image itself. It is odd that the book of Ezekiel fails to include a positive prediction for the personified city of Jerusalem, especially when it is considered alongside other literature dealing with similar issues of destruction and exile in which she receives numerous positive predictions. In Deutero-Isaiah, for example, Jerusalem receives words of comfort (Isa 40:1–2) and hope, especially in chapters 46–55, where salvation oracles addressed to her alternate with depictions of the suffering servant (49:15, 17–18, 22–23; 50:1). A similar message occurs in Trito-Isaiah as well (Isa 60; 62; 66:10, 12–13). The prophet proclaims to the city portrayed as a bereft mother the return of her children and other striking examples of the reversal of her fortunes. The appearance

---

31. See recently Kalinda R. Stevenson, *The Vision of Transformation: The Territorial Rhetoric of Ezekiel 40–48*, SBLDS 154 (Atlanta: Scholars, 1996); Odell, *Ezekiel*.

32. Middlemas, *The Templeless Age: The History, Literature, and Theology of the "Exile."* Louisville: Westminster John Knox, 2007) 115–36.

of positive prophecies to a female Jerusalem in contemporary literature raises the question of whether the context of Ezekiel may shed light on reasons for the lack of redemption in the prophetic book.

On one level, the nature of the difference in Ezekiel may have to do with the connection of the personified city (cities) with the issue of idolatry. The worship of images is presented as sexual promiscuity, as in Ezek 6:9:

> Those of you who escape shall remember me among the nations where they are carried captive, how I was crushed by their harlotrous heart that turned away from me, and their harlotrous eyes that turned after their dung idols. Then they will be loathsome in their own sight for the evils that they have committed, for all their abominations. (see also 20:30)

Ezekiel's two most favourite words for idols—"dung idols" and "abominations"—appear in conjunction with the sexual promiscuity being condemned. Outside of the association of harlotry and idol worship found in 6:9 and 20:30, the only other use of the term "harlot" appears in conjunction with the allegorical presentations of Jerusalem in chapters 16 and 23. The problem with personified Jerusalem is the same as that of the house of Israel—idol worship. We have already seen how the prophet creates a critical distance with respect to idols. The distancing of the imagery of womanhood applied to the city of Jerusalem (and, indeed, Samaria) may have to do with the close connection of idolatry and human worship.

On another level, Ezekiel expresses a clear concern about the creation of images in the form of human persons. It is widely believed that the statue of jealousy in Ezekiel 8 contains a vague allusion to the representation of a female figure (see Exod 20:4–6; Deut 5:8–10 on prohibitions against images). Especially if one translates 8:3 as "the lustful figure that causes lust" (along with some commentators), the deity is represented by a fertility statuette. Odell's alternative suggestion that the object represents a votive statue would also be problematic because of the representation of the human form or simply because of the use of an object in worship. While it is true as Kutsko has shown that Ezekiel's terminology for idols ("abominations," "dung idols," and "detestable things") debases them, it is difficult to see how the same concern carries equal force when the productions are in the likeness of men. Twice in the context of the allegorical representations of Jerusalem and Samaria, the issue at stake is the worship of figures of men—images of "a male" (זָכָר) (16:17) and "male figures" (אֲנָשִׁים) carved in the wall, looking like the figures of the Chaldeans (23:14). Ezekiel condemns the worship of idols as well as the figuration of items of worship in the shape of male persons. It is certainly possible that the city of Jerusalem—the holy city and the residence of Yahweh—as a woman evoked similar concerns.

The personified city of Jerusalem who makes no appearance in the final chapters of the book, indeed, for whom no redemption is made possible, may have fallen out of use in Ezekiel because of growing concerns about the use of images.[33] Even the holy city where Yahweh dwells with his people cannot be imaged. Personified Jerusalem (as well as personified Samaria) makes no appearance in the final vision of the restored temple community less because of objections to the idea of the city as a woman and more because of Ezekiel's aniconic stance. In his stance against the images of cities, Ezekiel exposes a reticence about the use of anthropomorphic imagery as well.

The Image of Yahweh

Thus far the prophetic book of Ezekiel evidences the power of the written word to influence ways of viewing and conceiving the world, through the presentation of idols and personified Jerusalem. With both, literary techniques were used to distance the image from the reality: divinity from constructions made by human hands and the figure of a woman from the city of Jerusalem. There is a paradox in Ezekiel's use of images, however, because the prophet employs dramatic graphic representations to convey his points while at the same time deploring their use, especially in conjunction with their worship. Adding complexity is the fact that reference is made to the book of Ezekiel in discussions about the *imago dei* (the creation of humankind, often with particular reference to the human male, in the image of God[34]) and about the

---

33. It may also have to do with concerns about the city goddesses known from the Mesopotamian laments, but this argument is outside the scope of this paper.

34. E.g., James Barr, "The Image of God in the Book of Genesis—A Study in Terminology," *BJRL* 51 (1969) 11–26; James M. Miller, "In the 'Image' and 'Likeness' of God," *JBL* 91 (1972) 289–304; Kutsko, *Between Heaven and Earth*; "Ezekiel's Anthropology," 120–25.

physical likeness of the deity in anthropomorphic, again usually male, terms.³⁵

In discussions about the image of God pride of place is given to the text of Gen 1:26–27, as indicative of the worldview of the Priestly writer. Kutsko presents one of the most recent and thorough discussions of the idea of the *imago dei* with particular reference to Ezekiel,³⁶ although Ezekiel has been tied to priestly thought elsewhere (Kutsko cites von Rad, as an example). Kutsko draws Ezekielian thought into a wider discussion about the use of humanity in the image of God as a clear rejection of the Mesopotamian emphasis on divine statues being fashioned in the likeness of deities. While his wider discussion is outside the scope of this paper, suffice it to say that even though it seems well established that the Priestly writers employ the concept of the צלם אלהים as a counter claim to the ideology of Mesopotamia,³⁷ the case is not so clear with respect to the book of Ezekiel. With respect to Ezekiel's contribution to the idea of the divine image, Kutsko cites Gen 1:26—the most recognized *imago dei* passage—"And God said 'Let us make man in our image, according to our likeness'" and asserts, "Clearly, Ezekiel's anthropomorphic description of God recalls P's description of human's creation in the image and likeness of God (Gen 1:26)."³⁸ Furthermore, he suggests that the Hebrew terms דמות and כמראה, which in his view specify concrete objects, evoke the Priestly concept of the divine image.³⁹ Does it make sense for Ezekiel to be resolutely anti-image with respect to the presentation of other deities and the city of Jerusalem, yet use concrete pictures in his representation of Yahweh-Elohim?

In two separate instances Ezekiel depicts the appearance of the presence of Yahweh in quite graphic terms. In distinction to what is

---

35. Rimon Kasher, "Anthropomorphism, Holiness and Cult: A New Look at Ezekiel 40–48," *ZAW* 110 (1998) 192–208. Because Kasher's arguments are dealt with in another article that focuses on aniconism and anthropomorphism, he will appear relatively rarely in the following discussion. See Jill Middlemas, 'Exclusively Yahweh: Aniconism and Anthropomorphism in Ezekiel', in J. Day (ed.), *Prophecy and the Prophets in Ancient Israel*, LHBOTS (New York: T. & T. Clark, forthcoming).

36. Kutsko, *Between Heaven and Earth*; "Ezekiel's Anthropology," 120–25.

37. For an overview, see Gerhard von Rad, *Old Testament Theology*, vol. 1, trans. D. M. G. Stalker (New York: Harper & Row, 1962) 144–48.

38. Kutsko, "Ezekiel's Anthropology," 132.

39. Ibid., 132–33.

argued by Kasher, who understands idiomatic expressions such as "the hand of God" as indicative of the figuration of the deity as a human being, James Barr has made it clear that it is only in theophanies, where Yahweh actually makes an appearance, that Yahweh is depicted in anthropomorphic details.[40] Human body parts used in descriptions of the deity function to connote attributes of the deity, such as power or sight, rather than depicting the deity as a human being. The כבוד־יהוה or "Yahweh's glory" signifying the divine presence actually makes an appearance in the three visions, termed the מראות אלהים, "visions of God" (Ezek 1:1; 8:3; 40:2; cf. 43:3). Another vision, that of the dry bones in chapter 37, falls into a different category. It is separated off from the visions of the divine presence through being called only a מראה, "vision," and by containing no depiction of the deity. The prophet encounters the כבוד־יהוה or "the glory of Yahweh" (1:28; 3:12, 23; 10:4, 18; 11:23; 43:4, 5; 44:4) and "the glory of the god of Israel" (8:4; 9:3; 10:19; 11:22; 43:2) three times, when the deity appears. In the first two visions, the prophetic visions are described using language and imagery consistent with a divine theophany.[41] Natural and supernatural phenomena like clouds (1:4, 28; 10:3, 4), brightness (1:4, 13, 27, 28; 10:4), fire (1:4, 15, 27; 8:2), and amber (1:4, 27; 8:2) accompany the appearance of the divine. It is worth noting that when Yahweh makes an appearance in the final chapters, far fewer theophanic elements accompany the event and the visual details are deemphasized.

In only two of the three encounters, Ezekiel attempts to define the figure of the deity more precisely. In his first vision by the river Chebar, the presence which is "seated above the likeness of a throne was something that seemed like a human form (אדם)" (1:26). Further, "upward from what appeared like its midsection[42] I saw something like

---

40. James Barr, "Theophany and Anthropomorphism in the Old Testament," in *Congress Volume: Oxford 1959* (Leiden: Brill, 1960) 31–38.

41. Jörg Jeremias, *Theophanie: Die Geschichte einer alttestamentlichen Gattung*, WMANT 10 (Neukirchen-Vluyn: Neukirchener Verlag, 1965).

42. MT מתניו usually translated "loins," but the English translation connotes a way of visualising the deity. Loins, although also used of those of women or of the side where one places a sword or even of the hips around which a belt appears, tends to be understood in the English translation as referring to male genitalia, and therefore supportive of perceptions of Yahweh as male. Preferring a less evocative term, I use "midsection" here to denote human figuration of unspecified form. Compare the change in meaning if the term "hips" were used for מתניו.

gleaming amber, something that looked like fire enclosed all around; and downward from what looked like its midsection I saw something that looked like fire, and there was splendour all around" (1:27). Again, the prophet depicts something about the presence of Yahweh in the second vision at the defiled temple site, "there was a figure that looked like fire; below what appeared to be its midsection it was fire, and above the midsection it was like the appearance of brightness, like gleaming amber" (8:2). Because אדם is used to describe Yahweh's presence in the first vision almost all commentators follow the Septuagint and emend the MT אש ("fire") to איש ("a man") in 8:2, translating, "there was a figure that looked like a man: below what appeared to be its loins it was fire." Moshe Greenberg, usually cautious in emending the text, cites the Septuagint as the better reading and understands an error in the Masoretic text creeping in from the depiction of the deity in the first vision, where the deity was also described as fire.[43] However, if that were the case, one wonders about the use of איש rather than אדם, since the equivalent closest to the divine form in 1:27 is the latter term. Moreover, it is not clear why precedence is given to the figure of the deity as a man when Yahweh in the first vision is described as fire as well as a human person.

It is not necessarily the case that the Septuagint rendering, ἀνδρός, should take priority over the Masoretic text. If Ezekiel struggles with imaging God (note the elusive type of language he uses in the visions and the frequent appearance of terms of comparison) and images of deities, does it follow that he is the most anthropomorphic of all the prophets? In the first two of three vision sequences in the book, Ezekiel employs multiple images in order to convey a greater sense of the presence of Yahweh instead of focusing on one image exclusively. Keil argues that the emendation of 8:2 to איש is based on arbitrary reasons and cites 1:27 where the figure is composed of fire in defense of the MT reading אש.[44] While it is true that the deity is likened to אדם in 1:26, the terms איש and אדם are not the same. In fact, איש is actually more specifically a reference to a human male than אדם, which is better understood with reference to an undifferentiated human person.[45] Ezekiel elsewhere fa-

43. Moshe Greenberg, *Ezekiel, 1–20*, AB 22 (New York: Doubleday, 1983) 166.

44. C. F. Keil, *Biblical Commentary on the Prophecies of Ezekiel*, vol. I.: *1–28*, trans. J. Martin (Grand Rapids: Eerdmans, 1966) 115.

45. Phyllis Trible, *God and the Rhetoric of Sexuality*, OBT (Philadelphia: Fortress, 1978).

vours more abstract language in conjunction with figuring the divine over the particular thereby raising a question of why the prophet would choose a more specific term in the second vision. Actually, the force of the image of Yahweh as אדם in the first vision is lessened within its immediate context when Yahweh's effulgence is comparable to a rainbow (1:27). Moreover, Yahweh's image can be fire as described in conjunction with the tabernacle, "On the day the tabernacle was established, the cloud covered the tabernacle, the tent of the covenant; and from evening until morning it was over the tabernacle, having the appearance of fire (כמראה אש)" (Num 9:15). Yahweh even appears to Moses in a burning bush (Exod 3:2–3). In addition, the fact that Ezekiel condemns idols created in the shape of men raises the question about whether it would then be acceptable for the prophet to depict Yahweh as a male.

What may be of assistance in clarifying 8:2 is a consideration of the term מראה. One use of מראה is with reference to the visions themselves. It refers back to prior visionary experiences (Ezek 8:4; 43:3, three times) and to the vision currently taking place (11:24, twice). In addition, at the conclusion of the first vision of the deity the expression "this was the vision of the form of the presence of Yahweh" summarizes what Ezekiel sees up until this point (1:28). It is set off from the use of מראה elsewhere in that it contains no additional detail about what the divine appearance is like; instead it captures what has been seen—i.e. the radiance of the vision is likened to how one perceives a rainbow in the sky on a cloudy day—bright, colorful, and filtered effusively through the particles of the cloud. The prophetic visualization is best characterized as elusive, insubstantial, and unspecific. A penchant favoring the abstract tells against the use of איש in the second vision, especially as "man" speaks more concretely about the divine form than אדם. Here is where Kutsko's first point breaks down. The Priestly writers also employed אדם and then became more specific by stating that the image of God was in the form of a male and female (זכר and נקבה; Gen 1:27). It is less likely that Ezekiel is interacting with Priestly concepts of the *imago dei* in figuring Yahweh as אדם. Rather, the prophet seeks to distance Yahweh from any specific image.

Furthermore, Ezekiel is cautious in his language by using comparatives such as the preposition "like" or "as." There is a lack of specificity in his recounting of the vision. In addition to language such as the preposition "like" that captures the details of the vision only partially, a unique expression דמות כמראה occurs in conjunction with depictions of the divine presence in 1:26 and 8:2 whose use speaks to the literary strategy of the prophet at these points. These terms (as an idiom, written in this order) are found nowhere else in Ezekiel or the Hebrew Bible.

A sense of what דמות and מראה mean in this idiom can be gathered from how they are used by Ezekiel in the descriptions of the variety of images that accompany the appearance of the divine presence as well as the likeness of the deity. The term מראה "vision" in the singular or the plural appears with or without the definite article or prepositions with reference to describing various objects Ezekiel sees accompanying the divine presence, such as the figures in the clouds (1:5, 13, 14), their wheels (1:16; 10:9), their faces (10:22), their wings (1:13), the dome over the figures (1:26), the cherub throne (1:27, 28), the man-like figure who guides Ezekiel around the temple to be rebuilt (40:3), and various objects at the new temple (41:21; 42:11). It is also used to compare the likeness of the divine presence with splendour (1:27), a rainbow (1:28), shining light (1:28), and brightness (8:2). Like מראה the word דמות is sometimes used more generally. It describes some aspect of the form or shape of the four living beings that appear in Ezekiel's vision (1:5, 10, 13; 10:21, 22), the wheels that accompany the creatures (1:16), the dome over them (1:22), as well as the divine cherub throne (1:26; 10:1).

Other terms used in conjunction with items in the visions appear to be more specific, as with תבנית, which indicates more exactly the shape of things. It is used of the hand that pulls Ezekiel to the defiled temple (8:3), the engravings being worshipped in Jerusalem (8:10), and the hands of the cherubim (10:8), but occurs in conjunction with דמות in 10:21, suggesting that the latter term can specify things more exactly. On occasion דמות elsewhere in the Hebrew Bible describes what objects appear like (oxen in 2 Chr 4:3) or are patterned after (the altar in 2 Kgs 16:10). In addition, it forms a parallel with צלם, "representative image," with reference to human beings in the likeness of God (Gen 1:26) and Adam's son being in his likeness (Gen 5:3),[46] as well as in an extra-biblical inscription from Tell Fakhariyeh.[47] In the Aramaic portion of a bilingual inscription inscribed on a statue of a bearded male

---

46. Silvia Schroer, *In Israel Gab es bilder: Nachrichten von darstellender Kunst im Alten Testament*, OBO 74 (Freiburg: Universitätsverlag, 1987) 322–32.

47. W. Randall Garr, "'Image' and 'Likeness' in the Inscription from Tell Fakhariyeh," *IEJ* 50 (2000) 227–34.

in Assyrian dress, the text identifies the figure with the supplicant of the text using דמותא and as the figure of the king using צלמא, with no apparent difference in meaning. As in Ezekiel, דמות can therefore represent the exact copy of something. It is used elsewhere in Ezekiel's visions to define more precisely the objects in the visions.

Objects of a more general nature observed by the prophet and indicated as such by the use of מראה (in the singular or plural) are made more precise when followed by דמות. The term דמות functions as a literary complement of מראה and describes in more detail one of the four wheels (Ezek 1:16; 10:10), the throne over the cherubim (1:26; 10:1), and the officers looking like Babylonians (23:15). These usages raise the question of whether דמות in the idiom דמות כמראה indicates the exact form of the deity.

Generally speaking, דמות qualifies מראה, except in conjunction with the divine form.[48] Significantly, Ezekiel employs כמראה after דמות in his depictions of the deity in the first two vision sequences. Because מראה occurs elsewhere to convey general observations, the implication must be that Ezekiel is at once capturing a sense of the image of the divine, by opening with דמות—the portrait or representation—and by following it with כמראה—like the more general figure. Imprecision follows specificity. Speaking more generally after opening with something more specific represents a brilliant rhetorical strategy to capture the sense of a visual experience, yet provide an element of distance and uncertainty at the same time. Ezekiel is much more cautious in his use of language than has been recognized. In fact, he shies away from characterizing the deity in any one form by using a general term (מראה) after the more specific one (דמות).

Kutsko uses the definition of the terms דמות and מראה to defend his argument that the form of the *imago dei* is in the image of human beings. Although he does not specifically refer to the deity in the shape of a human male, it is the case that he accepts uncritically the emendation to איש in 8:2 that would substantiate such a claim.[49] While arguing against accepting Ezekiel's language as cautious, he states, "I would emphasize that Ezekiel's language gives the additional impression that it is bridling something potentially dangerous because, in fact,

---

48. See also Kutsko, "Ezekiel's Anthropology," 131–32.
49. Kutsko, *Between Heaven and Earth*, 65, 88–89.

דמות and מראה imply a concrete representation. We must remember that Ezekiel, even more explicitly than P, is talking about the physical appearance of God" (67). Against his interpretation, however, it seems clear from the above that דמות and כמראה are not used in conjunction with the presentation of the divine form as precise representations. It is true that elsewhere, in the Hebrew Bible and in the Tell Fakhariyeh inscription, these terms are used this way. In Ezekiel, though, they are used slightly differently and the order in which they appear in conjunction with the divine effulgence speaks against Ezekiel portraying an exact copy of the deity. In addition, the use of the preposition -כ or "like" to modify the meaning of מראה, a point not mentioned by Kutsko, suggests that Ezekiel is again more subtle than P. Kutsko's second point about Ezekiel's contribution to the concept of the *imago dei* finds little support within the context of the book of Ezekiel. Ezekiel's rhetorical technique is consistent throughout the book—to distance divinity from specific forms.

It is not that for Ezekiel the likeness of the deity cannot be depicted as a human being (for Ezekiel the preferred term is אדם rather than איש), but that it should not be exclusively so. He strove throughout for multiple and fluid images without fixed features. Especially in the first two visions of the divine effulgence—where Ezekiel sees Yahweh—a plethora of imagery abounds. This aspect of how Ezekiel sketches his visual experiences appears to represent a strategy contrary to that found in conjunction with the illicit objects worshipped at the temple complex. When speaking of the veneration of idols, Ezekiel refrained from exact depictions of other deities or the ritual practices performed in their honor. As a rhetorical strategy this directs attention away from other gods and their worship, to focus instead on the objects employed in their worship. It is the very idols themselves that cause divine (and prophetic) consternation. With respect to the deity, the veritable cacophony of images elicits the exact opposite effect. The variety of images seen by Ezekiel draws attention away from the representation of Yahweh's divine form. It is a subtle, yet effective technique, used along with other rhetorical strategies (e.g., דמות כמראה) to distance the divinity from an exact representation. Ezekiel's aniconic and anti-anthropomorphic stance applicable even to the divine form suggest that any one image of Yahweh has the dangerous potential to itself become an idol.

In general, Ezekiel uses quite a lot of imagery in the first two vision sequences (chaps. 1–3 and 8–11), especially, but not exclusively, in conjunction with describing things or beings that accompany the appearance of the presence of the deity. Remarkably, as mentioned heretofore, almost no imagery occurs in the final vision of the return of the deity that takes place in conjunction with the purified temple to be built at some future point. Instead the text hints at the appearance of the divine by stating that "the earth shone with his presence" (43:2) and that the current vision is comparable to the first two (43:3). Even as the final vision has no elaborate description of the natural and supernatural phenomena that accompanied the coming of the deity, it has no depiction of the figure of Yahweh. Rather than literally capturing what the presence of the deity looked like, as in the first two visions, the final vision merely likens the scene to that experienced in the first (43:3). It is notable that in the visions of the כבוד יהוה in chapters 1–3 and 8–11, depictions of the deity's presence are graphic, full of minute details about the deity, other heavenly figures, and the cherub throne. The final vision is remarkable and distinctive by not containing a single descriptor of either the deity or the divine throne. Instead, the focus shifts away from what is seen to what is heard: the sound of Yahweh's appearance "was like the sound of mighty waters" (43:2). In spite of the fact that the prophet has been willing to graphically portray divine theophanies in two vision sequences, nothing comparable appears in the final vision. The long vision of the restored and purified temple focuses attention on the word of Yahweh and the temple itself. The image of the deity fades when the divine word holds sway (see 43:11, 12; 44:5).

The elevation of the divine word, even law, corresponds well to one of the observations about Ezekiel 40–48 made by Jon Levenson a number of years ago.[50] He noted correspondences between Moses and Ezekiel including typological similarities between Mt Zion (the location of Ezekiel's temple vision) and Mt Sinai as well as between the figures of Moses and Ezekiel. In addition, the final nine chapters of Ezekiel contain the only set of laws not delivered by Moses. Like the Ten Commandments, they are the only divine word to stem directly from the deity. The word of Yahweh takes precedence over, indeed supplants, the divine image in the concluding chapters of the book. The image of

---

50. Jon Levenson, *Theology of the Program of Restoration of Ezekiel 40–48*, HSM 10 (Missoula, MT: Scholars, 1976) 37–53.

Yahweh is transformed into the word of Yahweh. This observation is relevant to the discussion begun already by Karel van der Toorn who has argued that the Torah serves as a substitute image in ancient Israel.[51]

Conclusions

The foregoing analysis has examined how the visual representations of various figures appear in the book of Ezekiel in order to better understand the rhetorical strategies being employed. How Ezekiel uses items of a visual nature contributes to a wider discussion about the *imago dei* and theories about the closest representation of the deity of ancient Israel as a human being, most frequently thought of more specifically as male. Careful observation reveals that in every case, the book of Ezekiel establishes a type of distance between divinity and forms. One of the rhetorical strategies apparent is the evocation of images to abolish them. Arguments can be made for Ezekiel's contribution to discussions of the *imago dei* or anthropomorphism when taken out of the context of the literary strategies employed in the collection, but they become less persuasive when greater attention is placed on the ability of the written word to effect change. This study provides a contribution to this discussion by showing how Ezekiel transforms images. Images are employed in order to reject them. The rejection of other deities as unattractive objects, the cities as women, and the deity in any stable form show that the prophet is ultimately iconoclastic and aniconic. When the divine image fades from view—replaced by the divine word—the need and authorization for representative symbols ceases.

---

51. Karl van der Toorn, "The Iconic Book: Analogies between the Babylonian Cult of Images and the Veneration of the Torah," in *The Image and the Book: Iconic Cults, Aniconism, and the Rise of Book Religion in Israel and the Ancient Near East*, ed. Karel van der Toorn (Leuven: Peeters, 1997) 229–48.

Bibliography

Alster, Bendt. "Tammuz." In *Dictionary of Deities and Demons in the Bible*, edited by Karel van der Toorn, et al., 828–34. 2nd ed. Leiden: Brill, 1999.

Barr, James. "Theophany and Anthropomorphism in the Old Testament." In *Congress Volume: Oxford 1959*, 31–38. VTSup 7. Leiden: Brill, 1960.

———. "The Image of God in the Book of Genesis—A Study in Terminology." *BJRL* 51 (1969) 11–26.

Carley, Keith W. *Ezekiel Among the Prophets: A Study of Ezekiel's Place in Prophetic Tradition*. SBT 31. London: SCM, 1975.

Clements, Ronald E. "The Ezekiel Tradition: Prophecy in a Time of Crisis." In *Israel's Prophetic Tradition: Essays in Honour of Peter R. Ackroyd*, edited by Richard J. Coggins, et al., 119–36. Cambridge: Cambridge University Press, 1982.

Davis, Ellen F. *Swallowing the Scroll : Textuality and the Dynamics of Discourse in Ezekiel's Prophecy*. JSOTSup 78. Sheffield: Almond, 1989.

Day, John. *Molech: A God of Human Sacrifice in the Old Testament*. Cambridge: Cambridge University Press, 1989.

Day, Peggy L. "Adulterous Jerusalem's Imagined Demise: Death of a Metaphor in Ezekiel XVI." *VT* 50 (2000) 285–309.

Donner, Herbert and Wolfgang Röllig, *Kanaanäische und aramäische Inschriften*. Vol. 1. Wiesbaden: Harrassowitz, 1966.

Eichrodt, Walther. *Der Prophet Hesekiel Kapital 1–18*. ATD 22/1-2. Göttingen: Vandenhoeck & Ruprecht, 1959.

Galambush, Julie. *Jerusalem in the Book of Ezekiel: The City as Yahweh's Wife*. SBLDS 131. Atlanta: Scholars, 1991.

Garr, W. Randall. "'Image' and 'Likeness' in the Inscription from Tell Fakhariyeh." *IEJ* 50 (2000) 227–34.

Greenberg, Moshe. *Ezekiel, 1–20*. Anchor Bible 22. Garden City, NY: Doubleday, 1983.

Jeremias, Jörg. *Theophanie: Die Geschichte einer alttestamentliche Gattung*. WMANT 10. Neukirchen-Vluyn: Neukirchener, 1965.

Joyce, Paul M. *Ezekiel: A Commentary*. LHBOTS 482. New York: T. & T. Clark International, 2007.

Kasher, Rimon. "Anthropomorphism, Holiness and Cult: A New Look at Ezekiel 40–48." *ZAW* 110 (1998) 192–208.

Keil, C. F. *Biblical Commentary on the Prophecies of Ezekiel*. Vol. 1: *1–28*. Translated by J. Martin. Grand Rapids: Eerdmans, 1966.

Kutsko, John F. *Between Heaven and Earth: Divine Presence and Absence in the Book of Ezekiel*. Biblical and Judaic Studies from the University of California, San Diego 7. Winona Lake, IN: Eisenbrauns, 2000.

———. "Ezekiel's Anthropology and Its Ethical Implications." In *The Book of Ezekiel: Theological and Anthropological Perspectives*, edited by Margaret S. Odell and John T. Strong, 119–41. SBLSymS 9. Atlanta: Society of Biblical Literature, 2000.

Levenson, Jon D. *The Death and Resurrection of the Beloved Son: The Transformation of Child Sacrifice in Judaism and Christianity*. New Haven, CT: Yale University Press, 1993.

———. *Theology of the Program of Restoration of Ezekiel 40–48*. HSM 10. Missoula, MT: Scholars, 1976.

Lutzky, H. C. "On 'The Image of Jealousy.'" *VT* 46 (1996) 121–24.
Middlemas, Jill. *The Troubles of Templeless Judah*. OTM. Oxford: Oxford University Press, 2005.
———. *The Templeless Age: The History, Literature, and Theology of the 'Exile.'* Louisville: Westminster John Knox, 2007.
———. "Exclusively Yahweh: Aniconism and Anthropomorphism in Ezekiel." In *Prophecy and the Prophets in Ancient Israel*, edited by John Day. London: T. & T. Clark (forthcoming).
Miller, James M. "In the 'Image' and 'Likeness' of God." *JBL* 91 (1972) 289–304.
Moughtin-Mumby, Sharon. *Sexual and Marital Metaphors in Hosea, Jeremiah, Isaiah, and Ezekiel*. OTM. Oxford: Oxford University Press, 2008.
Odell, Margaret S. *Ezekiel*. SHBC. Macon, GA: Smyth & Helwys, 2005.
Rad, Gerhard von. *Old Testament Theology*. Vol. 1, *Theology of Israel's Historical Traditions*. Translated by D. M. G. Stalker. New York: Harper & Row, 1962.
Renz, Thomas. *The Rhetorical Function of the Book of Ezekiel*. VTSup 76. Leiden: Brill, 1999.
Schroer, Silvia. *In Israel Gab es bilder: Nachrichten von darstellende Kunst im Alten Testament*. OBO 74. Freiburg: Universitätsverlag, 1987.
Stavrakopoulou, Francesca. *King Manasseh and Child Sacrifice: Biblical Distortions of Historical Realities*. BZAW 338. Berlin: de Gruyter, 2004.
Stevenson, Kalinda R. *The Vision of Transformation: The Territorial Rhetoric of Ezekiel 40–48*. SBLDS 154. Atlanta: Scholars, 1996.
Taylor, John Glen. *Yahweh and the Sun: Biblical and Archaeological Evidence for Sun Worship in Ancient Israel*. JSOTSup 111. Sheffield: JSOT Press, 1993.
Toorn, Karel van der. "The Iconic Book: Analogies between the Babylonian Cult of Images and the Veneration of the Torah." In *The Image and the Book: Iconic Cults, Aniconism, and the Rise of Book Religion in Israel and the Ancient Near East*, edited by Karel van der Toorn, 229–48. Leuven: Peeters, 1997.
Trible, Phyllis. *God and the Rhetoric of Sexuality*. OBT. Philadelphia: Fortress, 1978.
Weinfeld, Moshe. "Burning Babies in Ancient Israel." *Ugarit Forschungen* 10 (1979) 411–13.
Zimmerli, Walther. *Ezechiel 1–24*. BKAT 13/1. Neukirchen-Vluyn: Neukirchener, 1979, original 1969.

5

Ezekiel and Moral Transformation

Paul M. Joyce

EZEKIEL THE PRIEST-PROPHET IS REMARKABLY BOLD IN THE WAY HE draws upon past tradition. In spite of sharing a good deal with the deuteronomistic tradition and with Jeremiah, we see Ezekiel as distinctive from them, not least in his use of "spirit" language. Other examples of his independence in relation to traditions abound. Chapter 16 is scathing in its critique of the Zion tradition (v. 3: "Your origin and your birth were in the land of the Canaanites; your father was an Amorite, and your mother a Hittite"), as elsewhere Ezekiel is radical in his downgrading of monarchy—king and messiah are marginalized, as indeed is the national history that the kings had shaped.[1] Another case, striking in view of Ezekiel's closeness to the priestly tradition, is found in his differences from pentateuchal legislation in chs. 40–48, however these are to be explained (compare, for example, Ezek 46:6 with Num 28:11). And we see Ezekiel's radical freedom in the handling of tradition even more clearly evidenced in ch. 20. Here alone in the Hebrew Bible Israel sins even in Egypt, before the Exodus (v. 8; cf. 23:3, 8). And here God gives "statutes that were not good and ordinances by which they could not live" (v. 25). In all of this Ezekiel works with an independent sense of authority and confidence rooted in his God-centered faith.

In no area was Ezekiel more radical in his transformation of the past than in the moral dimension. But wherein lies his innovation here? It has often been suggested that it is in the area of a significant move

---

1. See Paul M. Joyce, "King and Messiah in Ezekiel," in *King and Messiah in Israel and the Ancient Near East: Proceedings of the Oxford Old Testament Seminar*, ed. J. Day, 323–37, JSOTSup 270 (Sheffield: Sheffield Academic, 1998).

in the direction of the responsibility of the individual before God. In this essay the extent to which Ezekiel is indeed an individualist in this sense will first be explored. It will be argued that this in fact represents a significant misunderstanding of Ezekiel and of his contribution, which will then be shown to lie in a quite distinct aspect of the moral life.

Ezekiel and the Theological Crisis of Exile

The first twenty-four chapters of the book of Ezekiel contain one of the most sustained and vehement declarations of judgement to be found anywhere in the prophetic literature of the Hebrew Bible. These chapters speak of "disaster after disaster" (7:5), in language that is violent and at times crude: "My anger shall spend itself, and I will vent my fury on them and satisfy myself; and they shall know that I, the LORD, have spoken in my jealousy, when I spend my fury on them" (5:13). The wrath of YHWH expresses itself in judgement by fire, sword, wind, famine, wild beasts and pestilence (5:2, 16–17). So violent is the language used that it is hard not to regard this section of the book as containing a cruel and vindictive message, calling down upon the people the most dreadful calamities imaginable. It is as though Ezekiel wishes these things upon his own people. However, this must be read in the light of catastrophic events that had already come upon Israel, events that demanded theological interpretation. Ezekiel—already deported—offers a key to understanding the disaster that has engulfed the nation.

The context of the ministry of Ezekiel in early sixth-century Mesopotamia is a situation beset with profound theological questions posed by the Babylonian crisis. Judah had lost her land, and with it, it seemed, her status as the chosen people of YHWH. She had been stripped of her city, her temple, and not one but two kings. Robbed of all these elements of her identity, it is hardly surprising that profound theological questions were raised. The fate of the community formed a central and indispensable part of Israel's faith in her God. Had YHWH himself been defeated by the Babylonian gods? It does seem that some thought of imperial conquest in terms of the vanquishing of local gods by the imperial gods, and we have evidence that a number of Judahites in the early sixth century in fact embraced the worship of gods other than YHWH (Ezek 8; cf. Jer 44:18). Some managed to hold on to the belief that YHWH was powerful and indeed was responsible for what was happening to them; and yet, for many of these, profound questions were raised about the justice of a god who could permit such things (cf. Ezek 18:29, "Yet the house of Israel says, 'The way of the Lord is unfair'"). To quote John Austin Baker: "some drew the straightforward conclusion that their god was less powerful than the foreign gods; others decided that he was unjust. In both cases the result was that the nerve of their religion was cut, and that they lapsed into either paganism or despair."[2]

Too many discussions of the events of defeat and deportation by the Babylonians rush on to speak of the lessons that Israel learned from these experiences, and to show how growth came out of suffering; in so doing they fail to take the depth of the disaster with full seriousness.[3] This catastrophe might well have proved to be the end of Israel as a religious community. That it did not owed everything to a small group of theologians who boldly attempted to account for the disaster within the framework of faith in YHWH. In Judah, the prophet Jeremiah and also, it seems, the authors of the Deuteronomistic History struggled to give a Yahwistic account of events. Among the exiled community, this task apparently fell initially to just one person, namely Ezekiel.

Ezekiel, in this respect like Jeremiah, articulated the theological meaning of the national crisis: the present disaster was YHWH's powerful and just act, punishing his own people for their sins. The punishment fits the crime, an entirely appropriate response to the heinous sins of Israel, wherein YHWH's justice is vindicated. This may not seem a very edifying or even a theologically acceptable message to many modern readers; it depends upon the idea that Israel's God manipulates world events and uses war as an instrument to punish sin. But it is important to remember that Ezekiel is not a leisured work of systematic theology but rather an example of crisis literature written in an extreme situation. Ezekiel's theological message of judgement offered at least a glimmer of theological light to a people who had lost all; it made possible an initial assimilation of the traumatic disaster, which could eventually become the basis of subsequent more positive lessons.

---

2. John Austin Baker, *The Foolishness of God* (London: Darton, Longman & Todd, 1970) 30.

3. See, for example, C. F. Whitley, *The Exilic Age* (London: Longmans, Green and Co., 1957); D. Winton Thomas, "The Sixth Century B.C.: A Creative Epoch in the History of Israel," *JSS* 6 (1961) 33–46.

Any adequate Yahwistic response would have to vindicate both the power and the justice of the God of Israel. This was, of course, not the first time that such a task had been faced by the prophets of Israel. A century and a half before, the Assyrian empire had posed a dire threat to the Hebrew kingdoms; indeed, the northern kingdom of Israel fell c. 721 BCE and Judah nearly suffered the same fate around 700. During that period, four great prophetic figures attempted to give a theological explanation for this historical disaster. Amos and Hosea working in the north and Isaiah and Micah in the south advanced the view that, far from representing the routing of YHWH by Assyrian gods (cf. 2 Kgs 19:10–13), these events were the powerful and just act of YHWH who was angry with the sins of his people. Isaiah spoke of Assyria as a "rod" raised up by YHWH to beat his recalcitrant people (cf. Isa 10:5: "Ah, Assyria, the rod of my anger—the club in their hands is my fury!"). It is difficult to overstate the importance of this episode in "sharpening the tools" for the prophetic response to the Babylonian crisis at the start of the sixth century. Ezekiel and his Yahwistic contemporaries were confronted by a scenario remarkably similar to that which had faced the eighth-century prophets—only this time Jerusalem was not spared. Whereas in the Assyrian crisis the adequacy of the prophetic response was not tested to breaking point, since Judah survived intact (albeit under the shadow of imperial domination), the Babylonian crisis appeared to falsify all the promises of old. Thus the eighth-century prophets had provided invaluable resources—but could the same theological rationale for historical disaster bear all the weight that was now to be placed upon it?

The first twenty-four chapters of the book of Ezekiel assert in an unqualified way the responsibility of Israel for the fate that has befallen her. Given that everything that constituted the identity of Israel had been lost this time, it is hardly surprising that the theological explanation for this is given in the most thoroughgoing of terms. Ezekiel asserts that the events do not constitute meaningless chaos, but rather the just punishment of a sinful people by their powerful God. "For the land is full of bloody crimes; the city is full of violence. I will bring the worst of the nations to take possession of their houses" (Ezek 7:23–24)—this was indeed a hard message, but it at least offered theological meaning to a generation that was experiencing the loss of all that defined its identity. Moreover, Ezekiel's theology of judgement has broader theological implications. There is room for only one God who runs the affairs of the world as a whole. Implicit here are the nascent claims of monotheism as well as universalism, themes that would be articulated more explicitly in Isaiah 40–55 later in the exile.

The much-debated chapter 18 is devoted to making it clear that the present generation is punished for its own sins and not for the sins of previous generations. Ezekiel is consistent about this elsewhere too. For Ezekiel, the past is only ever *illustrative* of the nation's propensity to sin, as in 20:30, "Therefore say to the house of Israel, Thus says the Lord GOD: Will you defile yourselves after the manner of your ancestors and go astray after their detestable things?" and 16:44, "see, everyone who uses proverbs will use this proverb about you, 'Like mother, like daughter.'" Ezekiel is here distinctively different from a number of roughly contemporary theological witnesses. For example, towards the culmination of the Deuteronomistic History, 2 Kgs 23:26 reads: "Still the LORD did not turn from the fierceness of his great wrath, by which his anger was kindled against Judah, because of all the provocations with which Manasseh had provoked him." Lamentations 5:7 declares, "Our ancestors sinned; they are no more, and we bear their iniquities," and Jer 31:29, "In those days they shall no longer say: 'The parents have eaten sour grapes, and the children's teeth are set on edge.' But all shall die for their own sins; the teeth of everyone who eats sour grapes shall be set on edge." It is vital to recognize that the couching of this last text (superficially so similar to Ezek 18:2-4) as a hope for the future acknowledges that the present situation is unfair; as a result, the Jeremiah text and the Ezekiel text mean very different things.

While Ezekiel may be seen as the most radical of these witnesses in affirming the absolute responsibility of the present generation for its own fate, the "price" of this stance is an apparent failure to acknowledge the intergenerational effects of sin. The "sour grapes" saying so vigorously rejected in Ezek 18:2 was probably an established proverb, perhaps associated with the wisdom tradition.[4] Like all such material, it had no doubt been handed on because it was seen as encapsulating a

---

4. See Donn F. Morgan, *Wisdom in the Old Testament Traditions* (Atlanta: John Knox and Oxford: Blackwell, 1981) 109–10; and Katheryn Pfisterer Darr, "Proverb Performance and Transgenerational Retribution in Ezekiel 18," in *Ezekiel's Hierarchical World: Wrestling with a Tiered Reality*, ed. S. L. Cook and C. L. Patton, 199–223, SBLSymS 31 (Atlanta: SBL, 2004).

truth about life, in this case that children are affected by their parents' actions. It would be a mistake to read into Ezekiel's rejection of the saying a blanket denial of this traditional insight. Rather his purpose is a very precise one: to liberate his audience from the morale-sapping effects of passing the buck to others for the situation in which they found themselves.

Ezekiel and Individual Responsibility?

There has been a long tradition of interpretation that has insisted that a distinctive feature of Ezekiel's theology of judgement is its emphasis on individual responsibility, that is the moral independence of contemporary individuals. This has sometimes been seen as representing a landmark development in Israel's religious development.[5] However, this must be contested, particularly on the ground that Ezekiel's overriding concern is consistently to explain a disaster that is national and thereby collective. It is important to distinguish the issue of individual responsibility, in the sense of the moral independence of contemporary individuals, from the question of the moral independence of generations, though these two have often been confused in discussion of Ezekiel. Consideration of the nature of Israel's responsibility as presented in Ezekiel has focused especially on chapters 9, 14, and 18. These all assert unequivocally that the events of defeat and exile are YHWH's just punishment of Israel's sins, and in this respect they may be said to be typical of chapters 1–24 as a whole, dominated by the theme of the absolute responsibility of Israel for the punishment which is engulfing her.

The expression of this responsibility is throughout a good deal less individualistic than has often been suggested. Individualistic motifs feature in both chapter 9 (where a mark is to be put on the foreheads of those who sigh and groan over the abominations that are committed) and 14:12–23 (where it is implied that Noah, Daniel or Job would save at least their own lives by their righteousness if they were present), but these motifs are subordinate to a more collective primary theme, namely the imminent onset of the thorough judgement of the nation.

---

5. See, e.g., A. B. Davidson, *The Theology of the Old Testament* (Edinburgh: T. & T. Clark, 1904) 282–86; A. Causse, *Du groupe ethnique à la communauté réligieuse: le problème sociologique de la réligion d'Israël* (Paris: Alcan, 1937) 201; J. Lindblom, *Prophecy in Ancient Israel* (Oxford: Blackwell, 1962) 387.

The purpose of the mark on the forehead in chapter 9 is to make it quite clear that those who are to perish do so according to absolute justice. There seems to be no direct interest in the possibility that there may be some righteous to be spared. When the prophet asks "Ah Lord GOD! will you destroy all who remain of Israel as you pour out your wrath upon Jerusalem?" (9:8), the answer appears to be in the affirmative "The guilt of the house of Israel and Judah is exceedingly great"; and when the man clothed in linen returns at the end of the chapter we are not told whether he had found any righteous. As for Noah, Daniel and Job, these are legendary paragons of virtue; even they would not save their own children, so wicked is this nation. But of course they are not present at this dark time. Indeed the final verses of the chapter take it for granted that any chance survivors will be undeserving ones, whose sins will only serve to confirm the overall justice of the national judgement. Moreover, while 14:1–11 employs the admittedly individualistic concept of excommunication, it seems to envisage the "cutting off" of the idolatrous nation as a whole, rather than merely the punishment of individual idolaters.[6]

But it is chapter 18 of which most has been made, with its discussion of the "sour grapes" proverb. Ezekiel responds to a people who claim that they are suffering for the sins of their ancestors. This chapter has been seen as a charter for individual responsibility. However, it is vital to see that the context of the whole discussion is one in which Ezekiel and his audience have already been exiled. The context is one of a national calamity, which has to be explained. Ezekiel presents three hypothetical figures in vv. 1–20, a righteous man, his wicked son, and his righteous grandson. But although these cases are individual ones, Ezekiel is here as elsewhere reapplying the priestly case law format. Each individual here in fact stands for a generation, with the crucial case being the youngest, righteous generation. Ezekiel insists that if this last generation really were innocent, it would not be punished. In this subtle chapter we then see Ezekiel's audience protesting in verse 19 that this son (the righteous grandson) *should* suffer for his father's sin. They have a vested interest in defending a theory that would vindicate their innocence in spite of their suffering. But Ezekiel cleverly maneuvers them towards acknowledging

---

6. For discussion of this and other exegetical issues, see Paul M. Joyce, *Ezekiel: A Commentary*, LHBOTS 482 (New York and London: T. & T. Clark / Continuum, 2007).

that they are in fact sinful and that the justice of God is vindicated. The second half of the chapter turns to discuss what happens when the wicked turn from their sins or indeed when the righteous go to the bad. Ezekiel argues that the past is forgotten. Some, for example Raitt, have seen vv. 21–32 as making an individualistic offer.[7] But as with vv. 1–20, so this section too uses the examples of individuals to serve an argument about the community (addressed significantly as the "house of Israel"). The language of the liturgy of entrance into the sanctuary is reapplied to the discussion of a crisis that is inevitably communal and national. The "watchman" (or "sentinel") material of chapters 3 and 33 too must be read in the light of what is in fact always the context of Ezekiel's discourse, namely the overriding concern with the fate of the nation in an inevitably corporate catastrophe.

So not even these passages support the view that Ezekiel is the great exponent of individual responsibility some have portrayed. Moreover, the overwhelmingly corporate nature of the chapters dealing with judgement is echoed in the hopeful material in the book, where we find that renewal is consistently presented as a corporate experience. The promise of a "new heart" and a "new spirit" (36:26–27; cf. 11:19) is addressed to the "house of Israel" (36:22, 32). The "dry bones" of ch. 37 are said to be "the whole house of Israel" (37:11), and the promise of new life there is addressed by YHWH to "my people" (37:12, 13). Ezekiel 37:15–28 looks forward to the reunification of Judah and Israel; v. 22 emphasizes that they shall no longer be two nations but "one nation" under "one king," while v. 24 speaks of the promised king as "one shepherd" over the people (cf. 34:23). The final verses of ch. 37 (vv. 26–28) envisage the restored community gathered around the sanctuary, a theme that is explored at length in the last nine chapters of the book (40–48; cf. 20:40–44).

Furthermore, the common view that the contribution of Ezekiel marked a crucial stage in the evolution of individualism in Israel not only misrepresents the evidence concerning Ezekiel but also attempts to impose an excessively simple pattern upon language about collective and individual responsibility in the Hebrew Bible as a whole. If one sets Ezekiel within a broader context, one finds that the complexities that characterize the understanding of responsibility in the book of Ezekiel become less

---

7. Thomas M. Raitt, *A Theology of Exile: Judgment/Deliverance in Jeremiah and Ezekiel* (Philadelphia: Fortress, 1977) 49.

puzzling, indeed they may be seen as typical of the Hebrew Bible as a whole.[8] The variation between more individualistic elements and more collective elements may be seen as typical of the diversity that marked language relating to responsibility in all periods. The absence from Ezekiel of any sense that individualistic elements are being advanced as innovations is readily understandable in the light of the fact that notions of individual responsibility seem to have played a part in thought about responsibility in Israel from early times (in both legal practice, as in Deut 24:16, and narrative traditions, such as Genesis 18).

Nonetheless, it would be a mistake to *underestimate* the place of individualistic themes in Ezekiel's statement of Israel's responsibility. The individualistic dimension of the motif of the marking of the forehead in chapter 9 or the sparing of paragons of virtue in chapter 14 (or again of the judging "between sheep and sheep, between rams and goats" in 34:17–22) should indeed be taken seriously, even though, as we have noted, Ezekiel is unoriginal in all this. Discussion has been helpfully nuanced over recent years by several important contributions. Mein's notion of a moral "re-scaling" in the exilic context sheds light on the issue of Ezekiel's so-called individualism as well as on the theme of repentance: "Only moral actions on a more individual, domestic scale are possible . . . on the more domestic scale of relations between individuals and families, repentance remains an option."[9] Kaminsky argues persuasively for making more of the individualistic language of Ezekiel 18 as evidence for a real concern with the individual: "The primary focus may in fact be communal, but that does not preclude a strong concern for the individual. Just as the general context qualifies the individualistic language and indicates that it is being used in the service of a communal sermon, the individualistic language qualifies the communal elements in certain ways."[10] He continues: "such individualistic language may not indicate an attempt to assert the total moral autonomy of each individual, but it seems very likely that Ezekiel employs it as an attempt to arouse the individuals who compose the larger nation to accept responsibility for

---

8. Paul M. Joyce, *Divine Initiative and Human Response in Ezekiel*, JSOTSup 51 (Sheffield: JSOT Press, 1989); Joel S. Kaminsky, *Corporate Responsibility in the Hebrew Bible*, JSOTSup 196 (Sheffield: Sheffield Academic Press, 1995).

9. Andrew R. Mein, *Ezekiel and the Ethics of Exile*, OTM (Oxford: Oxford University Press, 2001) 214.

10. Kaminsky, *Corporate Responsibility*, 171.

the current state of the nation."[11] Nuanced contributions such as these should prevent us underestimating the place of individualistic themes in Ezekiel's statement of Israel's responsibility; but nonetheless the central points stand, that Ezekiel's discourse is always determined by the collective nature of the national crisis and that he has been grossly misunderstood by those who have seen him as a polemical exponent of individualism.

That Ezekiel deals with these matters on an "occasional" rather than a systematic basis is nowhere better illustrated than in some remarkable words found towards the end of the major section constituted by chapters 1–24: "say to the land of Israel, 'Thus says the LORD, "Behold, I am against you, and will draw forth my sword out of its sheath, and will cut off from you both righteous and wicked. Because I will cut off from you both righteous and wicked, therefore my sword shall go out of its sheath against all flesh from south to north""" (Ezek 21:8, 9 [Eng. 21:3, 4]) This would seem to confirm our interpretation that Ezekiel is not concerned with individual responsibility. These words have scant regard for any with a mark on the forehead, little respect even for any Noahs, Daniels or Jobs. They clearly pose a problem for any scholar wishing to present Ezekiel as a great individualist; thus, for example, Irwin claimed that the passage we have quoted from ch. 21 must come from early in the prophet's ministry, before he had reached the full maturity of his individualistic view.[12] But such special pleading is unnecessary, for Ezekiel's concerns are in no way systematic.

Ezekiel's Distinctive Contribution with regard to Moral Transformation

If the distinctive contribution of Ezekiel in the moral realm does not lie in the area of a new emphasis on the responsibility of the individual, where is it to be found? Given the bleakness of chapters 1–24 it is remarkable that Ezekiel ever comes to speak of a new future. This is only possible on the basis of the radical judgement he has announced. Ezekiel never says that a new future might depend on better behavior on Israel's part. There is indeed to be a future but it is undeserved and

---

11. Ibid., 171–72.

12. W. A. Irwin, *The Problem of Ezekiel: An Inductive Study* (Chicago: University of Chicago Press, 1943) 331–32.

depends solely on YHWH. As there was a call to righteousness that would nevertheless in no way avail to avert disaster, similarly among those enjoying deliverance there is abundant evidence of the sinful and undeserving nature of those involved. We see this in the recurrent motif of self-loathing on the part of survivors, whether accidentally spared or the recipients of God's undeserved deliverance. Self-loathing is found at 6:9; 20:43; 36:31. The related motif of shame is found at 16:52, 54, 61, 63; 36:32 (cf. 7:18; 43:10-11; 44:13).[13] In several cases survivors illustrate the deserved and just nature of the punishment that has taken place: 12:16 and 14:22-23 (cf. 6:8-10, 7:16). These motifs certainly serve to underline the vital fact that in Ezekiel the new future is never earned by righteousness; repentance is never the ground for a new beginning. When a new future is promised it is for God's own reasons; right behavior follows only afterwards, as a consequence (as in 36:22-32).

Helpful here is Mein's instructive emphasis on the shift from activity to passivity in the exilic situation:

> The people themselves take no action to bring about the revival of their fortunes, but are rather YHWH's pawns. There may be some connection between this movement from responsibility to passivity and the actual social circumstances of the exiles, who have gone from being people of some importance, with a wide range of moral possibilities open to them, to people for whom the relationships of individuals, family and business form the whole of their moral perspective.[14]

Not all appear to acknowledge that Ezekiel grounds the new beginning entirely in the divine initiative. Zimmerli dated chapter 18 to the period after the fall of Jerusalem in 587 because, he argued, a call to repentance then is more appropriate.[15] This apparently overlooks the

---

13. On the theme of shame in Ezekiel, see Margaret S. Odell, "The Inversion of Shame and Forgiveness in Ezekiel 16:59-63," *JSOT* 56 (1992) 101-12; Jacqueline E. Lapsley, *Can These Bones Live? The Problem of the Moral Self in the Book of Ezekiel*, BZAW 301 (Berlin: de Gruyter, 2000) 130-56; J. Stiebert "Shame and Prophecy: Approaches Past and Present," *Biblical Interpretation* 8 (2000) 255-75; *The Construction of Shame in the Hebrew Bible: The Prophetic Contribution*, JSOTSup 346 (Sheffield: Sheffield Academic, 2002) 129-62; Daniel L. Smith-Christopher, *A Biblical Theology of Exile* (Minneapolis: Fortress, 2002) 105-23.

14. Mein, *Ethics*, 215.

15. Walther Zimmerli, *Ezekiel 1: A Commentary on the Book of the Prophet Ezekiel, Chapters 1-24*, trans. Ronald E. Clements, Hermeneia (Philadelphia: Fortress, 1979) 377.

fact that repentance plays no determinative part in the restoration in Ezekiel. Lapsley writes of the exiles: "perhaps there is hope for them if they are of the right disposition."[16] This is misleading in so far as there is any suggestion here of a link with a future beyond exile; the conditional "if" has no place in Ezekiel as a ground for restoration. Matties sees chapter 18 as "an exhortation to the people to qualify for the return, which will include both temple and land in the presence of Yahweh."[17] But there is in fact in Ezekiel no question of the people having to qualify for the return, which will depend solely on YHWH's own purposes.

Both the righteousness that would not avert disaster and the sin that does not prevent deliverance highlight that all depends on God's continuity of providential activity. "Grace" is absolutely characteristic of Ezekiel. Although the word חן, often translated "grace," is not used, there is much in Ezekiel that shares affinities with what the Christian tradition has spoken of in terms of "grace." And far from this being an anachronistic imposition of New Testament ideas, it is Christianity that is the borrower here. Exilic theological developments are fundamental to New Testament and especially Pauline theology.[18]

Ezekiel's Thoroughgoing God-centeredness

In the use of a range of formulae and motifs in Ezekiel we find evidence of a distinctive emphasis on the absolute centrality of YHWH and his self-manifestation, a radical theocentricity that is of an order difficult to parallel anywhere in the Hebrew Bible. In a trio of seminal studies, Zimmerli established this in magisterial fashion.[19]

---

16. Lapsley, *Can These Bones Live?*, 76. While contesting this particular formulation by Lapsley, it must be acknowledged that her book makes an outstanding contribution to reflection on the themes addressed by this essay.

17. G. H. Matties, *Ezekiel 18 and the Rhetoric of Moral Discourse*, SBLDS 126 (Atlanta: Scholars Press, 1990) 186.

18. Cf. Frances Young and David F. Ford, *Meaning and Truth in 2 Corinthians*, BFT (London: SPCK, 1987) 60–84.

19. See W. Zimmerli, "Ich bin Yahweh," in *Geschichte und Altes Testament: A. Alt zum 70. Geburtstag dargebracht*, ed. W. F. Albright, 179–209, BHT 16 (Tübingen: Mohr/Siebeck, 1953); *Erkenntnis Gottes nach dem Buch Ezechiel. Eine theologische Studie*, ATANT 27 (Zürich: Zwingli-Verlag, 1954); "Das Wort des göttlichen Selbsterweises (Erweiswort), eine prophetische Gattung," in *Mélanges Bibliques rédigés en l'honneur de André Robert*, 154–64, Travaux de l'Institut Catholique de Paris 4 (Paris: Bloud et Gay, 1957). These have been collected in English in Zimmerli, *I am Yahweh*, ed. W. Brueggemann, trans. Douglas W. Stott (Atlanta: John Knox, 1982).

The so-called "Recognition Formula" or "Proof-Saying" is the most characteristic expression of the radical theocentricity (God-centeredness) of this prophet and of the tradition that he shaped: "and you (or they) shall know that I am YHWH" (NRSV: "The LORD"). The formula occurs in Ezekiel some fifty-four times in its basic form and over twenty more times with minor variations.[20] The basic pattern consists of a statement that YHWH will punish (or deliver) Israel (or the nations), followed by the words "and you (or they) shall know that I am YHWH." Generally the group for whom knowledge of YHWH is anticipated is the same as that which is said to be the object of YHWH's punishment or deliverance. However, this is not always the case; in fact a wide range of permutations is to be found, the consistent factor being that the formula is always associated with the account of an action of YHWH. What of the background of the formula? There are two parts of the Hebrew Bible where similar expressions occur, namely the books of Kings (e.g., 1 Kgs 20:13, 28) and the book of Exodus (e.g., Exod 7:17). The widespread view is that it had its origin in oracles against the nations.[21] By a paradoxical inversion of an established form the use of the formula has, at some point, been broadened to include oracles against Israel. The actions of YHWH are, it appears, deliberately directed toward the end that it may be known that "I am YHWH." This somewhat cryptic message is normally presented without elaboration. This gives our formula a certain aura of mystery, which serves to highlight the theocentricity of Ezekiel's presentation.[22] Moreover, the concern that it should be known that "I am YHWH" is at times so pressing that the specific recipients of this revelation fade into relative obscurity and it becomes unclear precisely who is being addressed—in such cases we are forcefully reminded that the focus is upon the God who is known rather than upon those by whom he is known. As Childs argued, the

20. Joyce, *Divine Initiative*, 91.

21. Zimmerli, "Das Wort des göttlichen Selbsterweises (Erweiswort)"; G. Fohrer, *Introduction to the Old Testament*, trans. David E. Green (London: SPCK, 1970) 104.

22. Lapsley (*Can These Bones Live?*, 31) criticizes my emphasis on Ezekiel's "radical theocentricity" as question-begging, for, in her words, "theocentricity is not so much an answer to the problem of the tensions in the book as it is part of the problem itself." But there really is a sense in which Ezekiel's presentation of the divine is self-referential and even circular. To put it another way, to step into the theological perspective of Ezekiel is to enter a world where the issue of divine identity is at the center and everything else is treated in a necessarily derivative fashion.

specificity of Ezekiel's situation and his audience is often blurred in what may be seen as the beginnings of the canonical process toward the final form of scripture.[23] It is no surprise that this should be particularly evident in the book of Ezekiel, for this is a prophet who is all but eclipsed by God.

A second important formula in this connection is the phrase "in the sight of the nations" or "in their sight." Closely related are the expressions "among the nations" and "among them." Characteristically they are used of YHWH himself as witnessed by the nations; some texts speak of the profanation of YHWH's name in the sight of the nations (20:9, 14, 22), while others look forward to his self-vindication in their sight (36:23). References to the nations are very bare and give no indication of any positive interest in their response for its own sake. The concern is not with the nations knowing or witnessing YHWH so much as with YHWH being known and witnessed. As with the "I am YHWH" formula, so here too we find abundant evidence of the radical theocentricity of Ezekiel. The overriding concern is that YHWH should be known as he is: "so I will display my greatness and my holiness and make myself known in the eyes of many nations. Then they shall know that I am the LORD" (38:23).

The third formula is "For the sake of my name." Why does YHWH act to save his people? Is it in order to punish the nations that he delivers Israel? Judgement on the nations plays a significant part in Ezekiel, but at no point does it appear to constitute in itself the primary motive of YHWH's actions (indeed, the oracles against the nations in Ezekiel seem more about teaching lessons to Israel). Is it, then, because Israel deserves favor that YHWH delivers her? On the contrary: "Thus says the Lord GOD: 'It is not for your sake, O house of Israel, that I am about to act'" (36:22). Admittedly, it is said that Israel will be cleansed (36:25), given a "new heart" and a "new spirit" (36:26), and made to walk according to YHWH's statutes (36:27), but all of this is a promise for the future, part and parcel of the gift of restoration, and certainly not a condition upon which it depends. It is in Ezekiel that the conviction that divine favor is undeserved is articulated more consistently than anywhere else in the Hebrew Bible: "'It is not for your sake that I will act,' says the Lord GOD, 'let that be known to you. Be ashamed and dismayed for your

---

23. Brevard S. Childs, *Introduction to the Old Testament as Scripture* (Philadelphia: Fortress, 1979) 361–62.

ways, O house of Israel'" (36:32). Is it, then, out of love for Israel that YHWH acts to deliver her? Even in ch. 16, which relates the story of the foundling girl, all the phrases used appear to be either legal or sexual; we do not find here much evidence of warmth of affection;[24] moreover, the reference is to the original election of Israel, from which she subsequently fell away, rather than to a promise of restoration. In ch. 23, the allegory of Oholah and Oholibah, the language of warmth and affection is absent too, and in ch. 24, in which the destruction of the sanctuary at Jerusalem is compared to Ezekiel's loss of his wife (24:16), at no point is the sanctuary spoken of as loved by YHWH himself. Neither the word אַהֲבָה ("love") nor the word חֶסֶד ("steadfast love, kindness"), or related forms, are ever used in Ezekiel in connection with YHWH. We shall not, it seems, find in the love of YHWH the basic reason for his restoration of Israel.

The primary motivation of the dramatic initiative of restoration is summed up rather in our third formula, that which speaks of YHWH acting for the sake of his "name" (שֵׁם). Ezekiel 36:22 provides a typical example: "It is not for your sake, O house of Israel, that I am about to act, but for the sake of my holy name, which you have profaned among the nations to which you came." There are fourteen references to the divine "name" in Ezekiel. On five occasions reference is made to YHWH "acting" for the sake of his name (20:9, 14, 22, 44; 36:22). He is also said to "have concern for" his name (36:21), to "sanctify" his name (36:23), to "make known" his name (39:7), and to "be jealous for" his name (39:25). It is of particular importance that the verb with which the divine "name" most frequently appears is חלל, "to profane." Profanation of the "name" is mentioned on no less than nine occasions (20:9, 14, 22, 39; 36:20, 21, 22, 23; 39:7). A high proportion of the cases of the word in Ezekiel occur in two significant passages. The first of these is ch. 20, which presents a survey of Israel's long history of sin, as an illustration of the wayward inclinations of this nation. Three times it is said that YHWH had resolved to punish his people as they deserved, but on each occasion he withheld his hand (20:9, 14, 22). YHWH's restraint is explained in all three cases (with only minor variations) in the words: "But I acted for the sake of

---

24. M. E. Shields, "Multiple Exposures: Body Rhetoric and Gender Characterization in Ezekiel 16," *Journal of Feminist Studies in Religion* 14 (1998) 5–18; reprinted in *Prophets and Daniel*, ed. A. Brenner, 137–53, A Feminist Companion to the Bible (Second Series) (London: Sheffield Academic, 2001).

my name, so that it should not be profaned in the sight of the nations, in whose sight I had brought them out." The other passage, 36:20–32, looks forward to YHWH's imminent deliverance of Israel; we read that when the people of Israel were exiled among the nations, they profaned YHWH's "holy name," for it was said of them, "These are the people of the LORD, and yet they had to go out of his land" (36:20). As a result, YHWH had concern for his "holy name," declaring "It is not for your sake, O house of Israel, that I am about to act, but for the sake of my holy name" (36:22). Both of these passages, then, speak of the profanation of the "name" of YHWH and state that it is for the sake of this "name" that YHWH acts to spare an undeserving Israel. In both it would seem that the primary purpose of YHWH's activity is the vindication of his reputation; but what aspect of his reputation is particularly in mind? The profanation of the divine "name" appears to consist essentially in the casting of doubt upon YHWH's power and effectiveness. The words that the nations utter in 36:20, "These are the people of the LORD, and yet they had to go out of his land," amount to a charge that YHWH was too weak to prevent other nations (aided presumably by their gods) from exiling his people. The nations express similar opinions elsewhere in Ezekiel too, as in 25:8 and 35:10. That it is essentially the power of YHWH that is questioned by the nations is confirmed by the fact that it is the restoration of Israel that will ultimately vindicate his "name" in their eyes. The nations have misinterpreted Israel's defeat as a sign of YHWH's weakness. He must now (even at the cost of waiving the rigor of his judgement) act to correct this misconception and vindicate his reputation as a powerful god. It would not be inaccurate to say that in Ezekiel YHWH in this way acts out of "divine self-interest."

The fourth and last feature of the language of Ezekiel that gives clear expression to his God-centered emphasis is the theme of divine holiness (Heb. קֹדֶשׁ). The "name" of YHWH often appears in the fuller form "holy name" (e.g., 36:22), while in 36:23 YHWH is spoken of as "vindicating the holiness of" (NRSV: "sanctifying") his "great name." It would seem, then, that there is in Ezekiel a close association between the divine "name" and words to do with holiness. In addition to the nine occasions when the noun קֹדֶשׁ, "holiness," is used with "name," the verb קדשׁ is frequently employed in closely related contexts. We find in the use of this verb in Ezekiel a strongly theocentric focus. This is underlined by the fact that the subject is normally YHWH himself (the verb generally having a reflexive sense: "I will vindicate my holiness," "I will sanctify myself"). The emphasis on the holiness of YHWH in Ezekiel is not without parallel elsewhere. There are particularly close affinities between Ezekiel and the Holiness Code (Lev 17–26), as was demonstrated by Reventlow.[25] It seems likely that Ezekiel's use of the root קדשׁ owes something also to previous prophetic usage, notably that of Isaiah of Jerusalem, as was argued by Bettenzoli.[26] Nevertheless, as Muilenburg wrote, "Ezekiel's awareness of the divine holiness is more awesome, more sublime and majestic, more cosmic and 'tremendous' than that of his prophetic predecessors."[27] The motif of divine holiness in Ezekiel gains particular force from the fact that it forms part of a network of interrelated themes. To a remarkable degree, language pertaining to the holiness of YHWH occurs together with and shares the emphases of the other formulae here reviewed. We may note also that the phrase "in the sight of the nations" or a related formula is almost always to be found where the verb קדשׁ is used in Ezekiel. Moreover, every such case occurs in conjunction with the "I am YHWH" formula (or a variation upon it). Furthermore, in those passages in which the verb קדשׁ is used, the theme of the vindication of YHWH's power is usually prominent (as in 28:22; 36:23; 38:23).

It is in such a context that we read of the gift of a "new heart" and a "new spirit" (36:26–27; cf. 11:19), the primary purpose of which is to preclude the otherwise inevitable danger of YHWH having to punish his people again, with the renewed risk of the profanation of his "name" that would bring. Israel's response is so important that YHWH himself promises to make it possible. This paradoxical conception raises the question of how far the responsibility of Israel remains intact. Echoes of the theme of Israel's responsibility do remain, even in chapter 36: Israel is to "be careful to observe my ordinances" (36:27) and she is to loathe herself for her iniquities and her abominable deeds (36:31). Ultimately, however, since obedience is guaranteed, it would seem that

---

25. Henning Graf Reventlow, *Das Heiligkeitsgesetz, formgeschichtlich untersucht*, WMANT 6 (Neukirchen: Neukirchener, 1961).

26. G. Bettenzoli, *Geist der Heiligkeit. Traditionsgeschichtliche Untersuchung des QDS-Begriffes im Buch Ezechiel*, Quaderni di Semitistica 8 (Florence: Instituto di Linguistica e di Lingue Orientali, 1979).

27. J. Muilenburg, "Ezekiel," in *Peake's Commentary on the Bible*, ed. M. Black and H. H. Rowley, 568–690 (London: Nelson, 1962) 622.

the responsibility of Israel has been subsumed in the overriding initiative of YHWH. At times even the presentation of judgement in Ezekiel is so God-centered that Israel's responsibility seems to be undercut. This is seen in the reference to the punishment of the prophet whom YHWH himself has deceived (14:9–10) and in the bizarre verse that speaks of YHWH giving to his sinful people "statutes that were not good and ordinances by which they could not live" (Ezek 20:25). Even such things as these can, it seems, be traced to this paradoxical God—"so that they might know that I am the LORD" (20:26). This trend is all the more marked in the material relating to deliverance. If in 20:25–26 YHWH enables sin that he might be known, in chapter 36 he enables obedience for the sake of his "name": "It is not for your sake, O house of Israel, that I am about to act, but for the sake of my holy name ... A new heart I will give you, and a new spirit I will put within you; and I will remove from your body the heart of stone and give you a heart of flesh. I will put my spirit within you, and make you follow my statutes and be careful to observe my ordinances" (36:22, 26–27). In this dramatic initiative of moral transformation of the nation, the God of Israel acts for the sake of his holy name. In short, YHWH acts because he is YHWH and must be known to be YHWH.

Ezekiel is not a great innovator in the area of individualism, as many have supposed. But he does give a presentation of the divine in relation to humanity so theocentric that his is in many ways the most God-centered book in the Bible. Here and nowhere else is to be found the core of Ezekiel's distinctive contribution to the moral transformation of Israel.

Bibliography

Baker, John Austin. *The Foolishness of God*. London: Darton, Longman & Todd, 1970.

Bettenzoli, G. *Geist der Heiligkeit. Traditionsgeschichtliche Untersuchung des QDS-Begriffes im Buch Ezechiel*. Quaderni di Semitistica 8. Florence: Instituto di Linguistica e di Lingue Orientali, 1979.

Causse, A. *Du groupe ethnique à la communauté religieuse: Le problème sociologique de la réligion d'Israél*. Paris: Alcan, 1937.

Childs, Brevard S. *Introduction to the Old Testament as Scripture*. Philadelphia: Fortress, 1979.

Darr, Katheryn Pfisterer. "Proverb Performance and Transgenerational Retribution in Ezekiel 18." In *Ezekiel's Hierarchical World: Wrestling with a Tiered Reality*, edited by S. L. Cook and C. L. Patton, 199–223. SBLSymS 31. Atlanta: SBL, 2004.

Davidson, A. B. *The Theology of the Old Testament*. Edinburgh: T. & T. Clark, 1904.
Fohrer, Georg. *Introduction to the Old Testament*. Translated by David E. Green. London: SPCK, 1970.
Irwin, W. A. *The Problem of Ezekiel: An Inductive Study*. Chicago: University of Chicago Press, 1943.
Joyce, Paul M. *Divine Initiative and Human Response in Ezekiel*. JSOTSup 51. Sheffield: JSOT Press, 1989.
———. *Ezekiel: A Commentary*. LHBOTS 482. London: T. & T. Clark, 2007.
———. "King and Messiah in Ezekiel." In *King and Messiah in Israel and the Ancient Near East: Proceedings of the Oxford Old Testament Seminar*, edited by J. Day, 323–37. JSOTSup 270. Sheffield: Sheffield Academic, 1998.
Kaminsky, Joel S. *Corporate Responsibility in the Hebrew Bible*. JSOTSup 196. Sheffield: Sheffield Academic, 1995.
Lapsley, Jacqueline E. *Can These Bones Live? The Problem of the Moral Self in the Book of Ezekiel*. BZAW 301. Berlin: de Gruyter, 2000.
Lindblom, J. *Prophecy in Ancient Israel*. Oxford: Blackwell, 1962.
Matties, G. H. *Ezekiel 18 and the Rhetoric of Moral Discourse*. SBLDS 126. Atlanta: Scholars Press, 1990.
Mein, Andrew R. *Ezekiel and the Ethics of Exile*. OTMS. Oxford: Oxford University Press, 2001.
Morgan, Donn F. *Wisdom in the Old Testament Traditions*. Atlanta: John Knox, 1981.
Muilenburg, J. "Ezekiel." In *Peake's Commentary on the Bible*, edited by M. Black and H. H. Rowley, 568–690. London: Nelson, 1962.
Odell, Margaret S. "The Inversion of Shame and Forgiveness in Ezekiel 16:59–63." *JSOT* 56 (1992) 101–12.
Raitt, Thomas M. *A Theology of Exile: Judgment/Deliverance in Jeremiah and Ezekiel*. Philadelphia: Fortress, 1977.
Reventlow, Henning Graf. *Das Heiligkeitsgesetz, formgeschichtlich untersucht*. WMANT 6. Neukirchen-Vluyn: Neukirchener, 1961.
Shields, M. E. "Multiple Exposures: Body Rhetoric and Gender Characterization in Ezekiel 16." *Journal of Feminist Studies in Religion* 14 (1998) 5–18. Reprinted in *Prophets and Daniel*, edited by A. Brenner, 137–53. A Feminist Companion to the Bible (Second Series). London: Sheffield Academic, 2001.
Smith-Christopher, Daniel L. *A Biblical Theology of Exile*. OBT. Minneapolis: Fortress, 2002.
Stiebert, J. "Shame and Prophecy: Approaches Past and Present." *BibInt* 8 (2000) 255–75.
———. *The Construction of Shame in the Hebrew Bible: The Prophetic Contribution*. JSOTSup 346. Sheffield: Sheffield Academic, 2002.
Whitley, C. F. *The Exilic Age*. London: Longmans, Green and Co., 1957.
Winton Thomas, D. "The Sixth Century B.C.: A Creative Epoch in the History of Israel." *JSS* 6 (1961) 33–46.
Young, Frances, and David F. Ford. *Meaning and Truth in 2 Corinthians*. Biblical Foundations in Theology. London: SPCK, 1987.
Zimmerli, Walther. "Das Wort des göttlichen Selbsterweises (Erweiswort), eine prophetische Gattung." In *Mélanges Bibliques rédigés en l'honneur de André Robert*, 154–64. Travaux de l'Institut Catholique de Paris 4. Paris: Bloud et

Gay, 1957. Reprinted in *Gottes Offenbarung: Gesammelte Aufsätze I*, 120–32. Theologische Bücherei 19. Munich: Kaiser, 1963.

———. *Erkenntnis Gottes nach dem Buch Ezechiel. Eine theologische Studie*. Abhandlungen zur Theologie des Alten und Neuen Testaments 27. Zürich: Zwingli-Verlag, 1954. Reprint, *Gottes Offenbarung: Gesammelte Aufsätze I*, 41–119. Theologische Bücherei 19. Munich: Kaiser, 1963.

———. *Ezekiel 1: A Commentary on the Book of the Prophet Ezekiel, Chapters 1–24*. Translated by Ronald E. Clements. Hermeneia. Philadelphia: Fortress, 1979.

———. *I am Yahweh*. Edited by W. Brueggemann. Translated by Douglas W. Stott. Atlanta: John Knox, 1982.

———. "Ich bin Yahweh." In *Geschichte und Altes Testament: A. Alt zum 70. Geburtstag dargebracht*, edited by W. F. Albright, 179–209. Beiträge zur historischen Theologie 16. Tübingen: Mohr/Siebeck, 1953. Reprint, *Gottes Offenbarung: Gesammelte Aufsätze I*, 11–40. ThBü 19. Munich: Kaiser, 1963.

6

Transformation of History in Ezekiel 20

Thomas Krüger

THE BOOK OF EZEKIEL IS THE RESULT OF A PROCESS OF THEOLOGICAL reflection and discussion. According to the dated oracles this process extended at least from 593 to 571 BCE. Additions in chapter 37[1] as well as the differences between MT and LXX[2] indicate that this process was still going on in the second century BCE. The scholarly discussion shows how difficult it is to reconstruct the literary development of the book as a whole and its various texts.[3] In the following considerations I will, therefore, largely abstain from redaction historical hypotheses. Instead, I will try to show some developments on the conceptual level that do not necessarily correspond to literary developments (since it is

---

1. Rüdiger Bartelmus, "Ez 37,1-14: die Verbform weqatal und die Anfänge der Auferstehungshoffnung," *ZAW* 97 (1985) 366-89.

2. Peter Schwagmeier, "Untersuchungen zu Textgeschichte und Entstehung des Ezechielbuches in masoretischer und griechischer Überlieferung," diss. theol., Zürich, 2004.

3. See, for example, the commentaries by W. Zimmerli (*Ezekiel 1 /2*, Hermeneia [Philadelphia: Fortress, 1979 and 1983]), L. C. Allen (*Ezekiel 1-19/20-48*, WBC 28/29 [Dallas: Word, 1994 and 1990]) and K-F. Pohlmann (*Das Buch des Propheten Hesekiel/Ezechiel 1-19/20-48*, ATD 22,1/2 [Göttingen: Vandenhoeck & Ruprecht, 1996 and 2001]), and the chapters on Ezekiel in E. Zenger et al., *Einleitung in das Alte Testament*, 6th ed. (Stuttgart: Kohlhammer, 2006); or C. H. Römer et al., *Introduction à l'Ancien Testament* (Geneva: Labor et Fides, 2004). Greenberg's hypothesis that the masoretic version is virtually the product of the prophet Ezekiel is highly improbable (M. Greenberg, *Ezekiel 1-20*, AB 22 [Garden City, NY: Doubleday, 1983] 18-27). For a comprehensive review of scholarly research on the book of Ezekiel in the last decades see K-F. Pohlmann, *Ezechiel: Der Stand der theologischen Diskussion* (Darmstadt: Wissenschaftliche Buchgesellschaft, 2008). On Ezekiel 20, in particular, see pp. 148-53.

not unusual that different texts written at the same time represent different levels of conceptual development), but may provide indications for their reconstruction.

Israel's History in Ezekiel 20[4]

The structure of Ezekiel 20 can be outlined as follows:[5]

—Introduction (vv. 1–3): *present*
    Setting: inquiry of the elders (v. 1)
    Speech of Yahweh: rejection of the inquiry (vv. 2–3)
—Speech of Yahweh (vv. 4–44)
    Introduction: order to the prophet to speak (vv. 4–5a): *present*
    Review of Israel's *past* (vv. 5a–29)
        Israel's first generation in Egypt (vv. 5a–10)
        Israel's first generation in the desert (vv. 11–17)
        Israel's second generation in the desert (vv. 18–26)
        The ancestors of the present Israelites in the land (vv. 27–29)
    Consequences for Israel's *present* (vv. 30–31)
    Future prospects (vv. 32–44)
        Judgment in the "desert of the nations" (vv. 32–38)
        Restitution of the "house of Israel" in the "land of Israel" (vv. 39–44)

The Present (vv. 1–5, 30–31)

The setting of Ezekiel 20 (vv. 1–4) is comparable to that of chapters 8 and 14: in the year 591 or 592 BCE certain elders of the exilic commu-

---

4. In addition to the commentaries, see J. Lust, *Traditie, redactie en kerygma bij Ezechiel: Een analyse van Ez., XX,1–26*, Verhandelingen van de Koninklijke Vlaamse Academie voor Wetenschappen, Letteren en Schone Kunsten van België, Klasse der Letteren 65 (Brussel: Paleis der Academie, 1969); T. Krüger, *Geschichtskonzepte im Ezechielbuch*, BZAW 180 (Berlin: de Gruyter, 1989); F. Sedlmeier, *Studien zu Komposition und Theologie von Ezechiel 20*, SBB 21 (Stuttgart: Katholisches Bibelwerk, 1990); S. Ohnesorge, *Jahwe gestaltet sein Volk neu: Zur Sicht der Zukunft Israels nach Ez 11,14–21; 20,1–44; 36,16–38; 37,1–14.15–28*, FB 64 (Würzburg: Echter, 1991); R. Bartelmus, "Menschlicher Misserfolg und Jahwes Initiative: Beobachtungen zum Geschichtsbild des deuteronomistischen Rahmens im Richterbuch und zum geschichtstheologischen Entwurf in Ez 20," *Biblische Notizen* 70 (1993) 28–47.

5. Krüger, *Geschichtskonzepte*, 202–3.

nity come to the prophet to consult Yahweh.⁶ As in chapter 14, Yahweh refuses to answer their questions, including perhaps questions concerning lawsuits within the community.⁷ Instead, he charges the prophet Ezekiel to judge his audience and to let them know the abominations of their ancestors. As in chapter 14, the elders and the community they represent are accused of worshipping idols and sacrificing their children,⁸ which is seen as incompatible with the worship of Yahweh. So they have no relationship with Yahweh, and Yahweh is not obliged to fulfill their requests. However, chapter 20 takes a step forward, accusing not only the present audience of the prophet but also their remote ancestors. And unlike chapter 14, Ezekiel 20 does not call on the audience to repent and turn away from their idols and abominations (see also chap. 18) but prompts them to go and serve their idols and to part with Yahweh and his cult (20:39). Apparently, Yahweh is no longer interested in Israel. Or should this order be understood ironically?

The Past (vv. 5–29)

Ezekiel 20:5–29 recounts the history of Israel from its beginnings in Egypt up to the present. The narrative focuses on the beginnings. Of the twenty-five verses, thirteen deal with the first generation of the exodus in Egypt and in the desert (vv. 5–17), nine verses are about the second generation in the desert and in the land (vv. 18–26), and only three verses tell of all the following generations of Israelites living in the land up to the exile (vv. 27–29).⁹ The strong focus on the beginnings of Israel's history in chapter 20 is contrary to the focus on Samaria's and Jerusalem's history in the land in chapter 23 (in chapter 16, Jerusalem appears to have been in the land of Canaan since its birth). In contrast

---

6. B. Lang, *Ezechiel: Der Prophet und das Buch*, EF 153 (Darmstadt: Wissenschaftliche Buchgesellschaft, 1981) 35 (August 14, 591); E. Kutsch, *Die chronologischen Daten des Ezechielbuches*, OBO 62 (Göttingen: Vandenhoeck & Ruprecht, 1985) 60 (August 24, 592).

7. To "judge" the people (20:4; cf. 22:2; 23:36) can mean to administer justice for them as well as to confront them with the divine judgment on them.

8. It is disputed whether (and how) the Israelites did really sacrifice children, e.g., W. Zwickel, "Menschenopfer," in *Neues Bibellexikon*, ed. by Manfred Görg and Bernhard Lang (Zurich: Benziger, 1995) 2:765–66.

9. Verses 27–29 are usually viewed as a later addition, see Allen, *Ezekiel 20–48*, 6; Sedlmeier, *Ezechiel 20*, 105, 275; S. Ohnesorge, *Jahwe gestaltet sein Volk neu*, 88; Pohlmann, *Hesekiel/Ezechiel 20–48*, 309.

to most other texts of the Book of Ezekiel, in chapter 20 the present situation of Israel, its dispersion among the nations, is not a consequence of its behavior in the land. Already in the desert, before he brought them into the land, Yahweh told the Israelites that he would "scatter them among the nations and disperse them through the countries" (v. 23).[10]

The presentation of Yahweh's attitude against Israel's first two generations in Egypt and in the desert in Ezek 20:5–26 is highly ambiguous. Yahweh turned toward the Israelites and "chose" them (v. 5) without any discernible reason. He promised them to bring them out of the land of Egypt (which is not explicitly called a "house of slavery," but is apparently understood so) into a land he had searched out for them (v. 6). Yahweh held to this promise and eventually fulfilled it, even though with some unforeseen delay (v. 10, 28). This delay was caused by the Israelite's tenacious refusal to actualize and complete their liberation from Egypt set off by Yahweh. They did not part with the gods whom they worshipped in Egypt and who held them in slavery or at least did not help them to get free (vv. 7–8). And they refused to follow the laws and instructions Yahweh gave them to perpetuate their freedom, and to keep the Sabbaths as social symbols of freedom and equality (v. 11–13, 16, 18–21, 24).[11] Israel's rebellion provoked Yahweh's anger. But Yahweh did not follow his just impulse to punish, or even kill, the Israelites, but rather "acted for the sake of his name, that it should not be profaned in the eyes of the nations" who had witnessed the promises he made to the Israelites and his actions to lead them out of Egypt (vv. 8–9, 13–14, 21–22). So Yahweh eventually fulfilled his promises, but at the same time announced to scatter the Israelites among the nations (v. 23).

Yahweh's treatment of the Israelites in the land (vv. 27–29) shows similar ambiguities. On the one hand, Yahweh appears to have lost any interest in the Israelites. He no longer admonishes them to change their behavior, as he did with the first two generations in the desert. His commentary about their cultic activities (v. 29) sounds rather mocking than reproving. Having given their ancestors bad laws and statutes "by which they could not live" (v. 25), Yahweh actually appears to have completely

---

10. Cf. Lev 26:27–33; Deut 4:25–28; 28:64–68; 31:16–29; 32.

11. It has to be pointed out that the text does not expressly connect the exodus from Egypt, the laws, the sabbaths and the "idols" with the topics of slavery and liberation. However, it appears reasonable to assume that the addressees of the text would make such associations. Cf. the metaphorical depiction of the "oppression" in Egypt in 23:2.

disabled Israel from repenting—even more, to "defile" them by acting according to his commandments (v. 26). "The notion that God misled the people so that He could then condemn them for it is found also in [Ezekiel] 14.9."[12] It may offend modern readers of the Bible. However, like the "hardening of the heart" of Israel in Isa 6:9ff. (cf. 63:17) or Pharaoh in Exodus 4–11,[13] Yahweh's bad laws and statutes in Ezekiel 20 prevent people who are already acting wrongly from changing their mind and behavior. There is no radical difference between this notion and the notion that Yahweh kills people who are guilty, which is widespread in the book of Ezekiel as well as in the whole Hebrew Bible. In both cases Yahweh does not treat the Israelites arbitrarily, but punishes them by misleading them or by killing them.

However, according to Ezek 20:26 Yahweh does not only "defile" (טמא, piel) the Israelites by giving them bad laws and statutes; another intention of his acting is described by the Hebrew verb שׁמם (hiphil; למען אשמם). It is translated as "devastate," "ravage," or the like or as "appall," "horrify," or the like.[14] With regard to Ezek 3:15 and 32:10, the latter translation appears to be preferable. At any rate, the text is at least ambiguous. It can be understood in the sense that Yahweh wants to "corrupt" the Israelites by their acting according to his bad laws. However, it can also be read as an expression of Yahweh's wish that the Israelites might be "appalled" at killing their firstborn animals and probably also their firstborn children (v. 31) and that they might stop doing so, even if a deity had commanded them to do so (The latter had not urged them to follow Yahweh's earlier statutes and ordinances!). If they had not recognized that Yahweh's earlier commandments helped them to preserve and to foster life, perhaps they would learn it when they had to obey commands that made them kill animals and humans. However, if Yahweh cherished hopes like that, they were frustrated. Unlike his earlier statutes and ordinances the Israelites readily followed his bad

---

12. M. A. Sweeney, "Ezekiel," in *The Jewish Study Bible*, ed. by Adele Berlin and Marc Zvi Brettler (Oxford & New York: Oxford University Press, 2004) 1078.

13. Greenberg, *Ezekiel 1–20*, 369.

14. BDB offers 1. "devastate," "ravage" (Ezek 20:26, 30:12, 14); 2. "appal," "shew horror" (Ezek 3:15, 32:10). HALOT suggests 1. "to cause to be deserted, cause to be desolated" (Ezek 30:12, 14); 2. "to cause to be dumbfounded, disconcerted, awestruck" (Ezek 3:15, 20:26, 32:10). LXX uses the verb ἀφανίσω ("to destroy, ruin"), but has no equivalent for למען אשר ידעו אשר אני יהוה. Peshitta uses אבד, aphel ("to make perish"). Vulgate translates למען אשמם as *propter delicta sua* (שׁם) = "guilt").

commandments and apparently were not appalled at them up to the present.

Thus, according to Ezekiel 20, Israel's past reveals a rather complex picture of the interactions between Yahweh and Israel which are witnessed by other nations. They cannot easily be classified as good or bad, salutary or baneful. It is also impossible to distinguish within Israel's past a period in which the relationship between Yahweh and Israel was intact and untarnished from a period in which Israel rebelled against Yahweh;[15] the Israelites rebelled against Yahweh already in the very beginning of their relationship. So every action of Yahweh can at the same time be understood (1) as an expression of his intention to create Israel as a community which is free and in which people can live in freedom, (2) as a consequence of his anger about Israel's permanent refusal to understand itself as such a community, and (3) as an attempt to establish for himself a good reputation as a god among the nations surrounding Israel.

These aspects or dimensions of Yahweh's actions sometimes fit together more or less neatly. In other instances there is some tension between them or they even mutually exclude each other. So for example, when Yahweh refuses to lead the Exodus generation into the promised land, it satisfies his intention to punish them, and at the same time opens the possibility that a new generation of Israelites would be more willing to act as a liberated community according to Yahweh's imagination. However, it also jeopardizes Yahweh's reputation among the nations. But this danger can easily be eliminated when Yahweh leads the next generation into the promised land. Later on, it appears to be more difficult to reconcile the different aspects of Yahweh's actions. When he leads the second generation into the land and at the same time announces that he will scatter them among the nations and give them bad laws and instructions, it can be understood as an expression of his anger about Israel's constant rebelliousness. However, does it mean that Yahweh failed in his attempt to create Israel as a community of freedom? And does not this failure jeopardize his reputation among the nations once again? Or is this whole period of Israel's living in the

---

15. See, for example, the contrast between the times of the exodus and the wandering in the desert as an ideal early period of the history of Israel and the negative view of the following period of Israel's living in Canaan in the book of Hosea (see K. Koch *Die Profeten I: Assyrische Zeit* [Stuttgart: Kohlhammer, 1995] 174ff.).

land up to the exile only one part of more comprehensive arrangements by which Yahweh will finally realize his original intentions and establish a good reputation among the nations? This will become clearer when we turn to the view of the future in Ezekiel 20.

Yahweh's actions and attitudes are complex and ambiguous, and Israel's are as well. After their constant rebellion against Yahweh and his commandments it is rather amazing that the Israelites apparently follow without reservation the bad laws and instructions which Yahweh gave them. It appears to be no problem for them that Yahweh demands their animals and probably also their children from them, whereas they refused to obey his former laws and commandments giving life and ensuring freedom. From the Israelites' point of view they do now, unlike their ancestors in the wilderness, follow Yahweh's instructions. But Yahweh apparently does not want them simply to do what he says. He wants them to do what is good, what advances life and freedom. In the view of the text, this distinguishes Yahweh from the other gods. Therefore Israel can only worship Yahweh *or* the other gods, but not Yahweh *and* the other gods.

The Future (vv. 32–49)

Ezekiel 20 closes with two predictions. The first one (vv. 32–38) begins with the statement that the Israelites' wish will never come about, namely, to be a people like all other nations and to worship their gods (including Yahweh, of whom they came to inquire, v. 1) just as all other people worship their gods (v. 32). For Yahweh will gather the Israelites from the nations and countries where they are scattered, bring them into "the desert of the nations," and single out the "rebels" among them.[16] Only those who pass this purgative judgment will enter the land of Israel and constitute a new community (v. 33–38). This implies that not all Israelites favor the program of cultural assimilation quoted in v. 32. There are also those who accept Yahweh's demand to be worshiped as Israel's only god and in a singular and distinct way according to his own (former) statutes and ordinances—including Ezekiel and like-minded

---

16. This judgment in the "desert of the peoples" is explicitly characterized as an analogue to the judgment on the Exodus generation in the "desert of the Land of Egypt." However, the latter had not been a judgment in which individual rebels were sorted out from the community, and it had not been very successful, since its survivors turned out to be equally rebellious as their parents.

persons—and possibly there will also be those who change their mind in light of the oracle delivered to them in this chapter. They will be the nucleus of a new Israel in its former homeland. All others will be excluded from the land of Israel and left behind in the "desert of the nations"—but obviously also stay alive there.

The second prediction (vv. 39–44) begins with a call to Israel to go and serve their idols. Thereafter, the text continues, the Israelites will certainly listen to Yahweh and no longer profane his holy name with their gifts and their idols (v. 39).[17] This appears to imply that the Israelites will in the course of time grow disgusted with their idolatrous worship, give it up and begin to worship Yahweh alone in a way that is compatible with his character as Israel's liberator (cf. Deut 4:27ff.). Verses 40–44 then describe Israel's future worship of Yahweh in the land. Now, Israel will be the community which Yahweh wanted it to be from the outset. So, finally, Yahweh has achieved his aim and manifested his holiness among Israel in the sight of the nations (v. 41). Israel's misconduct will not be ignored or forgotten. The Israelites will remember their corrupt deeds and will be ashamed by Yahweh's acting for his name's sake, not according to their evil ways (v. 44).

At first glance, the two predictions in vv. 32–38 and vv. 39–44 contradict and mutually exclude each other. Verse 32 tells the Israelites that they will fail if they try to be like the other nations and worship idols. Verse 39 calls them to do precisely that. Verses 33–38 announce a purgative judgment by which Yahweh will sort out all rebels from Israel and exclude them from the return to the land of Israel. According to vv.

---

17. This understanding of v. 39 is based on an interpretation of the conditional clause "if you will not listen to me ..." as an elliptic oath: "surely, you will listen to me and no longer profane my holy name ..." (so NIV and the German "Einheitsübersetzung," as well as the new "Zürcher Bibel"). The possible alternative translation "and afterwards, if you don't listen to me, you will no longer profane my holy name ..." makes little sense in the context (Krüger, *Geschichtskonzepte*, 260; Pohlmann, *Hesekiel/Ezechiel 20–48*, 301). The widespread interpretation of the imperatives "go and serve your idols" as ironic and the following "and/but afterward, if you will not listen to me ..." as "introducing an unspoken threat" is difficult, because it supposes that "to listen to Yahweh" here means not to do what he has said immediately before (K. Pfisterer Darr, "The Book of Ezekiel," in *The New Interpreter's Bible*, ed. by Leander E. Keck et al. [Nashville: Abingdon, 2001] 6:1290; see also, Greenberg, *Ezekiel 1–20*, 374; Allen, *Ezekiel 20–48*, 4). NRSV's translation "Go serve your idols, everyone of you now and hereafter, if you will not listen to me; but my holy name you shall no more profane ..." (so KJV, NJPS) would make sense in the context, but is hardly justifiable in view of the Hebrew text (וְאַחַר does not mean "now and hereafter").

40–44 the Israelites who finally return to the land will remember their wicked ways and deeds and know that they are not worthy of coming back to their homeland. These tensions and contradictions disappear if vv. 32–38 are removed. So it seems possible that this section of the text is a later insertion between v. 31 and vv. 39–44 which followed v. 31 immediately in the original text.[18]

However, it is also possible to read v. 32–44 as a meaningful sequence of events.[19] Verse 39 does not contradict v. 32 but affirms that statement: Even if the addressees "go and serve their idols" (v. 39) because they "want to be like the nations" (v. 32) they will eventually come back to Yahweh, so that their intention will finally be frustrated, as v. 32 said. When read after vv. 33–38, vv. 40–44 express the confidence that even the "rebels" who have been singled out in the "desert of the nations" (v. 38) will eventually return to Yahweh and join the new Israel, so that in the end "the *entire* house of Israel, *all* of them" (כל בית ישראל כלה) will worship Yahweh.[20] The memory of Israel's past wrongdoing will then be shared by all Israelites (v. 43)—and

---

18. The contradictions between vv. 32–38 and vv. 39–44 could also be removed by eliminating vv. 39–44 from the original text. However, it is difficult to understand v. 38 as the conclusion of chap. 20 in its original extent. See Pohlmann, *Ezechiel*, 149.

19. In *Geschichtskonzepte*, I proposed to understand vv. 32–38 and vv. 39–44 as alternative possibilities of the creation of a new Israel (270–73). T. Renz has characterized the alternative as "salvation by elimination or transformation" and argued that "vv. 39–44 may well presuppose and allude to a purification by elimination" as described in v. 32–38 (*The Rhetorical Function of the Book of Ezekiel*, SVT 76 [Leiden: Brill, 1999] 175, n. 116). I agree with Renz that vv. 32–38 and vv. 39–44 can (at least on the editorial level of the present text) be understood as a sequence of events. However, vv. 32–38 do not speak of an "elimination" of the "rebels" against Yahweh, and v. 39 can be understood to mean that even they will later return to Yahweh. (Renz follows the interpretation of v. 39 by the NRSV which is, in my view, philologically impossible [ibid., 174]). Therefore I would now propose to understand v. 32–38 as a depiction of the constitution of the new Israel and vv. 39–44 as a depiction of its completion (see v. 40: "all the house of Israel, all of them").

20. Thus Ezekiel 20 appears to anticipate (and its authors appear to look back on) a longer period of post-exilic (and post-diaspora) restoration with conflicts between earlier and later repatriates (Pohlmann, *Ezechiel*, 65ff.; *Ezechielstudien*; T. Krüger, "'An den Strömen von Babylon . . .': Erwägungen zu Zeitbezug und Sachverhalt in Psalm 137," in *Sachverhalt und Zeitbezug: Semitistische und alttestamentliche Studien, Adolf Denz zum 65. Geburtstag*, ed. by Rüdiger Bartelmus and Norbert Nebes [Wiesbaden: Harrassowitz, 2001] 79–84).

remind them that none of them has deserved to be a member of the new Israel which is established by Yahweh "for his name's sake" (v. 44).[21]

One significant difference between Israel's past and its future is that in the past Israel has always been a homogenous collective of rebels against Yahweh, whereas in the future there will be (at least for a while) a division between one part of Israel which is (already) loyal to Yahweh (and is living in the land of Israel), and another part of Israel which (still) assimilates to the other nations and their civilizations (among which it is living). But in the end "all the house of Israel, all of them, shall serve Yahweh in the land" (v. 40).

The text appears to be confident that the worship of Yahweh will finally prevail over the worship of other gods and idols, not because of the power of Yahweh and his threat to kill idolaters, but due to the experience that it is in the long run the better way of life. Therefore it does not call its addressees to "repentance"—even though it in all likelihood tries to convince them to share its view of Israel's past, present and future. In contrast to chapters 3, 18 and 33 there is no imminent danger of death which could be averted by changing one's behavior. All Israelites will be judged in the "desert of the nations"—and sooner or later all Israelites will join the new community in the former homeland. The individual Israelites possibly are able to define their place in the course of Israel's future history. However, some, if not most, of them at first may have to "live like the nations" in order to learn to estimate the advantages of worshiping Yahweh. The future history of Israel does not depend on the present decision of the individual Israelites, not because Yahweh determines it against or irrespective of their decisions, but because the worship of Yahweh will prevail in the long run by the power of persuasion.[22]

---

21. Obviously, even those who were not singled out as rebels in the "desert of the nations" should not think that they deserved to be members of a new Israel.

22. B. Schwartz, "Repentance and Determinism in Ezekiel," in *Proceedings of the Eleventh World Congress of Jewish Studies, Division A: The Bible and Its World* (Jerusalem: The Magnes Press, 1994) 123–30; "Ezekiel's Dim View of Israel's Restoration," in *The Book of Ezekiel: Theological and Anthropological Perspectives*, ed. by Margaret S. Odell and John T. Strong, SBLSymS 9 (Atlanta: Society of Biblical Literature, 2000) 43–67. Schwartz rightly points out that in Ezekiel 20 Israel's repentance is not a prerequisite of its restoration. One may call the view of history in this chapter "deterministic." However, that does not mean that there is absolutely no space for human freedom. One goal of Yahweh in his history with Israel is that the Israelites should learn to discern good and

Transformations of the View of Israel's History in Ezekiel 20

In his commentary, Karl-Friedrich Pohlmann rightly points out that Ezekiel 20 puts forward a reflection of history that widely outruns and encompasses all other statements in the book of Ezekiel.[23] In the present

---

evil actions and ways of life and to act and behave accordingly. This kind of divine determination does not collide with human freedom but provide human freedom, and it does not prevail by force but by the power of persuasion.

Lapsley, too, points out "the tension between the language of repentance and the language of determinism in the book" in view of texts like 3:16ff., 14:12ff., 18 and 33:1ff., on the one hand, and 16, 20 and 23f. as well as 11:19 and 36:26, on the other hand (J. E. Lapsley, *Can These Bones Live? The Problem of the Moral Self in the Book of Ezekiel*, BZAW 301 [Berlin: W. de Gruyter, 2000] 6; cf. also Joyce, *Divine Initiative*, and Pohlmann, *Ezechiel*, 168ff.). However, the problem appears to be rather the compatibility of human freedom and divine determination and the question whether repentance is caused by God or by humans themselves. Repentance is not always an act of freedom. So, for example, one can ask whether the repentance of the Ninevites in the book of Jonah—in the face of the threat of being killed!—is voluntary or forced and thus, in a way, "determined." (Note also, Lam 5:21, "Make us turn to you [or "repent"], Yahweh, and we will turn [or "repent"] . . ."; Jer 31:18, "Make me turn, and I will turn"; Isa 44:22; and Philippians 2:12f.) And by giving the Israelites a new heart, Yahweh makes it possible that they can keep his commandments, which is the main point of repentance according to chap. 18 (cp. also Deuteronomy 30:6–10, in which Yahweh will "circumcise" the Israelites' hearts so that they will love him and return to him [or "repent"].)

A. Mein sees in the book of Ezekiel a "movement from responsibility for judgment to passivity in the face of restoration" (*Ezekiel and the Ethics of Exile*, OTM [Oxford: Oxford University Press, 2001] 262). According to chap. 20 it is true that Israel's restoration is not the result of the Israelite's actions. However, that does not mean that they should passively wait for what will happen. Already in Israel's past the people have not been "responsible" for their liberation from Egypt, the laws, the Sabbaths, and their living in the land, all of which had been brought about by Yahweh for the sake of his "name."

23. "Das gesamte jetzt vorliegende Kapitel trägt eine die sonstigen Darlegungen des Ezechielbuches weit überholende und umgreifende Geschichtsreflexion vor . . ." (Pohlmann, *Hesekiel/Ezechiel 20–48*, 310). The conceptual and theological differences between the different texts in the book of Ezekiel limit the possibility of a coherent understanding of the contents and the function of the book as a whole. So, for example, Renz's summary of the "argument of the book of Ezekiel" (*Rhetorical Function*, 249–51) reflects a bird's eye view which has to ignore considerable parts of the text. Note the critical remarks of Pohlmann, in particular his note that Renz does not distinguish between exile- and diaspora-oriented texts (*Ezechiel*, 41ff.) and the more sophisticated study by K. Schöpflin, *Theologie als Biographie im Ezechielbuch*, FAT 36 (Tübingen: Mohr/Siebeck, 2002).

context it is not possible to demonstrate this in detail. It must suffice to sketch some main differences and developments in their basic outline.

Guilt and Punishment

The conquest of Jerusalem and Judah by the Babylonians in 597 and 587 BCE is generally interpreted in the book of Ezekiel as a consequence of the wrongdoing of the Israelites. So, for example, chapter 16 describes the conquest and destruction of Jerusalem by military forces as Yahweh's "judgment" on the city (vv. 35-43). In this judgment Jerusalem gets what she deserves for her guilt: "I have returned your deeds upon your head, says the Lord Yahweh" (v. 43).[24] Similarly, in chapter 18 Yahweh announces the Israelites: "I will judge you . . ., all of you according to your ways . . ." (v. 30).

By contrast, in chapter 20 Yahweh says that he will deal with the Israelites "for my name's sake, not according to your evil ways, or corrupt deeds" (v. 44). This corresponds with 36:22: "It is not for your sake, O house of Israel, that I am about to act, but for the sake of my holy name . . ." (v. 32). However, in 36:16ff. Yahweh's future course of action is contrary to his past behavior. When the Israelites defiled their land, Yahweh "poured out my wrath upon them" and "scattered them among the nations"; "in accordance with their conduct and their deeds I judged them" (vv. 17-19). By contrast, in chapter 20 Yahweh already in the past restrained his wrath and acted for the sake of his name (vv. 8-9, 13-14, 21-22). More precisely, in chapter 20 retribution and grace[25] are aspects of Yahweh's dealing that cannot be neatly separated. So, for example, when Yahweh waits until the generation of the exodus has died in the wilderness (v. 17), this is at the same time an act of judgment and retribution (Yahweh does not lead them into the promised land) and of grace (Yahweh does not destroy them). Therefore, in chapter 20 history is less clear and far more ambiguous than it is in other texts of the book of Ezekiel.

---

24. However, see the discussion of Ezek 16:59-63 under the heading "Covenant" below.

25. The book of Ezekiel generally refrains from speaking of Yahweh's "grace," "compassion," or "love" (but compare 20:17). However, the difference between Yahweh's grace and his not treating the Israelites according to their deeds pertains only to Yahweh's motivation, not to the effects of his acting.

Covenant (ברית)[26]

It is not clear whether the topic of covenant is present in Ezekiel 20 at all. In v. 37 MT reads

והעברתי אתכם תחת השבט והבאתי אתכם במסרת הברית

"I will make you pass under the staff, and will bring you within the bond of the covenant" (NRSV).

However, in the LXX version there is no mention of a covenant at all: καὶ διάξω ὑμᾶς ὑπὸ τὴν ῥάβδον μου καὶ εἰσάξω ὑμᾶς ἐν ἀριθμῷ, "and I will drive you under my (!) rod and bring you in by number (!)" (NETS). Peshitta and Vulgate parallel MT, whereas certain readings of the Vetus Latina tradition (Itala) confirm LXX (*et inducam uos in numero*). MT appears to be the more difficult reading. However, it is also very difficult to understand and can easily be explained as the result of a writer's error: if the original Hebrew text read במספר instead of במסרת הברית, a writer could easily have misread במסרת for במספר and הברית for the following וברותי (v. 38: dittography). The original Hebrew text could then be compared to 1 Chron 9:28 (כי במספר יביאום, "they brought them in by number").[27]

Looking at the MT version of Ezek 20:37, even if it is probably not the original one, it is clear that the covenant between Israel and Yahweh belongs strictly to the future (as it is the case also in 34:25 and 37:26). Yahweh's actions following the "election" of Israel can be understood as failed attempts to establish a covenant with Israel. He says: "I am Yahweh your God" (v. 5), but Israel is never called his people. He gives Israel his "statutes and ordinances" as well as "my Sabbaths, as a sign between me and them" (vv. 11–12), but Israel never accepts them. So it appears that there has never been a valid covenant between Yahweh and Israel up to the Babylonian exile.

---

26. See W. Gross, *Zukunft für Israel. Alttestamentliche Bundeskonzepte und die Debatte umden Neuen Bund*, SB 176 (Stuttgart: Katholisches Bibelwerk, 1998).

27. E.g., Zimmerli (*Ezekiel 1*, 403) and BHS who argue for the LXX's reading as the older one, and Greenberg (*Ezekiel 1-20*, 372f.) and Allen (*Ezekiel 20-48*, 4) who defend the MT. In 1989 I argued for the priority of MT (Krüger, *Geschichtskonzepte*, 268). However, in view of the findings of Schwagmeier, the priority of LXX appears to be more probable (P. Schwagmeier, "Ezechielbuches").

In contrast, chapter 17 speaks about a covenant with Yahweh which has been established in the past and is still valid in the present. However, this is not a covenant between Yahweh and Israel, but a treaty between the kings of Babylon and Judah, Nebuchadnezzar and Zedekiah. Since this treaty has probably been established before the deities of the covenant partners who function as witnesses and guarantors, Yahweh can call that treaty "my covenant" (v. 19 par. "the covenant" in v. 18). He warns Zedekiah not to break the covenant, otherwise not only Nebuchadnezzar but also Yahweh would turn against him.

In Ezekiel 16, a figurative presentation of the history of Jerusalem as a woman (and a wife of Yahweh), Yahweh entered into a covenant with Jerusalem when she was a young woman, and she became his wife (v. 8). In the course of time, however, Jerusalem committed adultery. So Yahweh will turn her over to judgment, i.e. the destruction of the city. This announcement was probably the end and the climax of the original oracle in vv. 1–43. In vv. 59–63, one of the later additions to the chapter,[28] Yahweh anticipates a future beyond the judgment. Jerusalem has broken the covenant with Yahweh, but Yahweh will remember this covenant and establish an everlasting covenant with Jerusalem (the exact relation between the "old" and the "new" covenant remains unclear).

This amounts to a fundamental change of Yahweh's dealing with Jerusalem. Up to the destruction of the city (which lies still in the future from the viewpoint of the text) Yahweh reacts to Jerusalem's behavior: "I will deal with you as you have done" (v. 59). Afterwards, however, he will act freely, without any obligation (v. 61: "not on account of a covenant with you"), and Jerusalem will react to Yahweh's dealing: "I will remember my covenant with you in the days of your youth, and I will establish with you an everlasting covenant; then you will remember your ways, and be ashamed . . ." (vv. 60–61).

Punishing Jerusalem for her unfaithfulness, Yahweh shows that he does not put up with Jerusalem thwarting his intention that she should be his wife. However, when Jerusalem is destroyed, Yahweh's intention is not realized either. So he decides to continue his story with Jerusalem, starting again with a covenant between himself and the city and hoping that the latter's mind and manners will be changed by the experience of judgment and undeserved grace. Jerusalem should be ashamed of her

---

28. Allen, *Ezekiel 1–19*, 233, 246; Pohlmann, *Hesekiel/Ezechiel 1–19*, 235. It is virtually impossible that vv. 59ff. belong to the original version of chap. 16.

past misdeeds as well as of her present unmerited wellbeing, and this should help her to act properly in the future. This view of history as the implementation of Yahweh's intentions against human opposition by way of judgment and grace as catalysts of a human learning process closely parallels Ezekiel 20. However, whereas in Ezekiel 20 this view permeates the whole chapter, in chapter 16 it is developed only in a later supplement at the end of the text.

Repentance

In most chapters of the book of Ezekiel Israel is viewed as an entity whose identity in the course of history poses no problem. Ezekiel 16 and 23 describe the histories of Jerusalem and Samaria as biographies of women. That human persons may be called to account for their deeds somewhat later in their lives appears to be acceptable for many. However, with regard to collective entities like Israel or Jerusalem their identity in the course of history is more problematic taking into consideration that they consist of several generations of individuals. That sons (and daughters) have to pay for the guilt of their fathers (and mothers) is not acceptable at all for a lot of people today.

In the book of Ezekiel it is expressly denied in the name of Yahweh in chapter 18: "The person who sins shall die. A son shall not suffer for the iniquity of a father, nor a father suffer for the iniquity of a child. The righteousness of the righteous shall be his own, and the wickedness of the wicked shall be his own" (v. 20).[29] Ezekiel 18 goes even one step further. Not only across the boundary between different generations shall there be no transfer of iniquity or righteousness, but also from an earlier phase of a person's life to a later phase—if that person "turns away" from its earlier (righteous or wicked) behavior and acts the other way round (see also 3:16-21; 33:1-9).

Ezekiel 20 integrates the insights from chapter 18 into its view of Israel's history. Israel is conceived as a succession of generations. Within the first generation there is also a clear distinction between successive phases of its life. Yahweh calls upon them to change their action and helps them with his statutes and ordinances to improve their way of life. He does the same with the second generation of Israelites, and the fol-

---

29. See Deut 24:16, 2 Kgs 14:6. This is also a guiding principle of the rewriting of the books of Kings in the books of Chronicles.

lowing generations too appear to have at least the possibility to change their lives, if it is true that Yahweh hopes they get horrified through their firstborn offerings (vv. 25–26) and realize the absurdity of their worship on the "high places" (במה, v. 29, 2x). Thus, Ezekiel 20 appears to agree at least in principle with chapter 18 that each generation of the Israelites has the chance to turn away from the "statutes, ordinances and idols" of their parents and even to distance itself from their own past and start a new life in accordance with the will of Yahweh and their insight into what is good and supports life.[30]

However, Ezekiel 20 at the same time contradicts chapter 18. All subsequent generations of Israel had to suffer Yahweh's sanctions for the misdeeds of the first and second generation. And the new Israel will include those who did not deserve it. These are "flagrant violation(s) of the principle of individual responsibility" established in Ezekiel 18.[31] However, there is also a tension in Ezekiel 18 between this principle of individual responsibility and the possibility of repentance. Taken literally, the principle that "the person who sins shall die" (v. 20) would imply that a sinner hardly had any chance to repent. That it is nevertheless possible that a sinner repents is secured by another principle, namely that Yahweh has no pleasure in the death of the wicked (v. 23) or of anyone (v. 32). Therefore he waits and looks to see whether a sinner repents before he executes the death sentence.

In Ezekiel 20 the principle that "the person who sins shall die" seems to be virtually given up. The first two generations of Israel are explicitly spared from being destroyed in the desert. Their successors in the land are finally scattered among the nations, but not killed. And those who will be sorted out as rebels and transgressors in the upcoming judgment in the "desert of the nations" apparently do not die im-

---

30. It is often overlooked (e.g., by G. Matties, *Ezekiel 18 and the Rhetoric of Moral Discourse*, SBLDS 126 [Atlanta: Scholars, 1990]) that chap. 18 argues against people who are living in the land of Israel (v. 2) and demands that children should suffer for the iniquities of their ancestors (v. 19), apparently in view of those in exile (11:14ff.). This rhetorical situation probably reflects conflicts between Israelites who are in their land and returnees (or earlier and later returnees). Ezekiel 18 holds that people who have changed their mind and behavior should be welcomed regardless of their former faults (Krüger, *Geschichtskonzepte*, 355–82). Chapter 20, similarly, appears to plead for a peaceful cohabitation of earlier (vv. 32ff.) and later (vv. 39ff.) returnees in the new Israel.

31. M. Fishbane, "Sin and Judgment in the Prophecies of Ezekiel," *Int* 38 (1984) 143.

mediately but are left to serve their idols and assimilate themselves to the nations, with the chance to come back to Yahweh and worship him alone later on. That Yahweh grants humans the possibility of repentance even when he judges them, is, however, in Ezekiel 20 not motivated by his distaste for death as in chapter 18, but by his will to carry out his intentions against a rebellious Israel. He deals with Israel "for his name's sake," not according to Israel's deeds and behavior.

Whereas in 20:39 Yahweh appears to be confident that the Israelites sooner or later will realize on their own that it is better for them to serve him and to keep his commandments than to serve other gods, 11:19-20 and 36:26-27 are, obviously, more skeptical in this regard:[32] the Israelites' mind ("heart" and "spirit") is so fatuous that Yahweh needs to replace it by a new one in order to make it possible for the people to know what is good for them. This seems to be a conceptual development that goes beyond chapter 20.[33] It does not replace free insight by divine manipulation, but accentuates the need to free the human mind from fatuousness so that free insight becomes possible.

Collective and Individual[34]

Most oracles in the book of Ezekiel are focusing on Israel or Jerusalem as collective entities. Other texts talk about individual persons like the prophet Ezekiel, kings, prophets and prophetesses, righteous or wicked individuals (see, among others, chaps. 13-14; 17-19). Ezekiel 18 states that human beings are judged by Yahweh according to their individual righteousness or wickedness. This is compatible with a collective punishment if and only if all Israelites without exception are wicked and deserve punishment. That appears to be the case for Jerusalem in chapter 22. However, even here mention is made of poor and needy people

---

32. T. Krüger regards it as possible that the Israelites get a new heart and a new spirit on their own ("Das menschliche Herz und die Weisung Gottes: Elemente einer Diskussion über Möglichkeiten und Grenzen der Tora-Rezeption im Alten Testament," in *Rezeption und Auslegung im Alten Testament und in seinem Umfeld*, ed. by R. G. Kratz and T. Krüger, OBO 153 [Freiburg and Göttingen: Universitätsverlag and Vandenhoeck and Ruprecht, 1997] 65-92).

33. Ezekiel 36:23bβ-38, which are missing in the LXX manuscript Pap967, possibly belong to the latest additions to the book of Ezekiel (Schwagmeier, "Ezechielbuches," 2004; Pohlmann, *Ezechiel*, 22ff., 127ff.

34. Krüger, *Geschichtskonzepte*, 382-94.

(v. 29) who appear to be rather victims than wrongdoers. Nevertheless, there is no one who is willing (and able) to counter the wickedness of the city's other inhabitants (v. 30). In the vision of Jerusalem's destruction in Ezekiel 9 "those who sigh and groan over all the abominations that are committed in it" (v. 4) are marked on their foreheads and escape being killed by the gang of angels who are destroying the city. This comes close to the statement in 14:12–20 that only just individuals will save their lives in the impending judgment. Even Noah could not save his sons and daughters, not to mention all the animals.

However, this postulate obviously did not agree with the experienced realities of 597 and 587 BCE and with what could be expected from disasters like the military destruction of a city. So Ezekiel 21 frankly announces that Yahweh will cut off from the land of Israel "both righteous and wicked" (vv. 3–4). However, there were also those who escaped the disaster, but not all (if any) of them were righteous. According to 12:16 and 14:21–23 there would be those who escaped the destruction of Jerusalem in 587 in order to show the people to whom they escaped how wicked they were and how much the other inhabitants of Jerusalem, who had been at least as wicked as they, had deserved their ruin.

Ezekiel 6:8–10 expects that those who escaped the catastrophe (apparently of 587) will realize that they have done wrong and turn back to Yahweh. In 11:14–21 it is Yahweh who will cause a change of mind in the exiles of 597 after having brought them home into the land of Israel.

In both instances the undeserved sparing of guilty individuals can be understood in the light of Ezekiel 18 as giving them a chance to change their moral conduct.

The mentioned sections in the book of Ezekiel show the difficulties in reconciling the expectation and experience of a collective catastrophe and its interpretation as divine judgment with the postulate that each individual should be treated by God according to its righteousness or wickedness. The texts try to cope with that problem without finding a resolution. Ezekiel 20 does not offer a resolution either. But here the problem is at least softened since Yahweh's judgments are not depicted as the killing of people but as a worsening of their living conditions: the first generation of Israelites is not led into the promised land and the subsequent generations in the land must live with bad divine statutes and ordinances and the impending threat of being scattered among the nations and countries. These judgments do not necessarily imply the dead of innocent individuals as a kind of collateral damage (albeit they probably did imply it).

The future judgment in the "desert of the peoples" will, according to Ezekiel 20, combine collective and individual justice since it will not destroy the collective (which will on the contrary be rebuilt by it) but sort out bad individuals from the community. This view which looks beyond the expected catastrophe to a restoration of Israel is shared by texts like chapters 13 (see esp. vv. 9 and 23); 14:1–11 and 34. It appears to be a peculiarity of Ezekiel 20 that even those who are purged out in the announced judgment have a second chance to change their minds and lives and join the new Israel.

Yahweh's "Statutes and Ordinances"

In Ezek 5:6-7; 11:12; 18 and 33 Yahweh's "statutes (חֻקּוֹת) and ordinances (מִשְׁפָּטִים)" define which kind of behavior is appropriate for Israel as a whole and for every single Israelite. According to Ezek 11:20; 36:27 and 37:24 the same will be true in the future (see also 43:11 and 44:24), and Yahweh will make sure that Israel never again transgresses his statutes and ordinances as the people had done in the past. In Ezekiel 20 Yahweh's statutes and ordinances are also valued as supporting life in vv. 11–24. However, according to v. 25 Yahweh also gave Israel "statutes that were not good and ordinances by which they could not live."[35]

Ezekiel 20:26 makes clear that these bad statutes and ordinances include the demand to offer the first child or animal that is born by a mother (בהעביר כל פטר רחם, literally: "to let pass over [from life to death] everything that breaches the womb"). In the Pentateuch only Exod 22:28–29 demands the offering of all firstborn sons (or children?) as well as of all (male?) firstborn animals. They must be "given" to Yahweh, i.e. probably be killed. According to Exodus 13:1–2, every "first to open the womb ... of human beings and animals" belongs to Yahweh and has to be "consecrated" to him. This is amplified in 13:11–13: Every male firstborn sheep or goat must be offered to Yahweh. The firstborn of a donkey has to be killed or to be "redeemed" with a sheep. The firstborn

---

35. This goes beyond the statement of Jer 8:8 that Yahweh's law has been fudged by the scribes.

male children of humans are to be "redeemed" with an animal offering (cp. Exod 34:19–20; Num 18:15–18). Deuteronomy 15:19–23 does not mention firstborn humans. In Genesis 22 God praises Abraham for his willingness to sacrifice his only son Isaac, but at the same time waives the execution of that offering. Micah 6:6–7 at least considers it possible that Yahweh could be pleased with the offering of a firstborn child. However, Jer 7 insists that Yahweh never commanded child sacrifices (vv. 30–31). In fact, he never commanded any sacrifices at all (v. 22)!

These different statements appear to reflect a discussion about the appropriateness of child sacrifices in connection with the worship of Yahweh. While Genesis 22 and the commandments in the Pentateuch imply that Yahweh can, at least in principle, demand the offering of a firstborn human, Jeremiah 7 vehemently denies that Yahweh could ever do so. Ezekiel 20 concedes that Yahweh indeed demanded firstborn sacrifices from the Israelites, but at the same time explains that demand as an expression of Yahweh's anger with Israel and his hope that the Israelites will come to their senses and see that what they are doing is not good and does not really please Yahweh.

Thus, in Ezekiel 20 religion is historically put into perspective.[36] Not everything Yahweh once has said or commanded remains valid and relevant in perpetuity. Religious traditions need to be critically evaluated before they can be applied to the present. And evil deeds that destroy life instead of supporting it cannot be vindicated or excused under reference to a divine order. The god of Ezekiel 20 would not have praised Abraham for his readiness to kill his child, but blamed him for not having shrunk back from such a horrible act—even if it had been demanded by a heavenly voice. If Ezek 11:19–20 and 36:26–27 announce that Yahweh will change the Israelite's "heart" (לב) and "spirit" (רוח), so that they will observe his "statutes and ordinances," this can be read as a relapse into an uncritical religious traditionalism ("in case the tradition appears to be unreasonable, it is reason that has to be changed")[37] or as an affirmation of the tradition-critical stance of Ezekiel 20. That is,

---

36. This notion is at least implied in the text, even if perhaps not intended by its author(s).

37. Jeremiah 31:33 appears to tend more clearly towards this view. Numbers 15:37–41 recommends to follow Yahweh's commands without any regard to one's "eyes" and "heart" (Krüger, "Das menschliche Herz").

one should not observe "statutes and ordinances" that contradict one's "heart" and "spirit," even if they are religiously authorized.

"For my name's sake" (למען שמי)

One of the characteristics of the view of history in Ezekiel 20 is the notion that Yahweh's actions are ultimately determined by his concern for his good reputation among the nations. "And you shall know that I am Yahweh, when I deal with you for my name's sake, not according to your evil ways and corrupt deeds, O house of Israel, says the Lord Yahweh," are the last words of the chapter (v. 44). They sound very much like what Yahweh says in chapter 36: "Thus says the Lord Yahweh: It is not for your sake, O house of Israel, that I am about to act, but for the sake of my holy name, which you have profaned among the nations to which you came" (v. 22, cf. v. 32). However, on closer examination it becomes evident that the meaning of the phrase "for my name's sake" in chapter 20 is considerably different from that in chapter 36.[38]

So the opposite of "for my name's sake" in the two statements quoted is on the one hand "for your sake" (36:22) and on the other hand "according to your evil ways and corrupt deeds" (20:44). In the first instance Yahweh insists that he will not restore Israel because of feeling sympathy towards the people; in the second instance he points out that he will not punish and destroy Israel but restore it. According to Ezekiel 20 already in Israel's past Yahweh abstained from punishing the Israelites for their rebelliousness, but acted "for his name's sake." By contrast, in 36:16ff Yahweh did punish the Israelites "in accordance with their conduct and their deeds" (v. 19) and scatter them among the nations, and it is exactly this punishment that is jeopardizing his reputation among the nations who say about Israel: "These are the people of Yahweh, and yet they had to go out of his land" (v. 20).

In chapter 36 Yahweh's reputation among the nations is put at risk because his actions do not comply with people's expectations from a deity. A god has to protect his people in their land. If the people are deported from their land, their god has obviously been unable to protect them.[39] By contrast, in chapter 20 Yahweh's reputation is jeopardized

---

38. This may indicate that 36:16–23(bα) represent an earlier stage of theological reflection than chap. 20 (Pohlmann, *Hesekiel/Ezechiel 1–19*, 31.

39. 2 Kgs 18:32–35.

when he does not fulfill what he himself has promised: to bring the Israelites out of Egypt into their own land. Therefore the dispersion of Israel among the nations is no menace for Yahweh's name, since Yahweh has announced it long ago. On the other hand, the dispersion of Israel implies that Yahweh's original intention to establish Israel as his people in its own land is eventually not realized. This can be understood as a threat to Yahweh's reputation, since he obviously was unable to prevail over the rebellious Israelites. However, since the Israelites have lived in their land for a considerable time one could also say that Yahweh has demonstrated his assertiveness but also allowed the Israelites to go their own ways.

However, according to 20:39 rather than the dispersion of Israel it is the manner how the Israelites worship Yahweh by which his name is jeopardized, namely their gifts (vv. 26 and 31) and their idols (the latter referring to the worship of other deities besides Yahweh and/or to the worship of images of Yahweh). This could suggest that Yahweh is a god like the gods of the nations and can be worshipped like them. So in Ezekiel 20 Yahweh does not restore Israel in order to comply with the common expectations from a deity as in chapter 36, but in order to make clear that he does not come up to the nations' notion of a deity.[40]

Summary: The View of History in Ezekiel 20

Ezekiel 20 depicts history as a temporal sequence of interactions between Yahweh, Israel and the nations. Yahweh and Israel are the main actors; the nations are the audience who evaluate what is happening before their eyes according to their perceptions and ideals. Yahweh is

---

40. Schwartz ("Dim View," 67) rightly points out that whereas in Jeremiah and Deutero-Isaiah Yahweh's "enduring love for his people makes their suffering intolerable to him," in Ezekiel "the glorification of his name" is the driving force of Yahweh's acting. "Thus, Ezekiel predicts, YHWH is bound and determined to embark on a most ungracious project of forced rehabilitation, in order to correct the failures of history once and for all and ultimately to derive the satisfaction for which he has striven so long." However, I do not understand why "this is anything but a relief" for Israel, as Schwartz states. It could also be understood as an attempt to assure the existence of Israel without any dependence on divine favor. Yahweh simply has to support Israel, whether he likes it or not. It should also be noticed that Yahweh's "name," his "reputation" among the nations according to Ezek 20 is based on his ability to free his people from foreign rule, to lead them into their own land and to teach them how to live and behave in a way that advances their life and freedom.

opposed to all other gods, the "idols" worshipped by the nations but also by Israel, whose existence he does not expressly deny, but with whom also he does not engage in any form of interaction. What distinguishes Yahweh from all other gods appears to be that he cares for Israel's freedom and life.

History develops from the antagonism between Yahweh's intention that Israel might live in freedom in its own land, and Israel's rebellion against Yahweh. Yahweh sets boundaries to Israel's resistance against his plans and waits for Israel's turning back to him, motivated by the people's experiences with him and with other gods. He appears to be confident that sooner or later the Israelites will understand that the worship of Yahweh helps them to become and to remain free and alive.

As against other views of Israel's history in the book of Ezekiel, in chapter 20 history is more complex and less clear. So, for example, it is not possible to divide it into epochs or episodes like an untroubled dawn of the relationship of Yahweh with Israel or Jerusalem, followed by a period of crisis induced by the disobedience of the people, which results in a time of catastrophe and judgment that brings about a rebound to a new period of salvation. Rather, the characteristics of those epochs are always present as aspects or dimensions of the historical process. Similarly God's and the people's actions are sometimes, if not mostly, ambiguous. So, for example, not every "statute and ordinance" of Yahweh is good and supports life, and for Israel it is not always good simply to do what Yahweh says. Nevertheless, history appears to be understood as a kind of educative process for Israel (and also for the nations) that leads to a better understanding of what is good for life and for freedom, and a better understanding of Yahweh as the force of life and freedom.

Further Developments

Developments within the Hebrew Bible

It is always problematic to speak of advancements in the history of ideas. Nevertheless, the view of history in Ezekiel 20 appears to be more appropriate to the complexity and ambiguity of historical reality than the more clear-cut models in older texts of the book of Ezekiel and other Old Testament books. However, it also has its problems and difficulties and raises new questions.

So, for example, one could ask whether Yahweh is interested exclusively in Israel's life and freedom or also in the life and freedom of the other nations,[41] and, if the latter is true, whether Yahweh can communicate with the other nations only indirectly through his acting with Israel or also in direct communication. The latter appears to be envisioned in Malachi 1 where Yahweh accuses the Israelites in Judah that they profane his name by offering him debased sacrifices, whereas his name is reverenced and great among the nations where incense and pure offerings are offered to him (vv. 11–14). It is possible to understand this as a statement about the worship of Yahweh by Jews in the diaspora. However, in view of the obvious allusions to Ezekiel 20 and 36[42] (above all in the topic of Yahweh's "name" in Israel and among the nations) it appears more likely that Malachi 1 contrasts the worship of the Israelites with that of the other nations, which is, then, not only expected in the future[43] but affirmed as a present reality.[44] This reflects either a profound ignorance of the real knowledge of Yahweh among the nations (which probably was negligible) or an idea that it is possible to worship Yahweh and hold him in high reputation without using the name "Yahweh."[45] Provided that Yahweh communicates directly with all nations,[46] he has no need to avoid possible misunderstandings of his acting with Israel on the side of the nations, as Ezekiel 20 presupposes; he can explain to them what he does and why he does it.

In Ezekiel 20 Yahweh in his acting in history time and again has to make compromises between his conflicting interests to establish and to sustain life, freedom and justice (this is also true of other texts of the book of Ezekiel and of the broader prophetic tradition). A state in which all three of these goals are realized in conjunction is only reached

---

41. E.g., Amos 9:7 but also the repeated articulation of Yahweh's interest to make himself known to the nations in Ezek 25–32 ("you/they shall know that I am Yahweh").

42. H. Utzschneider, *Künder oder Schreiber? Eine These zum Problem der "Schriftprophetie" auf Grund von Maleachi 1,6–2,9*, BEATAJ 19, (Frankfurt: Lang, 1989).

43. E.g., Zeph 3:9–10; Ps 102:16.

44. So Jonah and Ruth. The highly controversial exegetical discussion about Mal 1:11 is summarized by A. Meinhold, *Maleachi*, BKAT 14/8 (Neukirchen-Vluyn: Neukirchener, 2006) 125–33.

45. See the Ninevites in Jonah 3 who speak of "the god" instead of "Yahweh" (note also Dan 2:47; 3:28–29; 3:31–4:34; 6:26–28).

46. See Jonah and Isa 2:3f (= Micah 4:2f.) or Isa 42:3f; 49:6f.

at the expected goal of Yahweh's acting in history. Since this expectation has even now never been fulfilled, it is understandable that other concepts of history have been developed later on in the development of the Hebrew Bible. The main options were to see a balance between the ideals of life, freedom and justice already realized in the present world, or to expect the realization of such a balance not within the process of history but from a new creation after the end of history.

An example of the first option is the speech of Yahweh in the book of Job (chapters 38–41; cp. also the book of Qohelet). Here Yahweh depicts his creation as a habitat for different kinds of animals (including human beings). Yahweh is not indifferent about life, freedom and justice. He cares for the animals' food and for their reproduction (Job 38:39—39:4). He defends their freedom against the grasp of humans (39:5–12). And every morning he causes the dawn "to take hold of the skirts of the earth and shake the wicked out of it" (38:12–13). But within this broad framework of a well balanced order there remains a great deal to do for human beings who are free to disrupt the order of the world or to respect and sustain it. However, there is no overarching linear dynamic from chaos to cosmos, from unsatisfying compromises to an ideal balance in the world. History is not more than a reiterative variation of stable basic conditions (Qoh 1:4–11; 3:1–8) without a final goal.

The second option is present in the Hebrew Bible mainly in the book of Daniel and is further elaborated in the so-called apocalyptic writings of early Judaism (e.g., the Ethiopic book of Enoch). In their prognostic dreams and visions history appears to be completely predetermined by God. Humans are not expected to affect the course of history by their actions. History is the framework wherein individuals can and should prove themselves and qualify for the new world that will make an end to the process of history. The transition between the history of this world and the ideal and trans-historical new world is marked by a final judgment on the living as well as the dead that will sort out all those who are not qualified for the final salvation. This apocalyptic view of history can be understood as a transformation of the expectations developed in Ezekiel 20 from the process of history to an end of history and a new, trans-historical reality.

Present Perspectives

Two millennia after the texts discussed here, it appears that there have been historical developments or at least changes in the long run that exceed mere variations of relatively stable general conditions of life on our planet Earth. Such far-reaching historical changes have not been in view in any of the Old Testament texts discussed (or in any other text of the Bible). They challenge in particular the view of the book of Job (and Qohelet). However, our present cosmological and anthropological knowledge makes it also very difficult to sustain an apocalyptic worldview. So the prophetic conception of history developed in Ezekiel 20 still (or again) appears to be worthwhile to be thoroughly considered. However, history has taught us to be cautious in identifying God's actions and his purposes in the course of history. Too often humans have been misled by erroneous religious interpretations of their present to act cruelly and ruthlessly against their fellow creatures. History is first and foremost a realm of human freedom and responsibility (Job); if God acts in history, he does so mainly by helping humans learn to appreciate the value of life, freedom and justice (Ezekiel).

So the balance between life, freedom and justice as the main goals of historical change turns from a theological to an ethical problem. Not every action that supports life and freedom is also just. Justice limits freedom in order to protect it. Supporting life is the goal of justice, but not everything that supports life is also just. Thus humans acting in history and affecting the course of history are confronted with similar challenges to find viable compromises between their conflicting goals and purposes like Yahweh had in Ezekiel 20. If they learn from that chapter that it is often better to suppress one's (apparently) "just anger" in order to achieve greater and long-termed purposes, it was worthwhile to deal with that text.

Bibliography

Allen, Leslie C. *Ezekiel 1-19*. WBC 28. Dallas: Word, 1994.
———. *Ezekiel 20-48*. WBC 29. Dallas: Word, 1990.
Bartelmus, Rüdiger. "Ez 37,1-14: die Verbform weqatal und die Anfänge der Auferstehungshoffnung." *ZAW* 97 (1985) 366-89.
———. "Menschlicher Misserfolg und Jahwes Initiative: Beobachtungen zum Geschichtsbild des deuteronomistischen Rahmens im Richterbuch und zum geschichtstheologischen Entwurf in Ez 20." *Biblische Notizen* 70 (1993) 28-47.
Fishbane, Michael. "Sin and Judgment in the Prophecies of Ezekiel." *Int* 38 (1984) 131-50.
Greenberg, Moshe. *Ezekiel 1-20*. AB 22. Garden City, NY: Doubleday, 1983.
———. *Ezekiel 21-37*. AB 22A. Garden City, NY: Doubleday, 1995.
Gross, Walter. *Zukunft für Israel. Alttestamentliche Bundeskonzepte und die Debatte um den Neuen Bund*. Stuttgarter Bibelstudien 176. Stuttgart: Katholisches Bibelwerk, 1998.
Joyce, Paul M. *Divine Initiative and Human Response in Ezekiel*. JSOTSup 51. Sheffield: JSOT Press, 1989.
Koch, Klaus. *Die Profeten I: Assyrische Zeit*. Stuttgart: Kohlhammer, 1995.
Krüger, Thomas. *Geschichtskonzepte im Ezechielbuch*. BZAW 180. Berlin: de Gruyter, 1989.
———. "Das menschliche Herz und die Weisung Gottes: Elemente einer Diskussion über Möglichkeiten und Grenzen der Tora-Rezeption im Alten Testament." In *Rezeption und Auslegung im Alten Testament und in seinem Umfeld*, edited by Reinhard Gregor Kratz and Thomas Krüger, 65-92. OBO 153. Göttingen: Vandenhoeck & Ruprecht, 1997.
———. "'An den Strömen von Babylon...': Erwägungen zu Zeitbezug und Sachverhalt in Psalm 137." In *Sachverhalt und Zeitbezug: Semitistische und alttestamentliche Studien, Adolf Denz zum 65. Geburtstag*, edited by Rüdiger Bartelmus and Norbert Nebes, 79-84. Wiesbaden: Harrassowitz, 2001.
Kutsch, Ernst. *Die chronologischen Daten des Ezechielbuches*, Orbis biblicus et orientalis 62. Göttingen: Vandenhoeck & Ruprecht, 1985.
Lang, Bernhard. *Ezechiel: Der Prophet und das Buch*. Erträge der Forschung 153. Darmstadt: Wissenschaftliche Buchgesellschaft, 1981.
Lapsley, Jacqueline E. *Can These Bones Live? The Problem of the Moral Self in the Book of Ezekiel*. BZAW 301. Berlin: de Gruyter, 2000.
Lust, Johan. *Traditie, redactie en kerygma bij Ezechiel: Een analyse van Ez., XX,1-26*. Verhandelingen van de Koninklijke Vlaamse Academie voor Wetenschappen, Letteren en Schone Kunsten van België, Klasse der Letteren 65. Brussels: Paleis der Academie, 1969.
Matties, Gordon. *Ezekiel 18 and the Rhetoric of Moral Discourse*. SBLDS 126. Atlanta: Scholars, 1990.
Mein, Andrew. *Ezekiel and the Ethics of Exile*. OTM. Oxford: Oxford University Press, 2001.
Meinhold, Arndt. *Maleachi*, BK 14/8. Neukirchen-Vluyn: Neukirchener, 2006.
Ohnesorge, Stefan. *Jahwe gestaltet sein Volk neu: Zur Sicht der Zukunft Israels nach Ez 11,14-21; 20,1-44; 36,16-38; 37,1-14.15-28*. Forschungen zur Bibel 64. Würzburg: Echter, 1991.

Pfisterer Darr, Katheryn. "The Book of Ezekiel." In *The New Interpreter's Bible*, edited by Leander E. Keck et al., 6:1073–607. Nashville: Abingdon, 2001.

Pohlmann, Karl-Friedrich. *Ezechielstudien: Zur Redaktionsgeschichte des Buches und zur Frage nach den ältesten Texten*. BZAW 202. Berlin: de Gruyter, 1992.

———. *Das Buch des Propheten Hesekiel/Ezechiel 1–19*. ATD 22/1. Göttingen: Vandenhoeck & Ruprecht, 1996.

———. *Das Buch des Propheten Hesekiel/Ezechiel 20–48*. ATD 22/2. Göttingen: Vandenhoeck & Ruprecht, 2001.

———. *Ezechiel: Der Stand der theologischen Diskussion*, Darmstadt: Wissenschaftliche Buchgesellschaft, 2008.

Renz, Thomas. *The Rhetorical Function of the Book of Ezekiel*. VTSup 76. Leiden: Brill, 1999.

Römer, Thomas, et al. *Introduction à l'Ancien Testament*. Geneva: Labor et Fides, 1999.

Schwagmeier, Peter. "Untersuchungen zu Textgeschichte und Entstehung des Ezechielbuches in masoretischer und griechischer Überlieferung." Diss. theol., Zürich, 2004.

Schwartz, Baruch. "Repentance and Determinism in Ezekiel." In *Proceedings of the Eleventh World Congress of Jewish Studies, Division A: The Bible and Its World*, 123–30. Jerusalem: Magnes, 1994.

———. "Ezekiel's Dim View of Israel's Restoration." In *The Book of Ezekiel: Theological and Anthropological Perspectives*, edited by Margaret S. Odell and John T. Strong, 43–67. SBLSymS 9. Atlanta: Society of Biblical Literature, 2000.

Sedlmeier, Franz. *Studien zu Komposition und Theologie von Ezechiel 20*. SBB 21. Stuttgart: Katholisches Bibelwerk, 1990.

Sweeney, Marvin A. "Ezekiel." In *The Jewish Study Bible*, edited by Adele Berlin and Marc Zvi Brettler, 1042–138. Oxford: Oxford University Press, 2004.

Utzschneider, Helmut. *Künder oder Schreiber? Eine These zum Problem der "Schriftprophetie" auf Grund von Maleachi 1,6–2,9*. Beiträge zur Erforschung des Alten Testaments und des Antiken Judentums 19. Frankfurt: Lang, 1989.

Zenger, Erich, et al. *Einleitung in das Alte Testament*. 6th ed. Stuttgart: Kohlhammer, 2006.

Zimmerli, Walther. *Ezekiel 1*. Translated by R. E. Clements. Hermeneia. Philadelphia: Fortress, 1979.

———. *Ezekiel 2*. Translated by James D. Martin. Hermeneia, Philadelphia: Fortress, 1983.

Zwickel, Wolfgang. "Menschenopfer." In *Neues Bibellexikon*, edited by Manfred Görg and Bernhard Lang, 2:765–66. Zurich: Benziger, 1995.

7

Transforming the International Status Quo
Ezekiel's Oracles against the Nations

Paul R. Raabe

THE PROPHETS TYPICALLY ANNOUNCED DIVINE JUDGMENT AGAINST non-Israelite nations. It was an important part of their job description given the amount of space allotted to this kind of material (up to 20 percent). The reader of the Latter Prophets encounters it in the Books of Isaiah, Jeremiah, Joel, Amos, Obadiah, Micah, Nahum, Habakkuk, Zephaniah, and Zechariah. Therefore it is not surprising to see it in Ezekiel as well. In fact, Ezekiel's judgment speeches against nations in chapters 25–32 comprise 15 percent of the Book of Ezekiel.[1] In order to understand the overall vision of the Book, therefore, the reader must come to grips with this section.

In the Latter Prophets announcements of judgment against the various nations often appear together:

Isa 13–23	Babylon, Assyria, Moab, Damascus, Ephraim, Cush, Egypt, Dumah [= Edom?], Arabia, Jerusalem, Tyre and Sidon
Jer 46–51	Egypt, Philistia, Moab, Ammon, Edom, Damascus, Kedar and Hazor, Elam, Babylon

---

1. Word counts for the entire Hebrew Bible have been compiled by F. I. Andersen and A. D. Forbes, "'Prose Particle' Counts of the Hebrew Bible," in *The Word of the Lord Shall Go Forth: Essays in Honor of David Noel Freedman in Celebration of His Sixtieth Birthday*, eds. C. L. Meyers and M. O'Connor (Winona Lake, IN: Eisenbrauns, 1983) 165–83. Based on their word counts for the MT, Ezek 25–32 has 2805 words, comprising 15 percent of the entire book's length of 18,731 words.

Amos 1–2	Damascus, Philistia, Tyre, Edom, Ammon, Moab, Judah, Israel
Zeph 2–3	Philistia, Moab and Ammon, Cush, Assyria and Nineveh, Jerusalem
Zech 9	Aram, Tyre and Sidon, Philistia

The Book of Ezekiel follows this convention and collects the judgment speeches against nations into the same section.[2] There are seven nations targeted:

Ezek 25:1–7	Ammon
Ezek 25:8–11	Moab[3]
Ezek 25:12–14	Edom
Ezek 25:15–17	Philistia
Ezek 26:1–28:19	Tyre
Ezek 28:20–23	Sidon
Ezek 29:1–32:32	Egypt

The material we wish to explore is Ezek 25–32. To do so we will take the posture of a sympathetic reader who suspends disbelief and adopts the assumptions and viewpoints espoused in the material. So we will imagine ourselves among the Israelite exiles in Babylon, listening to the prophet Ezekiel, the son of Buzi. We want to hear the prophet's voice on its own terms rather than critique it or deconstruct it on the basis of our own modern Western viewpoints and sensitivities. The key questions at the forefront of our exploration will be: What does the material say? How does it say it? Why does it say it?

Dates of the Material

Chapter 24 records that the king of Babylon began to lay siege to Jerusalem in 588 BCE. During that time when the fall of Jerusalem took

---

2. Judgment speeches against the nations occur also outside of 25–32, in chapters 35 and 38–39.

3. The MT reads "Moab and Seir" while the Greek translation (LXX) lacks "Seir." How and why "Seir" was included in the MT are unknown. The unit deals only with Moab.

place the prophet pronounced God's judgment against foreign nations. Chapters 26–32 explicitly provide seven dates for the material, six of which belong to the Egyptian oracles of chapters 29–32.[4]

Ezek 24:1	9th year, 10th month, 10th day (Jan. 588)—beginning of siege on Jerusalem
Ezek 25:1–17	no date given (Is the reader to assume the same date as chapter 24?)—against Ammon, Moab, Edom, Philistia
1) Ezek 26:1	11th year, unstated month, 1st day (March/April 587–586)—against Tyre, against Sidon in 28:20–23
2) Ezek 29:1	10th year, 10th month, 12th day (Jan. 587)—against Egypt
3) Ezek 29:17	27th year, 1st month, 1st day (April 571)—against Egypt
4) Ezek 30:20	11th year, 1st month, 7th day (April 587)—against Egypt
5) Ezek 31:1	11th year, 3rd month, 1st day (June 587)—against Egypt
6) Ezek 32:1	12th year, 12th month, 1st day (March 585)—against Egypt
7) Ezek 32:17	12th year, unstated month, 15th day (March? 585)—against Egypt
Ezek 33:21	12th year, 10th month, 5th day (Jan. 585)—announcement of fall of Jerusalem

From the dates one can see that most of the proclamations against the nations fall between the beginning of Jerusalem's siege (24:1) and the report of her downfall (33:21). A notable exception is the Egyptian oracle of 29:17–21, which is chronologically out of place as the latest date given in the book (571 BCE). No doubt it was included here to keep all the Egyptian material together. The same goes for the two Egyptian oracles in chapter 32, which post-date the report of Jerusalem's fall by two months.[5]

---

4. On the dates in the book, see Moshe Greenberg, *Ezekiel 1–20*, AB 22 (Garden City, NY: Doubleday, 1983) 8–11.

5. The MT of Ezek 32:17 lacks a month but most scholars consider the date to be the same as that given in 32:1.

The reader naturally asks: Why do judgment speeches against foreign nations take place precisely around the time when Jerusalem was under siege? The purpose appears to be to create a tight interlocking between Jerusalem's downfall and that of the other nations.[6] The argument moves from the greater to the lesser. If strict judgment from God comes down on Jerusalem herself and even on his own temple as announced in chapters 4–24, then certainly it will come down on the non-Israelite nations as well. The other Levantine nations are not exempt (cf. Jer 25:29; 49:12).

Structure of the Material

Chapters 25–32 display different overlapping structures, wheels within wheels as it were. As mentioned earlier, there are seven nations and seven recorded dates. One could outline the section simply by one of those criteria. However, the major breaks seem to occur with the word-event formula ("the word of Yahweh came to me") followed by the vocative address to Ezekiel ("son of man"). On that basis the chapters are organized into seven sections with the seventh section itself blossoming into seven units. It is like a seven-branched menorah with the seventh branch itself becoming a seven-branched menorah:

1. Ezek 25:1–17—Ammon, Moab, Edom, Philistia
2. Ezek 26:1–21—Tyre
3. Ezek 27:1–36—Tyre
4. Ezek 28:1–10—Ruler of Tyre
5. Ezek 28:11–19—Ruler of Tyre
6. Ezek 28:20–23—Sidon

28:24–26—Summary material, interlude

7. I. Ezek 29:1–16—Pharaoh and Egypt
   II. Ezek 29:17–21—Egypt instead of Tyre

---

6. Note how key expressions used in the oracles against Judah are repeated in the oracles against the nations. See Lawrence Boadt, "Rhetorical Strategies in Ezekiel's Oracles of Judgment," *Ezekiel and His Book*, ed. J. Lust, BETL 74 (Leuven: Leuven University Press, 1986) 198; Thomas Renz, *The Rhetorical Function of the Book of Ezekiel*, VTSup 76 (Leiden: Brill, 1999) 93–101.

III. Ezek 30:1-19—Egypt
   IV. Ezek 30:20-26—Pharaoh and Egypt
   V. Ezek 31:1-18—Pharaoh and his multitude
   VI. Ezek 32:1-16—Pharaoh
   VII. Ezek 32:17-32—Pharaoh and his multitude

The summary material given after the Sidon oracle in 28:24-26 functions as the fulcrum for the two halves equal in length (25:1-28:23 / 29:1-32:32).[7] It is an important interlude in that it summarizes God's purposes for executing judgments against the foreign nations and anticipates Israel's restoration spelled out in chapters 34-37.

Interwoven through chapters 25-32 are other patterns. For example, we find interspersed sections of lamentation over Tyre (26:15-18; 27:1-36), over Tyre's king (28:11-19), over Pharaoh (32:1-16) and over Pharaoh and his multitude (32:17-32). Very often we see the sequence "because" a nation did such-and-such, "therefore" God will respond. We repeatedly encounter the recognition formula "they will know that I am Yahweh" or its variations. A refrain recurs in the Tyrian oracles (26:21; 27:36; 28:19). Finally, Ezekiel's prowess as a maker of metaphors comes through (cf. 20:49 [MT 21:5]).[8] Note how often Ezekiel employs extended metaphors by picturing Tyre as a seafaring vessel (27), Tyre's king as a guardian cherub in the garden of Eden (28), and Pharaoh as a sea monster (29; 32) or a great tree in the garden of Eden (31). In chapter 32 Ezekiel takes us on a tour of the underworld. The overlapping structures, refrains, and rich use of imagery have the effect of holding the disparate materials of chapters 25-32 together in an overall unity.

Summary of the Material

Chapter 25

In chapter 25 the prophet targets four small nations that immediately surround the land of Israel: Ammon, Moab, Edom, and Philistia. Each

---

7. See Daniel I. Block, *The Book of Ezekiel: Chapters 25-48*, NICOT (Grand Rapids: Eerdmans, 1998) 4-5.

8. See Carol A. Newsom, "A Maker of Metaphors: Ezekiel's Oracles Against Tyre," *Int* 38 (1984) 151-64; James A. Durlesser, *The Metaphorical Narratives in the Book of Ezekiel* (Lewiston, NY: Mellen, 2006).

judgment proclamation follows the same pattern: "because" the nation expressed hostility toward Israel, "therefore" God will punish it. Two paragraphs are devoted to Ammon while the other three nations receive one paragraph each. Each paragraph ends with the recognition formula, "they will know that I am Yahweh" or a variation of it.

Chapter 26

Chapter 26 begins a new section concerning Tyre. Its opening paragraph functions in a transitional way. It looks back to the previous short paragraphs in chapter 25 with the same "because—therefore" structure. Moreover, like the previous four nations the purpose of Tyre's downfall is stated with the recognition formula, that "they will know that I am Yahweh."

The opening paragraph also looks forward to the following material on Tyre by giving a brief summary statement of Tyre's fate, which in turn will be expanded in subsequent sections. God will bring up the nations against Tyre as the sea brings up its waves. The nations will destroy Tyre and make her a bare rock. Tyre's dependents on the mainland will be killed by the sword. These motifs will recur in the following Tyrian material.

In 26:7–13 the divine speech clarifies that God will destroy Tyre by bringing Nebuchadrezzar and the Babylonian army against her. The prophet presents a realistic portrayal of how an enemy army typically attacks, destroys, and plunders a city. At the end of this section we read that God will stop Tyre's music. That cessation of song anticipates a note that will be struck again and again in the Tyre section, the sound of lamentation. Verse 14 repeats two motifs stated earlier in vv. 4–5: Tyre will be made a bare rock and a place for drying fishing nets.

Verses 15–21 portray the response of the coastlands to Tyre's fall. Their princes will strip off their robes and raise a lamentation over Tyre. Tyre shall never again be inhabited or found; she will be submerged by the sea. The Tyrians will go down to the pit and join the inhabitants of the underworld. That motif will be picked up again concerning Egypt in chapters 31–32.

Chapter 27

Ezekiel's Tyre oracles follow the pattern of depicting the downfall and then the subsequent lamentation. We saw this sequence in chapter 26. Now in chapter 27 Ezekiel himself must raise a lamentation over Tyre, "the merchant of the peoples to many coastlands" (v. 3). Whereas chapter 26 gave a realistic picture of Tyre's demise, chapter 27 employs an extended metaphor by picturing Tyre as a beautiful ship. Basically the material has two parts. In vv. 3–25 Ezekiel extols the beauty and wealth of the merchant ship Tyre by providing an inventory list of her imports and exports. Then vv. 26–36 picture her shipwreck and the worldwide response. Heavily laden with goods from many nations she suffered shipwreck from a strong east wind and sank with all her wares and sailors. In response the other mariners take up a lamentation that resembles the prophet's lamentation. The coastlands are terror-stricken. Whereas in 26:19 Tyre the city is covered by the sea, in chapter 27 Tyre the ship sinks into the sea.

Chapter 28

Chapter 28 pairs two oracles against the ruler of Tyre.[9] In the first one (28:1–10) the prophet condemns the self-deifying pride of Tyre's ruler. The section follows the same "because—therefore" sequence evident in 25:1–26:6. Because Tyre's prince thinks he is a god who has enriched himself by his own commercial and business wisdom, therefore God will bring foreigners against him to defile his beauty and slay him.

Following the description—lament pattern for the city of Tyre, Ezekiel must now raise a lamentation (28:11–19) after picturing the death of Tyre's ruler. Whereas the previous section offered a realistic scenario (28:1–10), this one again makes rich use of imagery. It places the king in Eden, the garden of God, and lists the precious gems that adorned the king's royal robes. Then it speaks of the king as a guardian cherub on the mountain of God.[10] The section divides into two halves. Verses 12–15 extol his past splendor while vv. 16–19 depict his destruction. The description

---

9. The references to Tyre's "prince" (נגיד) and Tyre's "king" (מלך) are intended as interchangeable synonyms.

10. On the imagery of the king in the garden/mountain as a cherub, see Moshe Greenberg, *Ezekiel 21–37*, AB 22A (New York: Doubleday, 1997) 589–93; Block, *Ezekiel 25–48*, 113–21.

of his punishment intensifies from line to line: declared desecrated and barred from the mountain/garden; hurled down to the ground before kings; consumed by fire and turned to ashes before all.

In 28:20–23 Ezekiel announces judgment against Sidon, a fellow Phoenician city with Tyre. God will gain "glory" for himself and show his "holiness" by enacting judgments against Sidon. Those judgments include pestilence, bloodshed, and the sword. The purpose is that "they will know that I am Yahweh."

Verses 24–26 form an interlude that states the divine intent and purpose for executing judgments against the surrounding nations (see below).

Chapters 29–32

Chapters 29–32 contain seven oracles against Egypt, each of which is introduced with the word-event formula (ויהי / היה דבר־יהוה אלי לאמר).

In 29:1–16 Ezekiel proclaims judgment against Pharaoh and Egypt. The section divides into three units, each of which ends with the recognition formula. It begins with the metaphor of Pharaoh as a great sea monster/crocodile in the Nile. He is caught and hurled into the wilderness where he becomes food for the wild animals and birds.

The next two units follow the "because—therefore" sequence we have seen before. Because the Egyptians were a weak reed to Israel, therefore God will bring the sword against them and make the land a wasteland (vv. 6b–9a).

Verses 9b–16 flesh out the prospect of becoming a wasteland. Because Pharaoh claimed to be the Nile's creator and owner, therefore God will make the Nile and land a desolation to be uninhabited for forty years. The Egyptians will be dispersed among the nations. Verses 13–16 envision a surprising scenario. At the end of the forty years God will re-gather the dispersed Egyptians and bring them back to their land. Only this time they will be a weak and lowly kingdom that will never again be the object of Israel's trust.

The second Egyptian oracle in 29:17–21 is the last dated oracle in the book (571 BCE). Its location here serves to clarify that the Babylonian army will be God's instrument against Egypt but only after the siege of Tyre. After a 13 year siege Nebuchadrezzar failed to take

Tyre (588/7–573 BCE).[11] According to the divine speech, the Babylonian army was working for Yahweh but failed to receive wages for their labor. Therefore Yahweh will now compensate Nebuchadrezzar and his army with the land of Egypt and its wealth.

The third Egyptian oracle in 30:1–19 is the only Egyptian oracle that is undated. Its content exhibits links with both of the preceding sections in chapter 29. On the basis of the messenger formula—"Thus spoke the Lord Yahweh" (or simply "Thus spoke Yahweh")—one may organize the section into four units: vv 1–5, 6–9, 10–12, and 13–19.[12] According to the first two paragraphs, the day of Yahweh is coming. It is a time of doom for the nations, one of which is Egypt.[13] That will mean the downfall not only of Egypt but also those who support Egypt, such as Cush, Libya, Lydia, and "the children of the covenant land"—apparently foreign mercenaries in Egypt's army including some Israelites (v. 5). After hearing of Egypt's fall Cush will writhe in terror. In the third unit God promises to use as his weapon against Egypt's multitude Nebuchadrezzar and the Babylonian army, who will fill the land with the slain. Moreover, God threatens to dry up the branches and channels of the Nile. The fourth unit announces the coming destruction of Egypt's idols, the removal of any native ruler from Egypt, and the destruction of the various cities of Egypt.

The fourth Egyptian oracle (30:20–26) contrasts the king of Egypt with the king of Babylon. God says that he has broken Pharaoh's arm and it remains unhealed. The reference might be to Pharaoh Necho's defeat before Babylon at Carchemish (605 BCE), Pharaoh Hophra's failed attempt to assist Jerusalem (date unknown; cf. Jer 37:5–11), or the

---

11. On the siege of Tyre, see Martin Alonso Corral, *Ezekiel's Oracles against Tyre: Historical Reality and Motivations*, BiOr 46 (Rome: Pontifical Biblical Institute Press, 2002) 57–65.

12. Henry Van Dyke Parunak, "Structural Studies in Ezekiel" (Ph.D. diss., Cambridge: Harvard University, 1978) 390–93; Block, *Ezekiel 25–48*, 155. It is also possible to take the second messenger formula as part of a longer first unit with vv. 1–9, given that vv. 6–9 closely cohere with vv. 1–5. So, for example, Lawrence Boadt, *Ezekiel's Oracles against Egypt: A Literary and Philological Study of Ezekiel 29–32*, BiOr 37 (Rome: Biblical Institute Press, 1980) 57–58; Greenberg, *Ezekiel 21–37*, 627–28.

13. Note the parallel expressions "a time of nations" (v. 3) and "the day of Egypt" (v. 9). On the move from nations in general to one specific nation, see Paul R. Raabe, "The Particularizing of Universal Judgment in Prophetic Discourse," *CBQ* 64 (2002) 652–74.

battle between Egypt and Babylon near Egypt's border where both sides suffered heavy casualties (601 BCE).[14] The divine speech now proclaims that God will break both Pharaoh's arms so that he is unable to wield the sword.[15] In contrast God will strengthen the arms of Babylon's king who will stretch God's sword against Egypt. As a result the Egyptians will be dispersed among the nations.

The fifth Egyptian oracle (31:1–18) begins by asking Pharaoh and his multitude "To whom are you like in your greatness?" Pharaoh might rightly be compared to Assyria and the Assyrian king.[16] The section then pursues this comparison by depicting Assyria as a great and beautiful cedar that towered above all other trees and provided shade for many nations. Even the trees in the Garden of Eden envied it. But then it was cut down and abandoned. We are encouraged to read the tale of tree-Assyria as the tale of tree-Pharaoh. The comparison is spelled out in the Masoretic text of 31:10, "because you became lofty in height and he put his tree-top upward among clouds and his heart was exalted in his loftiness." The same sentence contains references to Pharaoh ("you") and Assyria ("he"), both depicted as trees. Given this comparison we expect tree-Pharaoh to be felled as well.[17] The end of the section repeats the question addressed to Pharaoh at the beginning: "To whom are you thus like in glory and in greatness among the trees of Eden?" (v. 18). But the same question asked in a different context evokes a different answer. Tree-Pharaoh is like the other trees in Eden in that it will be brought down to the Netherworld just like them. To emphasize that part of the comparison Ezekiel reverts back to literal language: "In the midst of the uncircumcised you [Pharaoh] will lie down with those slain by the sword" (v. 18).[18]

14. See Greenberg, *Ezekiel 21–37*, 633–34.

15. Perhaps Pharaoh's other healthy arm alludes to Egypt's navy that was assisting Tyre (Boadt, *Oracles against Egypt*, 85).

16. The word "Assyria" (אשור) (*šwr*) should not be emended to read "a cypress" (תאשור) as sometimes done by commentators. The text does not compare Pharaoh with two different trees but with the Assyrian king, "to *whom* are you like?" Then it gives a metaphorical portrayal of Assyria as a tree.

17. The verbs and pronouns in v. 11 continue to promote the equation of tree-Pharaoh with tree-Assyria: "I will give it [tree-Pharaoh] into the hand of a ram of nations ... I have expelled it [tree-Assyria]."

18. In his extended metaphors Ezekiel often inserts the literal referent into his imagery.

In the sixth Egyptian oracle in 32:1–16 the prophet raises a lamentation over Pharaoh. It begins with a contrast. Pharaoh likens himself to a lion of the nations that is able to prowl from land to land and capture prey. But Ezekiel compares him with a water bound sea-monster/crocodile that merely befouls the water.[19] He will be caught and hurled to the dry ground where the birds and beasts will feast on him. Ezekiel typically paints with shocking colors. So he goes on to say that God will strew the dragon's flesh all over and drench the land with its blood. Using imagery associated with the Day of the Lord and evoking the plague of darkness (Exodus 10), Ezekiel speaks of darkness covering the land of Egypt upon the death of Pharaoh (vv. 7–8). Then the other nations and kings will react with terror and fear for their own safety as well (vv. 9–10). The second unit (32:11–16) realistically portrays the Babylonian army slaying the people and beasts of Egypt, with the result that the waters of Egypt will run clear. The section ends with a colophon stating that the female mourners of the nations will chant Ezekiel's lament over Egypt's downfall (cf. 19:14).

The final Egyptian oracle in 32:17–32 gives a panoramic view of the Netherworld. The prophet is to lament over the multitude of Egypt and consign her to the underworld. There in the underworld are Assyria, Elam, Meshech-Tubal, Edom, the princes of the north and the Sidonians. Pharaoh and Egypt shall join them and lie down with the uncircumcised and those slain on the battlefield. By mentioning Edom and Sidon, two nations already covered, this final Egyptian oracle also provides a good conclusion to Ezekiel's oracles against foreign nations.

Divine Acts of Judgment against the Nations

Chapters 25–32 of Ezekiel present the God of Israel as announcing through his prophet that he will execute his wrath and do "judgments" (שׁפטים) against a particular place. Earlier the prophet announced "judgments" against Israel (e.g., 5:10, 15; 11:9; 14:21). Now he targets the foreign nations. These "acts of judgment" are cast in future tense. The prophet announces ahead of time what God will do.

In these chapters Ezekiel maintains his strongly theocentric vision. The "Lord Yahweh" is the chief actor for what is about to happen to the nations. The God of Israel is the Lord and judge of the foreign nations.

---

19. On the contrast given in 32:2 see Greenberg, *Ezekiel 21–37*, 657.

Moreover, these divine acts of judgment will take place concretely as destruction and exile. God will make use of earthly instruments to accomplish his ends. Against Ammon and Moab God will use "the sons of the East"—tent-dwelling nomads—(25:4, 10), and against Edom God's instrument will be restored Israel (25:14). God's chief weapon is the Babylonian army, against both Tyre and Egypt. Sometimes the prophet focuses on what God will do and other times on what Babylon will do. To show how both divine and human actions belong together, Ezekiel often oscillates between the two ways of speaking. He can even bring the two dimensions together into the same expression. For example, he speaks of Babylon wielding Yahweh's sword: "when I put my sword into the hand of the king of Babylon and he stretches it out against the land of Egypt" (30:25).

Why Divine Judgments against the Nations? Their Causes

Why are these divine "acts of judgment" going to happen? To answer that question we will make use of the Aristotelian distinction between efficient cause and final cause. Thus we will first look at the originating causes for the divine response and then at the purposes.

Chapters 25–32 frequently exhibit the pattern "because" nation X does such-and-such, "therefore" it will receive punishment. The "because—therefore" sequence occurs earlier in the Book of Ezekiel: against Jerusalem (5:7–10; 16:36–37); against false prophets and diviners (13:8, 22–23); and against Israel (22:19–22). Now the same standard operates against the foreign nations.

The pattern reveals several key features. These acts of divine wrath will come in response to the conduct of the particular nation. The divine responses are grounded on the behavior of the particular nation. They are not depicted as arbitrary, unpredictable acts "out of the blue" but as responses caused by and provoked by the actions of the nation. Just as the disasters against Jerusalem were not done "without cause" (14:23—חנם), so were the disasters against the nations. Ezekiel's theology is consistent.

Moreover, the standard of the judgment is the law of retaliation (*lex talionis*) expressed in the Pentateuchal legislation: "life for life, eye for eye, tooth for tooth" (Exod 21:23–25; Lev 24:20; Deut 19:21). There is a correspondence between the behavior and the punishment—as they have done, it shall be done back to them.[20] Thus the punishment is seen as fair, just, appropriate, and deserving. Just as Israel is judged "according to their ways"—an expression repeated frequently—so also the foreign nations. This *lex talionis* includes not only what people have done in the past but also what they wish would happen to others. As Deut 19:19 instructs the judges, "you shall do to him as he had meant to do to his brother."

Chapters 25–32 repeatedly evince judgment on the basis of the talionic standard. Sometimes the correspondence between action and punishment is reinforced by the repetition of key terms.

1. Because the Ammonites rejoiced over Judah when they went into exile, therefore God will hand the Ammonites over to another people, "the children of the East"—apparently a reference to tent-dwelling nomads (25:1–7).

2. Because Moab considered Judah like all the nations, therefore God will open up Moab's cities and "glory" to be possessed by "the children of the East." Thus Moab will be made like other nations, specifically like the Ammonites (25:8–11).

3. Because Edom acted vengefully against Judah, therefore God will lay his vengeance on Edom. Furthermore, the reversal will take place by Israel, who will enact God's anger (25:12–14).

4. Because the Philistines took vengeance, therefore God will enact vengeance against them (25:15–17).

5. Because Tyre exults that Jerusalem—called "the doors of the peoples"[21]—has been broken, therefore God will bring many nations against Tyre who will break down her walls and towers. Just

---

20. On the correspondence between sin and judgment in prophetic discourse, see Patrick D. Miller, *Sin and Judgment in the Prophets: A Stylistic and Theological Analysis*, SBLMS 27 (Chico, CA: Scholars Press, 1982).

21. Martin Alonso Corral (*Oracles against Tyre*, 144) takes the expression as a reference to Philistine ports, which provided Jerusalem's access to the sea. They were destroyed at the end of the 7th century. However, the Hebrew makes it clear that "Jerusalem" is the grammatical subject of the feminine singular verbs and that the phrase "the doors of the peoples" is used in apposition as a reference to Jerusalem. In the mid-eighth and seventh centuries Jerusalem was certainly a politically important city, and there is some evidence of it as a place of economic exchange as well (Greenberg, *Ezekiel 21–37*, 530).

as Tyre wanted to plunder Jerusalem, so Tyre will be plundered by other nations (26:1–6).

The texts above reveal one major cause for the divine response. Judgments are coming because these nations despise Jerusalem and Judah. In a summary statement Ezekiel calls these nations Israel's "neighbors who have treated them with contempt" (28:24, 26; cf. 16:57).[22] The initial judgment, which is against Ammon, illustrates the point:

> "Because you said, 'Aha!' over my sanctuary when it was profaned,
> and over the land of Israel when it was made desolate,
> and over the house of Judah when they went into exile." (25:3)

To despise the temple, land, and people is to despise Yahweh's sanctuary, Yahweh's land, and Yahweh's people. Yahweh's own honor and reputation is tied to Israel. By reproaching Yahweh's people the nations provoke Yahweh to wrath and bring down upon themselves his judgments. The divine speech in 36:1–7 emphasizes the causal connection. Because the land of Israel bore the humiliation of the nations, therefore the nations themselves will bear their own humiliation.

We should also note one related reason why Egypt is condemned. It is because Egypt was a "staff of reed" that collapsed when Israel leaned on it (29:6–9). Thus Egypt ended up hurting Israel by offering a false hope.

The second major cause that precipitates the response of divine judgment is human pride, traditionally one of the seven deadly sins.[23] There will be a reversal of fortunes. God targets the hubris of the kings and will bring down the high and mighty (cf. 17:24). This is another application of the *lex talionis*. The emphasis on pride is especially strong in the Tyre and Egypt oracles. The pattern of "because . . . therefore," which was noted earlier, occurs here as well (28:2–10; 29:9–12). The prince of Tyre thinks of himself as a god, because by his commercial wisdom he has enriched himself (28:1–10, 17). Pharaoh boasts that he made the

---

22. On the verb "to treat with contempt" (שאט), a very strong word, see Daniel Bodi, *The Book of Ezekiel and the Poem of Erra*, OBO 104 (Göttingen: Vandenhoeck & Ruprecht, 1991) 69–81.

23. On the theme of human pride in general, see Donald E. Gowan, *When Man Becomes God: Humanism and Hybris in the Old Testament*, PittsTMS 6 (Pittsburgh: Pickwick, 1975).

Nile for himself (29:1–16). He, like Assyria, towered high among the trees; the nations like birds and animals lived under its shade. As a result he became arrogant (31:1–18). Because of their overweening pride God will bring them down.

The above are the two major efficient causes behind the divine response. Next we turn to the final cause.

Why Divine Acts of Judgment? Their Purposes

The text of Ezekiel projects a picture in which the God of Israel announces that he will bring disaster upon various nations that surround Israel. Not only does he state what provoked him to this response but he also states what purposes will be served by this response. Why send destruction upon other nations? What good will that do? What is envisioned to result from the impending divine actions against the non-Israelite nations?[24]

One key purpose is to direct attention away from the nations and kingdoms of the world. The Ammonites and the Moabites will no longer be remembered among the nations (25:10). From now on all those who looked to Tyre for trade and with admiration will instead lament and be appalled (26:15–18; 27:28–36; 28:19). Tyre will no longer be the envy of the world. Egypt will no longer rule over others (29:15). The last oracle against Egypt emphasizes the point with the refrain that the nations "spread their terror in the land of the living" (32:23–30). That is what characterizes recent human history; the nations agitated, ruled, and terrorized. Now the God of Israel is about to act: "I spread my terror in the land of the living" (32:32). The one who deserves more attention than the nations is Yahweh.

As a corollary with the above, the coming disasters against the nations will serve a theocentric purpose.[25] They will direct attention away from the nations and toward Yahweh, the God of Israel, the one doing these things. This purpose is especially emphasized by the recognition

---

24. On the importance of this question, see Paul R. Raabe, "Why Prophetic Oracles against the Nations?" in *Fortunate the Eyes that See: Essays in Honor of David Noel Freedman in Celebration of His Seventieth Birthday*, ed. Astrid B. Beck et al. (Grand Rapids: Eerdmans, 1995) 236–57.

25. For an overview of Ezekiel's theocentric perspective, see Paul Joyce, *Divine Initiative and Human Response in Ezekiel*, JSOTSup 51 (Sheffield: Sheffield Academic Press, 1989) 89–105.

formula, an expression that appears frequently throughout the Book of Ezekiel.[26] The formula consists of the verb "to know" plus a self-identification clause: people "will know that I am Yahweh" (or with slight variations). The formula recurs throughout Ezekiel's oracles against the nations, typically at the end of a unit or section. There are eight occurrences for the first six nations and eight for Egypt:

- Ammon—2 times (25:5, 7)
- Moab—1 time (25:11)
- Edom—1 time (25:14)
- Philistia—1 time (25:17)
- Tyre—1 time (26:6)[27]
- Sidon—2 times (28:22, 23)
- Egypt—8 times (29:6, 9, 16; 30:8, 19, 25, 26; 32:15).

The logic behind the formula in chapters 25–32 operates this way. Currently the nations are treating Yahweh's Israel with contempt and are trivializing Yahweh's own identity and sovereignty. Ammon rejoices over Israel's downfall. Moab considers Judah just like the other nations. Edom and Philistia act with vengeful malice. Tyre seeks to exploit for herself the destruction of Jerusalem. Egypt claims lordship over the entire area. In response Yahweh will execute judgments against these nations. When the nations experience the upcoming disaster, they will know and acknowledge that the one who afflicted them is Yahweh, the God of Israel. They will discover and experientially know that the one who really deserves to be treated as God, the one who in fact defeats them, rules over them and judges them is Israel's God.

---

26. On the recognition formula, see the important essays by Walther Zimmerli, conveniently translated and collected in Walther Zimmerli, *I Am Yahweh*, trans. Douglas W. Stott, ed. Walter Brueggemann (Atlanta: John Knox, 1982). Also see Joyce, *Divine Initiative*, 89–95.

27. Why is there only one occurrence of the recognition formula in the lengthy Tyrian material? One possible explanation is given by John Strong, who connects the formula with Yahweh as divine warrior, a theme that did not fit the Tyrian situation very well. See John Strong, "Ezekiel's Use of the Recognition Formula in His Oracles against the Nations," *Perspectives in Religious Studies* 22 (1995) 115–33.

This theocentric purpose is succinctly stated in the Sidon oracle:

> "Behold, I am against you, O Sidon,
>   and I will glorify myself in your midst.
> And they will know that I am Yahweh
>   when I execute judgments in her
>   and I will show myself holy in her." (28:22)

Yahweh, whose holy name is profaned among the nations, will now glorify himself and show his holiness, his "God-ness," his separateness and sovereignty (cf. 36:20; 38:23). Then they will know Yahweh and his glory and holiness.

Another purpose served by the future judgments concerns the future post-exilic Israel. It is explicitly stated after the Sidon oracle (28:24–26). When the Israelites are restored to their land from exile, they will live in peace and security. No longer will hostile neighbors be a thorn in the flesh. No longer will they be allowed to treat Israel with contempt:

> "And they [=Israel] will dwell on it [=their land] in security
> and they will build houses and plant vineyards and dwell in security
> when I execute judgments on all those treating them with contempt
> from those around them." (28:26)

Ezekiel foresees a future restoration for Egypt after its punishment, but that future Egypt will be small and lowly. For what purpose? So that Israel will never again rely on Egypt (29:16). Divine judgment upon the nations will serve Israel's restoration and elicit Israel's exclusive loyalty to Yahweh.

Why Speeches of Judgment against the Nations?

So far we have asked about the announced actions of Yahweh, their originating causes and their purposes. We should also ask about the speeches themselves. Why did Ezekiel make these speeches? What were their rhetorical purposes?[28]

Ezekiel addressed these discourses to his fellow exiles in Babylon. Within that context and for those addressees one can readily see at least

---

28. On the importance of this question, see Raabe, "Why Prophetic Oracles against the Nations?"

two rhetorical purposes. First of all, by announcing divine judgment against the surrounding seven nations Ezekiel was warning the exiles. "Do not envy the glory and beauty of Tyre with her worldwide trade. Do not admire the greatness of Egypt. Stop expecting Egypt to come to the rescue." Earlier in the book Ezekiel condemned Israel for its desire to become just like the nations (11:12; 20:32; 23:30). To emulate the nations, Ezekiel says, is a dead end.

The second rhetorical purpose is to give the exiles hope for their future. The exiles were demoralized in deep and profound ways. Israel was publicly made a reproach to the other nations (5:14–15; 16:57; 22:4). Ezekiel articulates their hopelessness in his vision of the dry bones: "Our bones are dried up, and our hope is lost; we are clean cut off" (37:11). By announcing that Yahweh would soon remove the neighboring thorns and briers, Ezekiel was making the return from exile attractive. The future would not simply repeat the past. After their restoration and purification Israel will dwell in the land in security (28:24–26). They will no longer be a prey to the nations or suffer the reproach of the nations (34:28–29). That future prospect must have encouraged the despairing exiles.

Why Preserve the Oracles against the Nations?

Why were Ezekiel's oracles against seven particular nations preserved when some of the nations, Egypt for example, were no longer a concern during the Persian period? A clue presents itself in the Tyre oracles. In an oracle dated to the eleventh year (587–586) Ezekiel announced that Babylon would bring Tyre down (26:7). Later in the twenty-seventh year (571) Ezekiel proclaimed that Babylon would not conquer Tyre but would take Egypt instead (29:17–21). Yet the book keeps the earlier Tyre oracle. This clue suggests that the person or persons responsible for the book in its present form wanted to preserve all of the prophet's material, even the time-bound oracles.

What value would Ezekiel's oracles against seven particular nations have for later generations? Ezekiel's oracles were probably meant to be taken in a typological way. The announced judgment against these particular nations typified divine judgment against all nations (cf. chapter 36). Perhaps the ongoing significance of the material was facilitated by the theme of the day of the Lord (see 30:1–5). Certainly the theological witness of chapters 25–32 constitutes an important part of the book's overall outlook.

Location and Function in the Book

Finally we should ask about placement and function in the book. The oracles against foreign nations are located in the middle of the Book of Ezekiel, after the oracles of judgment against Israel and before the oracles announcing the restoration of Israel. Why are they located in this position? Their present location logically fits within the overall program of Ezekiel.

Ezekiel's overall vision basically envisions the following sequence of events:

Stage 1—Israel rebels against God.

Stage 2—Thereby Israel brings down upon themselves the judgment of God, who destroys Jerusalem and sends them into exile.

Stage 3—At Israel's plight the surrounding nations gloat and treat God's people and land with contempt. Tyre and Egypt exult in their arrogance.

Stage 4—God brings judgment against the surrounding nations.

Stage 5—God restores Israel back to its land, where they will enjoy security gathered around his sanctuary. God purifies their hearts so that they will now be his obedient and holy people.

Within this sequence stage 4 functions first of all as the divine response to stage 3. The nations will no longer profane God's holy name but instead will come to know and acknowledge Israel's God as their Lord and Judge.

Secondly, stage 4 provides a necessary preparation for stage 5. In order for Israel to be restored to its land and to dwell there in security God must first remove the thorns and briers that used to afflict them (28:24–26). Judgment against foreign nations will guarantee that restored Israel will no longer seek to emulate the proud ways of the other nations. No longer will they admire the wealth of Tyre or rely on Egypt. Perhaps Ezekiel 25–32 targets seven nations to suggest a typological correspondence between Israel's beginning and its postexilic future. Just as the seven nations of the land had to be removed before Israel could inherit the land (Deut 7:1), so the same kind of removal is necessary for Israel's restoration to the land.[29]

The location of chapters 25–32 fits logically within the outline of the book. Judgment against the non-Israelite nations is an essential part of the overall future scenario announced by the prophet Ezekiel. Therefore Ezekiel rightly devotes considerable attention to oracles against the nations.

Bibliography

Andersen, F. I., and A. D. Forbes. "'Prose Particle' Counts of the Hebrew Bible." In *The Word of the Lord Shall Go Forth: Essays in Honor of David Noel Freedman in Celebration of His Sixtieth Birthday*, edited by C. L. Meyers and M. O'Connor, 165–83. Winona Lake, IN: Eisenbrauns, 1983.

Block, Daniel I. *The Book of Ezekiel: Chapters 1–24*. NICOT. Grand Rapids: Eerdmans, 1997.

———. *The Book of Ezekiel: Chapters 25–48*. NICOT. Grand Rapids: Eerdmans, 1998.

Boadt, Lawrence. *Ezekiel's Oracles against Egypt: A Literary and Philological Study of Ezekiel 29–32*. BiOr 37. Rome: Biblical Institute Press, 1980.

———. "Rhetorical Strategies in Ezekiel's Oracles of Judgment." In *Ezekiel and His Book*, edited by J. Lust, 182–200. BETL 74. Leuven: Leuven University Press, 1986.

Bodi, Daniel. *The Book of Ezekiel and the Poem of Erra*. OBO 104. Göttingen: Vandenhoeck & Ruprecht, 1991.

Corral, Martin Alonso. *Ezekiel's Oracles against Tyre: Historical Reality and Motivations*. Biblica et Orientalia 46. Rome: Pontifical Biblical Institute, 2002.

Durlesser, James A. *The Metaphorical Narratives in the Book of Ezekiel*. Lewiston, NY: Mellen, 2006.

Gowan, Donald E. *When Man Becomes God: Humanism and Hybris in the Old Testament*. PittsTMS 6. Pittsburgh: Pickwick, 1975.

Greenberg, Moshe. *Ezekiel 1–20*. AB 22. Garden City: Doubleday, 1983.

———. *Ezekiel 21–37*. AB 22A. New York: Doubleday, 1997.

Hals, Ronald M. *Ezekiel*. FOTL 19. Grand Rapids: Eerdmans, 1989.

Joyce, Paul. *Divine Initiative and Human Response in Ezekiel*. JSOTSup 51. Sheffield: Sheffield Academic, 1989.

Miller, Patrick D. *Sin and Judgment in the Prophets: A Stylistic and Theological Analysis*. SBLMS 27. Chico, CA: Scholars, 1982.

---

29. Walther Zimmerli, *Ezekiel 2*, trans. James D. Martin, Hermeneia (Philadelphia: Fortress, 1983) 3; Ronald M. Hals, *Ezekiel*, FOTL 19 (Grand Rapids: Eerdmans, 1989) 180.

Newsom, Carol A. "A Maker of Metaphors: Ezekiel's Oracles against Tyre." *Int* 38 (1984) 151–64.

Raabe, Paul R. "Why Prophetic Oracles against the Nations?" In *Fortunate the Eyes that See: Essays in Honor of David Noel Freedman in Celebration of His Seventieth Birthday*, edited by Astrid B. Beck et al., 236–57. Grand Rapids: Eerdmans, 1995.

———. "The Particularizing of Universal Judgment in Prophetic Discourse." *CBQ* 64 (2002) 652–74.

Renz, Thomas. *The Rhetorical Function of the Book of Ezekiel*. VTSup 76. Leiden: Brill, 1999.

Strong, John. "Ezekiel's Use of the Recognition Formula in His Oracles against the Nations." *Perspectives in Religious Studies* 22 (1995) 115–33.

Van Dyke Parunak, Henry. "Structural Studies in Ezekiel." PhD diss., Harvard University, 1978.

Zimmerli, Walter. *Ezekiel 1*. Translated by R. E. Clements. Hermeneia. Philadelphia: Fortress, 1979.

———. *Ezekiel 2*. Translated by J. D. Martin. Hermeneia. Philadelphia: Fortress, 1983.

———. *I Am Yahweh*. Translated by Douglas W. Stott. Edited by Walter Brueggemann. Atlanta: John Knox, 1982.

8

Transformation of Royal Ideology in Ezekiel

Daniel I. Block

SCHOLARS HAVE LONG RECOGNIZED BOTH EZEKIEL'S DEPENDENCE upon earlier texts and traditions and his creative adaptation of earlier materials for his own rhetorical context. This is most obvious in his use of the Torah.[1] The purpose of this paper is to explore how Ezekiel adapts and transforms traditional and textual materials in his portrayal of Israel's monarchy. Our investigation will be divided into three parts: (1) Ezekiel's portrayal of the history of Israel's monarchy; (2) Ezekiel's portrayal of the monarchy in his day; (3) Ezekiel's portrayal of the future of the monarchy. Unlike other books in the prophetic corpus,[2] the book of Ezekiel lacks a formal introduction declaring the historical context of his ministry. Nevertheless, based on the information provided by the opening notice of the date of his inaugural vision and call to prophetic office, the prophet was born in 623 BCE, four years after Jeremiah's call to prophetic service (Jer 1:2), and seventeen years into the reign of Josiah (640–609 BCE). Therefore, for the purposes of this paper the accession to the throne of Josiah in 640 BCE (2 Kgs 21:18–25) marks the boundary between the past and present of Israel's monarchy, and the death of Jehoiachin in exile marks the boundary between the present and the future of the monarchy. We shall explore Ezekiel's disposition toward the monarchy in each of these three periods separately.

---

1. See most recently Michael A. Lyons, *From Law to Prophecy: Ezekiel's Use of the Holiness Code*, LHBOTS 507 (New York: T. & T. Clark, 2009). Also, R. Levitt Kohn, *A New Heart and a New Soul: Ezekiel, the Exile and the Torah*, JSOTSup 358 (Sheffield: Sheffield Academic, 2002).

2. Isa 1:1; Hosea 1:1; Amos 1:1; Micah 1:1; Jer 1:1–3.

Ezekiel's Portrayal of the History of Israel's Monarchy

From Ezekiel's revisionist histories of Israel in chapters 16 and 23, specifically his focus on Jerusalem and Samaria, the prophet was obviously aware of the separate political histories of the northern kingdom of Israel and the southern kingdom of Judah. Although these were the capital cities of separate nations, Ezekiel knew that their populations were ethnically related, for he refers to them as sisters in these chapters (cf. 16:46 and 23:4).[3] Inasmuch as the prophet explicitly refers to these two nations (שְׁנֵי גוֹיִם) as "two kingdoms" (שְׁתֵּי מַמְלָכוֹת; 37:22), it is also evident that Ezekiel knew that these two nations were ruled by kings.[4] But Ezekiel expresses no awareness of the circumstances that led to the creation of these two monarchies, nor even that there ever was a time when north and south were united under a single monarchy. Nor does he show any interest in the history of the northern kings.

Although hints of the history of Judah's monarchy are vague, from texts like 34:2–10 and 43:7–9 it is clear that Ezekiel had a negative view of the kings of Judah. In the former he accuses the רֹעִים יִשְׂרָאֵל, "shepherds of Israel," of exploiting their subjects for personal gain instead of caring for them. In 43:7–9 Ezekiel associates kings (מְלָכִים) with divine name-defiling actions involving harlotry (= idolatry), illicit funerary practices, and the encroachment of sacred space with construction projects. It is unclear in both cases whether these charges apply to Ezekiel's royal contemporaries or whether he has longstanding abuses of the office in mind.[5] Whatever the case, one gets the impression that the exilic prophet has intentionally suppressed much of the memory of Israel's monarchy, as if it were a bad dream. This impression is reinforced in several ways.

First, in Ezekiel's creative reconstruction (or should we say deconstruction?) of the history of Israel and Judah (16:1–34; 20:5–28;

---

3. This should not be pressed too far, since he also identifies Sodom as Jerusalem's sister in 16:46–52.

4. While the originality of מֶלֶךְ in the MT of 37:22 is disputed (Papyrus[967] and LXX read ἄρχων, on which see further below), שְׁתֵּי מַמְלָכוֹת is not. Papyrus[967] and LXX read δύο βασιλείας.

5. According to 2 Kgs 21:4–15 earlier prophets had responded to Manasseh's crimes by announcing the eventual destruction of the nation because of his crimes. But the history of court sponsored idolatry goes back much farther than Manasseh's reign to the time of Solomon (1 Kgs 11:1–8).

23:2-21) he never alludes to the human kings of Israel, let alone hints at their involvement in the crimes for which the nation is charged. When royal language occurs, the king is YHWH.⁶

Second, in contrast to Jeremiah, who identifies his royal contemporaries by name 100 times, and earlier kings more than twenty times,⁷ Ezekiel never mentions a king of Israel or Judah by name. David's name occurs four times (34:23, 24; 37:24, 25), but in each instance he has in mind a future king. And Jehoiachin's name appears in 1:2, but this verse derives from an editorial hand and actually represents the exception that proves the rule.

Third, instead of identifying Israel's rulers as מלכים, "kings," Ezekiel prefers to refer to them by the archaic expression, נשיאים, "princes." He does indeed use the former expression more than thirty times, especially when speaking of foreign kings (see Table below), and on occasion to refer to his royal contemporaries as kings.⁸ The only exception occurs in 43:7-9, where the prophet mentions that in the past, along with the people, their kings have defiled YHWH's holy name with harlotry and abominable funerary practices.

---

6. In 20:33 YHWH declares that in the future he will be king (מלך) over Israel. YHWH's kingship is also implied in 16:10-14, where YHWH lavishes on Jerusalem (representing Israel) the treasures and the culinary fare of an ancient monarch, and through his lavish generosity she attains royal status herself (מלוכה, v. 13). P. M. Joyce overlooks this text in his otherwise excellent discussion of the kingship of YHWH in Ezekiel: "King and Messiah in Ezekiel," in *King and Messiah in Israel and the Ancient Near East: Proceedings of the Oxford Old Testament Seminary*, ed. J. Day, JSOTSup 270 (Sheffield: Sheffield Academic Press, 1998) 332-36.

7. His contemporaries included: Josiah (18x), Jehoahaz (1x, as Shallum, 22:11), Jehoiakim (22x), Jehoiachin (10x, also as Coniah and Jeconiah), Zedekiah (49); earlier kings, David (14x), Solomon (1x), Hezekiah (3x), Manasseh (1x), Amon (2x).

8. Ezek 7:27 (indeterminate // נשיא); 17:12 (Jerusalem's king, i.e., Zedekiah); 17:16 (Zedekiah, caused to reign).

The Usage of מֶלֶךְ and נָשִׂיא in Ezekiel

Status	מלך	נשיא
Divinity (YHWH)	20:33 (YHWH will be king)	
King(s) of Judah	1:2 (Jehoiachin) 7:27 (indeterminate// נשיא) 17:12 (Jerusalem's king) 17:16 (Zedekiah, caused to reign) 37:22 (one king reigning over one kingdom 37:24 (My servant David, shepherd) 43:7 (plural, 2x) 43:9 (plural)	7:27 indeterminate // מלך 12:10 in Jerusalem (Zedekiah) 19:1 plural (Jehoahaz and Jehoiakim) 21:17[12]; plural delivered to sword 21:30[25]; wicked X of Israel (Zedekiah) 22:6; (former oppressive rulers) 22:25 (former oppressive rulers) 34:24; (My servant David, shepherd) 37:25; (My servant David) 45:8 (my princes will no longer oppress) 45:9 (princes, put away violence)
Patron of the Cult		44:3a, 3b; 45:7, 8, 9, 16, 17, 22; 46: 2, 4, 8, 10, 12, 16, 17; 48:21a 21b, 22a, 22b
Foreign Kings	Babylon 17:12; 19:9; 21:24[Eng 19], 26 [Eng 21]; 24:2; 26:7; 29:18, 19; 30:10, 24, 25a, 25b; 32:11.	
	Egypt, 29:2, 3; 30:21, 22; 31:2; 32:2 (pharaoh).	Egypt, 30:13 (no prince in Egypt = pharaoh)
	Tyre, 28:12	Gog, 38:2, 3; 39:1 (chief prince of Meshech)
	Edom, 32:29	
	Of the earth, 27:33 Of many peoples, 32:10	
	Of the coastlands, 27:35	26:16; (princes of the sea)
		27:21 (princes of Kedar) 32:29 (princes of Edom// מלכים) 39:18 (princes of the earth// גבורים)

Opinions on why Ezekiel avoided the term מֶלֶךְ when speaking of Israel's kings vary. Since outside this book references to the office of נָשִׂיא occur most frequently in the narratives concerning Israel's wandering in the desert, where leaders of tribes and clans were supposedly apolitical sacral figures, some suggest that by using this term the prophet was trying to reestablish this role as primary also for the monarch.[9] Others argue that Ezekiel prefers נָשִׂיא over מֶלֶךְ because the latter emphasizes the ruler's role as military leader, while the former speaks of his role as a moral and spiritual leader.[10] It seems more likely that Ezekiel avoids מֶלֶךְ because in his mind the expression carries overtones of independence and arrogance, while נָשִׂיא expresses, more appropriately, the king's status as a vassal of YHWH. This interpretation seems to be supported by his linkage of the latter term with עֶבֶד, "servant, vassal," in 34:23–24 and 37:24–25, his reference to past kings as נְשִׂיאַי, "my princes" in 45:8.[11] Ezekiel's problem is not with the monar-

---

9. Cf. J. Levenson, *Theology of the Program of Restoration of Ezekiel 40–48*, HSM 10 (Missoula, MT: Scholars, 1976) 142. However, not only is Ezekiel's perspective on the pre-monarchic period quite negative (cf. 20:10–26), but the image of the נָשִׂיא in chapters 40–48 also ill suits a wilderness context.

10. Accordingly to G. A. Cooke on 37:24–25 (*The Book of Ezekiel: A Critical and Exegetical Commentary*, ICC [Edinburgh: T. & T. Clark, 1946] 403), the Davidic king was to "have pastoral charge, to watch over the morals and religion of his people." Cf. B. Vawter and L. J. Hoppe (*A New Heart: A Commentary on the Book of Ezekiel*, ITC [Grand Rapids: Eerdmans, 1991] 204), who suggest he was "to devote himself entirely to the study of the Law (Deut 17:18–20)." This view is represented most recently by A. S. Crane, "The Restoration of Israel: Ezekiel 36–39 in Early Jewish Interpretation: A Textual-comparative Study of the Oldest Extant Hebrew and Greek Manuscripts," DPhil dissertation, Murdock University, Perth, Australia, 2006, 152: "Overall, we find one theology that has a resurrected and restored United Kingdom requiring a king, even a Davidic 'military' king, and then another theology where this Davidic נָשִׂיא would lead the people in spiritual pursuits, and not military activities." For an evaluation of Crane's view see further below.

11. Though the last kings are obviously also recognized as vassals of earthly foreign rulers: Zedekiah was a vassal of Nebuchadnezzar (12:10; 17:16 [he was "made king" (הִמְלִיךְ) by Nebuchadnezzar]; 21:30[25]); Jehoiakim was a vassal of the king of Egypt (19:4–9). According to S. S. Tuell, *The Law of the Temple in Ezekiel 40–48*, HSM 49 (Atlanta: Scholars, 1992), the נָשִׂיא in chapters 40–48 was a vassal of the king of Persia. However, 17:16 suggests that the distinction should not be overstated. If נָשִׂיא actually bears a stronger nuance of vassalage, it might have been more natural for Ezekiel to speak of Zedekiah as "installed, set up," as prince by the Babylonian overlord. Cf. 1 Kgs 11:34, where YHWH says, כִּי נָשִׂיא אֲשִׁתֶנּוּ כֹּל יְמֵי חַיָּיו, "for I will make him prince all the days of his life." I. M. Duguid, *Ezekiel and the Leaders of Israel*, VTSup 56 (Leiden: Brill, 1994) 57, rightly asserts that here נָשִׂיא obviously denotes a king.

chic institution in principle, but with the way those who have sat on the throne of David have exercised their power. Within his theocratic perspective, YHWH is Israel's real king, and the occupants of the throne, the descendants of David are his vassals. Because they have historically acted contrary to the divine will (Deut 17:14–20), and "done evil in the eyes of YHWH,"[12] they do not deserve the title מלך.

Ezekiel's Portrayal of the Monarchy in His Day

Our understanding of Ezekiel's disposition toward the history of Israel's monarchy in general and his adaptation of Israel's traditions is admittedly grounded largely on negative evidence—in this case absence of evidence is significant. As we explore his use of ancient texts and traditions to portray the last kings of Judah we witness an increasing transparency on this issue.

Josiah

The only possible allusions to Josiah surface in chapters 17 and 18. In the coda to the prophet's riddles concerning the eagle, the top sprig of a cedar tree from Lebanon, and the spreading vine, in 17:22–24 he uses a special expression to highlight the freshness of the sprig: רך, "tender." It is widely recognized that "the tender (sprig) from the topmost of its young twigs (מראש ינקותיו רך) is a harbinger of the messianic figure who will be presented in greater detail in later salvation oracles. However, Ezekiel's choice of this word also points backward. While the books of Kings in their present form cannot have been composed at the time of this oracle, Josiah's reputation as a ruler of piety and devotion to YHWH must have been well-known.[13] The word רך provides a remarkable link with 2 Kgs 22:19 (= 2 Chron 34:27), where the prophet Huldah speaks of the tenderness (רך) of King Josiah's heart, as demonstrated in his contrition before YHWH and his response to the hearing of the curses in the Torah. Although Antti Laato missed this connection, this

---

12. Ezekiel never uses the expression, though his colleague Jeremiah does (52:2), and the deuteronomistic historian uses it at least eighteen times (1 Kgs 15:26, 34; 22:53; 2 Kgs 8:18, 27; 13:2; 14:24; 15:9, 18, 24, 28; 17:2; 21:2, 20; 23:32, 37; 24:9, 19; cf. 2 Chron 21:6; 22:4; 33:2, 22; 36:5, 9, 12).

13. 2 Chron 35:26–27 suggests these may even have been available in some written form.

lexical link may buttress his thesis that Josiah provided the prophets with the model for the messianic king.[14]

While the case is somewhat weaker, this lexical connection may have influenced the arrangement of chapters 17–19, in which we find an oracle presenting a tri-generational succession of cases (18:5–17) sandwiched between two metaphorical oracles concerning the dynasty. Although a wider application was probably intended in the original rhetorical context,[15] according to this interpretation, Ezekiel has in mind the reigns of three of the last kings of Judah: Josiah (vv. 5–9), Jehoiakim (vv. 10–13), and Jehoiachin (vv. 14–20) respectively.[16] According to Laato:

> [T]he aim of Ezek 18 in its present context was to argue for Jekoniah's (or his family's) legitimate inheritance of the Davidic throne (as suggested in Ezek 17:22–24) in spite of the curse uttered in Jer 22:24–30. Jekoniah is responsible only for what he himself has done not for what his father has done. If he returns to YHWH and does not follow his father's evil acts he will prosper.[17]

Through this arrangement of oracles the editor urges the reader not to ascribe injustice to YHWH for the way he has treated the members of the royal house.

---

14. A. Laato, *Josiah and David Redivivus: The Historical Josiah and the Messianic Expectations of Exilic and Postexilic Times*, ConBOT 33 (Lund: Almqvist & Wiksell, 1992). Josiah is the only person in the Hebrew Bible who is recognized as being totally devoted to YHWH according to the paradigm of Deut 6:4–5. 2 Kgs 23:25 notes that there was no king in Israel who turned to YHWH "with all his heart/mind (לב), with all his being (נפש), and with all his possessions (מאד), according to the entire Torah of Moses."

15. On which see K. P. Darr, "Proverb Performance and Trans-generational Retribution in Ezekiel 18," in *Ezekiel's Hierarchical World: Wrestling with a Tiered Reality*, ed. C. Patton and S. Cook, SBLSymS (Atlanta: Society of Biblical Literature, 2004) 197–221; idem, "Ezekiel," in *The New Interpreter's Bible* (Nashville: Abingdon, 2001) 1257–62.

16. In addition to Laato (*Josiah and David Redivivus*, 162–64), see W. Zimmerli, *Ezekiel 1*, trans. R. E. Clements, Hermeneia (Philadelphia: Fortress, 1979) 72.

17. *Josiah and David Redivivus*, 358.

Jehoahaz

Two major oracles in Ezekiel focus on the fates of the last kings of Judah, viz., chapters 17 and 19. Both are highly poetic in style, cast in the form of extended metaphors. Only the latter involves Jehoahaz. While the preamble to chapter 19 identifies this text as a dirge, in reality it exhibits the features both of a riddle (חִידָה, cf. 17:2) and parody.[18] Ezekiel has taken the form of a *qinah* and infused it with alien content. This is not only a funeral song, but also a riddle that deals enigmatically with a living reality—the fate of the Davidic dynasty.

The preamble to the dirge announces that this oracle concerns the princes (נְשִׂיאִים) of Israel generally. The dirge itself concerns a pride of lions, specifically a mother lioness and two of her cubs. But whom do these lions represent? More precisely, what is the lioness?[19] One's first impulse is to identify the lioness as Hamutal, the wife of Josiah and mother of Jehoahaz and Zedekiah (2 Kgs 23:31; 24:18). However, this interpretation is excluded by the portrayal of her second cub in vv. 5–9, which most identify as Jehoiakim, who is identified elsewhere as the son of Zebidah, the daughter of Pedaiah of Rumah (2 Kgs 23:36). Perhaps the lioness functions symbolically for Judah or the Davidic dynasty,[20] but then Ezekiel should have used the masculine, לְבִיא. The switch to the feminine, לְבִיָּא, suggests the referent must be feminine, probably Jerusalem, which, like other geographic names, is consistently identified as feminine in the book.[21] If this is correct, Ezekiel minimizes their genealogical participation in the dynasty of David and highlights their geographical location.

Of the first cub the dirge says:

> She raised up one of her cubs; he became a young lion.
> He learned to capture prey; he devoured humans.
> The nations heard about him; in their pit he was caught.
> They dragged him off with hooks to the land of Egypt. (19:3–4)

---

18. G. A. Yee, "Anatomy of Biblical Parody: The Dirge Form in 2 Samuel 1 and Isaiah 14," *CBQ* 50 (1988) 565, defines a parody as "the literary imitation of an established form or style."

19. Note the form of the question and its answer with which the dirge opens: מָה אִמְּךָ לְבִיָּא, "What is your mother? A lioness!"

20. This was our interpretation in *Ezekiel Chapters 1–25*, 604.

21. So also M. S. Odell, *Ezekiel*, SHBC (Macon, GA: Smyth & Helwys, 2005) 237–39.

Since Jehoahaz was the only king of Judah taken to Egypt (2 Kgs 23:34), scholars generally agree the first lion represents the immediate successor to Josiah. Although Jehoahaz reigned only for three months, it was long enough for the deuteronomistic historian to characterize him as one "who did the evil in the sight of YHWH" (i.e., defection from YHWH to other gods) just as his predecessors had done (2 Kgs 23:31b).[22]

If Ezekiel's portrayal of this cub as a violent creature is natural, his metaphorical description of human rulers is traditional. The predatory habits of lions serve as a common figure for the violence of humans in the Hebrew Bible. The psalmists portray their enemies as ravaging lions,[23] and the prophets apply the metaphor to invading armies.[24] The vocabulary of Ezekiel's portrait of this lion suggests he may have adapted Nahum's description of the invading Assyrians (Nah 2:12–13 [11–12]):

Where now is the den of lions (אריות),

the feeding place of the young lions (כפרים);

Where the great feline (אריה), the lion (לביא) stalked

and the lion cub (גור אריה) with nothing to fear?

The lion (אריה) tore (טרף) victims for its cubs (גרות),

And strangled the prey for his lionesses (לבאתיו);

He filled his lairs with kill (טרף),

His dens with mangled flesh (טרפה).

But Ezekiel's lion is not satisfied with ordinary prey; he develops a particular appetite for human flesh.[25] His notoriety spreads quickly to the

---

22. Jeremiah has a short note on Jehoahaz (Shallum, Jer 22:10–12), but he adds nothing to the picture.

23. Ps 7:2; 10:9; 17:12; 22:13; 22:21. Cf. also Prov 28:15 and 1 Pet 5:8.

24. Isa 5:29; Hos 5:14.

25. For biblical references to humans being devoured by lions, see 1 Kgs 13:24–28; 20:35–36; 2 Kgs 17:25–26. The motif is common in ancient Near Eastern art. See the sandstone relief from Musawarat es-Sofra from early Ptolemaic Egypt (O. Keel, *The Symbolism of the Biblical World: Ancient Near Eastern Iconography and the Book of Psalms*, trans. T. J. Hallett [Winona Lake, IN: Eisenbrauns, 1997] 75, fig. 101), and the unfinished basalt carving from Nebuchadnezzar II's Babylon (fig. 102). See also the remarkable carved ivory plaque from the ninth century BCE palace of Ashurnasirpal II, which depicts a lion killing a Nubian. R. D. Barnett, *Ancient Ivories in the Middle East and Adjacent Countries*, Qedem, Monographs of the Institute of Archeology 14

surrounding nations, who combine forces to capture him and drag him off with hooks to Egypt. While our text is silent on why this upstart lion was taken to Egypt, the geographic reference offers the first concrete clue to the human behind the symbol.[26]

Jehoiakim

Though some argue that Ezek 18:10–13 applies to Jehoiakim, the only clear reference in Ezekiel to this king, the son of Josiah by a second wife, Zebidah (2 Kgs 23:36), occurs in the second part of this dirge (Ezek 19:5–9):

> When she realized her wait was in vain, and her hope had vanished,
> She took another one of her cubs, and appointed him a young lion.
> He strutted about among the lions, and he became a young lion.
> He learned to capture prey, and he devoured humans.
> He consorted with his widows, and laid waste their cities.
> The land and all its inhabitants were appalled, at the sound of his roaring.
> The nations from the surrounding provinces took up arms against him.
> They spread out their net against him; in their pit he was captured.
> With hooks they put him in a neck-stock, and brought him to the king of Babylon.

Although the second lion has been identified with Jehoiachin, Jehoiakim, and Zedekiah,[27] on balance, Jehoiakim seems the strongest candidate.[28] But even then Ezekiel plays loose and free with the histori-

---

(Jerusalem: Hebrew University 1982), pl. 49, fig. d; P. Amiet, *The Art of the Ancient Near East*, trans. J. Shepley and C. Choquet (New York: Henry N. Abrams, 1980), fig. 111; *IBD* 2:723. For further discussion of the ancient Near Eastern background to the imagery, see Block, *Ezekiel Chapters 1–24*, 600–601; B. Lang, *Kein Aufstand in Jerusalem: Die Politik des Propheten Ezechiel*, Stuttgarter Biblische Beiträge (Stuttgart: Katholisches Bibelwerk, 1981) 97–98.

26. Cf. Jeremiah's vague reference to Shallum being taken captive and dying in the land of his captors.

27. For discussion of the merits of each candidate see Block, *Ezekiel Chapters 1–24*, 604–6; C. Begg, "The Identity of the Princes in Ezekiel 19: Some Reflections," *ETL* 65 (1989) 358–65.

28. Two recent commentators have gone separate ways on this issue: Darr ("Ezekiel," 1270) follows our approach; Odell (*Ezekiel*, 235–36), prefers Zedekiah.

cal record, especially with the origins and the end of his reign. Whereas 2 Kgs 23:34–35 credits his elevation to kingship to Pharaoh Neco, Ezekiel has the lioness taking the initiative. Whereas the historian recounts in summary terms the transfer of his vassaldom to Nebuchadnezzar, his rebellion, his death and his succession by Jehoiachin, Ezekiel portrays him captured by a hunter and taken to the king of Babylon, to stifle his roar on the mountains of Israel. But the picture of the lion devouring human prey, laying waste the landscape, and terrifying the inhabitants with his roaring accords with the image of Jehoiakim's oppressive rule as painted by Jeremiah (Jer 22:13–23). When Ezekiel describes the exploitative and self-serving character of past rulers in 34:2b–6 the freshest illustration in his mind will have been Jehoiakim. The same applies to his allusion to earlier kings (נְשִׂיאִים) in 45:8–9. Within Ezekiel's lifetime, Jehoiakim in particular embodied this tyrannical style. Instead of promoting the health of the people, the hearts of Israel's kings were lifted high over their brothers (אֶחָיו, Deut 17:20), and they exploited them ruthlessly for selfish ends.

But this dirge also presents a curious irony. Because Israel's rulers are heartless and ruthless, intent on exploiting their subjects and tearing them up like lions tear up their prey, first the Egyptians and then the Babylonians are portrayed as deliverers, rescuing the people from their oppressors and ending their tyrannical reigns. Ezekiel paints a similar picture in 34:10, where YHWH declares that he will rescue his flock from the jaws of their shepherds, so they will no longer be prey for them. With the phrase וְהִצַּלְתִּי צֹאנִי מִפִּיהֶם, literally, "I will rescue my flock from their mouth," the prophet turns on its head the normal pastoral image of the shepherd rescuing his sheep from wild animals, and fulfilled by the ideal shepherd, David himself:

> Your servant used to keep sheep for his father; and whenever a lion or a bear came, and took a lamb from the flock, I went after it and struck it down, rescuing the lamb from its mouth; and if it turned against me, I would catch it by the jaw, strike it down, and kill it. Your servant has struck down both lions and bears, and this uncircumcised Philistine shall be like one of them, for he has defied the armies of the living God. (1 Sam 17:34–36, NRSV)

Amos paints a similar picture:

> Thus says YHWH: As the shepherd rescues from the mouth of the lion two legs, or a piece of an ear, so shall the people of Israel who live in Samaria be rescued, with the corner of a couch and part of a bed. (Amos 3:12)

Remarkably, these are the only texts in the entire Hebrew Scriptures where we encounter the idiom, הִצִּיל מִפֶּה, "to rescue from a mouth." Ezekiel hereby casts Israel's kings in an anti-Davidic mold. Not only have they not rescued the people from "every wild beast" (כל חית השדה, v. 5); they have morphed into ravenous lions themselves.

Having explored the referents for the principals in the dirge we may now consider the traditional and textual roots of Ezekiel's leonine metaphor. Although the lion was a common symbol for royalty in the ancient Near East,[29] the inspiration for Ezekiel's development of the figure in this dirge apparently derives from Jacob's blessing of Judah in Gen 49:8–9:

> Judah, your brothers will praise you;
> your hand will be on the neck of your enemies;
> your father's sons will bow down to you.
> You are a lion's cub (גור אריה), O Judah;
> you have gone up (עלית) from the kill (טרף), my son.
> Like a lion (אריה) he crouches (רבץ) and lies down.
> Like a lioness (לביא), who dares to rouse him?

These leonine terms, all of which are found in our text, show that the influence of Gen 49:8–9 extends beyond the central motif to the very words the prophet uses.[30] The echoes of Gen 49:8–9 in Ezek 19:1–9 suggest that as the heirs of Jacob's prophecy the last kings of Judah were utter failures and their captivity by foreign powers was perfectly justified. Beyond describing the demise of Jehoahaz and Jehoiakim, this dirge will go on to signal the end of the dynasty—at least as the Israelites have known it. The people may not bank on the dynastic promise of

---

29. The Medinet Habu relief of Rameses III places the representation of a lion beside the triumphant king; see O. Keel, The Symbolism of the Biblical World, 86, fig. 103. For a neo-Assyrian representation see the seal of Ashurbanipal, IBD 2:907. Cf. also the Israelite seal inscribed לשמע עבד ירובעם, "belonging to Shema' servant of Jeroboam [II]," with a beautifully carved lion emblem. See IBD 1:753.

30. In Rev 22:16 "Lion of the tribe of Judah" serves as a messianic title.

Gen 49:8–9 as grounds for their security in the face of the Babylonian threat.

Jehoiachin

Jehoiachin's name occurs only once in Ezekiel, in the editorial clarification of the context of the prophet's inaugural vision and commission as prophet (1:2). But he is the subject of two prophecies, the first part of the riddle of chapter 17, and the last part of the dirge of chapter 19.

Jehoiachin is described as the topmost sprig of a cedar (17:2–4). No text illustrates Ezekiel's bi-fold perspective on Israel's monarchy as dramatically as his metaphoric riddle in chapter 17. The chapter divides into four parts, which, based on the subject matter, are arranged chiastically as follows:

A The Riddle of the Cedar Sprig (vv. 2–3)

B The Riddle of the Vine (vv. 5–10)

B' The Interpretation of the Riddle of the Vine (vv. 11–21)

A' The Interpretation of the Riddle of the Cedar Sprig (vv. 22–24)

However, based on the function of the parts these segments exhibit a strange AA'BB' pattern, with the interpretation of the second riddle following immediately after the riddle itself, as we would expect, and the interpretation of the first being delayed until the end. Technically, only the first short segment and the first four clauses of v. 22 pertain to Jehoiachin. The remainder of the interpretation concerns a future far beyond him.

Although Ezekiel's main concern in the first scene of this extended and complex metaphor is Jehoiachin, the primary character in the first scene of this riddle is a magnificent eagle (v. 3). Throughout the ancient world the eagle served not only as a positive symbol of strength (Isa 40:31) and royal splendor,[31] but also as a fearful symbol of terror. Esarhaddon's boast, "Like a furious eagle I spread my pinions to de-

---

31. With Sennacherib's reference to the eagle as "the prince of the birds" (D. D. Luckenbill, *The Annals of Sennacherib* [1924; reprint, Eugene, OR: Wipf & Stock, 2005] 36), compare Pindar's "king of the birds" (*Olympian Odes* 13.21). On the eagle as a royal symbol in the ancient Near East see Lang, *Kein Aufstand*, 33–38.

stroy my enemies,"³² illuminates the meaning of Hosea's reference to the Assyrian hordes as "an eagle coming against the house of YHWH" (8:1). Ezekiel's nearer predecessor, Habakkuk, had described the Babylonians as "an eagle swooping down to devour" (1:8).³³ But this eagle is different; he is cast as a genuinely benevolent figure, plucking off a sprig of a cedar (that is about to be cut down?), taking it away to Babylon, and planting it there, apparently in very favorable circumstances.

By having the great eagle fly to Lebanon, where he plucked off the top of a cedar, Ezekiel has adapted a stock phrase, "cedars of Lebanon."³⁴ The association of these cedars with the royal constructions in Jerusalem³⁵ encourages an association with the dynasty. However, in an act quite uncharacteristic of eagles, the magnificent bird snipped off the "crown"³⁶ and carried the shoot of fresh growth³⁷ off to a foreign land, identified enigmatically as a commercial territory and a city of merchants. Ezekiel does not provide a motive for the eagle's actions. However, since in the Hebrew Bible a city is by definition a dwelling or group of buildings surrounded by defensive walls built for the protection of the residents, in contrast to the fields outside where crops and vineyards are planted, the purpose of bringing the sprig to this city of merchants presumably

---

32. R. Borger, *Die Inschriften Asarhaddons Königs von Assyrien*, AfO Beih. 9 (Graz: Selbsetverlage des Herausgebers, 1956), §44. Cf. also §65.

33. Cf. also Deut 28:49; Jer 4:13; 48:40; 49:22; Lam 4:19; and the reduction of Nebuchadnezzar to the level of the symbol of his pride in Dan 4:30–33.

34. Elsewhere Ezekiel himself will speak of "the cedar in Lebanon" (Ezek 31:3 [cf. vv. 15–16]) and "the cedar from Lebanon" (Ezek 27:5; cf. Ezra 3:7). The phrase "cedars of Lebanon" occurs often: Judg 9:15; Isa 2:13; 14:8; Ps 29:5; 104:16; cf. 1 Kgs 5:12[14]; Isa 37:24); "cedars in Lebanon" occurs in Ps 92:13; cf. 1 Kgs 5:13[4:33]; 2 Kgs 14:9); "Lebanon" and "cedars" occur in parallel lines in Jer 2:23; Zech 11:1; and Cant 5:15. References to foreigners importing cedar lumber from Lebanon are common: Israel (1 Kgs 5:22–28[8–14]; 2 Chron 2:7–15; Cant 3:9); Egypt (*ANET*, 243), Assyria (Isa 37:24), Babylon (*ANET*, 307).

35. One of Solomon's royal buildings was called "the house of the forest of Lebanon" (1 Kgs 7:2).

36. The expression צַמֶּרֶת, "crown," occurs only in Ezekiel. Here and in v. 22 it is paralleled with רֹאשׁ, "peak." In 31:3, 10, 14 the צַמֶּרֶת of the tree is very high, reaching into the clouds (cf. the place name Zemaraim, "twin peaks" (?) in Josh. 18:22). The form, derived from צֶמֶר, "wool," may have been suggested by the woolly appearance of clouds around the treetops.

37. The parallel expression רֹאשׁ יְנִיקוֹתָיו (from יָנַק, "to suck") concretizes the image of צַמֶּרֶת by referring to the fresh growth of the evergreen, which is still tender and easily plucked off by a bird (17:22).

was for safekeeping, as merchants protect their goods in warehouses within the walls of the city. In any case, both the image of the bird and his actions are painted in positive noble strokes.

Unlike the central core of this chapter, which consists of a second metaphor of the vine (vv. 5–10) and then follows this up immediately with an interpretation (vv. 11–21), the opening scene lacks an interpretation, leaving the reader to ponder over its significance—until the coda in vv. 22–24. While many delete the coda as a post exilic insertion,[38] without it the riddle of vv. 3–4 remains unresolved. As will be the case in the interpretation of the riddle concerning the vine, so vv. 22–24 declare that behind the actions of the magnificent eagle (Nebuchadnezzar) we are to see the actions of YHWH. Ultimately he is the one who plucks the sprig from the top of the cedar, and sets it (in a secure place), until the time is right to retrieve it and plant it on a high and lofty mountain.

But who does this sprig, this foremost of the fresh young twigs of the cedar (ראש ינקותיו) represent? If the cedar represents the Davidic dynasty, the freshness of the sprig suggests either a youthful king or one whose tenure was cut off shortly after assuming the throne.[39] These qualifications could apply either to Jehoahaz, the twenty-three year old son of Josiah who reigned only three months before he was taken away to Egypt (2 Kgs 23:31–34), or to Jehoiachin, the eighteen year old son of Jehoiakim, who also reigned only three months before he was taken away to Babylon (2 Kgs 24:8–16). However, since the interpretation to the riddle of the vine identifies the magnificent eagle with the king of Babylon and expressly declares that he came to Jerusalem and took its king (and the princes) back to Babylon, the sprig obviously refers to Jehoiachin. The significance of his transplant to Babylon cannot be fully established until we have considered the rest of the coda below. For the moment, we note simply that, contra 2 Kgs 24:9 and 2 Chron 36:9,[40] so far this riddle has nowhere suggested a negative reason for his removal from the cedar and his deportation to Babylon. On the contrary, the

---

38. For a defense of its inclusion, see Block, *Ezekiel Chapters 1–24*, 549–50.

39. Compare the characterization of the sprig as רך, "tender," in v. 22 with Prov 4:3–4, "When I was a son with my father, tender (רך), and my mother's favorite, he taught me and said to me, 'Let your heart hold fast my words; keep my commandments, and live.'"

40. This dim view of Jehoiachin is also shared by Jeremiah (Jer 22:24–30). In chapter 19 Ezekiel's evaluation of Jehoiachin will be quite negative.

reference to "the land of merchants" and the "city of traders" opens the door for a beneficent purpose.⁴¹

Jehoiachin is also described as the branch of a vine (19:10–13). Without warning the subject of the dirge in chapter 19 changes from a zoological (a pride of lions) to a horticultural metaphor (a vine). However, as in vv. 2–9 the primary figure (lioness, vine) is presented as the mother (אִמְּךָ) of the secondary figures (cubs, branches). Displaying strong lexical links with chapter 17, vv. 10–14 describe an extra-ordinary plant, planted beside abundant waters (מים רבים) and producing fine fruit and thick foliage. It sent out special kinds of branches: מטות עוז, "strong staves," and שבטי משלים, "scepters of rulers," which represent "the official insignia of a tribal chieftain."⁴² Its crown reached high into the clouds and could be seen for miles around, only to be uprooted and dried up and burned.

Whereas vines normally grow near the ground (cf. 17:6), this plant is a monstrosity, sending its profusion of branches up into the sky. If Ezekiel's audience had linked this image with the riddle of chapter 17, they might have interpreted its wild growth as a representation of hubris, which is answered by divine judgment.

Despite the links with 17:1–10, a shift in the symbolic significance of the vine is evident. Whereas the previous plant had represented an individual king, Zedekiah, in this instance, the vine (mother) represents either the tribe/nation of Judah, from which more than one ruler sprouts, or, the city of Jerusalem, since גפן is treated as feminine and the vine is portrayed as the "mother" of its branches.⁴³ But she has abandoned her natural function as a producer of grapes, and assumed the posture of a huge tree, a symbol of arrogance of nations.⁴⁴ In the story this self-aggrandizement provokes the wrath of YHWH, who punishes her by uprooting and humiliating her, subjecting her to the east wind

---

41. According to 2 Kgs 25:27–30, Nebuchadnezzar's successor Evil-merodach also had a favorable view of Jehoiachin.

42. Thus Jacob Milgrom, *Numbers*, JPS Torah Commentary (Philadelphia: Jewish Publication Society, 1990) 143, on Aaron's rod (Num 17:16–26[17:1–11]). Ezekiel's reference is reminiscent of Jer 48:17, which pairs מטה עז, "a mighty scepter," with מקל תפארה, "a magnificent rod." Ps 110:2 links the same expression with the Davidic dynasty.

43. Thus Odell, *Ezekiel*, 240–41. Compare Israel portrayed as a vine in chapter 15.

44. Cf. the portrayal of Assyria and Egypt as huge cedars in chapter 31.

(the Babylonians), and transplanting her in a foreign land. By this interpretation this is not only an indictment of Judah's kings, but also of Jerusalem herself, and the nation she represents.

In this part of the dirge the strong branches are best interpreted as a figure for the Davidic dynasty, the succession of royal rulers who have sprouted from the tribe of Judah in Jerusalem, with the מטות that serve as שבטי משלים, "scepters of rulers" representing not one, but two kings. The first, Jehoiachin, was torn off, withered and burned (removed from the throne), and then transplanted with the vine in the desert (deported to Babylon). By this interpretation the two dirges involving lions and the branches of the vine present the last four kings of Judah according to their historical order: Jehoahaz, Jehoiakim, Jehoiachin, Zedekiah.

Zedekiah

Ezekiel is more transparent in his hostility toward Zedekiah than toward any other king. His negative disposition is evident from the opening line of the book. Instead of dating his inaugural vision and commission to prophetic service according to the accession year of the regnant king, which was customary throughout the ancient Near East, he dates them according to his own birth date. And the editor adds insult to injury by synchronizing Ezekiel's thirtieth year, not with the year of Zedekiah's reign, but with the year of the previous king's exile (1:1–3). This attitude toward the king is evident in three oracles that concern him directly.

The sign-act (12:1–16). This prophecy consists of three parts: YHWH's charge to Ezekiel to perform a strange sign act (vv. 1–6); a summary report of the prophet's actions in response (v. 7); and YHWH's interpretation of the significance of the action (vv. 8–16). Although the interpretation ends with a prediction of the destruction of the nation—apparently in fulfillment of the covenant curses in Leviticus 26 and Deuteronomy 28—the focus is actually on "the prince" (הנשיא, vv. 10–13). The interpretation paints a shocking picture, casting YHWH in the role of a hunter who spreads his net over Zedekiah, captures him, and drags him away to Babylon (v. 13). Although the oracle suggests that the nation's demise is punishment for their rebellion (v. 2) and abominations (תועבות, v. 16), it offers no reasons for the king's fate. Its purpose is simply to demonstrate that the Judeans hope in rescue from the Babylonian threat based on the presence on the throne of a descendant of David (2 Samuel 7) is futile.

The renegade vine (17:5–21). The picture changes, however, in the metaphoric riddle of the renegade vine in chapter 17, the bulk of which concerns Zedekiah (vv. 5–21). Like the sign-act concerning this man in chapter 12, the present riddle about Zedekiah divides into two parts: the extended metaphor (vv. 5–10) and the interpretation (vv. 11–21). The link between these texts is reinforced by the description of YHWH's direct actions against the king (v. 20), which echo almost verbatim the earlier statement (12:13). However, whereas the interpretation of the sign-act in chapter 12 had been silent on Zedekiah's crimes, the explanation of the riddle charges Zedekiah with despising the oath and breaking the covenant (in which he had declared himself a faithful vassal of Nebuchadnezzar) by seeking the aid of Egypt against the Babylonians (vv. 13–18). But the prophet interprets this political treason as an act of treachery against YHWH (vv. 19–20).

But there is another element in presentation that deserves comment. The common element in the two parts to the riddle involving the cedar sprig (vv. 3–4) and the rebellious vine (vv. 5–10) is the magnificent eagle, cast in the roles a horticulturalist. Whereas in the first he had snipped off a tender cedar sprig and taken it away (to preserve it), here he takes a seed and plants it in extremely favorable conditions, so that it sprouts and grows into a large vine, sending its branches out in all directions.

With this riddle Ezekiel seizes upon traditional images and deliberately adapts and distorts them for rhetorical effect. According to Ps 80:9–20 (8–19), YHWH took a vine (Israel) from Egypt and with his right hand planted it in its own place (cf. Jer 2:21). Isaiah had added to the image by highlighting YHWH's special care for the vine, and describing how the plant had responded, producing only rotten grapes, illustrative of Israel's covenantal infidelity (Isa 5). Hosea associated the bad fruit explicitly with idolatry (Hos 10:1). In Jer 12:10 YHWH complains that many shepherds (rulers) have turned his vineyard into a wasteland. Earlier, in Ezek 15:1–7, the exilic prophet had taken the image a step farther, declaring that the vine was inherently worthless, fit only for fuel for fire.

In view of Ezekiel's previous denunciations of Judah's apostasy, and especially in light of his use of the metaphor of the vine in chapter 15, on first hearing, the reader is tempted to interpret the vine in chapter 17 as the nation of Israel, which was planted by YHWH (the eagle) in a fertile land,⁴⁵ but which turned from him, its source of life, to other gods (the second eagle). But the interpretation of the riddle takes the metaphor in a shocking new direction. The vinedresser is not YHWH but Nebuchadnezzar, and the vine is not the nation primarily, but the nobility of Jerusalem, if not the royal family and Zedekiah himself. Verses 12–14 allude to an earlier event when Nebuchadnezzar had apparently brought the king and his associates to Babylon and entered into a covenant relationship with them. Like the actions of the eagle involving the cedar sprig, this is portrayed as a positive development for the good of the king and his nation with him. However, the foolish vine abandoned its normal nature and function and sought its security elsewhere.⁴⁶ Because Zedekiah contemptuously violated the oath and broke his covenant as a vassal of Nebuchadnezzar by seeking the aid of Egypt (the second eagle), he is sentenced to death in Babylon (16–18).

But in vv. 18–21 Ezekiel adds a new twist. Because Nebuchadnezzar had appeared as YHWH's agent, treachery against him was treachery against YHWH, and for this the king had become the target of divine fury and his nation would be destroyed. Zedekiah represented the antithesis of the future David, who will be introduced as "my vassal" (עבדי, 34:23–24; 37:24, 25). With this announcement of the doom of the dynasty Ezekiel robs the people of one of the pillars on which they based their security—the presence of a descendant of David on the throne of Judah.

The doomed branch (19:14). Through the sign-act in 12:1–16 Ezekiel had predicted the doom of Zedekiah, and through the riddle of 17:15–21 he had justified his doom. The dirge for the dynasty in chapter 19 resumes the metaphor of the vine and ends with a brief reference to this last king of Judah:

> Fire has gone forth from the bough of its shoots.
> It consumed its fruit.
> No strong branch, no ruler's scepter, remained in it. (19:14)

---

45. H. Simian-Yofre ("Ez 17, 1–10 como enigma y parábola," *Bib* 65 [1984] 27–43) maintains this parable is open to several interpretations, and that the two provided in vv. 11–12 and 22–24 do not exhaust its meaning.

46. Cf. Lang, *Kein Aufstand*, 39.

This declaration lays no specific charge against Zedekiah; apparently his only problem was that he was a part of a dynasty characterized by arrogance (v. 11).

With the burning up of the vine, Ezekiel's riddle comes to a close. With Gen 49:8–12 as his point of departure, the prophet has retraced the events of Judah's final decades in four episodes, each of which revolves around the respective occupants of the Davidic throne. In the process he has declared the futility of any hopes based upon YHWH's covenant with the Davidic house. The promises of God to the ancestors are no guarantee of divine blessing for their descendants. Nor is the promise to the house of David of an eternal dynasty (2 Sam 7) an unconditional guarantee of their rule in Jerusalem.

The Wicked Prince (21:29–32 [24–27])

If the sign act of chapter 12 and the dirge of chapter 19 have been silent on the cause of YHWH's hostility to Zedekiah specifically, things change dramatically in a paraenetic appendix to an oracle announcing the imminent arrival of Nebuchadnezzar and his armies in 21:29–32 (24–27). After an impassioned announcement of doom against the people of Judah for their crimes in v. 29 (24), Ezekiel's tone reaches a fever pitch in vv. 30–32 (25–27):

> O you! O vile one! O criminal! O prince of Israel, whose day has arrived in time for your final punishment. Thus has the Lord YHWH declared: Remove the turban! And take off the tiara! Let nothing remain the same! Exalt the low and bring down the high! Topsy-turvy! Topsy-turvy! Topsy-turvy! That's what I will make it—a disaster without equal—until he comes to whom the judgment belongs, and to whom I will give it.

Forgetting completely YHWH's manipulation of Nebuchadnezzar's divinatory actions (vv. 16–17 [21–22], the prophet launches into a tirade against Zedekiah, unequalled in this book or any other prophet for its forthrightness and harshness. He focuses his hearers' attention on the king with a quadrupled vocative, "You! O vile one! O wicked one! O prince of Israel!" The prophet does not elaborate on the king's wicked actions, but he probably has in mind minimally the violation of his vassal oath (17:11–21), which will lead to his inevitable demise.[47]

---

47. Verse 30b (25b) is syntactically difficult. With Hebrew יומו אשר־בא, "whose day is coming," compare Ezekiel's reference to "the day of Egypt" in 30:9. For com-

Ezekiel's excitement becomes even more evident in vv. 31–32. Following the opening citation formula, Ezekiel calls on the king to relinquish authority by removing the insignia of royalty, to take off his turban and crown. With זֹאת לֹא־זֹאת, "This not this," viz., "Let nothing remain the same,"[48] the prophet calls for a ruthless upsetting of Judean social structures. The cry of "Exalt the low and bring down the high," that is, "Let the slaves rule, and the rulers be enslaved!" involves the same words we had seen in 17:24 with reference to trees. In this call for change Ezekiel foresees not only the termination of the dynasty but also a revolution affecting all strata of society.

The prophecy climaxes in v. 32 with the three-fold עַוָּה עַוָּה עַוָּה, which plays on עָוֹן (v. 30), from the same root, "to twist, to bend." The image presented recalls the cosmic and cataclysmic disintegration envisioned in Isa 24:1–3, the only other occurrence of the word:

> Look! YHWH will strip the earth bare, and lay it waste.
> He will twist (עִוָּה) its surface, and scatter its inhabitants.
> The layman shall be like the priest; the servant like his master.
> The maid like her mistress; the buyer like the seller.
> The lender like the borrower; the creditor like the debtor.
> The earth will be laid totally waste and completely despoiled,
> For YHWH has declared this word.[49]

The anarchy predicted for Jerusalem is not merely the result of social or political incompetence; it is YHWH who turns the world upside down.[50]

---

parable references outside Ezekiel, see Block, *Ezekiel Chapters 1–24*, 690. Hebrew בְּעֵת עֲוֹן קֵץ, literally "time of guilt, end!" speaks not only of the moment of Zedekiah's punishment, but also the termination of his iniquitous behavior.

48. M. Dijkstra and J. C. de Moor, "Problematic Passages in the Legend of Aqhâtu," *UF* 7 (1975) 204, translate "Whatever the outcome, . . ." based on Akkadian, *anniam la anniam* and *annnitam la annitam* (cf. *AHW*, p. 53; *CAD* 2:137) and Ugaritic *'an l'an yṣpṣ / 'an l'an 'il ygdrk* (*CTA* 6:IV:46–47). For a different understanding of this text (and different reference), see M. S. Smith, trans., "The Baal Cycle," in *Ugaritic Narrative Poetry*, ed. S. B. Parker, SBL Writings of the Ancient World 9 (Atlanta: Scholars, 1997) 159–60.

49. For a comparable extra-biblical description of anarchy see "The Admonitions of Ipu-Wer," in *ANET*, 442–43; *COS* 1:42 (p. 96).

50. Compare Esarhaddon's description of nature twisted out of shape because of the fury of Marduk over the moral and cultic crimes of the Babylonians. In heaven and on earth ominous signs concerning the ruin of humankind (*ḥalāq mitḫarti*) appeared (thus *CAD* 10/2.135; Borger, *Die Inschriften Asarhaddons*, 14–15; cf. *ARAB* 2 §§642, 649).

The oracle ends with a sinister reinterpretation of an ancient promise concerning Judah's hegemonic position within Israel. Earlier we had observed Ezekiel's exploitation of Gen 49:8–9 and 11–12 in the dirges of 19:2–9 and 10–14 respectively. Except for a reference to the scepter in 19:11, the prophet had skipped over Gen 49:10. He redresses this problem in 21:32 (27). The messianic/Christological interpretation of עד־בא אשר־לו המשפט ונתתיו, "until he comes to whom the judgment belongs," has a long history.[51] It imposes on this text a meaning of משפט, viz., "right, claim," found nowhere else in the book.[52] "Judgment" in the sense of "punishment" suits the context perfectly. The person to whom the task of "judgment" is delivered is none other than Nebuchadnezzar. Rather than delivering a ray of hope, Ezekiel envisions the imminent fall of Jerusalem, an event which no messiah would prevent.[53] This is not to say that Gen 49:10 is out of the picture. On the contrary, the prophet has turned a sacred text upside down, transforming an ancient promise on which his audience has staked its hopes, and transformed it into a frightening prediction of doom.[54] On Ezekiel's lips, Gen 49:10 is not about tribute and subordination of the world to Judah, but the judgment of Judah by the principal representative of that world that was to bow before the tribe.[55] With his condemnation of the Davidic house, the people may think Ezekiel has directly contradicted the Davidic tradition and the divine promises.[56] However, until and un-

---

51. See my commentary, *Ezekiel Chapters 1–24*, 692.

52. So also J. W. Wevers, *Ezekiel*, NCB (reprint, Grand Rapids: Eerdmans, 1982) 169. Elsewhere the word means "justice" (18:5, 19, 21, 27; 33:14, 16, 19) "judgment" (23:24) or "custom" (23:24; 42:11). Cf. J. Lust, "'Messianism and Septuagint," in *Congress Volume Salamanca 1983*, ed. J. A. Emerton, VTSup 36 (Leiden: Brill, 1985) 184–86.

53. For other non-messianic interpretations see F. Pili, "Possibili casi di metatesi in Genesi 49,10 e Salmo 2,11–12a," *Augustinianum* 15 (1975) 457–71, who proposes to reverse the letters of שיל ה, yielding הל ישׁ, viz., "Till the lion comes to whom the obedience of the peoples shall belong." Cf. Gen 49:9. A. Caquot, "La parole sur Juda dans le testament lyrique de Jacob (Genèse 49,8–12)," *Semitica* 26 (1976) 5–32 (followed by Lang, *Kein Aufstand*, 119) finds in Shiloh an abbreviation for Solomon.

54. Cf. M. Fishbane, *Biblical Interpretation in Ancient Israel* (Oxford: Clarendon, 1985), 502–3.

55. Cf. W. L. Moran, "Gen 49,10 and its Use in Ez 21,32," *Bib* 39 (1958) 424–25.

56. Like the psalmist in Ps 89:39–52 (38–51); cf. Cf. 2 Sam 7:1–16; Ps 89:2–5 (1–4), 20–38 (19–37); 132:10–12.

less the Israelites cease their rebellion (מרד) against YHWH, there is no security in David.⁵⁷

Ezekiel's Portrayal of the Future of the Monarchy

So much for the past and the present. What about the future? If the point of Ezekiel's judgment is to demolish the pillars on which the people have based their security, the aim of his restoration oracles is to declare that the judgment will not be the last word. Ultimately, because the promises of YHWH are in fact irrevocable, the people cannot be forever removed from the land; they will not be forever divorced from YHWH; YHWH will not abandon his temple forever; and the Davidic house will not be eliminated forever. After the judgment, in the distant future, the house will be reconstructed, which means that David will be back. Ezekiel's declarations on this subject are found in four texts.

The Cedar Sprig (17:22–24)

As Joyce rightly observes, this is the third of only four hopeful declarations of hope in the first twenty-four chapters.⁵⁸ Our earlier discussion of the cedar sprig in Ezekiel's riddle of chapter 17 had focused on vv. 3-4, which has the magnificent eagle (Nebuchadnezzar) plucking off one of the topmost twigs (ראש יניקות) and taking it to the land of merchants, the city of traders (Babylon). The eagle's purpose in transporting the sprig is not specified, though we suggested this may be interpreted as a benevolent act resulting in the sprig's preservation. The interpretation to this segment of the riddle provided by the coda of vv. 22-24 seems to confirm this understanding.

Several features of this passage deserve comment. First, as in vv. 19-20, behind the great eagle is YHWH himself. Ultimately he is the one who removed the sprig from the cedar. Second, the nature of YHWH's action in setting (נתן) the sprig is unclear. Apparently this is a shorthand expression for the divine equivalent to the eagle's action in bringing the sprig to the land of merchants and depositing it (שים) it in the city

---

57. One of his favorite epithets for the nation is בית מרי, "house of rebellion." Ezek 2:5-6; 3:9, 26-27; 12:2-3; 44:6.

58. Joyce, "King and Messiah in Ezekiel," 327. Each of the four messages of hope in chapters 1–24 seem to address one of these pillars: 11:14–21 (land), 16:59–63 (covenant relationship), 17:22–24 (king), and 20:4–44 (divine residence).

of traders (v. 22), presumably for safekeeping.⁵⁹ Whatever the action, it contrasts sharply with the fate of the branch that is burned in 19:14. Third, skipping over the sprig's exile in the land of merchants, YHWH takes the sprig and plants it on a very high mountain, where it provides a home for every kind of birds.⁶⁰ The tree itself is an enigma. On the one hand, it is a stately cedar (ארז אדיר, v. 23) but on the other hand, it yields fruit for food, and evoking admiration for its magnificence.⁶¹

Ezekiel's botanical imagery in vv. 22–24 is reminiscent of the language of other prophets, who had spoken of the messianic scion who would revive the Davidic line as a חטר, "shoot," and a נצר, "branch" (Isa 11:1) or as a צמח, sprout" (Jer 23:5).⁶² However, whereas Isa 11:1 creates an image of a stump that has been cut down (as an act of judgment, though because of the irrepressible life of the roots new shoots emerge from the stump), here the sprig is cut off by YHWH from the top, without any reference to judgment. Apparently this is as an act of benevolence, ensuring the survival of a branch of the tree until the judgment has passed.⁶³

The planting of the tree on the high mountain of Israel, and especially its growth into a fruitful and stately tree under which birds of every kind will rest, adapts a well-known extra-biblical and biblical motif of the cosmic tree.⁶⁴ Typically this tree is portrayed as a huge plant with its crown reaching into the heavens and its roots going down to the subterranean streams from which it draws its nourishment.⁶⁵ Although

---

59. The verbs שים in v. 4 and נתן in v. 22 function as virtual synonyms for שתל, "to transplant." Cf. the actions with respect to the vine (vv. 7, 8) and the sprig at the end (vv. 22, 23).

60. Hebrew כל צפור כל כנף, literally, "every bird, every wing," recalls Gen 7:14.

61. The triad of expressions, ענף, "boughs," פרי, fruit," and אדיר, "stately, noble" invites comparison with the eagle's intentions for the vine in v. 8, but this is an entirely different type of plant.

62. Cf. also Jer 33:15; Zech 3:8; 6:12.

63. As noted above, Ezekiel's characterization of the sprig as רך, "tender" hints at a Josianic figure. Cf. 2 Kgs 22:19; 23:25.

64. The birds that nest in the tree do not symbolize the nations but come as refugees. Cf. Isa 16:1–5; Amos 9:11–12; Zech 9:9–10. Similarly, Laato, *Josiah*, 163. The nations are represented by all the trees of the field that acknowledge YHWH in the next verse.

65. This tree is not to be associated with the "Tree of Life" in a paradisic garden. Cf. H. N. Wallace, *ABD* 6:658. For studies on the tree as a symbol of an ordered world in the face of the threat of death in ancient Near Eastern written and visual sources see U. Winter, "Der Lebensbaum in der altorientalischen Bildsymbolik," in ". . . *Bäume*

discussion of the tree is missing in cuneiform sources, according to S. Parpola, in Assyrian iconography the tree functions as an imperial symbol, representing "the divine order maintained by the king as the representative of the god Aššur, embodied in the winged disk hovering over the tree."[66]

While Ezekiel may have been first introduced to the "cosmic tree" motif in Babylon,[67] the present passage may also have been inspired by Isa 11:1–10, where the elements of a newly sprouted messianic shoot, the mountain of YHWH, and peaceful co-existence with wild animals are all conjoined. This tree is planted on the mountain of Israel, an obvious allusion to Mount Zion (cf. Isa 2:2–4; Mic 4:1–3). Although this mountain will become increasingly significant in later oracles, only here in Ezekiel are the motifs of Davidic line and Zion brought together.[68] In so doing the prophet reminds the exiles that YHWH had not forgotten his covenant with David (2 Sam 7). The dynasty would survive the deportation; it would be revived within the context of its original founding, and its protective influence would be felt all around the world.

The last verse highlights the universal impact of the tree with a complex version of the recognition formula. One might have anticipated that when all the trees, that is, all the dynasties of the earth as representatives of the nations, observe the splendor, productivity, and protection offered by the tree, they would fall down before it in hom-

---

braucht man doch!" Das Symbol des Baumes zwischen Hoffnung und Zerstörung, ed. H. Schweizer (Sigmaringen: Thorbecke, 1986) 57–88; D. E. Gowan, *When Man Becomes God: Humanism and Hybris in the Old Testament,* PittsTMS 6 (Pittsburgh: Pickwick, 1975) 102–106. Cf. also P. R. Frese and S. J. M. Gray, "Trees," *The Encyclopedia of Religion,* ed. M. Eliade (New York: Macmillan, 1987) 15:27–28; more recently, J. H. Walton, *Ancient Near Eastern Thought and the Old Testament: Introducing the Conceptual World of the Hebrew Bible* (Grand Rapids: Baker Academic, 2006) 175–76.

66. S. Parpola, "The Assyrian Tree of Life: Tracing the Origins of Jewish Monotheism and Greek Philosophy," *JNES* 52 (1993) 167. Parpola finds confirmation of this conclusion in the observation that the king sometimes takes the place of the tree between the winged genies. In these contexts the king represented the realization of the cosmic order in man. He was "a true image of God, the Perfect Man" (168).

67. In 31:1–18 Ezekiel develops the motif as a symbol of Egypt in much greater detail. In Daniel 4 the world tree represents Nebuchadnezzar.

68. The mountain motif is absent from 34:23–24 and 37:24–25. The present association is reminiscent of Ps 78:68–73 and 132:10–18, both of which juxtapose the election of David and the establishment of his dynasty with the choice of Mount Zion as YHWH's dwelling place. On Zion as a world mountain see R. J. Clifford, *The Cosmic Mountain in Canaan and the Old Testament,* HSM 4 (Missoula, 1972) 131–60.

age and submission. But this oracle is not about Davidic imperialism; it is about the cosmic sovereignty and fidelity of YHWH, which is highlighted by four sensitively constructed parallel lines:

> I bring down the high tree,
> I make high the low tree;
> I dry up the green tree,
> and I make the dry tree flourish.

These gnomic declarations recall many similar statements in the Hebrew Bible.[69] For a concrete illustration of bringing down the high, the listeners need look no farther than Zedekiah, whose fate had been described in vv. 19–21. As for the low being lifted up, this must refer to Jehoiachin. He may be currently languishing in captivity in Babylon, but his line will live. His scion will be restored to the throne of Israel, and elevated to the status of universal king.

To the exiles Ezekiel's words may have seemed like an impossible dream, but they are guaranteed in the final three lines. YHWH has spoken; he will act. The foundation for this oracle is found in his covenant with David, communicated four centuries earlier by Nathan the prophet (2 Sam 7). Not only had YHWH promised him eternal title to the throne of Israel; David had recognized its cosmic significance with his enigmatic interpretation of Nathan's oracle as "the instruction for humanity" (תורת האדם, 2 Sam 7:19). YHWH had not forgotten his ancient word. The dynasty would survive the exile. Indeed its best years were still to come.

Earlier in 11:5–12 Ezekiel had disputed the claims of those who had escaped the deportation of 597 BCE, arguing that this was a sign of YHWH's favor toward them. In response Ezekiel declared that Jerusalem should not be viewed as a pot protecting the people from danger, but as a trap holding them for the outpouring of divine fury, and the exile should be interpreted not as a sign of divine rejection, but of election. YHWH had removed them from Jerusalem to spare them the conflagration to come, and in Babylon he personally became their

---

69. Involving שפל and גבה, 1 Sam 2:7; 2 Sam 22:28 = Ps 18:28; Isa 2:11, 12, 17; 26:5; Ps 75:8; 147:6; also Sir 7:11. The most common pairing of roots involves שפל and רום. Other variations of the pair occur in Isa 10:33; 57:15; Ps 138:6; 147:6; Job 5:11; Qoh 10:6.

"small sanctuary."[70] Our text suggests that what the remnant of the exiles was to the future of the nation, Jehoiachin was to the dynasty. While the enemies wreak their havoc on the people, the land, the temple, and the dynasty, Babylon would provide refuge both for the exiles and for a remnant of the house of David.[71]

My Servant David, the נשיא / the מלך

Ezek 34:22–24 and 37:23–25 contain the most overtly messianic language in the book. There is no need here to retrace my analysis of these texts in an earlier article and in my commentary.[72] Our focus here will be on Ezekiel's use of antecedent traditions to present the future of monarchy.

Ezekiel 34:22–24

Ezekiel's first explicit reference to the Messiah occurs near the end of an extended restoration oracle in which YHWH poses as a benevolent divine shepherd, rescuing his beleaguered human flock from the tyranny of exploitative rulers and bullying members within the flock (34:1–31). For a brief moment, in vv. 23–24 the focus shifts to the appointment of David as [under]shepherd of YHWH's flock, followed by a presentation of the covenant of peace that YHWH establishes with his people.[73]

---

70. The enigmatic statement, "And I became to them a sanctuary in small measure (ואהי להם למקדש מעט) in the lands where they had gone" (v. 16) should probably be related to 37:27, "My sanctuary shall be over them" (והיה משכני עליהם). Greenberg (*Ezekiel 21–37*, 757–58) rightly sees in the latter a transformation of the tabernacle primarily as a symbol of God's dwelling amidst Israel to a sheltering presence over them.

71. The role of Babylon is analogous to that of Egypt in the narratives of Genesis. In Gen 45:7–11 and 50:20–21 Joseph informs his brothers that his presence in Egypt was part of God's plan to secure the existence of the chosen family while a famine devastated the region.

72. D. I. Block, "Bringing Back David: Ezekiel's Messianic Hope," in *The Lord's Anointed: Interpretation of Old Testament Messianic Texts*, ed. P. Satterthwaite, R. S. Hess, and G. J. Wenham (Grand Rapids: Baker, 1995) 172–83; idem, *Ezekiel Chapters 25–48*, NICOT (Grand Rapids: Eerdmans, 1998) 294–309; 406–24.

73. On these two features as fundamental elements of Jewish messianism in the Second Temple period, see S. H. Levey (*The Messiah: An Aramaic Interpretation. The Messianic Exegesis of the Targum* [Cincinnati: Hebrew Union College Press, 1974] xix, who defines the messianic age as follows:

These verses are packed with vital information on the new shepherd's status within Israel: (1) The ruler will be installed (הֲקִים) by YHWH himself after the exiles have returned to the land that YHWH would give them; (2) The ruler will be shepherd over (עַל) YHWH's people, but unlike the self-serving shepherds of vv. 1-10, he will actually tend the flock; (3) The ruler will be singular (רֹעֶה אֶחָד), reversing the division of Israel into northern and southern kingdoms that occurred after the death of Solomon (1 Kgs 11-12); (4) The ruler will be David, the name appearing here for the first time in the book; (5) The ruler will be the servant of YHWH; (6) The ruler will be a נָשִׂיא, "prince," in the midst of his people; (7) The ruler will function within the context of YHWH's covenant with Israel (cf. vv. 24a, 25).

Although chapter 34 as a whole represents an exposition of Jeremiah's oracle in Jer 23:1-6, Ezekiel's portrait of the future ruler makes heavy use of other antecedent texts and traditions.[74] His installation by YHWH after the exiles have returned to their patrimonial homeland recalls Deut 17:14. The king is not portrayed as a military figure who leads the Israelites in a battle of conquest. As shepherd he will not tend his people like the self-serving shepherds of vv. 1-10, but according to the ideal established for David in 2 Sam 7:7, 1 Chron 17:6, and Ps 78:70-72. Like the rest of the prophets, Ezekiel perceived the nation as one and recognized as legitimate only the Davidic dynasty.[75] In identifying the new ruler as David, Ezekiel follows a longstanding prophetic tradition, rooted ultimately in YHWH's eternal and irrevocable covenant with David (2 Sam 7; Ps 89:3-4, 19-29).[76] This understanding

---

The predication of a future Golden Age in which the central figure is a king primarily of Davidic lineage appointed by God.... It was believed that during the time of the Messiah the Hebrew people will be vindicated, its wrongs righted, the wicked purged from its midst, and its rightful place in the world secured. The Messiah will pronounce doom upon the enemies of Israel, will mete out reward and punishment in truth and in justice, and will serve as an ideal king ruling the entire world. The Messiah may not always be the active agent in these future events, but his personality must always be present, at least as the symbol of the glorious age which will be ushered in.

74. Cf. Block, *Ezekiel Chapters 25-48*, 275-76.
75. Ezekiel will expand on this notion in 37:15-24, where the term אֶחָד, "one," occurs no fewer than eleven times.
76. Cf. Isa 9:5-6; 11:1, 10; Hos 3:5; Amos 9:11; Jer 23:5. W. Gross, "Israel's Hope for the Renewal of the State," JNSL 14 (1988) 125-26, follows F. Hossfeld, *Untersuchungen zu Komposition und Theologie des Ezekielbuches*, FzB 20 (Würzburg: Echter, 1977) 230ff.

is reinforced by the epithet, עַבְדִּי, "my servant," which recalls the traditional view of David's willing subordination to YHWH. The expression is used of David twice in 2 Sam 7:5 and 8 and twenty-nine times elsewhere in the Hebrew Bible and mirrors ten-fold self-designation as עַבְדְּךָ, "your servant," in 2 Sam 7:19–29. The collapse of the Davidic house with the deportation of Jehoiachin in 597 BCE and the execution of Zedekiah in 586 BCE had raised doubts about YHWH's fidelity to his word. Ezekiel hereby reminds his hearers that in the immediate context YHWH may have suspended the benefits of his covenant with David, but he has not retracted it.

Ezekiel's use of the archaic title נָשִׂיא, "prince," contrasts with Hos 3:5 and Jer 3:5, both of which had referred explicitly to "David their king." However, it is consistent with his efforts elsewhere to downplay the roles of Israel's monarchs, and harks back to 1 Kgs 11:34, where it is said of Solomon, "I will make him נָשִׂיא all the days of his life for the sake of David my servant." Far from denying the ruler's true kingship, by referring to him as a נָשִׂיא rather than a מֶלֶךְ Ezekiel deliberately distinguishes him from the recent occupants of the office. Officially the נָשִׂיא may be "the promoted one," but as one in the midst (בְּתוֹךְ) of Israel, his heart will not exalted about his kinsfolk (cf. Deut 17:19–20).

In this arrangement, YHWH is the divine patron of the people; David is his representative and deputy. As David himself had acknowledged in 2 Sam 7:23–27, YHWH's granting his house eternal title to the kingship was not an isolated act, concerned only about the well-being of the king. That he appoints him within the context of his covenant relationship with the people is highlighted by the fact that this entire section (vv. 23–31) is framed by versions of the covenant formula (vv. 24, 30–31). This ruler's role is not to win allegiance to himself but to serve the relationship between people and deity.

Ezekiel's announcement of the appointment of a new David for Israel was intended to instill new hope in the hearts of the exiles. Contrary to appearance, the demise of the Davidic house in 586 BCE did not reflect divine impotence or indifference to previous commitments. These events had not only fulfilled previous prophetic utterances;[77] they

---

and 284ff., in deleting the reference to David as a late intrusion, dependent upon Ezek 37:24–25.

77. Cf. 12:1–16; 17; 19.

also set the stage for a dramatic new act of YHWH when the decadence of the old order would be removed. The prophet hereby challenges his people to look forward to a new day when YHWH's Davidic servant would be reinstated in accordance with his eternal and irrevocable covenant.

Ezekiel 37:22–25

The second reference to the restoration of the Davidic dynasty occurs in the interpretation of a sign act involving two pieces of wood on which are inscribed the names Judah and Joseph. Ezekiel is instructed to unite these two sticks as a symbolic gesture promising the eventual reunification of all the tribes of Israel in one nation (37:16–28).[78] The interpretation proper (vv. 21–28) offers an anthology of Ezekielian restoration ideas,[79] bringing his salvation oracles to a fitting conclusion. This verbal explanation divides into two parts (vv. 21–24a; 24b–28), each with its own covenant formula (vv. 23, 27). Verses 21–24a are preoccupied with the reunification of the nation under one shepherd; vv. 24b–28 with the eternality of YHWH's restorative acts. Accordingly, the specification of one shepherd over all Israel in v. 24a belongs to the preceding, rather than that which follows, and the identification of David as מלך in v. 24a ties in with the use of the same word in v. 22, but contrasts with Ezekiel's preferred designation for Israel's rulers, נשיא in v. 25. This division of vv. 21–28 results in two panels of approximately equal length.[80]

Although the first panel echoes key elements from 34:22–24,[81] here the distinctive emphasis is on creating "a single nation" (גוי אחד) under "one king" (מלך אחד) from two nations (שני גויים, v. 22a) and two kingdoms (שתי ממלכות). The textual tradition on the title for this ruler in 37:22, 24 is inconsistent. Where MT identifies this head as a מלך, "king," LXX and Papyrus[967] read ἄρχων, generally assumed to reflect נשיא, "prince," in the *Vorlage*.[82]

---

78. On which see K. Friebel, *Jeremiah's and Ezekiel's Sign-Acts: Rhetorical Nonverbal Communication*, JSOTSup 283 (Sheffield: Sheffield Academic Press, 1999) 362–69.

79. For summaries see J. Lust, "Ezekiel 36–40 in the Oldest Greek Manuscript," *CBQ* 43 (1981) 526–27.

80. In MT the first panel consists of 72 words; the second 68.

81. "My servant David," "one shepherd," the covenant formula.

82. Papyrus[967] is dated to the late second or early third century CE, hence prehexaplaric. For the publication see A. C. Johnson, H. S. Gehman, and E. H. Kase, Jr., eds.,

In view of the strong arguments of J. Lust and A. S. Crane, I can now accept that the *Vorlage* to the Old Greek text may well antedate the Hebrew text underlying MT.[83] However, I remain unconvinced that the *Vorlage* to the Old Greek text read נשיא rather than מלך.[84] On the one hand, LXX renderings of מלך when used of Israel's kings vary. On the other hand, the explanations for the shift in MT from נשיא to מלך strike me as unnecessarily speculative.[85] But even if MT reflects a change

---

The John H. Scheide Biblical Papyri: Ezekiel, Princeton University Studies in Papyrology 3 (Princeton: Princeton University Press, 1938).

83. See especially J. Lust, "Ezekiel 36–40 in the Oldest Greek Manuscript," *CBQ* 43 (1981) 517–33; idem, "Textual Criticism of the Old and New Testaments: Stepbrothers?" in *New Testament Textual Criticism and Exegesis*, ed. A. Denaux (Leuven: Leuven University Press, 2002), 28–31; idem, "Major Divergences between LXX and MT in Ezekiel," in *The Earliest Text of the Hebrew Bible: The Relationship between the Masoretic Text and the Hebrew Base of the Septuagint Reconsidered*, ed. A. Schenker, Septuagint and Cognate Studies 52 (Atlanta: Society of Biblical Literature, 2003), 83–92; A. S. Crane, "The Restoration of Israel," 255–328.

84. See K.-D. Schunck, "Die Attribute des eschatologischen Messias," *TLZ* 111 (1986) 651, n. 3; A. Rofé, "Qumranic Paraphrases: The Greek Deuteronomy and the Late History of the Biblical נשיא," *Textus* 14 (1988) 173, attributes LXX to a theological revision in the *Vorlage*. See further below.

85. Whereas Lust earlier attributed the changes in arrangement and the reading in this case in MT to Pharisaic reactions against apocalyptic views ("Ezekiel 36–40 in the Oldest Greek Manuscript," 532), he later admitted its "highly hypothetical" nature ("Textual Criticism of the Old and New Testaments: Stepbrothers?" 30. More recently Crane has argued that MT was produced as a Hasmonean "military call to arms" under a Davidic leader and "a call to purity or spiritual renewal." However, the former interpretation overplays the militaristic nature of מלך and underestimates the militaristic overtones of נשיא.

On the one hand, it is true that one of the roles of the מלך was to lead the nation in battle against foreign enemies (1 Sam 8:20), but this was only one of his roles. Along with vanquishing enemies, in the ancient Near East kings were expected to dispense justice internally, providing care and security for his subjects, and ensure the proper operation of the national cult. Indeed, Deut 17:14–20 expressly prohibits a militaristic stance: the primary task of the מלך was to read the Torah for himself, and his primary role is to embody covenant righteousness by walking in the ways of YHWH and not allowing his heart to be lifted up above his countrymen. Cf. D. I. Block, "The Burden of Leadership: The Mosaic Paradigm of Kingship (Deut. 17:14–20)," *BSac* 162 (2005) 259–78. Furthermore, while other prophets charged Israelite kings with pursuing overly militaristic policies, this is not a pronounced theme in Ezekiel. Admittedly, in chapter 17 he accuses Zedekiah of despising his oath of vassalage to Nebuchadnezzar by seeking an alliance with Egypt and sending envoys there that Pharaoh might aid him in his resistance to the Babylonian overlord. However, Ezekiel presents the king as relatively passive in this military context. Whereas centuries earlier the people had demanded a king who would go out before them and fight their battles (1 Sam 8:20), here Zedekiah

from נשיא to מלך,[86] those responsible for the change may simply have recognized that this נשיא is in fact a king. Not only do political entities identified as ממלכות, "kingdoms" (Greek reads βασιλείας) require a מלך at the head, but this is also virtually required by the reference to that nation as a גוי, which is by definition ruled by a king, rather than an עם, "people." For the moment Ezekiel offers no hints of the king's identity. He deals only with the issue of principle: a nation (גוי) is by definition a monarchy (ממלכה), which must by definition be ruled by a royal figure, a מלך.[87] If the emphasis on a single ruler symbolizes the nation's new unity, MT's reading of מלך instead of נשיא highlights the restoration of Israel to full nationhood.

The expansion of the covenant formula in vv. 23b–24a concretizes the spiritual renewal described in v. 23a by announcing his appointment of David as "king" in Israel. As YHWH's servant (עבדי) and as shepherd-king, he will tend the people after the divine model set out in

---

is portrayed as hiring outsiders to fight his battles. And even if this oracle paints him as a military leader, this is an isolated text.

On the other hand, this interpretation underplays the potentially militaristic overtones of נשיא. In the book of Numbers, which reflects the traditional use of the word, נשיאים were tribal and clan leaders whose responsibilities were primarily political and military. Accordingly, we read of them administering justice (Josh 22:32), leading in battle (Num 1:16, 44; 10:4; etc.), dividing the land (17:4), and negotiating with outsiders (Josh 9:18–19). E. A. Speiser, "Background and Function of the Biblical נשיא," CBQ 25 (1963) 115, rightfully comments "The נשיא represents (in Ex. 22:27) the chief political authority, comparable to later מלך." Similarly, B. Halpern, *The Constitution of the Monarchy in Israel*, HSM 25 (Chico: Scholars, 1981) 214. Furthermore, the non-military interpretation of נשיא also overlooks the fact that the most militaristic figure in the entire book of Ezekiel, Gog of Magog, is introduced three times as a "chief prince" (נשיא ראש, 38:2, 3; 39:1).

At the same time, this interpretation overplays the religious/liturgical role of the נשיא. The fact that "princes" provided offerings for the altar and the dedication of the tabernacle in Numbers 7 does not mean theirs was a sacral office. It means simply that they represented and acted on behalf of their tribes and clans. Where they are actually involved in cultic activity, the sacrifices are for themselves, not on behalf of the community (Lev 4:3, 31, 35). Indeed, when they attempted to seize a more significant role in the cult this was denied them (Num 16:1–3).

86. The reading of LXX and Papyrus[967] in vv. 22 and 24 may reflect an early reading of the text, perhaps a harmonization with v. 25, which declares expressly that "My servant David shall be their נשיא forever." A similar phenomenon may account for Ezek 28:12, where מלך is also rendered as ἄρχων by LXX, though in this instance the influence derives from נגיד, "prince," in v. 2, which LXX renders as ἄρχων. So also Duguid, *Ezekiel and the Leaders of Israel*, 23.

87. Cf. Duguid, *Ezekiel and the Leaders of Israel*, 24–25.

chapter 34, and apparently inspire them with his own conduct (cf. Deut 17:19–20) to walk in the ways of YHWH as called for in the covenant and the Deuteronomic Torah (v. 24b).

With his five-fold affirmation of the eternality of the restoration in the second panel (24b–28), YHWH transforms this oracle into a powerful eschatological statement, envisaging an entirely new existence, where the old historical realities are considered null and void, and the new saving work of God is perceived as final.[88] For Ezekiel eschatological events are neither ahistorical nor supra-historical; they are based upon YHWH's past actions in history and represent a final solution to the present historical crisis. But the scope of his eschatological hope extends beyond a renewal of YHWH's covenant with his people, incorporating all the other promises upon which the Israelites had based their security: YHWH's covenant with David, his establishment of Jerusalem as the place for his name to dwell, and his special interest in the land of Canaan as his land, offered as a gracious fiefdom to Israel to administer on his behalf.

In spite of the prophet's avoidance of specifically messianic designations,[89] the messianic significance of this oracle is obvious. The principal features of Ezekiel's Messiah are reflected in the titles and role designations he bears. As David he is heir to the eternal dynastic promises made by YHWH to Israel's greatest king. As עבדי, "my servant," he enjoys a special relationship with YHWH, ruling the people as his specially chosen agent. As נשיא, "prince, chieftain," he stands at the head of his people, not as a tyrannical ruler, but as one who has been called from their ranks to represent them. As מלך he symbolizes the nation's new unity. All other pretenders to the throne have been dismissed that Israel may be "one nation" (גוי אחד) under "one king" (מלך אחד) occupying the land of Israel. As רועה אחד "one shepherd," he seeks the welfare of the flock, according to the pattern of YHWH himself (chapter 34). In all these roles, Ezekiel's Messiah symbolizes the realities of the new age. Remarkably, he plays no part in the restoration of the nation. He neither gathers the people nor leads them back to their homeland. Unlike other prophets, Ezekiel does not speak of the Messiah as an agent

---

88. Cf. Block, "Bringing Back David," 180–81.

89. So also Targum Jonathan, on which see S. H. Levey, *The Targum of Ezekiel*, The Aramaic Bible 13 (Wilmington, DE: Glazier, 1987) 4–5; idem, *The Messiah*, 83–87.

of peace⁹⁰ or righteousness;⁹¹ these he attributes to the direct activity of God. The Messiah's personal presence symbolizes the reign of YHWH in the glorious new age.

The נשיא in Ezekiel 40–48

We conclude this discussion of the transformation of Ezekiel's royal vision with a few summary comments about the נשיא in chapters 40–48.⁹² Here the נשיא functions, not as a tribal chieftain, nor as a military leader, but as the leader of the people in the context of highly developed centralized economic and religious structures. We might summarize his role and function as follows:

1. Although the outer eastern gateway is forever closed to human traffic, the נשיא alone may sit in the gateway and eat his sacrificial meals there before YHWH (44:1–3).⁹³

2. The נשיא is assigned a special territorial grant, separate from the tribal allotments, consisting of two large tracts of land on either side, east and west, of the sacred reserve (45:7–9; 48:21).

3. The נשיא must provide the prescribed animals, grain and oil for sacrifices, which are to be offered on his and the people's behalf (45:21–25).

4. On weekly Sabbaths and new moon celebrations the נשיא shall stand in the inner court to watch the priests presenting the offerings on his behalf. Forbidden to step out onto the most sacred space of the inner court, he must prostrate himself on the threshold of the gate (46:1–7, 12).

5. At the appointed festivals, the נשיא must enter the sacred precinct with the rest of the lay worshippers. However, unlike the נשיא, the

---

90. Isa 9:5–6 [ET 9:6–7]; 11:6–9; Mic 5:5; Jer 23:6; Zech. 9:9–10.

91. Isa 5–6; 11:2–5; Jer 23:5–6. On the relationship of Ezekiel's Messiah with other biblical portraits, see A. Moenikes, "Messianismus im Alten Testament (vorapokalyptische Zeit)," *ZRGG* 40 (1988) 289–306.

92. For my discussion of this enigmatic figure see Block, "Bringing Back David," 183–88.

93. The notion of "sitting before YHWH" is relatively rare in the Hebrew Bible: Judg 20:26; 21:2; 2 Sam 7:18 = 1 Chr 17:16; 1 Kgs 8:25; 2 Chr 6:16.

common folk may not turn around inside the precinct and exit via the gate through which they entered (46:8–10).

6. The נשיא may present additional voluntary offerings to YHWH, but they must be presented like the Sabbath and new moon offerings, while he watches from inside the east gate. After the offerings are completed he must leave this gate and it shall be shut behind him (46:12).

7. The נשיא may apportion his property to his sons as their permanent possessions, but if he awards any of his land to his servants, in the year of liberation it must return to the prince (46:17).

8. The נשיא may not confiscate property of the people and give it to his sons as their own territorial grants (46:18).

My conclusions regarding the role of the נשיא in Ezekiel's closing vision still stand.[94] The primary concern in this vision is not political, but cultic. Unlike 34:23–24 and 37:22–24, the issue here is not the return of David, but the presence of YHWH. The role of the נשיא is facilitative, not regally symbolic. Unlike past kings, who perverted the worship of YHWH for selfish ends and/or sponsored the worship of other gods, this נשיא is charged with promoting the worship of YHWH in spirit and in truth. Uniquely in this vision, with its radically theocentric portrayal of Israel's future, the נשיא emerges as a religious functionary, serving the holy community of faith, which itself is focused on the worship of the God, who dwells in their midst. Where the presence of God is recognized, there is purity and holiness. Ezekiel's נשיא is not responsible for the administration of the cult. Not only does he not participate actively in the ritual; unlike previous kings he does not build the temple, design the worship, or appoint the priests; these prerogatives belong to YHWH. While departing from the historical roles of David and Solomon, this agrees with the image of the נשיא in 34:23–24, who is installed as under-shepherd by YHWH only after the latter has personally rescued Israel. In this ideological presentation the נשיא functions as YHWH's appointed lay patron and sponsor of the cult, whose activity ensures the continuance of harmonious relations between deity and subjects. The God of Israel has fulfilled his covenant promises, regathering the people and restoring them to their/his land.

---

94. "Bringing back David," 187–88.

More important, he has recalled the people to himself, and established his residence in their midst. Now let them celebrate, and let the נשיא lead the way.

Conclusion

In Ezekiel's mind, the kings of Israel, specifically David and his descendants, were YHWH's specially chosen agents appointed to govern his people in his place, and thereby secure their well-being.[95] Ezekiel's oracle against Israel's kings in 34:1–10 shares the theocratic vision of Deuteronomy, in which the king's primary role is to represent YHWH by embodying covenant righteousness and promoting the well being of those in his charge. His position within the tri-partite covenantal relationship may be illustrated as follows:

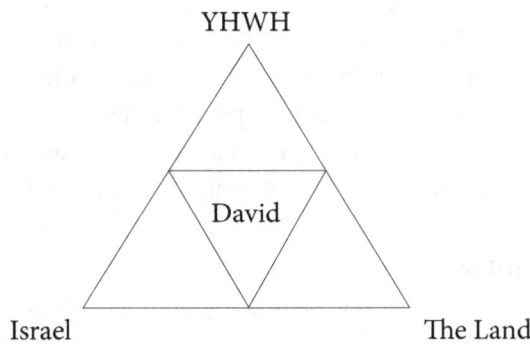

But in Ezekiel's mind the ideal and reality of the history of Israel's monarchy were miles apart. His comments about past kings tend to go in two directions.

On the one hand, in the past Israel's kings have failed miserably in their obligations as leaders of the people. For Ezekiel the dominant problem with Israel's monarchs was arrogance and the abuse of their role as מלך, expressed by violently exploiting their subjects for personal gain (34:2b–6; 45:8–9). Instead of promoting the health of the people, the hearts of Israel's kings were lifted high over their brothers

---

95. Just as at the cosmic level אדם, as the image of God, was charged to govern the world as God's viceroy (Gen 1:26–28; Ps 8), so at the national level the Davidic kings were appointed as vice-regents of YHWH, charged to govern as YHWH would, were he personally present.

(cf. Deut 17:20), and they terrorized and exploited them ruthlessly for selfish ends (19:3, 6–7). Indeed, in the final statement of that part of this pastoral oracle that concerns the shepherds of Israel, YHWH declares his determination to rescue his people from their own leaders (34:10).

In this event the king of Babylon plays a crucial role. Ezekiel envisions Nebuchadnezzar not only as a divine agent of judgment on the nation for their rebellion against him, but also as an agent of deliverance, rescuing the people from their oppressors, and providing a refuge for the exiles in Babylon while YHWH's fury rages all around at home. At the same time, in a remarkable twist, the coda of 17:22–24 portrays Nebuchadnezzar as the agent through whom the dynasty is rescued. Jehoiachin is removed to Babylon so that at the appropriate time, when YHWH has reconstructed the covenantal triangle, a representative of the Davidic house is available. This sets the stage for the final restoration oracles, according to which, having brought the remnants of all the tribes back to their ancestral homeland and reestablished justice among the people, YHWH will finally install the ideal David as shepherd, prince and king over his people. The ideational portrayal of the נשיא in the final vision highlights his facilitative role in ensuring that deity, people, and land permanently enjoy the ancient ideals.[96]

Bibliography

Amiet, P. *The Art of the Ancient Near East*. Translated by J. Shepley and C. Choquet. New York: Abrams, 1980.

Barnett, R. D. *Ancient Ivories in the Middle East and Adjacent Countries*. Qedem: Monographs of the Institute of Archeology 14. Jerusalem: Hebrew University, 1982.

Begg, C. "The Identity of the Princes in Ezekiel 19: Some Reflections." *ETL* 65 (1989) 358–65.

Block, Daniel I. "The Burden of Leadership: The Mosaic Paradigm of Kingship (Deut. 17:14–20)." *BibSac* 162 (2005) 259–78.

———. *Ezekiel Chapters 1–24*. NICOT. Grand Rapids: Eerdmans, 1997.

———. *Ezekiel Chapters 25–48*. NICOT. Grand Rapids: Eerdmans, 1998.

———. "Bringing Back David: Ezekiel's Messianic Hope." In *The Lord's Anointed: Interpretation of Old Testament Messianic Texts*, edited by P. Satterthwaite, R. S. Hess, and G. J. Wenham, 172–83. Grand Rapids: Baker, 1995.

Borger, R. *Die Inschriften Asarhaddons Königs von Assyrien*. Archiv für Orientforschung 9. Graz: Selbsetverlage des Herausgebers, 1956.

---

96. I am grateful to Jason Gile and Charlie Trimm for their helpful comments on an earlier draft of this paper.

Caquot, A. "La parole sur Juda dans le testament lyrique de Jacob (Genèse 49,8–12)." *Semitica* 26 (1976) 5–32.
Clifford, R. J. *The Cosmic Mountain in Canaan and the Old Testament.* HSM 4. Missoula, MT: Scholars, 1972.
Cooke, George A. *The Book of Ezekiel: A Critical and Exegetical Commentary.* ICC. Edinburgh: T. & T. Clark, 1946.
Crane, A. S. "The Restoration of Israel: Ezekiel 36–39 in Early Jewish Interpretation: A Textual-comparative Study of the Oldest Extant Hebrew and Greek Manuscripts." DPhil diss., Murdock University, Perth, Australia, 2006
Dijkstra, M. and J. C. de Moor. "Problematical Passages in the Legend of Aqhâtu." *UF* 7 (1975) 171–215.
Duguid, I. M. *Ezekiel and the Leaders of Israel.* VTSup 56. Leiden: Brill, 1994.
Fishbane, Michael. *Biblical Interpretation in Ancient Israel.* Oxford: Clarendon, 1985.
Friebel, K. *Jeremiah's and Ezekiel's Sign-Acts: Rhetorical Nonverbal Communication.* JSOTSup 283. Sheffield: Sheffield Academic, 1999.
Gowan, D. E. *When Man Becomes God: Humanism and Hybris in the Old Testament.* PittsTMS 6. Pittsburgh: Pickwick, 1975.
Gross, W. "Israel's Hope for the Renewal of the State." *JNSL* 14 (1988) 101–33.
Hossfeld, F.-L. *Untersuchungen zu Komposition und Theologie des Ezekielbuches.* FzB 20. Würzburg: Echter Verlag, 1977.
Johnson, A. C., H. S. Gehman, and E. H. Kase, Jr., editors. *The John H. Scheide Biblical Papyri: Ezekiel.* Princeton University Studies in Papyrology 3. Princeton: Princeton University Press, 1938.
Joyce, Paul M. "King and Messiah in Ezekiel." In *King and Messiah in Israel and the Ancient Near East: Proceedings of the Oxford Old Testament Seminary,* edited by John Day, 323–97. JSOTSup 270. Sheffield: Sheffield Academic, 1998.
Laato, A. *Josiah and David Redivivus: The Historical Josiah and the Messianic Expectations of Exilic and Postexilic Times.* CBOT 33. Lund: Almqvist & Wiksell, 1992.
Levenson, J. *Theology of the Program of Restoration of Ezekiel 40–48.* HSM 10. Missoula, MT: Scholars, 1976.
Keel, Othmar. *The Symbolism of the Biblical World: Ancient Near Eastern Iconography and the Book of Psalms.* Translated by T. J. Hallett. Winona Lake, IN: Eisenbrauns, 1997.
Levitt Kohn, R. *A New Heart and a New Soul: Ezekiel, the Exile and the Torah.* JSOTSup 358. Sheffield: Sheffield Academic, 2002.
Lang, B. *Kein Aufstand in Jerusalem: Die Politik des Propheten Ezechiel.* SBB. Stuttgart: Katholisches Bibelwerk, 1981.
Levey, S. H. *The Messiah: An Aramaic Interpretation. The Messianic Exegesis of the Targum.* Cincinnati: Hebrew Union College Press, 1974.
Luckenbill, D. D. *The Annals of Sennacherib.* 1924. Reprint, ATT. Eugene, OR: Wipf & Stock, 2005.
Lust, J. "Major Divergences between LXX and MT in Ezekiel." In *The Earliest Text of the Hebrew Bible: The Relationship between the Masoretic Text and the Hebrew Base of the Septuagint Reconsidered,* edited by A. Schenker, 83–92. SGS 52. Atlanta: Society of Biblical Literature, 2003.

———. "Textual Criticism of the Old and New Testaments: Stepbrothers?" In *New Testament Textual Criticism and Exegesis*, edited by A. Denaux, 15–32. Leuven: Leuven University Press, 2002.

———. "'Messianism and Septuagint.'" In *Congress Volume Salamanca 1983*, edited by J. A. Emerton, 174–91. VTSup 36. Leiden: Brill, 1985.

———. "Ezekiel 36–40 in the Oldest Greek Manuscript." *CBQ* 43 (1981) 517-33.

Lyons, Michael A. *From Law to Prophecy: Ezekiel's Use of the Holiness Code*. LHBOTS 507. New York: T. & T. Clark, 2009.

Milgrom, Jacob. *Numbers*. JPS Torah Commentary. Philadelphia: Jewish Publication Society, 1990.

Moenikes, A. "Messianismus im Alten Testament (vorapokalyptische Zeit)." *Zeitschrift für Religions und Geistesgeschichte* 40 (1988) 289–306.

Moran, W. L. "Gen 49,10 and its Use in Ez 21,32." *Bib* 39 (1958) 424–25.

Odell, M. S. *Ezekiel*. SHBC. Macon, GA: Smyth & Helwys, 2005.

Parpola, S. "The Assyrian Tree of Life: Tracing the Origins of Jewish Monotheism and Greek Philosophy." *JNES* 52 (1993) 161–207.

Pfisterer Darr, K. "Proverb Performance and Trans-generational Retribution in Ezekiel 18." In *Ezekiel's Hierarchical World: Wrestling with a Tiered Reality*. Edited by C. Patton and S. Cook. SBLSemS. Atlanta: SBL Press, 2004.

———. "The Book of Ezekiel." In *The New Interpreter's Bible*, vol. 6, edited by Leander Keck et al., 1073–607. Nashville: Abingdon, 2001.

Pili, F. "Possibili casi di metatesi in Genesi 49,10 e Salmo 2,11–12a." *Augustinianum* 15 (1975) 457–71.

Rofé, A. "Qumranic Paraphrases: The Greek Deuteronomy and the Late History of the Biblical נשיא." *Textus* 14 (1988) 37–46.

Schunck, K.-D. "Die Attribute des eschatologischen Messias." *Theologische Literaturzeitung* 111 (1986) 641-52.

Simian-Yofre, H. "Ez 17, 1–10 como enigma y parabola." *Bib* 65 (1984) 27–43.

Speiser, E. A. "Background and Function of the Biblical נשיא." *CBQ* 25 (1963) 1-17.

Tuell, Steven S. *The Law of the Temple in Ezekiel 40–48*. HSM 49. Atlanta: Scholars, 1992.

Vawter, B., and L. J. Hoppe. *A New Heart: A Commentary on the Book of Ezekiel*. ITC. Grand Rapids: Eerdmans, 1991.

Wevers, John W. *Ezekiel*. NCBC. Grand Rapids: Eerdmans, 1982.

Winter, U. "Der Lebensbaum in der altorientalischen Bildsymbolik," In ". . . *Bäume braucht man doch!" Das Symbol des Baumes zwischen Hoffnung und Zerstörung*, edited by H. Schweizer, 57–88. Sigmaringen: Thorbecke, 1986.

Zimmerli, W. *Ezekiel 1: A Commentary on the Book of Ezekiel, Chapters 1–24*. Translated by R. E. Clements. Hermeneia. Philadelphia: Fortress, 1979.

PART THREE

Transformation of Ezekiel in the Versions and New Testament

9

Transformation in Ezekiel's Textual History
Ezekiel 7 in the Masoretic Text and the Septuagint

Timothy Mackie

Introduction

THE CREATIVE REUSE OF EARLIER BIBLICAL TRADITIONS IS A DOMINANT feature of the book of Ezekiel, as the essays in the present volume suggest. This is not only a fitting characterization of the prophet himself, but also of the tradents and scribes who passed down the literary collection of his oracles. As the book of Ezekiel became a part of the emerging collection of sacred Scripture in the Second Temple period, this inclusion had a decisive impact on the book's textual shape. Some scribes of this period were intent not only on transmitting the sacred scrolls but also on coordinating their parts via compositional and textual means, and in the case of Ezekiel, this meant integrating his message with other prophetic texts in the collection of sacred writings. As I will attempt to show below, processes of textual expansion and coordination played a crucial role in the final stages of Ezekiel's composition history, and are discernible to us by carefully comparing its textual witnesses. The way in which the book reached the compositional shape found in the Masoretic Text (hereafter, MT) can be empirically traced by comparison with the Septuagint, which preserves a text that is shorter and in some places has a different arrangement. Such a state of textual affairs is now familiar from the existence of multiple literary editions of biblical books preserved in the Septuagint and the Hebrew manuscripts from

Qumran, particularly Jeremiah and Samuel.[1] However, the textual development of Ezekiel displays a particular feature that makes it relevant to the themes of this volume. The many textual additions made to Ezekiel that are found in the MT edition (and, less often, in the Septuagint) are not merely the result of the book's internal textual development, as if it were transmitted in solitude. They very often represent attempts to coordinate Ezekiel with other biblical texts, or to highlight certain elements of his oracles and develop them in tandem with other prophetic texts. In other words, they contribute to our understanding of the phenomenon of inner-biblical exegesis.[2] This kind of study in the overlap and intersection between compositional and textual history is a ripe and burgeoning field in Hebrew Bible studies today,[3] and Ezekiel studies in particular.[4] However, there are a number of methodological refinements that need to be made in this connection, and, in my view, the role of an emerging Scripture collection has not played as important a part in the discussion as it should. The judgment oracle of Ezekiel chapter seven offers an ideal setting to see how these two fields overlap, as well as how the book of Ezekiel both contributed to and was affected by the development of a Scripture collection in the latest stages of its formation.

1. See the chapter on the relationship between textual and literary criticism in Emanuel Tov, *Textual Criticism of the Hebrew Bible*, 2d rev. ed. (Minneapolis: Fortress; Assen: Van Gorcum, 2001).

2. A similar state of affairs in the 1QIsa[a] scroll has been well-studied. From a previous generation of scholarship, see Patrick Skehan, "The Qumran Manuscripts and Textual Criticism," in *Volume du Congrès, Strasbourg, 1956*, ed. G. W. Anderson, 148–60, VTSup 4 (Leiden: Brill, 1957) and Shemaryahu Talmon, "DSIa as a Witness to Ancient Exegesis of the Book of Isaiah," *ASTI* 1 (1962) 62–72. For more current studies, see Paulson Pulikottil, *Transmission of Biblical Texts in Qumran: The Case of the Large Isaiah Scroll 1QIsa[a]*, JSPSup 34 (Sheffield: Sheffield Academic, 2001).

3. See the essays in Adrian Schenker, ed., *The Earliest Text of the Hebrew Bible: The Relationship of the MT and the Hebrew Base of the Septuagint* (Atlanta: Scholars, 2003). Also very useful is the up-to-date survey of the scholarly discussion in the early chapters of M. N. van der Meer, *Formation and Reformulation: The Redaction of the Book of Joshua in the Light of the Oldest Textual Witnesses*, VTSup 102 (Leiden: Brill, 2004).

4. See Johan Lust, ed., *Ezekiel and His Book: Textual and Literary Criticism and their Interrelation*, BETL 74 (Leuven: Peeters, 1986); "The Ezekiel Text," in *Sôfer Mahîr: Essays in Honor of Adrian Schenker*, ed. Yohanan A. P. Goldman et al., 153–68 (Leiden: Brill, 2006); E. Tov, "Recensional Differences Between the Masoretic Text and the Septuagint of Ezekiel," in *The Greek and Hebrew Bible: Collected Essays on the Septuagint*, 397–410 (Leiden: Brill, 1999).

This study of Ezek 7 is generated by a simple textual fact: the Old Greek translation (hereafter, OG) presents us with a text that is shorter, and in a different order of arrangement than that of the MT.[5] It will be argued on the basis of recent studies on the translation technique of OG Ezekiel that the translation is based on a Hebrew text that quantitatively differed from the MT, that its Hebrew *Vorlage* preserves an earlier edition of the judgment oracle, and that the MT represents a secondary compositional stage. The editorial work reflected in the MT edition was designed to coordinate the details of the oracle in Ezek 7 with the depiction of the "king of the North" in the visions of Dan 7–12, and, most importantly, was prompted by a preexisting textual relationship between the two books. I will conclude with some reflections on the composition of Ezekiel in relation to the emergence of a Scripture collection in the period of the Second Temple, and how the resulting processes and effects of inner-scriptural interpretation played a decisive role in the textual shape of the Hebrew Bible.

The Greek Translation of Ezekiel and its Translation Technique

As is well known, the individual books of the Septuagint vary widely in the nature and character of their translations. Thus, any discussion about the Hebrew text lying behind the Greek translation presupposes a thorough study of the translation technique employed in any given book. The secondary literature on this subject in Septuagint studies has grown in recent decades and has stimulated more precise discussion about what it means for a translation to be "literal" in relation to its source text.[6] The defining features of literal translation most often dis-

---

5. The term "Septuagint" originally referred particularly to the translation of the Torah into Greek, and only later became a term for the entire translation of the Prophets, Writings, and Apocryphal works in the Christian tradition. To distinguish the original Greek translation of Ezekiel from the connotations of the word "Septuagint," I will refer to it as the "Old Greek," i.e., the earliest reconstructed form of the translation from the available manuscripts, as found in the edition of Joseph Ziegler, *Ezechiel*, Septuaginta: Vetus Testamentum Graecum Auctoritate Academiae Scientiarum Gottingensis editum XVI/1, 2d rev. ed. (Göttingen: Vandenhoeck & Ruprecht, 1977).

6. The most influential studies have been those of James Barr, "The Typology of Literalism in Ancient Biblical Translations," *Mitteilungen des Septuaginta-Unternehmens* 15 (1979) 279–325; and Tov, *The Text-Critical Use of the Septuagint in Biblical Research*, 2nd rev. ed. (Jerusalem: Simor, 1997) 54–60. R. T. McLay has contributed an impor-

cussed are (1) the degree to which the translation represents the formal and/or structural features of the source text, particularly in relation to word order and quantitative representation of words and phrases, and (2) the consistent use of translation equivalents for particular words in the source text, known as "stereotyped" translation equivalents.[7] When a translation displays such features to a high degree, we can speak with greater certainty about the text which lay before the translator.

It is only in recent years that the translation technique of OG Ezekiel has been systematically analyzed using such criteria. The most comprehensive analysis to date has been provided by Galen Marquis.[8] He has studied the way in which OG Ezekiel's syntax and word order was chosen to match that of the Hebrew as well as how consistently the translator chose specific Greek words to translate the Hebrew vocabulary. With regard to syntax and word order agreement between OG and MT Ezekiel, Marquis examined Ezek 1–39 (1013 verses) and found that only 9.9% of the Greek text (100 vv.) contained some sort of word order variation in relation to the Hebrew, while 90.1% (913vv.) displayed basic word order agreement.[9] In relation to the translator's consistent use of Greek translation equivalents for certain Hebrew words, Marquis found that there is a 95.6% consistency in the translator's rendering of nouns, and an 89.6% consistency for verbs.[10] While Tov and Wright

---

tant corrective to the discussion by arguing that studies which focus on criteria for the "literal" nature of the translation do not help in developing a holistic evaluation of a translator's approach to the source text. He proposes a more descriptive model that incorporates study of "literalistic" features as well more linguistically informed criteria, such as comparative language structure and syntagmatic lexical choice. See his detailed discussion in *The Use of the Septuagint in New Testament Research* (Grand Rapids: Eerdmans, 2003) 44–99.

7. Barr, "Typology of Literalism," 294–314; Tov, *Text-Critical Use*, 17–31.

8. Galen Marquis, *The Translation Technique Reflected in LXX-Ezekiel* [Hebrew] (MA thesis, Hebrew University, 1982); "Word Order as a Criterion for the Evaluation of Translation Technique in the LXX and the Evaluation of Word-Order Variants as Exemplified in LXX-Ezekiel," *Textus* 13 (1986) 59–84; "Consistency of Lexical Equivalents as a Criterion for the Evaluation of Translation Technique in the LXX of Ezekiel," in *VI Congress of the International Organization for Septuagint and Cognate Studies*, ed. C. Cox, 405–24 (Atlanta: Scholars, 1987).

9. Marquis, "Word Order," 63–64. Because of the nature of MT Ezekiel's consistent additions in relation to OG, only those elements where OG and MT overlap were taken into consideration, so as to gain independent evidence for making judgments about their quantitative differences.

10. Marquis, "Consistency," 416–17. The lower percentage in lexical equivalence for verbs is related to contextual semantics, especially for verbs with a wide semantic

have found examples of both variation and strict consistency in how OG Ezekiel renders certain syntactic constructions, they still admit that it is an extremely literal translation.[11] All said, those who have attempted to statistically quantify elements of the "literalness" of OG Ezekiel have affirmed that the translation overwhelmingly "mimics" the Hebrew text in representing its structural and quantitative features as well as adopting stereotyped translation equivalents for the Hebrew vocabulary.[12]

The characterization of OG Ezekiel as "literal" does not, however, address the whole issue. Many of the differences between the OG and MT of Ezek 7 involve not simply word order or lexical diversity, but "quantitative differences" (i.e., large amounts of the MT are not represented in OG, or vice-versa) as well as "differences of sequence" (i.e. material common to both OG and MT is in a different arrangement). As Aejmelaeus has argued, such differences of sequence and quantity belong to a completely different category than what she calls smaller level "word variants," namely differences of word order and lexical equivalence.[13] If a translator makes small-scale deviations from the Hebrew word order or syntax to produce more coherent Greek, it does not follow that the same translator is therefore also responsible larger scale differences of sequence or quantity, i.e., of "omitting" material or rearranging the contents of the text. The latter are not the result of the translation process, but are differences of an editorial nature. Therefore it must be demonstrated, not assumed, that the translator of OG Ezekiel

---

range. For example, the verb נשא can be used in the sense of physical "lifting" (ἐξαιρω, 1:19), of metaphorical "bearing" of guilt (λαμβανω, 4:5) or disgrace (κομιζω, 16:52), of "bearing" fruit (φερω, 17:8) or prideful "exaltation" (ὑψόω, 29:15). Such an example does not show the translator's *inconsistency* in rendering the word נשא, but rather his sensitivity to context in each case (cf. Marquis, 410–11).

11. Emanuel Tov and Benjamin G. Wright, "Computer-Assisted Study of the Criteria for Assessing the Literalness of the Translation Units in the Septuagint," in *The Greek and Hebrew Bible: Collected Essays on the Septuagint*, ed. E. Tov, 219–37 (Leiden: Brill, 1999) 237.

12. The theoretical concept of "mimesis" in translation theory is drawn from the helpful discussion of Michael V. Fox, "Translation and Mimesis," in *Bible Translation in Context*, ed. F. W. Knobloch, 207–21 (Bethesda: University Press of Maryland, 2002).

13. Anneli Aejmelaeus, "What Can We Know about the Hebrew *Vorlage* of the Septuagint?" in *On the Trail of the Septuagint Translators*, 77–115 (Kampen: Kok Pharos, 1993) 111–12. The same position has recently been argued in detail by M. Zippor, *Tradition and Transmission: Studies in Ancient Biblical Translation and Interpretation* [Hebrew] (Tel Aviv: Hakibbutz Hameuchad, 2001) 16–53.

was an editor as well as a translator. The evidence of Marquis' detailed studies of OG Ezekiel's translation technique render highly improbable the suggestion that the translator was involved in large-scale reorganization and consistent shortening of his *Vorlage*. It is almost certain that these phenomena took place at another point in the text's history. Tov's conclusion summarizes the issue well:

> Evidence from translation technique [of OG Ezekiel] thus supports the view that the short text of the LXX reflects a short Hebrew *Vorlage* which is not known from other manuscripts ... Rather than taking the LXX as a short text, we should thus take MT as an expanded text.[14]

In addition to the literal character of OG Ezekiel, we also have the supporting examples of different literary editions found in the Qumran biblical manuscripts that correspond to the Septuagint. These preserve alternate editions of whole books (e.g., Jeremiah[15]), large sections of books (Joshua, Judges[16]) or particular literary units (e.g., 1 Sam 2[17]). While the scanty Qumran manuscript evidence for Ezekiel offers no significant variations from the MT textual tradition, this is no argument against our case.[18] Even in the instance of Jeremiah and Samuel, texts both agreeing and disagreeing with the (proto-)MT tradition are attested from the Qumran scrolls.[19] Given the random nature of the manuscript finds at Qumran, the presence or absence of proto-MT manuscripts for any biblical book found in the caves is no basis for an argument. It should not surprise us that for books without much at-

---

14. Tov, "Recensional Differences," 400.

15. See Tov, "The Literary History of the Book of Jeremiah in the Light of Its Textual History," in *Empirical Models for Biblical Criticism*, ed. J. H. Tigay, 211–37 (1985; reprint, Eugene, OR: Wipf & Stock, 2005).

16. Alexander Rofé, "The Editing of the Book of Joshua in the Light of 4QJosh^a," in *New Qumran Texts and Studies*, ed. George J. Brooke, STDJ 15 (Leiden: Brill, 1994) 73–80; Julio Trebolle Barrera, "Textual Variants in *4QJudg^a* and the Textual and Editorial History of the Book of Judges," *RevQ* 54 (1989) 229–45.

17. Tov, "Different Editions of the Song of Hannah," in *Tehilla le-Moshe: Biblical and Judaic Studies in Honor of Moshe Greenberg*, ed. M. Cogan et al., 149–70 (Winona Lake, IN: Eisenbrauns, 1997); Lust, "Ezekiel Manuscripts in Qumran: Preliminary Edition of 4Q Ez a and b," in *Ezekiel and His Book: Textual and Literary Criticism and their Interrelation*, ed. J. Lust, BETL 74 (Leuven: Peeters, 1986) 90–100.

18. Lust, "Ezekiel Manuscripts in Qumran."

19. For details, see Tov, *Textual Criticism*, 319–27.

testation in Qumran manuscripts, the Septuagint is our prime witness to significant textual differences. This corollary evidence, combined with the extremely formal and literal character of the OG translation of Ezekiel, give us compelling reason to believe that when the translation displays differences of quantity and arrangement in relation to the MT it is preserving an alternate edition.

Based on this conclusion, I will proceed on the supposition that the OG of Ezek 7 accurately reflects the structural and editorial organization of its Hebrew *Vorlage*, and thus presents us with an earlier edition of the oracle. By comparing the expansions and editorial rearrangements present in the MT, we have empirical means of studying the oracle's composition history.

Differences of Sequence and Quantity in MT and OG Ezek 7:1–11

There are many textual differences between OG and MT Ezek 7, ranging from single word or phrase-length expansions to the addition or relocation of multiple sentences. I will focus on two examples of large-scale differences. It will become evident that at least these two editorial changes are related to one another and make a decisive contribution to the shape and meaning of the MT edition.

The first case is a combination of *differences of sequence and quantity* (see Appendices I and II: Comparison between OG and MT Ezek 7:2–10): a large block of material in the OG edition of the oracle (Ezek 7:7–9 in OG) is found in a different location in the MT edition (Ezek 7:3–5a in MT). Also, along the edges of this material one finds a number of phrases that have been added (indicated by italics in Appendix I). These appear directly after the differently located material in the MT (Ezek 7:5b–7a) and also later on in the oracle (MT Ezek 7:10b–c). The fact that these additions occur near the edges of the unit makes it likely that all of these textual differences are related and took place at the same time.[20]

---

20. For this editorial principle, note J. Trebolle Barrera's comments on scroll editing in the ancient world by means of "cutting and pasting" (προς ἀλληλα κολλων τε και ἀφαιρων, Plato, *Phaedrus,* 278). In such cases, material added in the editing process was chiefly located at the beginning or ending of text units; see Trebolle Barrera, *The Jewish Bible and the Christian Bible* (Leiden: Brill, 1998) 96–97.

Two related explanations for this textual discrepancy have been put forward in modern scholarship. Zimmerli (building on Cornill's work) argued that because the differently located material (MT Ezek 7:3a–5a) is almost identical to the section of text found in MT Ezek 7:8–9, it is therefore an extraneous doublet that was secondarily added to the text. In an early period, according to Zimmerli, the Greek translation was assimilated to the proto-MT text which already had the secondary addition, but it was accidentally added into the wrong place in the translation, resulting in the difference of sequence.[21] He sees the other MT additions as unrelated and attributes them to a later stage in the oracle's development.[22] Tov represents a related, but distinct view which also holds that the transposed material is not original to the oracle, but he describes more cogently the scribal mechanics behind the different sequences:

> [A] textual mishap such as a doublet must be supposed here ... The different sequence of the LXX may point to a late insertion of the section. Probably one of the two parts was added in MT in one place and in the LXX in another. At first the added section was placed in the margin and from there it reached two different places in the text.[23]

With regard to the sequence differences in the oracle, these explanations are compelling. The hypothesis that the section was a marginal doublet of a unit in the main text appeals to the well-known phenomena of marginal variants.[24] While a doublet of this size (about 30 words) is strikingly large, there are similar examples found in the Qumran biblical manuscripts.[25] However, the explanations of Zimmerli and Tov

---

21. Walther Zimmerli, *Ezekiel 1*, trans. Ronald E. Clements, Hermeneia (Philadelphia: Fortress, 1979) 193–94.

22. Zimmerli, *Ezekiel*, 194: "After the conclusion of this process, yet further additions were made in M." In this conclusion he follows Carl Heinrich Cornill, *Das Buch des Propheten Ezechiel* (Leipzig: Hinrichs, 1886) 214: "Wir haben in beiden Recensionen eine Duplette, welche schon durch ihre bei beiden verschiedene Stellung als nicht ursprünglich erwiesen wird und *ausserdem ist M noch vielfach von Glossen und Zusätzen überwuchert*" (emphasis mine).

23. Tov, "Recensional Differences," 398.

24. See Tov, "Glosses, Interpolations, and Other Types of Scribal Additions in the Text of the Hebrew Bible," in *The Greek and Hebrew Bible: Collected Essays on the Septuagint*, 70–72 (Leiden: Brill, 1999).

25. For a discussion on marginal or interlinear variants of shorter length see S. Talmon, "Double Readings in the Masoretic Text," *Textus* 1 (1960) 144–84; "Synonymous

do not account for all of the textual issues in the chapter, as they have lumped together two different kinds of textual phenomena that need to be analyzed separately. Their arguments for considering the differently located material as a doublet are convincing. We have two parallel textual units, with the kinds of minor differences that are characteristic of the textual transmission of other parallel biblical texts. Whether the different position of the material in OG and MT is the result of the OG's transmission in Greek (Zimmerli, Cornill) or of the transmission history of the oracle in Hebrew (Tov), it seems fairly likely that we are dealing with a textual doublet that was entered into the main text.[26] However, the doublet does not encompass all of the textual differences in this section. There also occur a number of textual expansions present only in the MT edition of the oracle (MT Ezek 7:5b–6 and 7:10b–c, the italicized material in Appendix I). Regardless of how one explains the presence of the textual doublet in the oracle, the location and significance of these editorial additions are separate issues which need to be considered apart from the problematic doublet. That these additions are related to one another is clear from their content:

> MT 7:5b–6: A singular calamity, a calamity, look, its comes; an end comes ... it arises against you; look, it comes; the *ṣephirah* comes!

> MT 7:10b–c: Look, it comes; the *ṣephirah* has come out!

Readings in the Textual Traditions of the Old Testament," *Scripta Hierosolymitana* 8 (1961) 335–85; "Aspects of the Textual Transmission of the Bible in the Light of Qumran Manuscripts," *Textus* 4 (1964) 95–132. For examples of much longer doublets, cf. 1QIsa[a] XXXII, where a doublet of 13 words (Isa 38:19–20) has been preserved in the main text; cf. also the margin of 4QJer[a] III, where a large portion of the text (over 100 words) was omitted by the original scribe, and later added in the margin by another hand, cf. Eugene Ulrich et al., *Qumran Cave 4: The Prophets*, DJD XV (Oxford: Clarendon, 1997) 155–56.

26. P.-M. Bogaert's argument that the OG *Vorlage* displays a chiastic structure and that the MT is the result of editorial restructuring is very unlikely; cf. his "Les deux rédactions conserves (LXX et TM) d'Ézéchiel 7," in *Ezekiel and His Book*, ed. J. Lust, BETL 74 (Leuven: Peeters, 1986) 21–47, esp. 23–25. Because the doublets appear right next to each other in the OG, he proposes that the last phrase in MT 7:9/OG 7:6, וידעתם כי אני יהוה מכה ("and you will know that I am YHWH who strikes") is the center of a chiasm. But this is entirely unconvincing. The entire verse is the parallel unit of its doublet in MT 7:4/OG 7:8, וידעתם כי אני יהוה ("and you will know that I am YHWH"), and does not stand outside the unit as a chiastic member.

These additions introduce a new feature to the judgment oracle. In the OG edition it is YHWH himself who brings judgment (OG Ezek 7:6, "I am YHWH who strikes"), yet in the MT edition a more particular facet of the coming disaster is identified: the calamity is connected to the coming of the *ṣephirah* (הַצְּפִירָה), a word found only in the expansions of the MT (7:6c–7a, 10b–c). These editorial expansions are interrelated and represent an attempt to *introduce a specific agent of YHWH's judgment: the ṣephirah.*

Before we move on to the meaning and significance of these additions, we need to consider another major textual difference in Ezek 7:12–14 that is connected to the additions discussed above. The following table illustrates the differences between the OG and MT.

A Comparison of OG and MT Ezek 7:12–14

	Old Greek	Masoretic Text	
7:12a	The time has come! Look, the day!	The time has come! The day has approached!	7:12a
7:12b	Let the buyer not rejoice, nor the seller weep,	Let the buyer not rejoice, nor the seller weep,	7:12b
7:12c	-----	*for anger is against all of its horde!*	7:12c
7:13a	for the seller will not return to that which is sold,	for the seller will not return to that which is sold,	7:13a
7:13b	-----	*even while they are both alive.*	7:13b
7:13c	-----	*For the vision is about all its horde, it will not be reversed.*	7:13c
7:13d	and no one will retain the eye of his life	and no one will retain his life by iniquity.	7:13d
7:14a	blow the trumpet, and render decision about everything!	Blow the trumpet, and prepare everything!	7:14a
7:14b	-----	*and no one goes out to war,*	7:14b
7:14c	-----	*for my anger is against all of its horde.*	7:14c

While there are numerous "word-variants" in these verses which can be attributed to the translation process, the sentence-long expansions belong to the category "quantitative differences," and, as I argued above, are editorial in nature and cannot be attributed to the translator.[27] Additionally, the expansions MT Ezek 7:12c, 13c, and 14c are clearly similar in form and content, which lends credence to the idea that these are related to one another and were added at the same time:

7:12c כי חרון אל כל המונה
7:13c כי חזון אל כל המונה לא ישוב
7:14c כי חרוני אל כל המונה

7:12c *For anger is against all of its horde!*
7:13c *For a vision is about all of its horde! It will not be reversed!*
7:14c *For my anger is against all of its horde!*

This refrain underscores the importance of the horde. The center refrain (Ezek 7:13c) states that "the vision," i.e., the oracle of Ezek 7, is irreversible, and concerns "its" horde, while the outer refrains (Ezek 7:12c, 14c) repeat that "its" horde will face the divine wrath. The obviously outstanding feature of these expansions is the obscurity surrounding "all its horde" (כל המונה). To whom or what does "its" refer? The third feminine suffix "its" on המונה has no antecedent referent in the immediate sentence; the horde does not belong to the "buyer" or "seller" or "day" of Ezek 7:12 (all masculine nouns). The only possible referent for the feminine suffix in these editorial additions is the previous feminine noun *ṣephirah*, found only in the MT expansions (Ezek 7:7, 10). It is clear, then, that these three refrains are to be understood as part of the same layer of editorial activity that took place in vv. 1–10.

While there are many other expansions found in the MT edition (Ezek 7:16c, 19b, 24a, 27a) which may also be related to the editorial

---

27. Using Aejmaleus' terminology (cf. "What Can We Know," 112), "word-variants" are differences that originate in the translator's different interpretation of the same consonants in the MT. For example, in 7:13d the MT בעונו ("by his iniquity") is represented in the Greek by ἐν ὀφθαλμῷ ("by his eye"), in which case the translator's *Vorlage* may have contained בעינו ("by his eye") or, because of the negligible difference between *waw* and *yod* in the square script, may have been read as בעינו. For discussion of these options, see Lust et al., "Notes to the Septuagint." Because I am focusing here on the *quantitative differences* between OG and MT, other small scale differences in these verses do not have any significant bearing on the discussion.

activity in vv. 1–14, they do not have any explicit connection. Some of these are more accurately characterized as "contextually secondary elements," comments that are made only in relation to their immediate context in the sentence. For example, the long addition in MT Ezek 7:19b ("their silver and their gold will not be able to deliver them in the day of YHWH's wrath") is, in addition to being a citation of Zephaniah 1:18, linked to the key words of the first half of Ezek 7:19 ("their silver . . . and their gold").[28] Thus while it is not impossible that these other MT pluses are related to those in vv. 1–14, they do not contain any unambiguous connections with them, and so will not be discussed.

To summarize the argument so far: the OG edition of Ezek 7 preserves an earlier form of the judgment oracle, which announced an imminent act of judgment by YHWH. The MT edition has been expanded with the additions in Ezek 7:5b–7a, 10b–c, by which the *ṣephirah* is introduced as the agent of YHWH's judgment. But as the editorial refrains added in Ezek 7:12–14 make clear, although it is the agent of YHWH's judgment, the divine wrath will eventually turn against the *ṣephirah* and "its horde" as well. Now that we have an accurate picture of the textual differences between OG and MT, we are now in a position to step back and evaluate the significance of these additions for the composition history of Ezek 7.

The Hermeneutical Significance of the Editorial Changes to the MT Edition

Clearly, the *crux interpretum* of this entire matter revolves around the meaning and identification of the *ṣephirah*, whose appearance and downfall is the highlight of additions made in the MT edition. The word in its absolute form (צְפִירָה) occurs only here in Biblical Hebrew. The only other possible occurrence of the word is in Isa 28:5, לִצְפִירַת תִּפְאָרָה ("for a beautiful crown"), where it clearly refers to a "wreath" or "crown" of some sort, in light of its parallel term "a glorious diadem" (לַעֲטֶרֶת צְבִי).[29] Philological studies of Isa 28:5 have appealed

---

28. For more description of the category "contextually secondary element," see Tov, "Glosses," 70–72. For another example, the plus in MT 7:16c כְּיוֹנֵי הַגֵּאָיוֹת "like doves of the valleys" appears to be an addition meant to expand the image of the refugees "moaning" (הֹמוֹת) in the immediate context.

29. Isa 28:5 reads:
בַּיּוֹם הַהוּא יִהְיֶה יְהוָה צְבָאוֹת לַעֲטֶרֶת צְבִי לִצְפִירַת תִּפְאָרָה לִשְׁאָר עַמּוֹ

to the cognate Arabic verb *ṣafara* "to braid/interweave," and on this basis have posited the existence of a (*qatīl* base) nominal form in Hebrew with the meaning "wreath."[30] It is exceedingly unclear, however, what such a word would mean in Ezek 7, where the *ṣephirah* is an active subject whose coming is linked with an imminent calamity. Nevertheless, a nominal (*qatīl*) form of the Arabic cognate with a "figurative" sense has been proposed, so that the Arabic verb "weave, interweave" is associated with "a turn of events," and the nominal form with "doom."[31] A more recent explanation hypothesizes a different meaning from the cognate root: it refers to a woven object such as a "lasso" or "woven cord," which symbolizes the Judean deportation.[32] Targum Jonathan has relied upon the phrase in Isa 28:5 and interpreted the word as "kingdom," as have some modern commentators.[33] Both Rashi and David Kimḥi explained *ṣephirah* by appeal to an Aramaic word with the same consonants, צַפְרָא, "morning," and understand it as a reference to the time of the coming calamity.[34] At least one modern commentator refused to trans-

---

"In that day, YHWH of Hosts will become a beautiful crown, and a glorious diadem for the remnant of his people." For discussion of the word's meaning in this context, cf. Hans Wildberger, *Isaiah 28-39*, CC (Minneapolis: Fortress, 2002) 5.

30. Cf. Rudolf Smend, *Der Prophet Ezechiel*, KeH (Leipzig: Hirzel, 1880) 42. Smend traced this philological suggestion for Ezek 7:7 back to G. B. Winer's revision of J. Simonis' lexicon; cf. Winer, *Lexicon manuale hebraicum et chaldaicum in Veteris Testamenti libros post J.G. Eichhornii curas denuo castigavit, multisque modis auxit G.B. Winer*, 4th ed. (Leipzig: 1828) 831. This tradition appears even earlier in the revisions of G: Theodotion, ἡ πλοκή "woven work"; Aquila, συστολη "contraction." These are followed by Jerome (*contraction*).

31. This view is represented by most modern commentators: G. A. Cooke, *A Critical and Exegetical Commentary on the Book of Ezekiel*, ICC (Edinburgh: T. & T. Clark, 1936) 77-78, 85; Moshe Greenberg, *Ezekiel 1-30*, AB (New York: Doubleday, 1983) 148; Cornill, *Ezechiel*, 214-15; and by modern English versions (NRSV, NAS). The JPS Tanakh (1985) has based its translation ("the cycle has come round") on the earlier stage of the figurative sense's development.

32. M. Masson, "ṣepîrâ (Ezéchiel vii 10)," *VT* 37 (1987) 301-11; Daniel I. Block, *The Book of Ezekiel: Chapters 1-24*, NICOT (Grand Rapids: Eerdmans, 1997) 251-52.

33. Targum Jonathan reads תְּגַל יְאַת מַלְכוּתָה, "the kingdom is revealed" for both occurrences of the word in Ezekiel 7. See also Richard Kraetzschmar, *Das Buch Ezekiel*, HKAT (Göttingen: Vandenhoeck & Ruprecht, 1900) 74-75; Alfred Bertholet, *Das Buch Hesekiel erklärt*, KHC (Freiburg: Mohr/Siebeck, 1897) 39-40.

34. David Kimḥi:

באה הצפירה הגזירה באה לך בקר מתרגום בקר בצפרא

"the *ṣephirah* has come—the decree has come to you *in the morning*—from the (Aramaic) translation of 'morning' (בקר) as 'morning' (צפרא)." Rashi:

late the term altogether.³⁵ While this welter of suggestions has long existed in the interpretive tradition, none of them can be regarded as ultimately satisfactory. The use of the word *ṣephirah* is directly connected to the editorial history of the oracle, and any solution for the word's meaning must provide a philological solution that also elucidates the chapter's textual development.

P.-M. Bogaert has proposed an explanation that takes into account the fact that *ṣephirah* appears only in the MT edition and is integrally related to the editorial changes made to the oracle.³⁶ He argued that (1) *ṣephirah* is a feminine nominal form of the masculine noun צָפִיר, "goat,"³⁷ (2) that the editors of MT Ezek 7 understood the earlier OG edition of the oracle to be closely related to the visions of Dan 7–11, particularly chapter 8 (the vision of the ram and the goat, הַצָּפִיר, Dan 8:5ff.), and (3) that the editorial changes resulting in the MT edition were made to introduce a veiled reference to Daniel's "insolent king" into Ezekiel's oracle. Bogaert gives the following support for his argu-

---

בא ושקע מאור השחר, "it has come, and the morning star has gone down . . ." Interestingly, the Authorized Version of 1611 follows this interpretive tradition in its translation, "the morning is come unto thee." This is likely due to the influence of medieval Jewish exegesis on the translators of the AV; see Erwin I. J. Rosenthal, "Rashi and the English Bible," *BJRL* 24 (1940) 138–67.

35. Zimmerli, *Ezekiel 1*, 195–96.

36. Bogaert, "Les deux rédactions," 21–47. He is followed by Lust et. al., "Notes to the Septuagint of Ezekiel 7," *ETL* 77 (2001) 384–94.

37. Bogaert, "Les deux rédactions," 41–44. The morphological variation between feminine and masculine nominal forms is not uncommon in BH, e.g., אשמה / אשם, "guilt"; גדר / גדרה, "wall"; שיר / שירה, "song." For further examples and discussion of such "gender doublets," see Hans Bauer and Pontus Leander, *Historische Grammatik der hebräischen Sprache des Alten Testaments* (1922; reprint, Hildesheim: Olms, 1962) §62; Bruce Waltke and Michael O'Connor, *An Introduction to Biblical Hebrew Syntax* (Winona Lake, IN: Eisenbrauns, 1990) 106. It is possible that the Syriac Peshitta also saw the he-goat here in its rendering *spry'* which could be vocalized as (1) *ṣephraya'* "he-goat" or (2) as *ṣaphraya'* "morning"; cf. Jessie Payne-Smith, ed., *A Compendious Syriac Dictionary* (Oxford: Clarendon Press, 1903) 483. The reason for the feminine form in the Hebrew word hrypc is unclear. Lust et al. ("Notes to the Septuagint," 385) argue that it is because the *ṣephirah* represents the Greek people, but no parallel examples are offered. The feminine form may be explained as a broadening of the term צְפִיר־עִזִּים in Daniel, the first noun being masculine and the second feminine (cf. BDB, *ad loc*). Another possibility is that because the *ṣephirah* refers specifically to the horn of the he-goat in Dan 8, a feminine form was chosen to reflect the gender of the word "horn" (קֶרֶן).

ment.³⁸ One can see in MT's editorial work the prominent place given to "a singular coming calamity" (רעה אחת באה, MT Ezek 7:5b), which is identified with the *sephirah*. Daniel too, after the vision of the he-goat in ch.8, highlights "a calamity" (הרעה) in his penitential prayer (cf. Dan 9:12–14, the only occurrences of הרעה in the book). Bogaert believes that Daniel's description of "the insolent king . . . who will greatly destroy and prosper" (Dan 8:23–24) as "the single horn" (קרן אחת, Dan 8:9) is connected with the "single calamity" (רעה אחת) of Ezek 7:5. In Dan 8:7 the he-goat "comes near" (הגיע) and "strikes" (ויך), both of which are descriptions of the calamity in Ezek 7: v. 12 "the day *comes near*" (הגיע היום) and v. 9 "YHWH who *strikes*" (יהוה מכה).

Not all of Bogaert's arguments are equally persuasive, but his suggestion is important and opens up the possibility for a new solution. There are a large number of additional connections between Daniel and Ezek 7 that Bogaert did not mention, and these allow us to develop this idea into a much more compelling and comprehensive solution. It is well known that Ezekiel's judgment oracles (particularly chapter 7), along with other important prophetic texts, were a direct source for much of the language and imagery employed in the visions of Dan 7–12.³⁹ The announcement of the "end" (קץ) and the "time" (עת) are prominent in Ezek 7 (vv. 2, 3, 6, 7, 12), and in fact, the use of these terms together in the phrase "time of the end" occurs only in Ezekiel and Daniel. The author of Daniel's visions has clearly drawn upon the language of Ezek 7 at this point: Dan 8:17 "the vision is for the *time of the end*" (לעת קץ החזון); 11:35 and 12:4 "until the *time of the end*" (עד עת קץ); 11:40 "the *time of the end*" (עת קץ). Another example of borrowing occurs where the author of Daniel's visions drew upon the imagery of the temple's defilement in Ezek 7:21–24 and 24:21. In Ezek 7, YHWH announces that "the pride of their strength" (Ezek 7:24 עזם והשבתי גאון)⁴⁰ will be "defiled" in the coming calamity (Ezek 7:21, 22 וחללו; 7:24 וחללהו), and in Ezek 24:21, "I will defile my sanctuary, the pride of your strength" (הנני מחלל את מקדשי גאון עזכם).

---

38. Bogaert, "Les deux rédactions," 41–47.

39. Michael Fishbane has devoted an entire discussion to the way in which the visions of Daniel draw upon Isa 10, 28, 53, Jer 25, Hab 2, and Num 24. See his *Biblical Interpretation in Ancient Israel* (Oxford: Clarendon, 1985) 482–95.

40. Reading with the OG "their strength" (της ἰσχυος αὐτων = עֻזָּם) against the MT "the strong" (עָזִּים).

Dan 11:31 draws directly on these passages when it describes how the forces of the king of the North will "defile the strong sanctuary" (וחללו מקדש המעוז). These examples give ample evidence that the oracle of Ezek 7 and its description of the temple's defilement were an important resource in the composition of Daniel's visions.

It is these strong connections that already existed between Dan 7–12 and Ezek 7 that motivated the expansions we have been examining. These expansions reflect an attempt to establish a further relationship between these texts. This point is crucial in distinguishing this study from those of Bogaert and Lust, for it shows that there was a pre-existing relationship between the two texts (namely, Daniel's use of Ezek 7) that generated the expansions. The additions about the *ṣephirah* are an attempt to identify the *agent* of judgment in Ezekiel's oracle as the "insolent king" in Daniel's visions (Dan 8:23); he is the one who will carry out the destruction of the temple described in Ezek 7:21–24. Further, the three expansions that appear in Ezek 7:12–14 describe the complex role this king will play in the divine plan. The thrice repeated mention of "all of its [the *ṣephirah*'s] horde" (כל־המונה) is derived from the description of the armed forces of the king of the North ("his great horde," המון רב, Dan 11:13).[41] More specifically, the middle refrain (Ezek 7:13c) states that the *vision* (חזון) which is about the *ṣephirah*'s horde will inevitably be fulfilled.[42] The first and last refrains (MT Ezek 7:12c, 14c) tell us that YHWH's "wrath" (חרון) is *against* all its horde." Although the *ṣephirah* and "its horde" are the divinely chosen agents of judgment against Israel, YHWH's wrath will ultimately be turned against him in the end.[43] This is consistent with the depiction of the

---

41. In Dan 11:10–13 the word "horde" (המון) is used five times to describe the armies of the king of the North.

42. The language of the refrain of 7:13c is very close to the formulation in Hab 3:3, "For the vision is still for an appointed time ... it will not disappoint," a passage heavily drawn upon in Dan 8–12.

43. This depiction is also present in the *Vorlage* of OG 7:11. The MT reads as follows: החמס קם למטה רשע, "violence has arisen as a rod of the wicked." The OG and its corresponding *Vorlage* reads: καὶ συντρίψει στήριγμα ἀνόμου = ושבר למטה רשע, "and he [YHWH?] will break the rod of the wicked." This is a clear allusion to Isa 14:5, where the destruction of Babylon is announced, despite its role as YHWH's instrument of judgment: שבר יהוה מטה רשעים, "YHWH will break the rod of the wicked." Isaiah 14 plays a crucial role in the visions of Dan 8–10 (cf. the use of שבר in Dan 8:7–8, 22, 25), for the selection of Babylon as an agent of judgment and its later downfall is the model upon which Daniel's visions are constructed. It is likely

insolent king in Daniel's visions, who after executing his role in the divine plan is filled with arrogance (Dan 7:20-21; 8:25; 11:36-39) and is consequently destroyed (Dan 7:26; 8:25; 11:45).[44]

It is possible now to step back and gain an overview of the argument as a whole. We can discern two stages in the development of the MT edition of Ezek 7. First, the earlier edition of the judgment oracle (represented by the OG's *Vorlage*) contained a message of imminent, divine wrath upon Israel, a judgment (Ezek 7:9b) that would involve the defilement of the temple (Ezek 7:20-24). The language and imagery of this edition of the oracle was drawn upon in the composition of the visions in Dan 7-12, where the insolent king, the horn of the he-goat, and the king of North all describe the one who would defile the temple. The second stage involved the expansions in Ezek 7, which introduce allusions to Daniel's "insolent king" to represent his complex role in the divine plan as both an agent and recipient of God's wrath.

To sharpen the nature of the argument, it will be useful at this point to note a distinction between the approaches of Bogaert and Lust to the different editions of Ezek 7 and what is being proposed here. Lust states that the MT editor "presents a re-reading of the text from his historical point of view, after the events during the reign of Antiochus IV," and that "the main objective of the MT redaction appears to be the insert of this allusion to the disastrous events happening in the Seleucid period."[45] In other words, Lust describes the expansions in the MT edition as allusions to Antiochus IV and his desecration of the temple. In this study I have attempted to characterize the situation in a more nuanced way. It is probable that the actions of Antiochus IV were part of the impetus for these textual processes, but the way in which these events are described and interpreted in the MT additions is more sophisticated. The expansions do not simply allude to the historical events surrounding Antiochus IV; the language employed in the expansions to describe them is drawn directly from the *text* of Dan

---

that OG's *Vorlage* is secondary in relation to the MT, but it attests to the same processes of inner-biblical allusion to the visions of Daniel by means of editorial alteration.

44. The pattern is a familiar one in the prophets, particularly in Isaiah's depiction of Assyria (Isa 10:5-19, 24-34), and in fact, the portrait of the insolent king in Daniel was likely made in dependence upon these Isaiah texts. See Jürgen C. H. Lebram, "König Antiochus im Buch Daniel," *VT* 25 (1975) 737-72.

45. Lust et al., "Notes on the Septuagint," 385, 387.

7–12. In other words, the scribes interpreted these historical events in the light of another crucial event, namely, the emergence of a scriptural collection that includes Daniel. This collection created a "textual world," so to speak, in which Ezekiel's and Daniel's visions were seen as integrally related and in need of mutual clarification. The historical events related to Antiochus IV acted as the flash point that generated this complex of inner-biblical interpretation and textual expansion in Ezek 7. Instead of simply saying that the MT edition of Ezek 7 includes allusions to Antiochus IV, we must take into account the hermeneutical and textual dimensions involved. The allusions are made on the basis of a close reading of Dan 7–12, and can be described as an effort of *textual and hermeneutical coordination* between Daniel and Ezekiel in light of the events surrounding Antiochus IV. The expansions in Ezek 7 are an attempt to show that Ezekiel's judgment oracle did not refer to the happenings of his own day, but rather to the events described in the visions of Daniel.[46] Thus, the emerging scriptural collection exerted a kind of force upon itself, one in which inner-scriptural interpretation and composition functioned as a primary means for coordinating and shaping what would become the "canon."[47] Brevard Childs has argued for a similar relationship in describing the book of Isaiah's influential role in the composition history of Micah. His comments are fitting in this discussion:

> The point is not to deny that later historical events influenced the redactors, but to contest a direct and intentional move on their part to adjust the tradition to each new historical situation. Rather, the editors of Micah sought to understand God's purpose ... by means of interpreting the growing body of sacred lit-

---

46. The temporal reference of Ezekiel's oracles was the source of much discussion in the Second Temple Period, as the Qumran fragments of 4QPseudo-Ezekiel (4Q385) attest; see the discussion in Florentino García-Martínez, "The Apocalyptic Interpretation of Ezekiel in the Dead Sea Scrolls," in *Interpreting Translation: Studies on the LXX and Ezekiel in Honour of Johan Lust*, ed. F. García-Martínez and M. Vervenne, 163–76, BETL 192 (Leuven: Peeters, 2005).

47. I have in mind here the same phenomena that generated the compositional activity found in Deuteronomy 34 and Malachi 4, described at length by Stephen Chapman, *The Law and the Prophets: A Study in Old Testament Canon Formation*, FAT 27 (Tübingen: Mohr/Siebeck, 1999). I have, however, avoided using the word "canon" in relation to this due to the current debates about the anachronistic use of the term; see E. Ulrich, "The Notion and Definition of Canon," in *The Canon Debate*, ed. Lee M. McDonald and James A. Sanders, 21–35 (Peabody, MA: Hendrickson, 2002).

erature. Thus the effect of the changing historical situation was mediated through an interpretation of scripture.⁴⁸

This kind of formulation is much more suited to what we see happening in Ezek 7, and can lead us to some final thoughts on the significance of this study for the relationship between the composition history of Ezekiel and the emergence of a scriptural collection.

Implications for Understanding Ezekiel's Relationship to the Emerging Scriptural Collection

The conclusions reached here contribute significantly to two interrelated subjects, namely the composition history of Ezekiel and the relationship between text and a scriptural collection. Tov and Lust have argued that MT Ezekiel is not simply an expanded text, but represents a further editorial stage of the book, and our study has borne out this view in relation to Ezek 7. In examining the relationship between OG and MT Ezekiel, we are observing a stage of the book's composition history. This issue has been widely discussed in relation to the work of Eugene Ulrich, who has developed the concept of multiple literary editions of biblical books.⁴⁹ Building on the work of James Sanders,⁵⁰ Ulrich has applied the model of the biblical text's "stability and adaptability" within the religious communities of ancient Israel and Judaism. In Sanders' model, these texts were authoritative and yet still open to modification in light of the experiences of the community. However, I have attempted to show that the hermeneutical processes involved were more complex. Textual shaping or modification was not merely a response to historical events; it was also a response to an emerging corpus of literature held to be sacred Scripture by its tradents. One of the key historical realities in the life of post-exilic Israel was the emergence and consolidation of this collection of sacred texts. As the individual parts of the textual collection came to be viewed as a coherent whole, it became necessary to coordinate them by means of various techniques, namely, textual expansion, further composition, and inner-biblical

---

48. Brevard S. Childs, *Introduction to the Old Testament as Scripture* (Philadelphia: Fortress, 1979) 434.

49. See Ulrich, *The Dead Sea Scrolls and the Origins of the Bible* (Grand Rapids: Eerdmans, 1999).

50. James Sanders, *Torah and Canon* (Philadelphia: Fortress, 1972).

interpretation, all of which reflect what Seeligmann called a "canon-consciousness" (*Kanonbewusstsein*).[51] In the case of Ezek 7, the purpose of the MT expansions was to show that Ezekiel's oracle referred not to his own day, but to the events described in Daniel's visions. The composition history of Ezek 7 was directly affected by the emergence of a scriptural collection in which Daniel exerted determinative influence.

In conclusion, what we find in the textual development of Ezek 7 is the interconnectedness of inner-biblical interpretation, scriptural composition, and textual transmission. It illustrates for us how in the Second Temple period one of the dynamics at work in the development of the scriptural books was the emergence of the scriptural collection itself.

---

51. Isac Leo Seeligmann, "Voraussetzungen der Midraschexegese," in *Congress Volume. Copenhagen 1953*, ed. G. W. Anderson et al., 150–81, VTSup 1 (Leiden: Brill, 1953) 152.

Appendix I: Comparison between the OG and MT of Ezek 7:2–10

MT expansions in italics

	Masoretic Text		Old Greek	
7:2a	And you son of man:	And you, son of man:	7:2a
7:2b	Thus says the Lord YHWH to the land of Israel:	Say: thus says the Lord to the land of Israel:	7:2b
7:2c	An end, the end comes upon the four corners of the land.	An end has come, the end has come upon the four corners of the land	7:2c
7:3a	Now, the end is upon you, I will send my anger against you;		
7:3b	and I will judge you according to your ways;		
7:3c	and I will set upon you all your abominations;		
7:4a	and my eye will not spare you, nor will I have compassion;		
7:4b	for I will set your ways upon you,		
7:4c	and your abominations will be in your midst.		
7:4d	And you will know that I am YHWH		
7:5a	Thus says the Lord YHWH		
7:5b	*A singular calamity,*		
7:5c	*a calamity, look, it comes*		
7:6a	*an end comes*		
7:6b	the end comes	the end comes	7:3
7:6c	*it arises against you*		
7:6d	*look, it comes*		
7:7a	*the ṣephirah comes*		

	Masoretic Text	**Old Greek**	
7:7b	against you, O inhabitant of the land.	against you, O inhabitant of the land.	7:4a
7:7c	the time has come near, today!	the time has come near, today!	7:4b
7:7d	Confusion, and not shouting on the mountains.	Not with an uproar, nor with pangs,	7:4c
7:8a	Now, so I will pour out my wrath against you,	Now, I will pour out my wrath upon you,	7:5a
7:8b	and I will expend my anger on you;	and I will expend my anger on you	7:5b
7:8c	and I will judge you according to your ways;	and I will judge you by your ways	7:5c
7:8d	and I will set against you all your abominations;	and I will set against you all your abominations	7:5d
7:9a	and my eye will not spare, nor will I have compassion.	my eye will not spare, nor will I have compassion	7:6a
7:9b	I will set your ways against you;	for, I will set your ways against you,	7:6b
7:9c	and your abominations will be in your midst.	and your abominations will be in your midst	7:6c
7:9d	And you will know that I am YHWH who strikes.	And you will know that I am YHWH who strikes.	7:6d
		Now the end is against you, and I will send against you;	7:7a
		and I will judge you according to your ways;	7:7b
		and I will set against you all your abominations;	7:7c
		my eye will not spare you, nor will I have compassion;	7:8a
		for I will set your way against you;	7:8b

Transformation in Ezekiel's Textual History 271

	Masoretic Text	Old Greek	
		and your abominations will be in your midst.	7:8c
		And you will know that I am YHWH.	7:8d
		For thus says YHWH:	7:9
		Look, an end comes,	7:10a
7:10a	Look, the day	Look, the day of the Lord	7:10b
7:10b	*Look, it comes,*		
7:10c	*the ṣephirah has come out!*		

Appendix II: Comparison between the OG and MT of Ezek 7:2-10

Masoretic Text	MT	OG	Old Greek Retroverted	Old Greek
ואתה בן אדם	7:2a	7:2a		και συ υιε ἀνθρωπου
כה אמר אדני יהוה לאדמת ישראל	7:2b	7:2b	לאדמת יהוה לאדמת ישראל	εἰπον ταδε λεγει κυριος τη γη Ισραηλ
קץ	7:2c	7:2c		περας ἥκει
בא הקץ על ארבעת כנפות הארץ	7:2d	7:2d	הקץ בא על ארבע כנפות הארץ	το περας ἥκει επι τας τεσσαρας πτερυγας της γης
עתה הקץ עליך ושלחתי אפי בך	7:3a			
ושפטתיך כדרכיך	7:3b			
ונתתי עליך את כל תועבתיך	7:3c			
ולא תחוס עיני עליך ולא אחמול	7:4a			
כי דרכיך עליך אתן	7:4b			
ותועבותיך בתוכך תהיין	7:4c			
וידעתם כי אני יהוה	7:4d			
כה אמר אדני יהוה	7:5a			
רעה אחת	7:5b			

ממגד הדה אמרי	7:5c			
קץ בא	7:6a			
בא הקץ	7:6b	7:3	בא הקץ	ἥκει τὸ πέρας
הקיץ אליך	7:6c			
הנה באה	7:6d			
הצאת אלין	7:7a			
בא העת אליך	7:7b	7:4a	אליך יושב הארץ	ἐπὶ σὲ τὸν κατοικοῦντα τὴν γῆν
קרוב היום מהומה	7:7c	7:4b	בא העת קרוב היום	ἥκει ὁ καιρός ἤγγικεν ἡ ἡμέρα
מהומה ולא הד הרים	7:7d	7:4c	מהומה ולא הד הרים (?)	οὐ μετὰ θορύβων οὐδὲ μετὰ ὠδίνων
עתה מקרוב אשפוך חמתי עליך	7:8a	7:5a	נון עתה מקרוב אשפך חמתי עליך	νῦν ἐγγύθεν ἐκχέω τὴν ὀργήν μου ἐπὶ σὲ
וכליתי אפי בך	7:8b	7:5b	וכליתי אפי בך	καὶ συντελέσω τὸν θυμόν μου ἐν σοι
ושפטתיך כדרכיך	7:8c	7:5c	ושפטתיך כדרכיך	καὶ κρινῶ σε ἐν ταῖς ὁδοῖς σου
ונתתי עליך את כל תועבותיך	7:8d	7:5d	ונתתי עליך את כל תועבותיך	καὶ δώσω ἐπὶ σὲ πάντα τὰ βδελύγματά σου

Masoretic Text	MT	OG	Old Greek Retroverted	Old Greek
לֹא תָחוֹס עֵינִי עָלַיִךְ וְלֹא אֶחְמוֹל	7:9a	7:6a	לֹא תָחוֹס עֵינִי עָלַיִךְ וְלֹא אֶחְמוֹל	οὐ φείσεται ὁ ὀφθαλμός μου οὐδὲ μὴ ἐλεήσω
	7:9b	7:6b	כִּי דְרָכַיִךְ עָלַיִךְ אֶתֵּן	διότι τὰς ὁδούς σου ἐπὶ σὲ δώσω
	7:9c	7:6c	וְתוֹעֲבוֹתַיִךְ בְּתוֹכֵךְ תִּהְיֶינָה	καὶ τὰ βδελύγματά σου ἐν μέσῳ σου ἔσονται
כִּי דְרָכַיִךְ עָלַיִךְ אֶתֵּן	7:9d	7:6d	וִידַעְתֶּם כִּי אֲנִי יְהוָה מַכֶּה	καὶ ἐπιγνώσῃ διότι ἐγώ εἰμι κύριος ὁ τύπτων
וְתוֹעֲבוֹתַיִךְ בְּתוֹכֵךְ תִּהְיֶינָה		7:7a	עַתָּה מִקָּרוֹב אֶשְׁפֹּךְ חֲמָתִי עָלַיִךְ	νῦν τὸ πέρας πρὸς σὲ καὶ ἀποστελῶ ἐγὼ ἐπὶ σὲ
וִידַעְתֶּם כִּי אֲנִי יְהוָה		7:7b	וְנִקַּמְתִּי בָךְ בִּדְרָכָיִךְ	καὶ ἐκδικήσω σε ἐν ταῖς ὁδοῖς σου
		7:7c	וְנָתַתִּי עָלַיִךְ אֵת כָּל תּוֹעֲבוֹתָיִךְ	καὶ δώσω ἐπὶ σὲ πάντα τὰ βδελύγματά σου
		7:8a	לֹא תָחוֹס עֵינִי עָלַיִךְ וְלֹא אֶחְמוֹל	οὐ φείσεται ὁ ὀφθαλμός μου ἐπὶ σὲ οὐδὲ μὴ ἐλεήσω
		7:8b	כִּי דַרְכֵּךְ עָלַיִךְ אֶתֵּן	διότι τὴν ὁδόν σου ἐπὶ σὲ δώσω
		7:8c	וְתוֹעֲבוֹתַיִךְ בְּתוֹכֵךְ תִּהְיֶה	καὶ τὰ βδελύγματά σου ἐν μέσῳ σου ἔσται

			7:8d	הנה יהוה אל יצאה	και ἐπιγνωση διοτι ἐγω κυριος
			7:9	הנה כה אמר יהוה	διοτι ταδε λεγει κυριος
			7:10a	הנה קץ בא	ἰδου το περας ἤκει
	7:10a	הנה היום	7:10b	הנה יהוה	ἰδου ἡμερα κυριου
	7:10b	הנה באה			
	7:10c	הנה נפצאתה			
	7:10d	יצץ המטה	7:10c	יצץ המטה	και ἡ ῥαβδος ἠνθηκεν
	7:10e	פרח הזדון	7:10d	פרח הזדון	ἡ ὕβρις ἐξανεστηκεν

Bibliography

Aejmelaeus, Anneli. "What Can We Know about the Hebrew *Vorlage* of the Septuagint?" In *On the Trail of the Septuagint Translators*, 77–115. Kampen: Kok Pharos, 1993.
Barr, James. "The Typology of Literalism in Ancient Biblical Translations." *Mitteilungen des Septuaginta-Unternehmens* 15 (1979) 279–325.
Bauer, Hans, and Pontus Leander. *Historische Grammatik der hebräischen Sprache des Alten Testaments*. 1922. Reprint, Hildesheim: Olms, 1962.
Bertholet, Alfred. *Das Buch Hesekiel erklärt*. KHC. Freiburg: Mohr/Siebeck, 1897.
Block, Daniel I. *The Book of Ezekiel: Chapters 1–24*. NICOT. Grand Rapids: Eerdmans, 1997.
Bogaert, Pierre-Maurice. "Les deux rédactions conserves (LXX et TM) d'Ézéchiel 7." In *Ezekiel and His Book*, edited by J. Lust, 21–47. BETL 74. Leuven: Peeters, 1986.
Chapman, Stephen. *The Law and the Prophets: A Study in Old Testament Canon Formation*. FAT 27. Tübingen: Mohr/Siebeck, 1999.
Childs, Brevard S. *Introduction to the Old Testament as Scripture*. Philadelphia: Fortress, 1979.
Cooke, G. A. *A Critical and Exegetical Commentary on* the *Book of Ezekiel*. ICC. Edinburgh: T. & T. Clark, 1936.
Cornill, Carl Heinrich. *Das Buch des Propheten Ezechiel*. Leipzig: Hinrichs, 1886.
Fishbane, Michael. *Biblical Interpretation in Ancient Israel*. Oxford: Clarendon, 1985.
Fox, Michael V. "Translation and Mimesis." In *Bible Translation in Context*, edited by F. W. Knobloch, 207–21. Bethesda: University Press of Maryland, 2002.
García-Martínez, Florentino. "The Apocalyptic Interpretation of Ezekiel in the Dead Sea Scrolls." In *Interpreting Translation: Studies on the LXX and Ezekiel in Honour of Johan Lust*, edited by F. García-Martínez and M. Vervenne, 163–76. BETL 192. Leuven: Peeters, 2005.
Greenberg, Moshe. *Ezekiel 1–30*. AB 22. New York: Doubleday, 1983.
Kraetzschmar, Richard. *Das Buch Ezekiel*. HKAT. Göttingen: Vandenhoeck & Ruprecht, 1900.
Lebram, Jürgen C. H. "König Antiochus im Buch Daniel." *VT* 25 (1975) 737–72.
Lust, Johan, ed. *Ezekiel and His Book: Textual and Literary Criticism and Their Interrelation*. BETL 74. Leuven: Peeters, 1986.
———. "Ezekiel Manuscripts in Qumran: Preliminary Edition of 4QEz a and b." In *Ezekiel and His Book: Textual and Literary Criticism and their Interrelation*, edited by J. Lust, 90–100. BETL 74. Leuven: Peeters, 1986.
———. "The Ezekiel Text." In *Sôfer Mahîr: Essays in Honor of Adrian Schenker*, edited by Yohanan A. P. Goldman et al., 153–68. Leiden: Brill, 2006.
Lust, Johan, et al. "Notes to the Septuagint of Ezekiel 7." *ETL* 77 (2001) 384–94.
Marquis, Galen. "Consistency of Lexical Equivalents as a Criterion for the Evaluation of Translation Technique in the LXX of Ezekiel." In *VI Congress of the International Organization for Septuagint and Cognate Studies*, edited by C. Cox, 405–24. Atlanta: Scholars, 1987.
———. *The Translation Technique Reflected in LXX-Ezekiel* [Hebrew]. MA thesis, Hebrew University, 1982.

———. "Word Order as a Criterion for the Evaluation of Translation Technique in the LXX and the Evaluation of Word-Order Variants as Exemplified in LXX-Ezekiel." *Textus* 13 (1986) 59–84.
Masson, M. "Ṣepīrâ (Ezéchiel vii 10)." *VT* 37 (1987) 301–11.
McLay, R. Timothy. *The Use of the Septuagint in New Testament Research*. Grand Rapids: Eerdmans, 2003.
Payne Smith, Jessie, editor. *A Compendious Syriac Dictionary*. 1903. Reprint, ALR. Eugene, OR: Wipf & Stock, 1999.
Pulikottil, Paulson. *Transmission of Biblical Texts in Qumran: The Case of the Large Isaiah Scroll 1QIsaᵃ*. JSPSup 34. Sheffield: Sheffield Academic, 2001.
Rofé, Alexander. "The Editing of the Book of Joshua in the Light of 4QJoshᵃ." In *New Qumran Texts and Studies*, edited by George J. Brooke, 73–80. STDJ 15. Leiden: Brill, 1994.
Rosenthal, Erwin I. J. "Rashi and the English Bible." *BJRL* 24 (1940) 138–67.
Sanders, James. *Torah and Canon*. Philadelphia: Fortress, 1972.
Schenker, Adrian, editor. *The Earliest Text of the Hebrew Bible: The Relationship of the MT and the Hebrew Base of the Septuagint*. Atlanta: Scholars Press, 2003.
Seeligmann, Isac Leo. "Voraussetzungen der Midraschexegese." In *Congress Volume. Copenhagen 1953*, edited by G. W. Anderson et al., 150–81. VTSup 1. Leiden: Brill, 1953.
Skehan, Patrick. "The Qumran Manuscripts and Textual Criticism." In *Volume du Congrès, Strasbourg, 1956*, edited by G. W. Anderson, 148–60. VTSup 4. Leiden: Brill, 1957.
Smend, Rudolf. *Der Prophet Ezechiel*. KeH. Leipzig: S. Hirzel, 1880.
Talmon, Shemaryahu. "Aspects of the Textual Transmission of the Bible in the Light of Qumran Manuscripts." *Textus* 4 (1964) 95–132.
———. "Double Readings in the Masoretic Text." *Textus* 1 (1960) 144–84.
———. "DSIa as a Witness to Ancient Exegesis of the Book of Isaiah." *ASTI* 1 (1962) 62–72.
———. "Synonymous Readings in the Textual Traditions of the Old Testament." *Scripta Hierosolymitana* 8 (1961) 335–85.
Tov, Emanuel. "Different Editions of the Song of Hannah." In *Tehilla le-Moshe: Biblical and Judaic Studies in Honor of Moshe Greenberg*, ed. M. Cogan et al., 149–70. Winona Lake, IN: Eisenbrauns, 1997.
———. "Glosses, Interpolations, and Other Types of Scribal Additions in the Text of the Hebrew Bible." In *The Greek and Hebrew Bible: Collected Essays on the Septuagint*, 70–72. Leiden: Brill, 1999.
———. "The Literary History of the Book of Jeremiah in the Light of Its Textual History." In *Empirical Models for Biblical Criticism*, edited by J. H. Tigay, 211–37. 1985. Reprint, Eugene, OR: Wipf & Stock, 2005.
———. "Recensional Differences Between the Masoretic Text and the Septuagint of Ezekiel." In *The Greek and Hebrew Bible: Collected Essays on the Septuagint*, 397–410. Leiden: Brill, 1999.
———. *The Text-Critical Use of the Septuagint in Biblical Research*. 2nd rev. ed. Jerusalem: Simor, 1997.
———. *Textual Criticism of the Hebrew Bible*. 2nd rev. ed. Minneapolis: Fortress, 2001.

Tov, Emanuel, and Benjamin G. Wright. "Computer-Assisted Study of the Criteria for Assessing the Literalness of the Translation Units in the Septuagint." In *The Greek and Hebrew Bible: Collected Essays on the Septuagint*, edited by E. Tov, 219–37. Leiden: Brill, 1999.

Trebolle Barrera, Julio. *The Jewish Bible and the Christian Bible*. Grand Rapids: Eerdmans, 1998.

———. "Textual Variants in 4QJudg^a and the Textual and Editorial History of the Book of Judges." *RevQ* 54 (1989) 229–45.

Ulrich, Eugene. *The Dead Sea Scrolls and the Origins of the Bible*. Grand Rapids: Eerdmans, 1999.

———. "The Notion and Definition of Canon." In *The Canon Debate*, edited by Lee M. McDonald and James A. Sanders, 21–35. Peabody, MA: Hendrickson, 2002.

Ulrich, Eugene, et al. *Qumran Cave 4: The Prophets*. DJD 15. Oxford: Clarendon, 1997.

Meer, Michaël N. van der. *Formation and Reformulation: The Redaction of the Book of Joshua in the Light of the Oldest Textual Witnesses*. VTSup 102. Leiden: Brill, 2004.

Waltke, Bruce, and Michael O'Connor. *An Introduction to Biblical Hebrew Syntax*. Winona Lake, IN: Eisenbrauns, 1990.

Wildberger, Hans. *Isaiah 28–39*. Translated by Thomas H. Trapp. Continental Commentaries. Minneapolis: Fortress, 2002.

Winer, Georg Benedikt. *Lexicon manuale hebraicum et chaldaicum in Veteris Testamenti libros post J. G. Eichhornii curas denuo castigavit, multisque modis auxit G. B. Winer*. 4th ed. Leipzig: Fleischer, 1828.

Ziegler, Joseph. *Ezechiel*. Septuaginta: Vetus Testamentum Graecum Auctoritate Academiae Scientiarum Gottingensis editum 16/1. 2nd rev. ed. Göttingen: Vandenhoeck & Ruprecht, 1977.

Zimmerli, Walther. *Ezekiel 1: A Commentary on the Book of the Prophet Ezekiel, Chapters 1–24*. Translated by Ronald E. Clements. Hermeneia. Philadelphia: Fortress, 1979.

Zippor, M. *Tradition and Transmission: Studies in Ancient Biblical Translation and Interpretation* [Hebrew]. Tel Aviv: Hakibbutz Hameuchad, 2001.

10

Transformation of Ezekiel in John's Revelation

Beate Kowalski

Introduction

THE REVELATION OF JOHN REFERS MORE OFTEN TO EZEKIEL THAN do all other NT writings. The following contribution deals with the transformation of Ezekiel in Revelation, the only example of sustained apocalyptic or prophetic writing in the NT.

It is well known that the Book of Revelation often refers to the OT and that Ezekiel plays a particularly important role in Revelation. John references Ezekiel on diverse levels: in the form of citations, allusions on the level of sentences or entire verses, references that relate the situation of Ezekiel and his addressees to the situation of John and his addressees, parallel theological ideas, and overall structure.[1] Although interest in the topic of intertextuality and in particular the reception of Ezekiel in Revelation has increased dramatically during the last decade, there has been little research that has comprehensively compared both books and done so using clear terminology and methodology. In this article I seek to address these issues.

The State of Research[2]

The use of Ezekiel in Revelation is part of a larger area of research on the OT in the NT. This area of research has grown as exegetes have

---

1. See below for the definitions of "citation" and "allusion" as used here.
2. I use the technical term "Old Testament" and not "First Testament," which was introduced to scholars by E. Zenger, *Das Erste Testament: Die jüdische Bibel und*

discovered more and more the unity of both parts of the Christian Bible and the Jewish background of the NT.³ Refined methods of exegesis are additional reasons for this development.⁴ In particular, the last book of the NT, the Revelation of John, has received central attention. There is a clear consensus among scholars that the final book of the NT is characterised by the use of the OT, and more specifically by the use of prophetic books and intertestamental apocalyptic writings.⁵ However, not all problems related to the influence of the OT and other Jewish writings on the different linguistic levels of Revelation have been solved. The issue of whether the traditions received by the author were oral or written is disputed. Assuming that written *Vorlagen* were used, there is also significant debate about the use of either the MT or the LXX (or both) as pre-texts by the author of Revelation.⁶

---

die Christen, 2nd ed. (Düsseldorf: Patmos, 1992) 144–54; idem, *Am Fuß des Sinai: Gottesbilder des Ersten Testaments* (Düsseldorf: Patmos, 1993). The reason is the fact that publications on the reception of the OT in Revelation use the older term. Furthermore, it is our intention to use the uniform term "Old Testament" with the high appreciation with which the NT writings and the Church have understood it (cf. the document of the Pontifical Biblical Commission, *Jewish People*, II.A.1 n. 37: "For the origin of this title, see above no. 2. Today in certain circles there is a tendency to use "First Testament" to avoid any negative connotation attached to "Old Testament." But "Old Testament" is a biblical and traditional expression which of itself does not have a negative connotation: the Church fully recognises the importance of the Old Testament.").

3. Cf. the short surveys of research on Ezekiel from K. Pfisterer Darr, "Ezekiel among the Critics," *CRBS* 2 (1994) 9–24, and in more detail U. Feist, *Ezechiel. Das literarische Problem des Buches forschungsgeschichtlich betrachtet*, BWANT 138 (Stuttgart: Kohlhammer, 1995), who focuses his view in particular on the literary problem of Ezekiel. The position of B. Duhm is very interesting in this context as he regards Ezekiel as "father" of apocalyptic and the *Schriftgelehrtentum* (cf. Feist, 132–36).

4. S. E. Porter, "The Use of the Old Testament in the New Testament: A Brief Comment on Method and Terminology," in *Early Christian Interpretation of the Scriptures of Israel*, ed. Craig A. Evans and James A. Sanders, JSNTSup 148 (Sheffield: Sheffield: Academic, 1997) 79.

5. E. Böhl, *Die alttestamentlichen Citate im Neuen Testament* (Wien: Braumüller, 1878) 333ff. appropriately states already in 1878: "Die Apokalypse ... ist so mit dem A.T. verwachsen, dass es hier unthunlich erscheint, das Eigenthum des Sehers auf Patmos von dem Eigenthum Mose's und der Propheten in dieser Arbeit wenigstens zu sondern. [...] Die Apocalypse ist durchgängig eine Reproduction der Schriften Mose's und der Propheten, von denen besonders Jesaia, Daniel, Sacharja und Ezechiel benutzt sind, jedoch mit solcher Freiheit, dass man eigentliche Citate wie in den übrigen apostolischen Schriften nirgends findet."

6. Regarding use of Scripture in Revelation, cf. A. Lancelotti, *Sintassi ebraica nel greco dell'Apocalisse, I. Uso delle forme verbali*, Collectio Assiniensis 1 (Assisi: Studio

Several studies have been recently published on the use of particular OT writings and early Jewish apocalyptic texts in Revelation, including several on Ezekiel.[7] The first attempt at a comprehensive analysis of all quotations and allusions was an article published in 1962 by A. Vanhoye, S.J.[8] His disciples A. Lancelotti, B. Marconcini, A. Gangemi, and G. Deiana followed the footsteps of their master and published articles on Ezekiel, Daniel, and Zechariah (Lancelotti), Isaiah (Marconcini), Deutero-Isaiah (Gangemi), and Jeremiah (Deiana) in Revelation.[9] They were followed by J. M. Vogelgesang (1985), whose monograph explored the literary dependence of Revelation on Ezekiel on diverse levels.[10] J.-P. Ruiz (1989) has analyzed Rev 16:17—19:10.[11] Among the German scholars, K. Berger (1994; 2nd ed.1995) was the first to describe Revelation as a midrash on Ezekiel due to similar structural features.[12] L. Wei (1999) submitted an (unpublished) PhD dissertation on Ezekiel in Revelation. M. D. Goulder (1999) claimed that the similarities between the two books were due to Revelation's dependence on the liturgical reading

---

teologico "Porziuncola," 1964) and H. M. Parker, "The Scripture of the Author of the Revelation of John," *Iliff Review* 37 (1980) 35–51. Lancelotti tried to prove the Hebrew character of Johannine language: cf. Lancelotti, "Predominante paratassi nella narrativa ebraizzante dell'Apocalisse," *SBFLA* 30 (1980) 303–16; "Il kai narrativo di 'consecuzione' alla maniera del wayyiqtol ebraico nell'Apocalisse," *SBFLA* 31 (1981) 75–104; "Il kai 'consecutivo' di predizione alla maniera del weqataltî ebraico nell' Apocalisse," *SBFLA* 32 (1982) 133–46.

7. H. B. Swete assumes that Revelation is dependent exclusively upon OT texts: "The apocalyptic portions of Ezekiel, Zechariah, and Daniel are continually present to his mind; and though it is less certain that he made use of Enoch or any other post-canonical apocalypse, he could scarcely have been ignorant of their existence and general character." See Swete, *The Apocalypse of St John. The Greek Text with Introduction Notes and Indices*, 3rd ed. (1908; reprint, Grand Rapids: Eerdmans, 1951) xxviii.

8. A Vanhoye, "L'utilisation du livre d'Ézéchiel dans l'Apocalypse," *Bib* 43 (1962) 436–76.

9. Lancelotti, *Sintassi*; B. Marconcini, "L'utilizzazione del T.M. nelle citazioni Isaeiane dell'Apocalisse," *RivBib* 24 (1976) 113–36; A. Gangemi, "L'utilizzazione del Deutero-Isaia dell'Apocalisse di Giovanni," *ED* 27 (1974) 109–44, 311–39; G. Deiana, "Utilizzazione del libro di Geremia in alcuni brani dell' Apocalisse," *Lat* 48 (1982) 125–137.

10. J. M. Vogelgesang, "The Interpretation of Ezekiel in the Book of Revelation" (PhD diss., Harvard University, 1985).

11. J.-P. Ruiz, *Ezekiel in the Apocalypse. The Transformation of Prophetic Language in Revelation 16,17–19,10*, European University Studies 23/376 (Frankfurt: Lang, 1989).

12. K. Berger, *Theologiegeschichte des Urchristentums. Theologie des Neuen Testaments*, UTB für Wissenschaft, 2nd ed. (Tübingen: Francke, 1995) 622.

sequence of Ezekiel, a hypothesis that is very difficult to prove.[13] S. Bøe (1999) worked on the reception of Gog and Magog (Ezek 38–39) in Revelation.[14] M. Jauhiainen (2005) analysed the reception of Zechariah in Revelation.[15]

My own study (2003) was the first comprehensive analysis of all quotations, allusions, and structural similarities between Ezekiel and Revelation.[16] I also explored the linguistic influence of the Hebrew and Greek texts of the OT on the design of Revelation and the question of the subsequent theological and hermeneutical consequences. In particular, I was interested in the following questions: How did John communicate with his addressees through the use of the OT? How did John understand the OT?[17] What consequences does the influence of the OT and other Jewish writings have on our understanding of Revelation as visionary literature? Is the author's self-conception influenced by the use of the OT? What is the relationship between his creative use of Scripture and his understanding of inspiration? How can his understanding of inspiration best be described?[18] These systematic questions

13. M. D. Goulder, "The Apocalypse as an Annual Cycle of Prophecies," *NTS* 27 (1981) 342–67.

14. S. Bøe, *Gog and Magog: Ezekiel 38–39 as Pre-Text for Revelation 19,17–21 and 20,7–10*, Studiebibliothek for Bibel og Mission 5 (Oslo: Biblia/Fjellhaug Skoler, 1999).

15. M. Jauhiainen, *The Use of Zechariah in Revelation*, WUNT 199 (Tübingen: Mohr Siebeck, 2005).

16. B. Kowalski, "Die Rezeption des Propheten Ezechiel in der Offenbarung des Johannes" (*Habilitationsschrift*, University of Innsbruck, 2003). See now *Die Rezeption des Propheten Ezechiel in der Offenbarung des Johannes*, SBB 52 (Stuttgart: Katholisches Bibelwerk, 2004).

17. H. Hübner, "Eine hermeneutisch unverzichtbare Unterscheidung: Vetus Testamentum und Vetus Testamentum in Novo receptum," in *Texts and Contexts. Biblical Texts in Their Textual and Situational Contexts: Essays in Honor of Lars Hartman*, ed. T. Fornberg and D. Hellholm (Oslo: Scandinavian University Press, 1995) 906ff. points to the distinction between the OT per se and its reception in the NT. He speaks about an openness of the OT, which could be interpreted Christologically. He asks: "Gibt es identisches Verstehen für Vergangenheit und Gegenwart?" Every text recited is understood on the basis of the particular author's approach to reality. That means for Revelation, John understands Ezekiel according to his approach to reality. One must ask why this book in particular has inspired him most.

18. A. T. Hanson emphasised this aspect in particular: "John the Divine is so free and creative in his use of scripture that we are driven occasionally to wonder whether he really regarded scripture as inspired"; Hanson, *The Living Utterances of God: The New Testament Exegesis of the Old* (London: Darton, Longman and Todd, 1983) 175. Cf. R. Nicole, "A Study of the Old Testament Quotations in the New Testament with

can only be answered with a precise exegesis of all allusions to Ezekiel in Revelation.

The Revelation of John: A Mosaic of OT Texts?

Intertextual relationships between Ezekiel and Revelation can be discerned on diverse levels. These levels exist in both the source text (e.g., the multiple [LXX and MT] textual traditions of Ezekiel) and in the borrowing text (e.g., the use of quotation or allusion). According to many scholars, John never quotes from the OT because he never uses an introductory formula,[19] the usual indicator of direct quotation.[20] However, John does make explicit reference to the OT when he mentions Moses' song (Rev 15:3b), although it is impossible to assign this reference to a specific pre-text.[21]

A good number of implicit allusions in Revelation guide the reader's attention to the OT as one important source of the macrotext. John refers to different OT characters, institutions, and places, many of which have theological significance.[22] For example, his central image of God, as expressed by the *Dreizeitenformel* (see below), refers to God's self-revelation in Exod 3:14. Furthermore, John alerts his readers to his use of the OT by employing linguistic solecisms. Revelation is there-

---

Reference to the Doctrine of the Inspiration of the Scriptures" (MST thesis, Gordon College of Theology and Missions, 1940) who deals with the connection between the reuse of scripture and the doctrine of inspiration.

19. Cf. references to (1) fulfilment (πληρόω) of the γραφή in Matt 21:42; 26:54; Mark 14:49; Luke 4:21; 12:10; 24:27; John 13:18; 17:12; 19:24, 36; Acts 1:16; Jas 2:23, (2) fulfilment of the prophets in Matt 1:22; 2:5, 15, 17, 23; 4:14; 8:17; 12:17; 13:14, 35; 21:4; 26:56; 27:9; John 12:38, (3) fulfilment of the "writings of the prophets" in Matt 26:56, and of the Torah in John 15:25. References to the "law and prophets" appear in Matt 5:17; 22:40; Luke 16:16, to prophets in Matt 3:3; 24:15; Mark 1:2; Luke 1:70; 3:4; 4:17; 24:25, to "Moses and all the prophets" in Luke 24:27, and to the fulfilment of "Moses, the prophets and the psalms" in Luke 24:44. There is no direct quotation in Philemon; cf. Porter, "Use," 89–94.

20. J. T. A. G. M. van Ruiten, *Een begin zonder einde. De doorwerking van Jesaja 65:17 in de intertestamentaire literatuur en het Nieuwe Testament* (Sliedrecht: Uitgeverij Merweboek, 1990) 14: "Men maakt voortdurend gebruik van schriftteksten, zonder dat men dit vermeldt."

21. Cf. already Vanhoye, "L'utilisation," 437.

22. J. Fekkes, *Isaiah and Prophetic Traditions in the Book of Revelation. Visionary Antecedents and their Development*, JSNTSup 93 (Sheffield: Sheffield Academic, 1994) 68ff.

fore rightly considered to be a mosaic built from OT texts.²³ In what follows, I will offer a survey of John's signals for directing the reader (*Leserlenkungssignale*), which can be found on the level of stylistic and thematic parallels.

The Song of Moses

The song of those who are victorious over the beast, his image (cf. Rev 13:15), and the number of his name (13:17–18) is called the "song of Moses and the Lamb" (cf. 15:2-4). It is the only song in Revelation that has a title. A precise identification of the hymn (Rev 15:3b-4) with one of the two songs in the Pentateuch assigned to Moses (Exod 15:1-19; Deut 32:1-44) is not possible.²⁴

Nevertheless, both of Moses' songs have something in common, which John probably had in mind. Both are located at crucial parts of the OT. Moses' song after the Exodus is the first prayer in the OT that responds to YHWH's liberation after slavery in Egypt.²⁵ Moses' song at the end of Deuteronomy not only completes the life of Moses, but also the Pentateuch. Above all, it builds a bridge to the narratives of the giving of the land to God's people. Moreover, both songs are sung in a situation of victory: Moses' song at the sea praises God after the experience of the victory over the Egyptian power, and Moses' song at the end

---

23. F. Jenkins, *The Old Testament in the Book of Revelation* (Marion, IN: Cogdill, 1972; reprint, Grand Rapids: Baker, 1976) 21; A. van Schaik, "De Apocalyps als Tekstmozaïek," *Schrift* 114 (1987) 231-34.

24. Vanhoye, "L'utilisation," 436ff.; W. Fenske ("'Das Lied des Mose, des Knechtes Gottes, und das Lied des Lammes' [Apokalypse des Johannes 15,3f.]. Der Text und seine Bedeutung für die Johannes-Apokalypse," *ZNW* 90 [1999] 257ff.) refers to Deut 32; J. A. Du Rand ("David and Goliath in the Apocalypse of John?" *Ekklesiastikos Pharos* 76 [1994] 25-30) regards Deut 32 and Jer 11 as pre-texts. Cf. also Du Rand, "The Song of the Lamb Because of the Victory of the Lamb," *Neot* 29 (1995) 203-10. R. Bauckham discusses the OT references extensively and comes to the following result: "Revelation's version of the song of Moses is not, as has usually been thought, a medley of Old Testament phrases with no relation to the song of Moses in Exodus 15. On the contrary, it is a careful interpretation of the song, achieved by skilful use of recognized exegetical methods. The effect is to interpret the song in line with the most universalistic strain in Old Testament hope: the expectation that all the nations will come to acknowledge the God of Israel and worship him" (*The Climax of Prophecy. Studies on the Book of Revelation* [Edinburgh: T. & T. Clark, 1993] 296-307, esp. 306).

25. G. Fischer, "Das Schilfmeerlied Exodus 15 in seinem Kontext," *Bib* 77 (1996) 32-47.

of Deuteronomy honours God's power over history (cf. Deut 32:7) in the life of Moses and the people of Israel.[26]

Revelation 15:3b entitles the song of the victors over the beast, its name, and image as the "song of Moses and the Lamb."[27] This new "song of Moses" is also a song of victory. This becomes obvious through the narrative link of Rev 15:1ff with the previous chapter, in which the Lamb and its followers, the 144,000 from all tribes of Israel (cf. 7:4–8), also begin to sing a "new song" (Rev 14:3). Both songs follow from experiences of difficulties. The "new song" in Rev 14:3 succeeds the dramatic climax of Rev 12 and 13, in which the threat of the beasts is described.[28] The "song of Moses and the Lamb" is a result of the threat of judgment in Rev 14:6–20. The singers are those who do not stand under this judgment, the ones who are victorious over the Empire Cult.[29] The position and function of both songs in Revelation are reminiscent of those of the two songs of Moses in the OT.[30]

The Dreizeitenformel

Another indication that John is referencing the OT is his use of the *Dreizeitenformel*: ὁ ὢν καὶ ὁ ἦν καὶ ὁ ἐρχόμενος (1:4, 8; 4:8; 11:17[31]) or ἐγώ εἰμι ὁ πρῶτος καὶ ὁ ἔσχατος καὶ ὁ ζῶν (1:17f), which unfolds the revelation of God's name in Exod 3:14.[32] The grammatical

---

26. Like Miriam's song (Exod 15:21b), the song of Moses asks the nations and the people of Israel to praise God (Deut 32:43).

27. Only a few exegetes wonder about this title; cf. Fenske ("*Lied*," 250, 250 n.2) who points to the scholarly discussion and provides reasons for the title of the song "Song of Moses and the Lamb." The reference to Moses and the Lamb is interpreted typologically, saying "daß Völker Gott anbeten, weil durch das Lamm Satzungen offenbar wurden wie Mose dem Volk Gebote übergeben hat" (cf. 264).

28. The polemical parallelism, which is used several times in Revelation, is characteristic of this chapter, in which the three agents of the forces of evil are developed.

29. The sentencing of Babylon (Rev 14:8; the fall of Babylon is expressed with an aorist as if it happened already, although it is first narrated in 17–18) and the worshippers of the beast (14:9ff.) is pronounced.

30. J. J. O'Rourke, "The Hymns of the Apocalypse." *CBQ* 30 (1968) 400–422 and K.-P. Jörns, *Das hymnische Evangelium. Untersuchungen zu Aufbau, Funktion and Herkunft der hymnischen Stücke in der Johannesoffenbarung*, SNT 5 (Gütersloh: Mohn, 1971).

31. In Rev 4:8, ἦν appears first, whereas in 11:17 the reference to the future coming of God is omitted.

32. H. Giesen, *Die Offenbarung des Johannes*, RNT (Regensburg: Friedrich Pustet, 1997), 74 points to examples of Jewish exegesis of Exod 3:14 (Targum Pseudo-Jonathan on Deut 32:39; Exodus Rabbah 3 [69c]), which are closer to the *Dreizeitenformel*.

solecism ἦν could point to the use of the Hebrew text, where the finite verb אֶהְיֶה is used as a non-declined name and subject.[33]

The use of this formula (which is a *leitmotif* in Rev 11)[34] points to God's trustworthiness, exclusiveness, infinity, and inability to be reduced to human disposal. By referring to Exod 3:14 and integrating it into his theological message, John emphasizes that God's powerful liberation from Egypt in the past retains significance for his addressees in Asia Minor. In order to express God's concrete nearness and exalted status, John does not employ the actual name of God here.[35]

OT Institutions

John's references to the twelve tribes of Israel, Zion, and Jerusalem are other signals that point to OT material. The first such reference is the christological title "The Lion of the tribe of Judah" (ὁ λέων ὁ ἐκ τῆς φυλῆς Ἰούδα) in Rev 5:5. Revelation 7:4 mentions that the 144,000 are sealed "out of every tribe of the sons of Israel." In the list that follows, the leading position of the tribe of Judah (Rev 7:5; cf. 5:5) and the omission of Dan are worthy of note. The next reference to the twelve tribes is connected with the description of the vision of the New Jerusalem (21:12). The names of the twelve tribes are inscribed on twelve gates. Whoever enters the heavenly city must pass under the umbrella of the tribes' names, which signifies protection. The redeemed Christians can enter the New Jerusalem only through the gates of God's work in Israel. These gates create a twelvefold access to the city. With this vision John

---

33. See J. Frey, in M. Hengel and J. Frey, *Die johanneische Frage. Ein Lösungsversuch*, WUNT 67 (Tübingen: J. C. B. Mohr, 1993) 360 n. 202. Cf. also G. K. Beale, "Solecisms in the Apocalypse as Signals for the Presence of Old Testament Allusions: A Selective Analysis of Revelation 1–22," in *Early Christian Interpretation of the Scriptures of Israel*, ed. C. A. Evans, JSNTSup 148 (Sheffield: Sheffield Academic Press, 1997) 426–28, who identifies signals for directing readers (*Leserlenkungssignale*) and discusses the reception of Exod 3:14 in the later Jewish tradition. Another interpretation is supported by H. Giesen, "Das Gottesbild in der Johannesoffenbarung," in *Der Gott Israels im Zeugnis des Neuen Testaments*, ed. U. Busse, QD 201 (Freiburg: Herder, 2003) 164ff., who argues that there is no past form of εἶναι and that the existence of the form ὁ γεγονώς in other books implies that John created a grammatically impossible word to describe God.

34. Revelation speaks of the future coming kingdom of God in 1:7; 2:16 (ταχύ); 3:11 (ταχύ); 16:15 (ἔρχομαι); 22:7 (ταχύ), 12 (ταχύ), 20 (ταχύ).

35. Giesen (*Offenbarung*, 74) relates this to God's sovereign action in history.

demonstrates his understanding of the OT and the people of Israel in order to connect Christian hope and salvation with the OT and Jewish roots.

The concept of the twelve tribes was an central ideal in Israel's history, and is connected with Zion-Jerusalem theology. The Lamb and his followers stand "on Mount Zion" (Rev 14:1; ἐπὶ τὸ ὄρος Σιών is only mentioned here and in Heb 12:22).[36] It is the place from which John observes the holy city, Jerusalem, coming down out of heaven (Rev 21:10). Furthermore, Rev 12:1–6 portrays a heavenly woman with a crown of twelve stars. She is a symbol for the daughter of Zion. Jerusalem is the gift promised to those in the church in Philadelphia who "conquered" (Rev 3:12). In contrast to this positive depiction, the earthly Jerusalem is "allegorically called Sodom and Egypt" (11:8).[37]

John's emphasis on the ideal of the covenant of the twelve tribes and on Zion-Jerusalem theology are very obvious signals that point to the roots of the author's theology.[38] It was particularly during the

---

36. J. Roloff, "Irdisches und himmlisches Jerusalem nach der Johannesoffenbarung," in *Zion—Ort der Begegnung, Festschrift für Laurentius Klein zur Vollendung des 65. Lebensjahres*, ed. F. Hahn et al., BBB 90 (Bodenheim: Athenaum Hain Hanstein, 1993) 93, who refers to the similarity between Hebrews and Revelation. Σιών is mentioned in Matt 21:5; John 12:15; Rom 9:33; 11:26 and 1 Pet 2:6. The reference to the pillar in God's temple (στῦλος, Rev 3:12) may point to Zion, which Fohrer takes as etymologically related to צִיּוֹן "pillar" (cf. G. Fohrer and E. Lohse, "Σιών, Ιεροσυαλήμ, Ιεροσόλυμα, Ιεροσολυμίτης," in *TWNT* 7:293.

37. J. Roloff comes to a negative result: "... die Stadt Jerusalem in ihrer Bedeutung als Mitte Israels und Ort der endzeitlichen Sammlung des Gottesvolkes bewusst ignoriert. Namen und Bezeichnung 'Jerusalem' bleiben allein der vollendeten Heilsgemeinde vorbehalten (21,2.10). Sie allein ist heilige Stadt, Ort der Gegenwart Gottes unter seinem Volk" (*Die Kirche im Neuen Testament*, GNT 10 [Göttingen: Vandenhoeck & Ruprecht, 1993] 181). P. G. R. de Villiers ("The Lord was Crucified in Sodom and Egypt. Symbols in the Apocalypse of John," *Neot* 22 [1988] 133–35) discusses the meaning of symbolic language in Revelation and interprets Sodom and Egypt as Babylon. M. Bachmann ("Himmlisch: Der 'Tempel Gottes' von Apk 11.1," *NTS* 40 [1994] 474–80) argues for a different date of Revelation and does not identify the temple as earthly in chapter 11. In the same way, de Villiers argues against Charles that the city must be Rome. A reason is the expression "great city" (τῆς πόλεως τῆς μεγάλης), which means Babylon or Rome in Rev 16:19 (18:10, 16, 18, 19, 21). In 17:18 the great city is identified with the great whore Babylon. The reference to an allegorical reading points to this interpretation (11:8, ἥτις καλεῖται πνευματικῶς).

38. See also Roloff (*Kirche*, 186), who states: "Die Impulse für solche Interpretation gewinnt der Verfasser primär aus dem Alten Testament. Er greift auf Jes 60–66 sowie Ezek 40–48 zurück..."

Babylonian Exile and the following phase of restoration that Zion-Jerusalem theology was further developed in order to overcome the crisis. The two exilic prophets Isaiah (60–66) and Ezekiel (40–48), both of whom influenced Revelation to a great extent, each conclude with a final note of emphasis on Zion-Jerusalem.[39] With the manifold references to Jerusalem at crucial positions, John leads his readers to these prophetic sources and points to their use as models for crisis management during and after the Babylonian Exile. He parallels the crisis of the Christian churches of Asia Minor with Israel's crisis.

John's reference to the cultic institution of the temple (ναός, Rev 3:12; 7:15; 11:1, 2, 19 [2x]; 14:15, 17; 15:5, 6, 8 [2x]; 16:1, 17; 21:22 [2x]; σκηνή, Rev 13:6; 15:5; 21:3) and its furnishings (the altar, 6:9; 8:3 [2x], 5; 9:13; 11:1; 14:18; 16:7; the ark of the covenant, 11:19) are signals which point to the OT and Jewish tradition.[40] Both Lee and Stevenson have inquired into the reasons the temple is mentioned in Revelation.[41]

---

39. ציון is used 154 times in the OT, very often in Isaiah, Jeremiah and in the Book of Psalms. One third of the references are connected with other nouns (such as mountain, daughter, gate); cf. Fohrer and Lohse, "Σιών," 292. Cf. also E. Otto, "ציון," in *TWAT* 6: 994–1028, and G. Fohrer, "Zion-Jerusalem im Alten Testament," in *Studien zur alttestamentlichen Theologie und Geschichte (1949-1966)*, ed. G. Fohrer, BZAW 115 (Berlin: de Gruyter, 1969) 213. Cf. U. Berges, who refers to the Book of Lamentations and its attempt to overcome the crisis of the exile with Zion theology ("'Ich bin der Mann, der Elend sah' [Klgl 3,1]. Zionstheologie als Weg aus der Krise," *BZ* 44 [2000] 1–20).

40. "A survey of the text of Revelation reveals an abundance of temple and cultic language" (G. Stevenson, *Power and Place. Temple and Identity in the Book of Revelation*, BZNW 107 [Berlin: de Gruyter, 2001] 2). Another Jewish institution mentioned in Revelation is the synagogue (cf. Rev 2:9; 3:9), which emerged from the Jewish diaspora. H. Frankemölle, "συναγωγή," in *EWNT* 3:710, speaks about anti-Jewish tendencies in connection with this reference.

41. P. Lee, *The New Jerusalem in the Book of Revelation. A Study of Revelation 21–22 in the Light of its Background in Jewish Tradition*, WUNT 129 (Tübingen: Mohr Siebeck, 2001). Note in particular Stevenson's observation that ". . . John, in addressing a mixed cultural audience in Asia Minor, employs the symbol that communicated powerfully to both cultural groups [Jew and Gentile Christians], marking it an appropriate vehicle for this message" (*Power*, 3). Further he maintains: "In the attempt to resolve these issues, certain patterns arose. To varying degrees, all of these documents reveal similarities with Ezekiel. . . . Furthermore, in all of these documents the temple is connected to issues of power and identity" (211). Revelation differs from the OT with regard to how the temple is understood. On the *motivgeschichtliche* context of the temple motif, see R. A. Briggs, *Jewish Temple Imagery in the Book of Revelation*, Studies in Biblical Literature 10 (New York: Peter Lang, 1999).

OT Characters

Revelation refers to various OT characters including Balaam (Rev 2:14), Balak (2:14), Jezebel (2:20), David (3:7; 5:5; 22:16), Moses (15:3), Michael (12:7), Gog and Magog (20:8) and Abaddon (9:11).[42] In the letter to the church in Pergamon John mentions Balaam and Balak (2:14), and in the letter to the church in Thyatira, the false prophetess Jezebel (2:20). In both cases he is speaking about the problem of false teachers and heresies. While in Num 22–24 Balaam is a prophet from the Euphrates commissioned by YHWH, John underlines negative aspects of his role according to other OT passages (LXX Num 31:16; cf. 25:1ff.) and early Jewish traditions (Philo, *De vita Mosis* 1.48–55; Josephus, *Ant.* IV 126ff.; *Sifre Num* 131; 157[43]), which portray him as someone who seduces Israel into idolatry. Jezebel is a non-Israelite, the daughter of Ethbaal, king of the Sidonians; she married King Ahab (1 Kgs 16:29–34), deceived Israel into idolatry (cf. 2 Kgs 9:22), and killed the prophets with the sword (1 Kgs 19:1ff.). Elijah pronounced God's sentence against her and her husband Ahab (1 Kgs 21:17–26). By using these names, John references OT stories describing idolatry and the conflict between true and false prophecy. These references function as a warning to the churches.

The references to King David (Rev 3:7; 5:5; 22:16) have a messianic function. In the letter to the church in Philadelphia, John refers to the "key of David" as a metaphorical expression of Christ's power. John refers to David again when using messianic titles for the Lamb ("root of David"; "root and offspring of David," 22:16).

Other famous OT characters include Moses (Rev 15:3; see the discussion above) and Michael (Rev 12:7), who plays an important role in the apocalyptic tradition (Daniel, Enoch). He is regarded as the patron of Israel and mediator between God and human beings, the one who keeps the key to the kingdom of heaven.[44] In Rev 12 he protects a daughter of Israel and her child.

---

42. Fekkes (*Isaiah*, 69) mentions the following list of *dramatis personae*: Balaam, Balak, Jezebel, David, prophets, Moses, Elijah, Michael, the Lamb, the serpent, the beast, the whore, Gog and Magog, four living beings, Abaddon. It is striking that he lists Elijah, who is not mentioned explicitly. Jenkins (*Testament*, 125–27) mentions only Balaam and Jezebel as OT characters in Revelation.

43. References from Giesen, *Offenbarung*, 102.

44. The significance of Michael in the OT and other Jewish traditions explains the throwing down of the great dragon in Rev 12:7–10. Michael protects the daughter of

A signal to which scholars have paid only a little attention is the use of two different language traditions in Rev 9:11 and 16:16.⁴⁵ John names the angel of the bottomless pit bilingually in Greek and Hebrew (9:11: ὄνομα αὐτῷ Ἑβραϊστί Ἀβαδδών, καὶ ἐν τῇ Ἑλληνικῇ ὄνομα ἔχει Ἀπολλύων), and the place name Armageddon is described as a Hebrew word (16:16: τὸν καλούμενον Ἑβραϊστί Ἁρμαγεδώ). With both references John points to Hebrew, and in 9:11 he reveals that he knows both Hebrew and Greek.⁴⁶

OT Geographical Traditions

Besides his references to OT characters, John reminds his readers of geographical traditions that have great significance in the OT. Mount Zion (Rev 14:1; cf. also 21:10)—in the NT mentioned only in Revelation and in Heb 12:22—and Jerusalem are places of the promise of salvation. The destruction of Jerusalem is expressed metaphorically by the references to Sodom and Egypt (Rev 11:8). Armageddon (the gathering-place of God's opponents, Rev 16:16) and Babylon (a reminder of the Babylonian Exile and a symbolic name for the Roman Empire, Rev 14:8; 16:19) stand in contrast to Zion-Jerusalem. Furthermore, John alludes to the Euphrates (9:14), which plays a role in the creation narrative (Gen 2:10–14).⁴⁷

Other References

Some of the motifs and metaphors which John takes from the OT are not based on institutions, characters, or geographical locations. For example, the two olive trees which metaphorically describe the two wit-

---

Israel (and her child) in both writings and he serves as mediator between God and humans.

45. Swete, *Apocalypse*, clvi: "But the forms Ἀβαδδών (ix. 11) and Ἁρ Μαγεδών (xvi. 16) seem to imply acquaintance on the writer's part with Hebrew or Aramaic, and this inference is supported, as we have seen, by the style and manner of his work." Frey (Hengel, *Frage*, 340 n. 72) maintains: "In gewissem Sinne fremdartig, aber eben 'biblisch-hebräisch' sind natürlich auch Eigennamen wie Ἀβαδδών Apk 9,11 (vgl. Prov 15,11; Ps 87,12; Hi 26,6 Q' und 28,22 Q') und Ἁρμαγεδών Apk 16,16."

46. See the research to date in N. F. Marcos, *Introducción a las versiones griegas de la Biblia*, Textos y Estudios "Cardenal Cisneros" 23, 2nd ed. (Madrid: Consejo Superior de Investigaciones Científicas, 1998), in particular chapters 10–11.

47. Giesen, *Offenbarung*, 362.

nesses (Rev 11:3ff.) are reminiscent of the messianic visions in Zech 4:3, 14.[48] The morning star (Rev 2:28; 22:16) is a metaphor evoking OT messianic expectations (cf. Num 24:17), here applied to Christ. The tree of life which is connected with the heavenly Jerusalem (Rev 22:2) refers to the creation narrative (Gen 2; 3; cf. also Ezek 47:12), and the hidden manna (Rev 2:17) to Israel's journey through the desert (Exod 16).

Summary

Throughout his writing, John refers to OT traditions, many of which have theological significance. The reference to the "Song of Moses," the *Dreizeitenformel*, and the references to OT institutions, characters, and places are deliberate signals,[49] which must have been recognised by readers or hearers with a Jewish-Christian background in Asia Minor.[50] They are rooted in another, non-Hellenistic, cultural context with which John argues his mission and message for his churches. These signals point to the writings of Israel in order to provide solutions in John's contemporary crisis.

The Transformation of Ezekiel in Revelation

In the following discussion of the transformation of Ezekiel in Revelation, three observations should be noted: first, Revelation is not an interpretation of the OT. Rather, it is a "revelation of Jesus Christ" (Rev 1:1). None of the various "rules" (e.g., the *middôt* of Rabbi Hillel and Rabbi Eliezer) or genres of Jewish exegesis can describe John's reception of Ezekiel.[51] He does not deal with the OT by using the form of

---

48. Olive oil (ἔλαιον) was used very often in Antiquity and in the Orient; cf. H. Schlier, "ἔλαιον," in *TWNT* 2:468–70. The reference to the two olive trees in Rev 11:3f does not refer to cultural traditions in Asia Minor but recalls Jewish messianic expectations.

49. Modern exegesis pays attention to the use of signals for directing the reader (*Leserlenkungssignale*). Both allusions and direct quotations can be regarded as deliberate signals, though it is difficult to determine whether all of the parallels between the OT and Revelation are accidental or deliberate.

50. S. van Tilborg, *Reading John in Ephesus*, NTS 83 (Leiden: Brill, 1996).

51. G. Stemberger and C. Dohmen, *Hermeneutik der Jüdischen Bibel und des Alten Testaments*, Studienbücher Theologie I,2 (Stuttgart: Kohlhammer, 1996) 38–109. Fekkes (*Isaiah*, 287–90) is emphatic that Revelation is not a kind of exegesis of the OT: "John merely strengthens the prophet's own haggadic integration of *Urzeit* and *Endzeit* by adding ζωῆς" (99 n. 76). See also E. Schüssler Fiorenza, *The Book of Revelation: Justice*

a pesher nor by using the form of the Targumim. Therefore Revelation cannot be regarded as a midrash on Ezekiel.[52]

Second, the same pictures and motifs have different connotations according to the circumstances of time and culture.[53] No word of human language and no metaphor has the same meaning and effect within different contexts. In particular, the use of poetic language creates changes in the way words typically function in the process of communication.

Third, biblical scholars describe the transformation of Ezekiel in Revelation on various levels according to modern methods of text interpretation, rather than according to an ancient understanding of Scripture—which of course is only visible in hindsight.[54] It would be

---

and Judgment (Philadelphia: Fortress, 1985) 135: "He does not interpret the OT but uses its words, images, phrases, and patterns as a language arsenal in order to make his own theological statement or express his own prophetic vision. He adapts or borrows whole OT text sequences as patterns for his own original compositions but never refers to the OT as authoritative Scripture." S. Moyise, *The Old Testament in the Book of Revelation*, JSNTSup 115 (Sheffield: Sheffield Academic Press, 1995) 115, supports this view: "By incorporating allusions into his work, John has created a new figuration whereby the old words are given a new context and principally derive their meaning from that."

52. This disagrees with Berger, *Theologiegeschichte*, 622 ("Apk nimmt nicht nur mit Anspielungen auf Ez [und viele andere] Bezug, sondern ist in den wesentlichen Elementen seiner Gesamtkonstruktion an Ez orientiert und versteht sich daher als fortlaufender Midrasch zu diesem Buch"). G. Stemberger notes that the NT is often described as midrash, although this description is quite modern (*Einleitung in Talmud und Midrasch*, Beck'sche Elementarbücher, 7th ed. [München: C. H. Beck, 1982] 222–28). The literary genre midrash is hardly defined. It is a form of creative Jewish exegesis. Midrashim have a distinct present-day relevance.

53. J. Cambier, "Les images de l'Ancien Testament dans l'Apocalypse de S. Jean," *NRTh* 7 (1955) 118: "Un fait que frappe celui qui étudie la signification des images de l'Apocalypse est leur continuité: une même image servira à évoquer des époques différentes de l'histoire religieuse." H. Hübner ("Eine hermeneutisch unverzichtbare Unterscheidung: Vetus Testamentum und Vetus Testamentum in Novo receptum," in *Texts and Contexts. Biblical Texts in Their Textual and Situational Contexts: Essays in Honor of Lars Hartman*, ed. T. Fornberg and D. Hellholm [Oslo: Scandinavian University Press, 1995] 906ff.) points to the difference between the OT and the reception of these writings. He speaks about an openness of the OT which can be interpreted christologically. Furthermore, he asks: "Gibt es identisches Verstehen für Vergangenheit und Gegenwart?"

54. S. Moyise ("Seeing the Old Testament Through a Lens," *IBS* 23 [2001] 36–42) mentions the problem. Cf. the discussion between Moyise and Beale and Paulien's comments in *AUSS* 39 (Moyise, "Authorial Intention and the Book of Revelation," 35–40; Beale, "A Response to Jon Paulien on the Use of the Old Testament in Revelation," 23–34; and J. Paulien, "Dreading the Whirlwind: Intertextuality and the Use of the Old Testament in Revelation," 5–22).

wrong to assume that John has carefully and scientifically studied the various translations and traditions of the text of the OT and early Jewish writings in order to compose his own writing.

Technical Terms

The transformation of Ezekiel in Revelation can be described on different levels. Technically, we can distinguish between citations, allusions, mixed allusions, and contextual and non-contextual use of Ezekiel in Revelation.

I define a citation as a sequence of at least five words which are unique in Ezekiel and Revelation. Introductory formulae or other kinds of authorial self-reflection are not required. An allusion on the verbal level is defined as agreement of at least two relevant words. Allusions on the level of structure alone need to have one agreement of a relevant word which is supported by the context.

Mixed allusions are defined as the influence of two or more verses of the same writing within one verse in Revelation.[55] The term also can be applied to the influence of multiple text segments. Many texts in Revelation which are strongly shaped by the order and selection of motifs in Ezekiel are simultaneously influenced by other OT writings.

Authorial self-reflection is lacking in Revelation. John does not discuss his recourse to OT texts overtly. There are no introductory formulae or attached commentaries. Even signals that guide the reader (*Leserlenkungssignale*) in a specific direction and point to the general use of the OT cannot be regarded as overt reflection by the author. So while John's use of text markers points the addressees of Revelation to the extensive use of the OT, the absence of deliberate self-reflection does not imply plagiarism. Nor does it merely indicate that John was familiar with the OT. If this were the case, the readers would have been hindered in understanding Revelation. John's writing shows his deliberate intent to communicate (cf. Rev 22:10), as can be seen by the epistolatory style and form of the macrotext and by the seven letters to the churches in Asia Minor.

---

55. G. K. Beale, "The Various Ways John Uses the Old Testament," in *John's Use of the Old Testament in Revelation*, ed. G. K. Beale, JSNTSup 166 (Sheffield: Sheffield Academic, 1998) 63.

Contextual usage of the OT in the NT pays attention to both the original context and to the intention behind the use of the OT in its new context.[56] Non-contextual usage regards the OT as a kind of quarry—a source of material to exploit, whether the original text fits into the new context or not. The use of Ezekiel in Revelation results from continuous contextual usage, as can be seen by the high degree of affinity in subject and theme between the two texts.

Allusions to material that is spread across several verses are noticeable as well. Allusions and citations are often examined at the verse level; but this leads to an atomized understanding of the text and ignores the fact that chapters and verses are secondary developments. One example of an overlapping allusion is the order of the four plagues in Rev 6:8 which uses Ezek 14:21 and the entire text segment Ezek 14:12-23.

OT motifs can be repeatedly used in a single NT text.[57] The double or even multiple use of motifs and text segments from Ezekiel is a characteristic feature in Revelation.[58] J. Fekkes describes this as "repetition of OT texts."[59] Another attested feature is the connection of two or more text segments of the OT with each other when used in the NT.[60] This is discernable in John's use of Ezekiel: his final vision of the heavenly Jerusalem alludes to Ezekiel's vision of Jerusalem and to the lamentation over Tyre in Ezek 26-28 at the same time.

---

56. Ibid., 67.

57. S. Bøe, *Gog and Magog. Ezekiel 38-39 as Pre-text for Revelation 19,17-21 and 20,7-10*, WUNT II 135 (Tübingen: J. C. B. Mohr, 2001) 366, 371ff., and Vanhoye, "L'utilisation," 462, who speaks about "double utilisation."

58. Already Ezekiel uses motifs twice: "Ezekiel 39 recapitulates the same battle narrated in Ezekiel 38. This would suggest that if John is following any model in Rev. 19:17-21 and 20:7-10, he would be following the generally acknowledged pattern of recapitulation in Ezekiel 38-39 . . ." (G. K. Beale, *The Use of Daniel in Jewish Apocalyptic Literature and in the Revelation of St. John* [Lanham: University Press of America, 1984] 365). Such doublets are characteristic of Ezekiel and prophetic literature. Beale (*Use*, 367) calls them "flashback" ("Most see the concluding comments about restoration from exile in 39:25-29 as a summary or retrospective reflection on the same theme in chs. 34-37, serving as a transition between 34:1-39:24 and chs. 40-48"; cf. 367).

59. Fekkes, *Isaiah*, 283ff.

60. Ibid.

Transformation of Language

The transformation of OT writings in the NT can be observed on the levels of language and style (semitisms, septuagintisms).[61] In Revelation the many grammatical irregularities which function as signals to direct the reader (*Leserlenkungssignale*) point to this fact. It can also be seen in the use of characteristic rhetorical forms and sentence structures which occur within comparable contexts or literary genres. Two examples include the use of the rhetorical question from Ezek 37:3 ff. in Rev 7:13 ff., and of the sentence structure οὐ μὴ ... ἔτι from Ezek 26:13, 14 in Rev 18:21, 22, 23.

Transformation of Structure

The use of Ezekiel has also influenced the structure of Revelation. In regard to the literary dependency of OT and NT texts, the level of the structural form of text segments and the level of the overall composition have to be distinguished. The structural transformation of text segments in Revelation can be observed best in a comparison of the final visions in that the order and composition of the two are similar. The structure of Rev 18–22 runs parallel to Ezek 37–48. Such a replication of the structure of an OT text in its linear order is unique in the entire Bible.

Ezek 37–48	Rev 18–22
Preparation of the final battle (Ezek 38:1–39:10)	Preparation of the final battle (Rev 16:12–16)
Final battle against Gog and Magog (Ezek 38–39)	Final battle against the beast (Rev 19:17–21)
Meal of the birds (Ezek 39:4, 17–20)	Meal of the birds (Rev 19:11–21)
	First resurrection and Messianic reign (Rev 20:4–6)
Battle against Gog (Ezek 38:17–39:10; 39:11–16)	Final battle against Gog and Magog (Rev 20:7–10)
Revival of the dry bones (Ezek 37)	Second resurrection (Rev 20:11–15)
	Last judgment (Rev 20:11–15)
Vision of the New Temple and the New Israel (Ezek 40–48)	Descent of the heavenly Jerusalem (Rev 21–22)

---

61. Cf. Beale, "Ways," 125ff.

Another characteristic feature of the author's transformation of entire text segments from Ezekiel is a noticeable tendency to abbreviate, simplify, or clarify.[62] Examples include the transformed description of the vision of God from Ezek 1–3 in Rev 4–5, the description of the harlot Babylon (Rev 17) according to the description of prostitution in Israel and Judah (Ezek 16; 23), the usage of the Gog-Magog tradition (Ezek 38–39), and the final vision of the renewed Jerusalem (Ezek 40–48) in Rev 21–22.

Literary genres which are typical of OT writings can serve as literary prototypes and be transformed in NT writings.[63] This procedure is applied in Revelation. In particular, it can be seen in the transformation of the vocation account in Ezekiel, which combines two genres—the reports of an encounter (*Begegnung*) and a vision. Both of these are used in Rev 1:9–20 and Rev 4–5. Further examples of the transformation of literary genres can be seen in John's use of the vision narrative and the prophetic performance of measuring the temple.[64]

Transformation of Content

Transformations on the level of content can take many different forms. One way NT writers transform their OT source texts is by the creation of analogies.[65] Such transformation can be found in most of the references to Ezekiel in Revelation; comparisons of individual motifs in the various text segments demonstrate this.[66] John's preferred method is the

---

62. Vanhoye, "L'utilisation," 463–65 and Ruiz, *Ezekiel*, 427, who speaks about three different ways of reception: "The reappropriation of Ezekielian material can be described under three interrelated headings: a) simplification, b) rearrangement, c) reintegration." An example of "simplification" is the use of Ezek 27:12–25a in Rev 18:12ff. "Rearrangement" can be observed in Rev 18:12–13 (which "does not follow the order of Ezek 27:12–25a"; cf. Ruiz, *Ezekiel*, 431). Regarding "reintregration," Ruiz remarks: "items in Rev 18,12–13 also found in Ezek 27,12–25a are familiar from elsewhere in the Apocalypse, and that five of the first eight echo the Rev 17,4 description of the Great Prostitute whose judgment is the theme of the vision" (ibid., 436).

63. Beale, "Ways," 75–79.

64. Beale ("Ways," 76ff) points to the following examples: Ezek 37–48 in Rev 20–22; Ezek 1–2 in Rev 4:1–5:1; Ezek 26–27 in Rev 18:9–19, 23; Ezek 40–48 in Rev 21:9–22:5.

65. Ibid., 94ff.

66. Beale ("Ways," 99) mentions the following examples: judgment (Ezek 1 and Rev 4–5; Ezek 2 and Rev 10); victory of the faithful against the enemy (Ezek 38–39 and Rev 20:8); idolatry (Ezek 16:15 and Rev 17).

combination of two older texts by analogy (e.g., the living beings in Rev 4–5 are taken from a combination of Isa 6 and Ezek 1; 10; the plagues are taken from a combination of Exod 7–10 and numerous other texts, particularly the prophetic writings; the vision of the heavenly worship in Rev 4–5 is taken from a combination of texts, particularly from Ezekiel and Isaiah).[67]

Typological readings of the OT have long been popular in Christian interpretation.[68] One example in Revelation is the description of the two beasts (Rev 13), which reflects a typological reading of Daniel. The sealing of the 144,000 (Rev 7:2–8) could be understood as a typological transformation of the sealing of the faithful in Jerusalem (Ezek 9:3–4).[69]

Universalization of OT statements occurs where NT authors transform promises addressed to one recipient (e.g., Israel) into promises addressed to a wider group.[70] For example, when John refers to Ezekiel's final vision of the renewed Jerusalem, he does not use Ezekiel's arrangement of the land (Ezek 45:1–8; 47:13–48:35), but rather emphasizes that the heavenly Jerusalem will be offered as a homeland to many peoples (Rev 21:24, 26).[71]

---

67. Fekkes, *Isaiah*, 283ff.

68. Bøe, *Gog*, 366ff. In a typological reading, certain historical characters of the OT are understood to anticipate later historical characters (cf. Rom 5:14ff). This understanding is also applied to historical events or institutions (so Moyise, *Old Testament*, 83).

69. Moyise, *Old Testament*, 83.

70. Beale, "Ways," 100–111. See further Vanhoye ("L'utilisation," 466), who mentions the following examples: Ezek 3:11 in Rev 10:11; Ezek 37:26 in Rev 7:15; Ezek 10:2 in Rev 8:4; Ezek 7:1–26; 21:14–19 in Rev 6:4; 8:13; Ezek 27:29–34 in Rev 17:5; 18:9; Ezek 44:9 in Rev 21:3. He concludes: "Cette universalisation est la marque de l'esprit chrétien, mais elle ne va pas contre le sens de l'A.T., elle en constitue au contraire l'accomplissement."

71. Other examples: the promise of God's presence and healing for Israel is applied to the nations (Ezek 37:27; 44:9; 48:35 in Rev 21:3; Ezek 47:12 in Rev 22:2); the description of the destruction of Tyre is applied to the "whore Babylon" (Ezek 26:16–18; 27:29–35 in Rev 17:1–3; 18:9). Beale (*The Book of Revelation*, NIGTC [Grand Rapids: Eerdmans, and Carlisle: Paternoster, 1998] 979) states that "Ezekiel 39 recapitulates the battle narrated in Ezekiel 38." And further: "Nevertheless, there still may be some degree of universalization here in the Apocalypse (Rev 20:8), since the nations in Ezekiel 38–39 appear to come only from, at most, two major directions, while in Rev. 20:8 they proceed from all four points of the compass. John has already recorded the fulfilment of the same Ezekiel prophecy in 16:14–16 and 19:17–21" (1023).

NT authors may personify certain characters in terms of characters (or things) described in the OT. In the transformation of Ezekiel two examples of personification are discernable: firstly, the identification of "Gog and Magog"[72] with the peoples (Rev 20:8); secondly, the personification of "God and the Lamb" as a temple (Rev 21:22).[73]

John transforms many images of God from Ezekiel, but avoids all kinds of anthropomorphisms that are characteristic of OT descriptions of God.[74] Numerous examples can be mentioned; in particular, when John uses and transforms Ezek 1-3, he omits Ezekiel's anthropomorphic descriptions.[75] This avoidance of OT anthropomorphisms is deeply rooted in two characteristics of the Johannine image of God which culminates in two crucial sentences: "Our Lord and God" (Rev 4:11: ὁ κύριος καὶ ὁ θεὸς ἡμῶν), and "for you alone are holy" (Rev 15:4: ὅτι μόνος ὅσιος).

John's transformation of his source text may result in descriptions in Revelation which are antithetical to those in Ezekiel.[76] For example, John uses the precious stone list from Ezek 26-28 to illustrate the heavenly Jerusalem (Rev 21:19-20), not to describe the whore Babylon (cf. its use in Ezekiel to describe Tyre).[77]

72. Cf. LXX Amos 7:1, where one locust of the swarm is identified as "Gog the king."

73. The spiritualisation of the temple can also be observed in rabbinic literature. It is an attempt to overcome the catastrophe of 70 CE; cf. C. Thoma, "Auswirkungen des jüdischen Krieges gegen Rom (66-70/73 n.Chr.) auf das rabbinische Judentum," *BZ* 12 (1968) 193-206.

74. Anthropomorphisms are characteristic features of the OT depiction of God, cf. J. Hempel, "Die Grenzen des Anthropomorphismus Jahwes im Alten Testament," *ZAW* 57 (1939) 82; M. Saebø, "Den ene Gud og Herre. Bemerkninger til det gammeltestamentlige gudsbegrep," *TTK* 48 (1977) 241-53; A. Deissler, "Der Gott des Alten Testaments," in *Die Frage nach Gott*, ed. J. Ratzinger, QD 56 (Freiburg: Herder, 1973) 45-58; G. Fohrer, "Das Gottesbild des Alten Testaments," in *Studien zur alttestamentlichen Theologie und Geschichte (1949-1966)*, ed. G. Fohrer, BZAW 115 (Berlin: de Gruyter, 1969) 163-75; V. Maag, "Das Gottesverständnis des Alten Testaments," in *Kultur, Kulturkontakt und Religion. Gesammelte Schriften zur allgemeinen und alttestamentlichen Religionsgeschichte*, ed. H. H. Schmid and O. H. Steck (Göttingen: Vandenhoeck & Ruprecht, 1980) 256-99 and H. Schrade, *Der verborgene Gott. Gottesbilder und Gottesvorstellung in Israel und im Alten Orient* (Stuttgart: Kohlhammer, 1949).

75. Contrast Ezek 1:26 with Rev 4:2, 3; 20:11, and note the reservation in describing God in Rev 4:3.

76. Moyise, *Old Testament*, 114.

77. Beale, "Ways," 122-24. Moyise (*Old Testament*, 114) mentions a second example,

It is noticeable that John often takes great liberties in his creative transformation of Ezekiel: "Nous avons rappelé combien l'imagerie d'Apoc. relevait de L'Ancien Testament; la liberté avec laquelle déjà la valeur historique relative; il reste à préciser cette dernière expression."[78] The degree of freedom that an author takes when using an earlier text has been described in various ways. In order to describe John's use of Ezekiel, J.-P. Ruiz uses the term "imitation," which he describes in a fourfold manner: (1) reproductive imitation, which means a precise reproduction; (2) eclectic usage of different sources without giving priority to one source;[79] (3) heuristic imitation, which indicates the actualization of the pre-text; (4) dialectic imitation, which disagrees with the pre-text.[80]

The relationship between OT and NT can also be described with the terms "continuity" and "discontinuity."[81] Theological motifs and ideas, OT institutions and laws, etc., may be brought over into the NT (continuity) or be cancelled (discontinuity). Revelation very often displays continuity. Some examples of discontinuity should be mentioned here: John does not adopt the Ezekelian theology of the land nor the cultic instructions and building code of the temple in Jerusalem. Furthermore, the community structures are changed. These examples can be explained by the centrality of the Christ event in John's thought.

Hermeneutical Questions

The transformation of Ezekiel in Revelation raises a number of hermeneutical questions. In particular, it raises the question of the relationship between the OT and the NT. Much research has been done on this question.[82] The following models may be mentioned.

---

the description of the temple in Ezek 40–48, which John modifies antithetically in Rev 21:22.

78. Cambier, "Images," 118.

79. Rev 16:17–21 is an example; all the references to lightning, earthquakes, etc. (4:5; 8:5; 11:19) help create the climax in 16:18–21.

80. Moyise (*Old Testament*, 118–23) points to the thesis and typology of T. M. Greene (*The Light in Troy: Imitation and Discovery in Renaissance Poetry* [New Haven: Yale University Press, 1982] 16–53), regarding different imitations.

81. Moyise, *Old Testament*, 110.

82. C. Dohmen and T. Söding, eds., *Eine Bibel—zwei Testamente*, UTB 1893 (Paderborn: Schöningh, 1995).

One very old model to describe the relationship between the two parts of the Bible is that of promise and fulfilment. The OT is understood as pronouncement of the Christ event. One can distinguish between informal, direct, and indirect (typological) prophetical fulfilment of the OT.[83] On the basis of my research this model cannot be applied to the transformation of Ezekiel in Revelation. Numerous promises in Ezekiel retain validity as promises in Revelation; they are not regarded as having been fulfilled. This also applies to the motif of the seal as a symbol of protection, and to the promise of the renewed Jerusalem. Finally, the promise of judgment and resurrection can be mentioned (Rev 19:17–21; 20:7–10), which John does not regard as having been previously fulfilled.

Another model can be described as re-reading. The OT has been re-read in two ways: first, as a Jewish *relecture* (e.g., the use of the OT in rabbinic texts); second, as a re-reading in the light of Christ. J. Fekkes speaks about a christological "exploitation" of Hebrew parallelisms.[84] This twofold reception suggests that a *relecture* cannot replace the original meaning.[85] A *relecture* of the OT in the light of Christ can be recognized in John's transformation of Ezek 37 in Rev 11 and 20.

Conclusion

John drew upon various OT writings, in particular prophetic writings such as Isaiah, Daniel, Jeremiah and Ezekiel. But no text has influenced Revelation more than Ezekiel. Both Ezekiel and John conceive of themselves as prophets in exile. Both writings have the same structure (four

---

83. Beale, "Ways," 111–16; Bøe, *Gog*, 364–67. Also, Beale (*Revelation*, 88) argues the thesis that the author of Revelation "utilized [OT patterns] as lenses through which past and present eschatological fulfillment is understood." Ruiz (*Ezekiel*, 223) argues the converse: "... reappropriate biblical metaphors through the lens of Revelation itself." τελέω (fulfill) occurs in Rev 10:7; 11:7; 15:1; 17:17; 20:3, 5, 7. Schüssler Fiorenza (*Revelation*, 13) states: "Rev. does not distinguish either between John and the prophets or between the OT and early Christian prophets. The observation that the use of Scripture in Revelation resembles that of Qumran is correct." Schüssler Fiorenza distinguishes between early Christian homily and exegesis that interpret Scripture, and early Christian prophecy that pronounces judgment and salvation (cf. 137).

84. Fekkes, *Isaiah*, 283ff. Perhaps it is better to speak of a "re-reading" instead of a Christian eisegesis.

85. Pontifical Biblical Commision, *Jewish People*, II.A.2 "This new interpretation does not negate the original meaning."

vision narratives with a change of location). No other OT writing is alluded to so often in Revelation as Ezekiel. No other OT prophet is similarly transported by the Spirit to various places. John is also influenced by the theology of Ezekiel in terms of eschatology, prophetic mission, and the image of God. Both speak about the same plagues and the same living beings. Both are developments of Merkabah-mysticism. Both share the same formal elements and literary forms (vocation narrative, lamentation, vision narrative, etc.). The theology of both is prophetic and priestly at the same time. The theology of Ezekiel and of John is Jerusalem-centered. Both live in a time of heteronomy.

These similarities in theology, structure, form, linguistic features, and authorial self-conception have led Steve Moyise to the following conclusion: "The most obvious explanation is that John has taken on the 'persona' of Ezekiel. Through meditation and study (of which there are ample precedents), John has absorbed something of the character and mind of the prophet. This is why he can make so many allusions to the book without ever actually quoting it. It is possible that he does not quote it as Scripture because he does not see it as an external source. He has taken on the mind of Ezekiel and writes 'in the spirit' (εν πνευματι)."[86] It seems that John could identify closely with Ezekiel's personality and theology. Ezekiel helped him express his visions and message to the churches in Asia Minor.

---

86. Moyise, *Old Testament*, 78f.

Appendix: Comprehensive List of Allusions to Ezekiel

References which are not mentioned in NA^{27} or GNT^4 are presented in square brackets.

Rev	Ezek (word level)	Ezek (structural level)
Rev 1:10 (cf. 4:1; 17:3; 21:10)	Ezek 3:12 (cf. 2:2)	
Rev 1:13	Ezek 1:26; 9:2, 11 LXX	
Rev 1:15 (cf. 14:2; 19:6)	Ezek 1:7, 24 MT (cf. 43:2)	
Rev 1:17 (cf. 19:10; 22:8)	Ezek 1:28; 3:23; 11:13; 43:3; 44:4 MT	Ezek 2:6; 3:9
[Rev 2:4]	[Ezek 16:8 MT]	
Rev 2:7	Ezek 31:8 (quotation), 9b	
Rev 2:20		Ezek 13:17
Rev 2:23	Ezek 33:27	
Rev 2:27 (cf. 7:17; 19:15)	Ezek 34:23	
Rev 3:12	Ezek 48:35	
[Rev 4:1 (corresponds to 19:11)]	[Ezek 1:1]	
Rev 4:2 (cf. 1:10; 17:3; 21:10)	Ezek 1:26; 2:9, 10	
Rev 4:3	Ezek 1:26f, 28; 28:13	
Rev 4:5 (cf. 1:4; 3:1; 5:6)	Ezek 1:13	
Rev 4:6	Ezek 1:5, 13, 18, 22; 10:12	
Rev 4:7	Ezek 1:10; 10:14 MT	
Rev 4:8	Ezek 1:5, 6, 18; 10:12	
Rev 4:9	Ezek 1:26	
Rev 4:10	Ezek 1:26	
Rev 5:1	Ezek 1:26; 2:9, 10	
Rev 5:7	Ezek 1:26	
Rev 5:13	Ezek 1:26	
[Rev 6:4]	[Ezek 14:17; 21:14, 16, 19]	

Rev	Ezek (word level)	Ezek (structural level)
Rev 6:6	Ezek 45:10 LXX	
Rev 6:8	Ezek 5:12 LXX, 17; 14:21; 33:27	Ezek 5:16–17; 14:13, 15, 17, 19
Rev 6:12 (cf. 11:13; 16:18)	Ezek 3:12; 38:19	
Rev 6:16	Ezek 1:26	
Rev 7:1 (cf. 20:8)	Ezek 7:2 (quotation)	
Rev 7:2		Ezek 43:2
Rev 7:3 (cf. 9:4; 13:16; 14:13; 17:5; 22:4)	Ezek 9:4	Ezek 9:6
Rev 7:10	Ezek 1:26	
Rev 7:13	Ezek 37:3	
Rev 7:14	Ezek 37:3	
Rev 7:15	Ezek 1:26	
Rev 7:17 (cf. 2:27; 19:15)	Ezek 34:23 MT	
Rev 8:4	Ezek 8:11	
Rev 8:5 (corresponds to Rev 4:5)	Ezek 1:13	
Rev 8:7	Ezek 5:2, 12 MT; 38:22	
Rev 8:12	Ezek 32:7	
Rev 9:4 (cf. 7:3; 13:16; 14:1, 9; 17:5; 22:4)	Ezek 9:4	
Rev 9:17 (cf. 9:18; 14:10; 19:20; 20:10; 21:8)	Ezek 38:22	
Rev 9:21	Ezek 43:7, 9 LXX	
Rev 10:1 (cf. 4:2)	Ezek 1:28	
Rev 10:2	Ezek 2:9	
Rev 10:8	Ezek 2:9	
Rev 10:9	Ezek 2:8 LXX; 3:1f, 14	

Rev	Ezek (word level)	Ezek (structural level)
Rev 10:10	Ezek 3:3 (quotation); 3:14 MT	
Rev 10:11	Ezek 3:11; 25:2	
Rev 11:1 (cf. 21:15)	Ezek 40:3, 5, 47; 41:1; 42:16–19; 43:13	
Rev 11:8	Ezek 11:6	Ezek 37:1
Rev 11:11	Ezek 37:5 LXX, 10	
Rev 11:13 (cf. 6:12; 16:18)	Ezek 3:12; 38:19, 23 LXX	
Rev 12:3	Ezek 29:3	
Rev 12:14	Ezek 17:3, 7	
Rev 13:15	Ezek 37:10	
Rev 14:1 (cf. 7:3; 9:4; 13:16; 14:1, 9; 17:5; 20:4; 22:4)	Ezek 9:4	
Rev 14:2 (cf. 1:15; 19:6)	Ezek 1:24 (cf. 43:2) MT	
Rev 14:10 (cf. 9:17f; 19:20; 20:10; 21:8)	Ezek 38:22	Ezek 23:25
Rev 15:6	Ezek 9:2, 3, 11	
Rev 16:1	Ezek 14:19; 20:8 (cf. Ezek 7:5; 9:8; 20:13, 21; 22:22, 31; 30:15; 36:18; 39:29)	
Rev 16:6	Ezek 24:6; 35:6	
Rev 16:14		Ezek 38:4, 7, 13, 15
Rev 16:15	Ezek 16:7, 22, 39; 23:29	
Rev 16:16		Ezek 38:4, 7, 13, 15
Rev 16:17	Ezek 3:12	
Rev 16:18 (cf. 6:12; 11:14)	Ezek 3:12; 38:19	
Rev 16:19	Ezek 16:38	Ezek 23:25; 31f
Rev 17:1	Ezek 16:15–17; 23:3	

Transformation of Ezekiel in John's Revelation

Rev	Ezek (word level)	Ezek (structural level)
Rev 17:2	Ezek 16; 23; 27:33	
Rev 17:3 (cf. 1:10; 4:2; 21:10)	Ezek 2:2; 20:35f	
Rev 17:1–3	Ezek 20:35f	
Rev 17:4	Ezek 16:13; 28:13	
Rev 17:5 (cf. 7:3; 9:4; 13:16; 14:1, 9; 22:4)	Ezek 16:15	
Rev 17:6	Ezek 23:45	
Rev 17:16	Ezek 16:39; 23:25, 26, 29	
Rev 18:1	Ezek 43:2 MT	
Rev 18:3	Ezek 27:12, 18	Ezek 16:15; 23:19
Rev 18:7		Ezek 16:13 MT
Rev 18:9	Ezek 26:16f; 27:31b MT, 32, 33–35	
Rev 18:11	Ezek 27:31b MT	
Rev 18:12	Ezek 27:12 LXX	Ezek 27:7, 22; 28:13
Rev 18:13	Ezek 27:13	Ezek 16:13; 27:17
Rev 18:15	Ezek 27:31b MT, 33	
Rev 18:16	Ezek 16:13	Ezek 27:7
Rev 18:17	Ezek (26:19); 27:27–29	Ezek 27:27
Rev 18:18	Ezek 27:32 MT (quotation)	
Rev 18:19	Ezek 27:30, 31b MT	
Rev 18:21	Ezek 26:21 MT	
Rev 18:22	Ezek 26:13	
Rev 18:24	Ezek 24:6, 7; 36:18 MT	
Rev 19:2		Ezek 23:45
Rev 19:4	Ezek 1:26	
Rev 19:6 (cf. 1:15; 14:2; 19:6)	Ezek 1:24 MT (cf. 43:2)	
Rev 19:8	Ezek 16:10	
Rev 19:11 (cf. 4:1)	Ezek 1:1	Ezek 38:4, 22

Rev	Ezek (word level)	Ezek (structural level)
Rev 19:15 (cf. 1:16; 2:12 [Ezek 5:1]); (cf. 2:27; 7:17; 19:15 [Ezek 34:23])	Ezek 5:1; 34:23	
Rev 19:17	Ezek 39:4, 17, 18, 20	Ezek 38:4, 7, 13, 15
Rev 19:18	Ezek 39:17f, 20	Ezek 38:4; 39:20
Rev 19:19		Ezek 38:4, 7, 13, 15
Rev 19:21	Ezek 39:4	Ezek 38:4; 39:17
Rev 20:4	Ezek 37:10	
Rev 20:5	Ezek 37:3	
Rev 20:8 (cf. 7:1; 9:17f; 14:10; 19:20; 20:10)	Ezek 7:2; 38:2	Ezek 38:4, 7, 13, 15
Rev 20:10 (cf. 1:10; 4:1; 17:3)	Ezek 38:22	
Rev 20:12	Ezek 18:30	
Rev 21:5	Ezek 1:26	
Rev 21:7	Ezek 11:20 LXX (quotation)	
Rev 21:10	Ezek 40:1f (cf. 2:2; 3:12, 14, 24; 8:3; 11:1, 24; 43:5)	
Rev 21:11	Ezek 43:2	
Rev 21:12	Ezek 48:31–34	
Rev 21:13	Ezek 48:31–34	
Rev 21:15 (cf. 11:1)	Ezek 40:5; 42:16–18	
Rev 21:16	Ezek 41:4; 43:16; 45:2f; 48:20	
Rev 21:17	Ezek 40:5; 41:4f; 43:16; 45:2f	
Rev 21:19	Ezek 28:13	
Rev 21:22		Ezek 48:35
Rev 21:27	Ezek 44:9	

Rev	Ezek (word level)	Ezek (structural level)
Rev 22:1	Ezek 47:1	Ezek 47:8f
Rev 22:2 (cf. 2:7)	Ezek 47:7, 12 MT	
Rev 22:4	Ezek 9:4	
Rev 22:11	Ezek 3:27	
Rev 22:19	Ezek 47:12	

Bibliography

Bachmann, M. "Himmlisch: Der 'Tempel Gottes' von Apk 11.1." *NTS* 40 (1994) 474–80.

Bauckham, R. *The Climax of Prophecy: Studies on the Book of Revelation.* Edinburgh: T. & T. Clark, 1993.

Beale, G. K. "A Response to Jon Paulien on the Use of the Old Testament in Revelation." *AUSS* 39 (2001) 23–34.

———. "Solecisms in the Apocalypse as Signals for the Presence of Old Testament Allusions. A Selective Analysis of Revelation 1–22." In *Early Christian Interpretation of the Scriptures of Israel*, edited by C. A. Evans, 421–46. JSNTSup 148. Sheffield: Sheffield Academic, 1997.

———. *The Book of Revelation.* New International Greek Testament Commentary. Grand Rapids: Eerdmans, 1998.

———. *The Use of Daniel in Jewish Apocalyptic Literature and in the Revelation of St. John.* Lanham, MD: University Press of America, 1984.

———. "The Various Ways John Uses the Old Testament." In *John's Use of the Old Testament in Revelation*, edited by G. K. Beale, 60–128. JSNTSup 166. Sheffield: Sheffield Academic, 1998.

Berger, K. *Theologiegeschichte des Urchristentums: Theologie des Neuen Testaments.* UTB für Wissenschaft. 2nd ed. Tübingen: Francke, 1995.

Berges, U. "'Ich bin der Mann, der Elend sah' (Klgl 3,1): Zionstheologie als Weg aus der Krise." *BZ* 44 (2000) 1–20.

Bøe, S. *Gog and Magog: Ezekiel 38–39 as Pre-Text for Revelation 19,17–21 and 20,7–10.* Studiebibliothek for Bibel og Mission 5. Oslo: Biblia/Fjellhaug Skoler, 1999.

———. *Gog and Magog. Ezekiel 38–39 as Pre-text for Revelation 19,17–21 and 20,7–10.* WUNT 2/135. Tübingen: Mohr/Siebeck, 2001.

Böhl, E. *Die alttestamentlichen Citate im Neuen Testament.* Wien: Braumüller, 1878.

Briggs, R. A. *Jewish Temple Imagery in the Book of Revelation.* Studies in Biblical Literature 10. New York: Lang, 1999.

Cambier, J. "Les images de l'Ancien Testament dans l'Apocalypse de S. Jean." *La nouvelle revue théologique* 7 (1955) 113–22.

Deiana, G. "Utilizzazione del libro di Geremia in alcuni brani dell' Apocalisse." *Lateranum* 48 (1982) 125–137.

Deissler, A. "Der Gott des Alten Testaments." In *Die Frage nach Gott*, edited by J. Ratzinger, 45–58. Quaestiones disputatae 56. Freiburg: Herder, 1973.

Dohmen, C., and T. Söding, eds. *Eine Bibel— zwei Testamente.* UTB 1893. Paderborn: Schöningh, 1995.

Du Rand, J. A. "David and Goliath in the Apocalypse of John?" *Ekklesiastikos Pharos* 76 (1994) 25–30.

———. "The Song of the Lamb Because of the Victory of the Lamb." *Neot* 29 (1995) 203–10.

Feist, U. *Ezechiel. Das literarische Problem des Buches forschungsgeschichtlich betrachtet.* Beiträge zur Wissenschaft vom Alten und Neuen Testament 138. Stuttgart: Kohlhammer, 1995.

Fekkes, J. *Isaiah and Prophetic Traditions in the Book of Revelation: Visionary Antecedents and Their Development.* JSNTSup 93. Sheffield: Sheffield Academic, 1994.

Fenske, W. "'Das Lied des Mose, des Knechtes Gottes, und das Lied des Lammes' (Apokalypse des Johannes 15,3f.). Der Text und seine Bedeutung für die Johannes-Apokalypse." *ZNW* 90 (1999) 250–64.

Fischer, G. "Das Schilfmeerlied Exodus 15 in seinem Kontext." *Bib* 77 (1996) 32–47.

Fohrer, G. "Das Gottesbild des Alten Testaments." In *Studien zur alttestamentlichen Theologie und Geschichte (1949-1966)*, 163–75. BZAW 115. Berlin: de Gruyter, 1969.

———. "Zion-Jerusalem im Alten Testament." In *Studien zur alttestamentlichen Theologie und Geschichte (1949-1966)*, edited by G. Fohrer, 195–241. BZAW 115. Berlin: de Gruyter, 1969.

Fohrer, G., and E. Lohse. "Σιών, Ιεροσυαλήμ, Ιεροσόλυμα, Ιεροσολυμίτης." In *TWNT* 7:291–338.

Frankemölle, H. "συναγωγή." In *Exegetisches Wörterbuch zum Neuen Testament* 3 (1982) 700–10.

Gangemi, A. "L'utilizzazione del Deutero-Isaia dell'Apocalisse di Giovanni." *Euntes Docete* 27 (1974) 109–44, 311–39.

Giesen, H. "Das Gottesbild in der Johannesoffenbarung." In *Der Gott Israels im Zeugnis des Neuen Testaments*, edited by U. Busse, 162–92. QD 201. Freiburg: Herder, 2003.

———. *Die Offenbarung des Johannes*. Regensburger Neues Testament. Regensburg: Friedrich Pustet, 1997.

Goulder, M. D. "The Apocalypse as an Annual Cycle of Prophecies." *NTS* 27 (1981) 342–67.

Greene, T. M. *The Light in Troy: Imitation and Discovery in Renaissance Poetry*. New Haven: Yale University Press, 1982.

Hanson, A. T. *The Living Utterances of God: The New Testament Exegesis of the Old*. London: Darton, Longman & Todd, 1983.

Hempel, J. "Die Grenzen des Anthropomorphismus Jahwes im Alten Testament." *ZAW* 57 (1939) 75–85.

Hengel, M., and J. Frey. *Die johanneische Frage: Ein Lösungsversuch*. WUNT 67. Tübingen: Mohr/Siebeck, 1993.

Hübner, H. "Eine hermeneutisch unverzichtbare Unterscheidung: Vetus Testamentum und Vetus Testamentum in Novo receptum." In *Texts and Contexts: Biblical Texts in Their Textual and Situational Contexts. Essays in Honor of Lars Hartman*, edited by T. Fornberg and D. Hellholm, 901–10. Oslo: Scandinavian University Press, 1995.

Jauhiainen, M. *The Use of Zechariah in Revelation*. WUNT 199. Tübingen: Mohr/Siebeck, 2005.

Jenkins, F. *The Old Testament in the Book of Revelation*. 1972. Reprint, Grand Rapids: Baker, 1976.

Jörns, K.-P. *Das hymnische Evangelium: Untersuchungen zu Aufbau, Funktion und Herkunft der hymnischen Stücke in der Johannesoffenbarung*. Studien zum Neuen Testament 5. Gütersloh: Mohn, 1971.

Kowalski, B. *Die Rezeption des Propheten Ezechiel in der Offenbarung des Johannes*. SBB 52. Stuttgart: Katholisches Bibelwerk, 2004.

———. "Die Rezeption des Propheten Ezechiel in der Offenbarung des Johannes." *Habilitationsschrift*, University of Innsbruck, 2003.

Lancelotti, A. "Il *kai* 'consecutivo' di predizione alla maniera del *weqataltî* ebraico nell'Apocalisse." *SBFLA* 32 (1982) 133-46.

———. "Il *kai* narrativo di 'consecuzione' alla maniera del *wayyiqtol* ebraico nell'Apocalisse." *SBFLA* 31 (1981) 75-104.

———. "Predominante paratassi nella narrativa ebraizzante dell'Apocalisse." *SBFLA* 30 (1980) 303-16.

———. *Sintassi ebraica nel greco dell'Apocalisse, I. Uso delle forme verbali*. Collectio Assiniensis 1. Assisi: Studio teologico "Porziuncola," 1964.

Lee, P. *The New Jerusalem in the Book of Revelation: A Study of Revelation 21-22 in the Light of its Background in Jewish Tradition*. WUNT 129. Tübingen: Mohr/Siebeck, 2001.

Maag, V. "Das Gottesverständnis des Alten Testaments." In *Kultur, Kulturkontakt und Religion: Gesammelte Schriften zur allgemeinen und alttestamentlichen Religionsgeschichte*, edited by H. H. Schmid and O. H. Steck, 256-99. Göttingen: Vandenhoeck & Ruprecht, 1980.

Marconcini, B. "L'utilizzazione del T.M. nelle citazioni Isaeiane dell'Apocalisse." *Rivista biblica italiana* 24 (1976) 113-36.

Marcos, N. F. *Introducción a las versiones griegas de la Biblia*. Textos y Estudios "Cardenal Cisneros" 23. 2nd ed. Madrid: Consejo Superior de Investigaciones Científicas, 1998.

Moyise, S. "Authorial Intention and the Book of Revelation." *AUSS* 39 (2001) 35-40.

———. "Seeing the Old Testament Through a Lens." *IBS* 23 (2001) 36-42.

———. *The Old Testament in the Book of Revelation*. JSNTSup 115. Sheffield: Sheffield Academic, 1995.

Nicole, R. "A Study of the Old Testament Quotations in the New Testament with Reference to the Doctrine of the Inspiration of the Scriptures." MST thesis, Gordon College of Theology and Missions, 1940.

O'Rourke, J. J. "The Hymns of the Apocalypse." *CBQ* 30 (1968) 400-422.

Otto, E. "Νωψξ." In *TWAT* 6:994-1028.

Parker, H. M. "The Scripture of the Author of the Revelation of John." *Iliff Review* 37 (1980) 35-51.

Paulien, J. "Dreading the Whirlwind: Intertextuality and the Use of the Old Testament in Revelation." *AUSS* 39 (2001) 5-22.

Pfisterer Darr, K. "Ezekiel among the Critics." *CRBS* 2 (1994) 9-24.

Pontifical Biblical Commission. "The Jewish People and their Sacred Scriptures in the Christian Bible." No pages. Accessed March 29, 2008. Online: http://www.vatican.va/roman_curia/congregations/cfaith/pcb_documents/rc_con_cfaith_doc_20020212_popolo-ebraico_en.html

Porter, S. E. "The Language of the Apocalypse in Recent Discussion." *NTS* 35 (1989) 582-603.

———. "The Use of the Old Testament in the New Testament: A Brief Comment on Method and Terminology." In *Early Christian Interpretation of the Scriptures of Israel*. edited by Craig A. Evans and James A. Sanders, 79-96. JSNTSup 148. Sheffield: Sheffield: Academic, 1997.

Roloff, J. *Die Kirche im Neuen Testament*. Grundrisse zum Neuen Testament 10. Göttingen: Vandenhoeck & Ruprecht, 1993.

———. "Irdisches und himmlisches Jerusalem nach der Johannesoffenbarung." In *Zion—Ort der Begegnung, Festschrift für Laurentius Klein zur Vollendung des 65. Lebensjahres*, edited by F. Hahn et al., 85–106. BBB 90. Bodenheim: Hanstein, 1993.

Ruiten, J. T. A. G. M. van. *Een Begin zonder Einde: De Doorwerking van Jesaja 65:17 in de Intertestamentaire Literatuur en het Nieuwe Testament*. Sliedrecht: Uitgeverij Merweboek, 1990.

Ruiz, J.-P. *Ezekiel in the Apocalypse: The Transformation of Prophetic Language in Revelation 16,17–19,10*. European University Studies 23/376. Frankfurt: Lang, 1989.

Saebø, M. "Den ene Gud og Herre. Bemerkninger til det gammeltestamentlige gudsbegrep." *Tidsskrift for Teologi og Kirke* 48 (1977) 241–53.

Schaik, A. van. "De Apocalyps als Tekstmozaïek." *Schrift* 114 (1987) 231–34.

Schlier, H. "ἔλαιον." In *TWNT* 2:468–70.

Schrade, H. *Der verborgene Gott: Gottesbilder und Gottesvorstellung in Israel und im Alten Orient*. Stuttgart: Kohlhammer, 1949.

Schüssler Fiorenza, E. *The Book of Revelation: Justice and Judgment*. Philadelphia: Fortress, 1985.

Stemberger, G. *Einleitung in Talmud und Midrasch*. Beck'sche Elementarbücher. 7th ed. Munich: Beck, 1982.

Stemberger, G., and C. Dohmen. *Hermeneutik der Jüdischen Bibel und des Alten Testaments*. Studienbücher Theologie I,2. Stuttgart: Kohlhammer, 1996.

Stevenson, G. *Power and Place: Temple and Identity in the Book of Revelation*. BZNW 107. Berlin: de Gruyter, 2001.

Swete, H. B. *The Apocalypse of St John: The Greek Text with Introduction Notes and Indices*. 3rd ed. 1908. Reprint, Grand Rapids: Eerdmans, 1951.

Thoma, C. "Auswirkungen des jüdischen Krieges gegen Rom (66–70/73 n.Chr.) auf das rabbinische Judentum." *BZ* 12 (1968) 30–54, 186–210.

Tilborg, S. van. *Reading John in Ephesus*. NTS 83. Leiden: Brill, 1996.

Vanhoye, A. "L'utilisation du livre d'Ézéchiel dans l'Apocalypse." *Bib* 43 (1962) 436–76.

Villiers, P. G. R. de. "The Lord was Crucified in Sodom and Egypt: Symbols in the Apocalypse of John." *Neot* 22 (1988) 125–38.

Vogelgesang, J. M. "The Interpretation of Ezekiel in the Book of Revelation." PhD diss., Harvard University, 1985.

Zenger, E. *Am Fuss des Sinai: Gottesbilder des Ersten Testaments*. Düsseldorf: Patmos, 1993.

———. *Das Erste Testament. Die jüdische Bibel und die Christen*. 2nd ed. Düsseldorf: Patmos, 1992.

Scripture Index

Old Testament

Genesis

1	99
1:25–26	99
1:26	99, 128, 132
1:26–27	128
1:26–28	70, 80, 243
1:27	131
2	291
2:10–14	290
3	291
5:3	132
6:4	98
7:14	231
7:23	99
9:3	100
10	65, 78, 82, 84
10:2	94, 100, 101
10:2–3	58, 65, 94
10:2–8	65
10:3	94
10:4	65
10:6	94
10:6–8	94
10:7	65, 96
10:28	65, 96
18	147
19	70
19:24	99
20:12	16
22	178
25:3	65, 96
31:18	96
34:23	96
36:6	96
38	16
45:7–11	234
48:12	54
48:18	54
48:21	88
49:1	97
49:8–9	219, 220, 229
49:8–12	227
49:9	229
49:10	229
49:11–12	229
50:20–21	234

Exodus

1:13–14	7
2:11	98
2:23	98
3:2–3	131
3:10	68, 95
3:12	68, 95
3:14	xxv, 283, 285, 286
3:17	23
4–11	163
6:8	95
7–10	297
7:4	23, 68, 95
7:17	151
10	197
11:8	68, 95
12:17	23
12:31	68, 95
13:1–2	177
13:5	95
13:9	23
13:11	95

Exodus (cont.)

13:11–13	177
14:4	102
14:17	102
14:18	102
15	xxv
15:1–19	284
15:21	285
16	291
20:4–6	126
20:17	16
21:2–6	7
21:17	14
21:23–25	198
22:28–29	177
23:10–11	73
23:29	18
25:9	37
25:40	37
31:13	15
34:10	77
34:19–20	178

Leviticus

4:3	239
4:31	239
4:35	239
7:23–27	75, 76, 80, 103
10:3	102
10:10	13, 21
10:10–11	xviii
11:35	45
11:44	37
14:45	23, 45
15:26	16
17–26	xvii, 2, 3, 4, 9, 13, 155
17:13	11
17:15–16	74
18	45
18–20	14
18:3	6
18:4–5	13, 19, 21, 28
18:5	12, 14, 20
18:7	15
18:7–9	12
18:9	16
18:15	12, 16
18:17	12, 15
18:19	12, 15, 16, 20
18:19–20	12, 18
18:20	16, 20
18:21	71, 101
18:25–28	74
18:26	16
18:27	16
18:29	16
18:30	16
19:3	14, 15
19:8	15
19:12	71, 101
19:13	15, 16
19:16	15
19:26	11
19:29	15
19:30	15
19:31	45
19:34	13
19:36	23
20:2	13
20:3	13, 45, 71, 101, 105
20:5	13
20:6	13
20:9	14, 15
20:10	16, 19, 20
20:11	15
20:12	16
20:13	16
20:14	15
20:17	16
20:25	13, 21
21:1–3	12, 13, 21
21:1–8	21
21:5	13, 21
21:6	71, 101
21:7	11, 13, 21
21:10	13, 21

Leviticus (cont.)

21:10–15	21
21:11	12, 13, 21
21:14	11, 13, 21, 22
21:23	6
22:2	15, 71, 101, 105
22:4	74
22:8	21
22:9–10	21
22:15	15
22:32	71, 101, 105
22:33	23
24:20	198
25	10
25:1–7	73
25:18	24, 68, 95, 96, 97, 101, 105
25:19	24, 68, 95, 96, 97, 101, 105
25:25–28	10
25:31	96
25:35	7
25:36	12, 16, 20
25:36–37	19
25:37	20
25:39	7
25:43	7
25:44	7
25:45	7
25:45–46	13
25:46	7, 11
25:53	7
26	9, 13, 16, 17, 18, 25, 28, 61, 88, 224
26:1	43
26:2	15
26:3	25
26:4	9, 10, 12, 24, 25
26:4–6	24
26:5	24, 25, 68, 95, 96, 97, 105
26:5–6	12
26:6	13, 24, 25, 105
26:9	12, 13
26:12	88
26:13	23, 24, 25
26:14–39	25
26:15	88
26:17	13
26:18	18
26:20	24
26:21	18
26:22	11, 12, 13, 17, 18, 25
26:23	18
26:25	12, 18, 104
26:25–26	17
26:26	12, 18, 26
26:27–33	162
26:29	8
26:30	9, 44, 45
26:30–31	8, 9
26:31	6
26:31–32	87
26:32	87
26:33	12, 13, 17, 18
26:33–35	11
26:34	105
26:36	105
26:38	105
26:39	7, 8, 105
26:40	104, 105
26:40–41	27
26:40–42	26
26:41	105
26:43	88
26:43–44	11
26:44	88, 105
26:45	13, 22, 23, 83, 99, 105
26:46	25

Numbers

1:16	239
1:44	239
7	239
9:15	131
10:4	94, 100, 239
11:25	78

Numbers (cont.)

11:29	78, 79
14:3	68, 95
14:8	68, 95
14:24	68, 95
15:37–41	178
15:41	23
16:1–3	239
17:4	239
17:16–26	223
18:15–18	178
18:32	15
19:16	102
21:5	23
22–24	xix, 289
23–24	64, 82
23:14	64
24	64, 65, 263
24:7	64, 94, 97, 99, 100, 102
24:14	97
24:17	291
25:1	289
28:11	139
31:16	289
33:4	102
33:52	43, 44, 118
35	45
36:1	94, 100

Deuteronomy

1–4	40, 44
1:12	95
1:27	23
2:28	87
3:1	64
3:5	68, 96
3:13	64
4	35, 37, 40
4:1	20
4:1–40	39
4:2	39
4:5–6	39
4:9	39
4:15	39
4:15–18	38
4:16	36, 37
4:17–18	38
4:19	36, 38
4:25	38
4:25–28	39, 162
4:27	40, 166
4:28	36, 41
4:29	88
4:30	97
4:34	40
4:37	23, 40
4:47	64
5:8–10	126
5:21	16
5:31	77, 104
6:4–5	214
7:1	206
7:5	37, 42, 45
7:26	40
8:7	95
9:28	95
12:1	77, 104
12:2	37, 42
12:3	37, 42, 45
12:10	24, 95, 96, 97, 105
12:31	16
13:15	16
15:19–23	178
17:3	36
17:9	98
17:11	77, 104
17:14	235
17:14–20	213, 238
17:18–20	212
17:19	88
17:19–20	236, 240
17:20	218, 244
18:9	16
18:10	36, 41
18:12	41
19:17	98

Deuteronomy (cont.)

19:19	199
19:21	198
20:1	23
20:18	16
21:1	100
22:24	16
24:16	8, 147, 173
26:3	98
27:22	16
28	86, 224
28:26	25, 72, 100
28:29	88
28:36	36, 41, 87
28:37	87
28:48	87
28:49	221
28:63	88
28:64	36, 41
28:64–68	162
29:16	36, 40, 41, 45
29:17	36
30:2	88
30:3	68, 95
30:6–10	169
30:16	20
31:16	88
31:16–29	162
31:17	58, 104, 105
31:17–18	87
31:18	58, 104, 105
31:20	88, 105
31:21	95
31:29	97
32	xxv, 162, 284
32:1–44	284
32:7	285
32:20	58, 104
32:39	285
32:43	285
32:51	104, 105
34	266

Joshua

5:5	95
9:18–19	239
18:22	221
20:2	98
20:4	74, 102
20:6	98
21:44	104
22:32	239
24:6	23
24:17	23

Judges

2:1	23
2:18	88
7:22	69
9:15	221
9:37	68, 96
16:24	104
17:6	98
18:1	98
18:7	24
19:1	98
20:6	15
20:26	241
20:27	98
20:28	98
20:36	74, 102
21:2	241
21:25	98

1 Samuel

2	254
2:7	233
3:1	98
8:8	23
8:20	238
9:22	74, 102
12:8	23
12:11	24
14:20	69
17:34–36	218

1 Samuel (cont.)

27:5	74, 102
28:1	98
28:17	98

2 Samuel

7	224, 227, 232, 233, 235
7:1–16	229
7:5	236
7:7	235
7:8	236
7:18	241
7:19	233
7:19–29	236
7:23–27	236
7:23–32	236
7:24	236
7:30–31	236
16:23	98
22:28	233

1 Kings

5:5	24
5:12	221
5:13	221
5:22–28	221
7:2	221
8:16	23
8:25	241
8:48	105
8:53	98
8:56	98
10:32	98
11–12	235
11:1–8	209
11:34	212, 236
12:11	87
12:15	98
13:24–28	216
14:18	98
14:24	16
15:26	213
15:29	98
15:34	213
15:37	98
16:12	98
16:29–34	289
16:34	98
17:16	98
18:5	18
19:1	289
20:1	98
20:2	98
20:13	151
20:28	151
20:35–36	216
21:17–26	289
22:23	78
22:53	213

2 Kings

8:18	213
8:27	213
9:7	98
9:22	289
9:36	98
10:10	98
10:32	98
11:16	54
13:2	213
14:6	173
14:9	221
14:24	213
14:25	98
15:9	213
15:18	213
15:24	213
15:28	213
15:37	98
16:10	132
17:2	213
17:7	23
17:13	98
17:23	98
17:25–26	216

2 Kings (cont.)

18:32–35	179
19:7	78
19:10–13	142
19:35–37	69
20:1	98
21:2	16, 213
21:4–15	209
21:7	117
21:10	98
21:11	16
21:14	88, 104
21:18–25	208
21:20	213
22:3	xxiii
22:19	213, 231
23:4–20	61
23:10	74, 102
23:17	102
23:25	214, 231
23:26–27	2
23:26	143
23:31–34	222
23:31	215, 216
23:32	213
23:34	216
23:34–35	218
23:36	215, 217
23:37	213
24:2	98
24:8–16	222
24:9	213, 222
24:18	215
24:19	213
24:20	2
25:27–30	223

1 Chronicles

5:4	64
9:28	171
17:6	235
17:16	241

22:2	55

2 Chronicles

2:7–15	221
4:3	132
6:16	241
7:13	18
7:22	23
18:22	78
21:6	213
22:4	213
23:15	54
32:23	23, 83
33:2	16, 213
33:7	37, 117
33:15	37, 117
33:22	213
34:8	xxiii
34:27	213
35:26–27	213
36:5	213
36:8	16
36:9	213, 222
36:12	213

Ezra

3:7	221

Nehemiah

6:13	102
9:20	78
9:27	104
9:29	14, 21
12:44	55

Esther

3:1	64
4:16	55
9:24	64

Job

5:11	233
11:19	25
17:11	15
26:6	290
28:22	290
31:11	15
38–41	183
38:12–13	183
38:39—39:4	183
39:5–12	183

Psalms

3:7	55
4:9	24
8	243
10:9	216
11:6	70
17:12	216
18:28	233
22:13	216
22:21	216
22:25	105
26:10	15
29:5	221
38:10	105
43:3	72
46:9–10	73
50:13	103
66:7	83
67:7	24
75:8	233
78:19	103
78:68–73	232
78:70–72	235
79	63, 72
79:1–4	xix, 60, 62, 63, 81
80:9–20	225
84:12	77
85:13	24
87:12	290
89	2
89:2–5	229
89:3–4	235
89:19–29	235
89:20–38	229
89:26	54
89:39–52	229
92:13	221
98:2	23, 83
102	63
102:16	182
104:16	221
105:16	18
107:3	105
110:2	223
115:1	77
119:150	15
132:10–12	229
132:10–18	232
138:6	233
147:2	55
147:6	233

Proverbs

3:29	24
4:3–4	222
6:29	16
10:23	15
11:13	15
15:11	290
20:19	15
20:20	14
21:27	15
24:9	15
28:15	216
30:11	14

Qohelet

1:4–11	183
2:8	55
3:1–8	183
3:5	55
10:6	233
12:7	78

Canticles

3:9	221
5:15	221

Isaiah

1:1	208
1:7	18
2:2	84, 97
2:2–4	232
2:3	182
2:11	233
2:12	233
2:13	221
2:17	233
5	225
5–6	241
5:10	83
5:29	216
6	xxi, 297
6:9	163
7:18	96
7:21	96
7:23	96
8:17	104, 105
9:2–5	101
9:5	73
9:5–6	235, 241
10	66, 68, 81, 82, 84, 263
10:2	96, 101
10:3	67, 95
10:3–6	67, 82
10:5	67, 142
10:5–19	265
10:6	67, 73, 96, 101
10:7	96
10:20	96
10:24–34	265
10:27	25, 96
10:33	233
11:1	231, 235
11:1–10	232
11:2–5	241
11:6–9	241
11:10	96, 235
11:11	96
11:12	105
13–23	xxii, 187
14	xix, 72, 81, 264
14:2	101
14:4–21	72, 82
14:5	264
14:8	221
14:13	58, 68, 72, 94, 97, 100
14:25	99
16:1–5	231
17:2	25, 105
17:4	96
20:6	101
22:20	96
23:2	101
23:6	96, 101
23:15	96
24:1–3	228
24:21	96
25:6–7	75, 103
26:5	233
26:15	102
27:12	96
27:13	96
28	263
28:5	260, 261
32:7	15
34	76
34:2	75
34:6	103
34:6–7	58, 75, 79, 82, 103
37:7	78
37:24	221
37:36–38	69
38:1	98
38:19–20	257
40–55	143
40–66	77, 78, 91
40:1–2	125
40:31	220
42:1	78

Isaiah (cont.)

42:3	182
42:8	77, 104
42:23–25	2
44:22	169
46–55	125
47:8	24
48:11	77, 104
49:6	182
49:11	99
49:15	125
49:17–18	125
49:22–23	125
50:1	2, 125
52:10	23, 77, 104
53	263
54:8	104, 105
55	xxiii
56:4	15
56:9	75, 103
57:15	233
58:2	77
60	125
60–66	288
60:21	26
61:3	26
62	125
62:2	77, 104
62:4	18
63:17	163
66:5–16	78
66:10	125
66:12–13	125
66:15	69, 99
66:19	77, 78, 79, 104

Jeremiah

1:1–3	208
1:2	208
2:15	18
2:20	25
2:21	225
2:23	221
3:5	236
4:7	18
4:9	96
4:12–13	95, 97
4:13	221
4:27	18
5:5	25
5:8	16
5:24	24
6:8	18
6:15	16
6:22–23	58, 94, 97, 100
6:28	15
7:10	16
7:22	23, 178
7:25	98
7:30–31	178
7:30–34	74, 102
7:31	116
7:33	25, 105
8:8	177
9:3	15
9:32	96
10:9	96
10:22	99
11	284
11:11	87
12:10	225
12:11	18
13:27	15
14:16	102
15:21	88
16:14	23
16:17	105
18:16	18
19:5	116
20:5	104
21:12	87
22:10–12	216
22:13–23	218
22:24–30	214, 222
23:1–6	235
23:1–8	87

Jeremiah (cont.)

23:3	105
23:5	231, 235
23:5–6	241
23:6	241
23:20	97
24:10	18
25	263
25:9–10	87
25:11	18
25:29	99, 190
25:38	18
26:5	98
28:2	25
28:4	25
28:10	25
28:11	25
28:12	25
28:13	25
29:17	18
29:19	98
29:23	16
30:8	25, 96
30:10	25, 105
30:24	97
31:8	105
31:16	105
31:18	169
31:21	102
31:29	98, 143
31:32	88
31:33	178
32:35	16
32:37	24, 105
32:43	18
33	xxiii
33:15	98, 231
33:16	98
34:16	71
34:20	104
34:21	104
35:15	98
37:5–11	195
44:4	98
44:18	140
44:20–23	2
44:22	16, 18
46–51	187
46:10	58, 75, 103
46:27	25, 105
48:17	223
48:40	221
48:47	97
49	xix, 66, 68, 82, 84
49:12	190
49:22	221
49:30	67, 96
49:30–31	97
49:30–33	67, 79, 82, 90
49:31	24, 67, 96
49:32	67, 96, 101
49:33	67
49:39	97
50:3	18
50:20	98
50:25–27	58, 75, 103
51:29	18
51:40	103
52:2	213

Lamentations

1:10	77
4:19	221
5:7	143
5:21	169

Ezekiel

1	296, 297
1–2	296
1–3	xv, 114, 135, 296, 298
1–24	144, 148, 230
1–37	71
1–39	252
1:1	54, 129, 302, 305
1:1–3	xxiii

Ezekiel (cont.)

1:2	54, 210, 211, 220
1:4	129
1:5	132, 302
1:6	302
1:7	302
1:10	132, 302
1:13	129, 132, 302, 303
1:14	55, 132
1:15	129
1:16	132, 133
1:18	302
1:19	253
1:22	132, 302
1:24	302, 304, 305
1:26	129, 130, 132, 133, 298, 302, 303, 305, 306
1:27	129, 130, 131, 132
1:28	129, 131, 132, 302, 303
2	296
2:2	302, 305, 306
2:5	26
2:5–6	230
2:6	26, 302
2:7	26
2:8	26, 303
2:9	302, 303
2:10	302
3	146, 168
3:1	303
3:3	304
3:6	94, 95, 97, 99
3:7	26
3:9	26, 230, 302
3:11	54, 297, 304
3:12	99, 129, 302, 303, 304, 306
3:13	99
3:14	303, 304, 306
3:15	54, 163
3:16	169
3:16–21	173
3:19	55
3:20	55
3:23	129, 302
3:24	306
3:26	26
3:26–27	230
3:27	26, 307
4–24	190
4:5	253
4:16	18
4:16–17	4
4:17	7
5–6	114
5:1	306
5:1–2	3, 4
5:2	4, 54, 140, 303
5:5	65
5:6–7	177
5:7	102
5:7–10	198
5:7–17	123
5:8	23, 52, 83, 94, 99, 100, 105
5:10	8, 54, 197
5:11	19, 36, 40, 54, 118
5:11–13	3
5:12	12, 19, 54, 104, 303
5:13	52, 99, 140
5:14	95, 102
5:14–15	204
5:15	100, 101, 197
5:16	18
5:16–17	140, 303
5:17	12, 13, 18, 52, 56, 57, 99, 100, 101, 303
6	53, 61, 62, 63, 68, 84
6:1–7	4
6:1–10	61, 90
6:1–14	xix, 60, 61, 62, 63, 80, 81
6:2	52, 61, 94, 95, 100, 103
6:3	9, 18, 52, 61, 62, 95, 99, 100, 103
6:3–7	3
6:4	9, 44
6:4–7	9
6:5	9, 54, 102
6:6	9, 37, 42, 44, 95

Ezekiel (cont.)

6:7	62
6:8	12, 54, 95
6:8–10	123, 149, 176
6:9	126, 149
6:10	62
6:11	12
6:12	12, 19, 104
6:13	37, 42, 61
6:14	18, 54, 62
7	xxiv, 53, 102, 251, 253, 255, 259, 260, 261, 262, 263, 264, 265, 266, 267, 268
7:1–10	259
7:1–11	255
7:1–14	260
7:1–26	297
7:2	62, 263, 269, 272, 303, 306
7:2–10	255, 269, 272
7:3	41, 263, 269, 272
7:3–5	255, 256
7:4	19, 41, 54, 257, 269, 272
7:5	101, 140, 263, 269, 272, 273, 304
7:5–6	257
7:5–7	255, 260
7:6	101, 263, 257, 258, 269, 273
7:6–7	258
7:7	62, 259, 261, 263, 269, 270, 273
7:7–9	255
7:8	41, 78, 257, 270, 273
7:8–9	256
7:9	19, 41, 54, 257, 263, 265, 270, 274
7:10	101, 255, 257, 258, 259, 260, 271, 275
7:11	264
7:12	258, 259, 263, 264
7:12–13	4, 10
7:12–14	258, 260, 264
7:13	55, 258, 259, 264
7:14	258, 259, 264
7:15	12
7:16	149, 259, 260
7:18	149
7:19	259, 260
7:19–22	123
7:20	36, 40, 44, 116, 118
7:20–24	265
7:21	96, 101, 102, 263
7:21–24	263, 264
7:22	263
7:23	62
7:23–24	142
7:24	259, 263
7:27	62, 210, 211, 259
8	34, 36, 37, 38, 40, 43, 44, 46, 126, 140, 160
8–11	xv, xxii, 114, 135
8:2	41, 129, 130, 131, 132, 133
8:3	36, 37, 116, 117, 120, 121, 126, 129, 132, 306
8:3–6	121
8:4	120, 129, 131
8:5	36, 37, 116, 117, 121
8:5–6	37
8:6	16, 41, 55
8:7–12	8, 37
8:9	16, 41, 118
8:10	36, 37, 105, 118, 132
8:11	303
8:12	43, 53, 62, 118
8:13	16, 41, 55, 118
8:13–14	38
8:14	116
8:14–15	119
8:15	41, 55
8:15–16	38
8:16	36, 38
8:16–17	116
8:16–18	118
8:17	16, 38, 41, 55, 62
8:18	19, 54
9	144, 145, 147
9:2	302, 304
9:3	129, 304

Ezekiel (cont.)

9:3–4	297
9:4	16, 176, 303, 304, 307
9:5	19, 54
9:6	303
9:8	78, 145, 304
9:9	62
9:10	19, 54
9:11	55, 302, 304
10	xv, 297
10:1	132, 133
10:2	297
10:3	129
10:4	129
10:8	132
10:9	132
10:10	133
10:12	302
10:14	302
10:18	129
10:19	129
10:21	132
10:22	132
11:1	306
11:1–13	8
11:3	53
11:5–12	233
11:6	304
11:8	18, 36
11:9	197
11:10	104
11:12	177, 204
11:13	302
11:14	174
11:14–17	2
11:14–21	27, 176, 230
11:15	8, 26, 53, 62
11:16	12, 54, 234
11:17	13, 40, 54, 55, 62, 96
11:17–20	71
11:18	21, 40
11:19	78, 105, 146, 155, 169
11:19–20	27, 28, 79, 81, 175, 178
11:20	25, 177, 306
11:21	36, 40, 118
11:22	129
11:23	129
11:24	54, 131, 306
11:25	54
11:26	78
11:27	78
11:36	78
12	114, 225, 227
12:1–6	224
12:1–16	8, 224, 226, 236
12:2	26, 224
12:2–3	230
12:3	26, 54
12:4	54
12:7	54, 224
12:8–16	224
12:9	26
12:10	211, 212
12:10–13	224
12:11	54
12:12	62
12:13	224, 225
12:14	52, 54, 94, 95, 99, 100
12:15	12, 13, 40, 54
12:16	12, 149, 176, 224
12:17–20	8
12:19	62, 102
12:20	18, 62, 95
12:22	53, 62, 99
12:24	105
12:25	26, 100, 101
12:27	53, 95
12:28	100, 101
13	53, 57, 177
13–14	175
13:2	94, 97, 100
13:4	95
13:8	52, 94, 100, 198
13:9	62, 105, 177
13:10	57

Ezekiel (cont.)

13:10–11	99
13:11	52, 57, 99
13:12	57, 99
13:13	52, 57, 99
13:14	54, 57, 99
13:14–15	57
13:15	99
13:17	52, 94, 97, 100, 302
13:22	55
13:22–23	198
13:23	177
14	114, 144, 147, 160, 161
14:1–11	4, 145, 177
14:3–8	13
14:4	96
14:6	26, 55
14:7	96
14:8	13
14:9	54, 97, 101, 163
14:9–10	156
14:12	169
14:12–13	4
14:12–19	56
14:12–20	176
14:12–23	144, 294
14:13	12, 18, 54, 62, 303
14:13–21	17
14:15	11, 12, 13, 18, 62, 303
14:16	18, 62
14:17	12, 18, 62, 302, 303
14:19	12, 18, 52, 57, 62, 99, 303, 304
14:21	12, 13, 18, 197, 294, 303
14:21–23	176
14:22–23	149
14:23	198
14:34	177
15	223, 225
15:1–7	225
15:4	100
15:6	100
15:6–8	13
15:7	13
15:8	18, 62
16	26, 36, 53, 114, 123, 126, 139, 153, 161, 169, 170, 172, 173, 209, 296, 305
16:1–34	209
16:1–43	172
16:3	62, 139
16:5	54
16:7	304
16:8	172, 302
16:10	305
16:10–14	210
16:13	210, 305
16:14	52, 94
16:15	102, 296, 305
16:15–17	304
16:17	44, 116, 118, 127
16:20–36	118, 120
16:21	116
16:22	41, 304
16:25	41, 102
16:27	15, 54
16:35–43	170
16:36	41, 54
16:36–37	198
16:37	54
16:38	304
16:39	45, 304, 305
16:43	15, 41, 170
16:44	143
16:44–45	26
16:46	209
16:46–52	209
16:47	41
16:49	96
16:50	16, 41
16:51	16, 41
16:52	41, 105, 149, 253
16:53	105
16:53–63	71
16:54	27, 105, 149
16:57	54, 200, 204
16:58	15, 41

Ezekiel (cont.)

16:59	88, 172
16:59–63	170, 172, 230
16:60–61	172
16:60–63	27
16:61	27, 149, 172
16:61–63	105
16:63	27, 149
17	172, 213, 215, 220, 223, 225, 230, 236, 238
17–19	175, 214
17:1–10	223
17:2	105, 215
17:2–3	220
17:2–4	220
17:3	220, 304
17:3–4	222, 225, 230
17:4	231
17:5	62
17:5–10	220, 222, 225
17:5–21	225
17:6	223
17:7	231, 304
17:8	231, 253
17:9	94, 95, 97, 99
17:11–12	226
17:11–21	220, 222, 225, 227
17:12	26, 210, 211
17:12–14	226
17:13	62
17:13–18	225
17:15	94, 95, 97, 99
17:15–21	226
17:16	210, 211, 212
17:16–18	226
17:17	97
17:18–21	226
17:19	172
17:19–20	225, 230
17:19–21	233
17:20	99, 104, 225
17:21	52, 94, 95, 99, 100, 101, 104
17:22	220, 221, 222, 231
17:22–24	xxiii, 213, 214, 220, 222, 226, 230, 231, 244
17:23	231
17:24	100, 101, 200, 228, 233
18	xx, 8, 21, 53, 143, 144, 145, 147, 149, 150, 161, 168, 169, 173, 174, 175, 176, 177, 213, 214
18:1–20	145, 146
18:2	53, 62, 99, 143, 174
18:2–3	7
18:2–4	143
18:5	229
18:5–9	214
18:5–17	214
18:6	12, 15, 16, 20
18:8	12, 16, 20, 55
18:8–9	4, 20
18:9	20
18:10–13	214, 217
18:11	11, 16, 20
18:12	16, 55
18:13	12, 16, 20
18:14–20	214
18:15	11, 16, 20
18:17	16, 20, 55
18:19	145, 174, 229
18:20	7, 173, 174
18:21	20, 55, 229
18:21–32	146
18:23	55, 174
18:24	16, 55
18:25	53
18:26	55
18:27	55, 229
18:28	53, 55, 141
18:30	55, 170, 306
18:30–32	26
18:32	55, 174
19	56, 215, 220, 222, 223, 226, 227, 236
19:1	211
19:1–9	219

Ezekiel (cont.)

19:2–9	223, 229
19:3	244
19:3–4	215
19:4	56
19:4–9	212
19:5–9	215, 217
19:6–7	244
19:7	95
19:9	52, 56, 95, 100, 103, 211
19:10–13	223
19:10–14	223, 229
19:11	227, 229
19:14	197, 226, 231
20	xxi, 14, 26, 35, 46, 53, 83, 139, 153, 159, 160, 161, 162, 163, 164, 165, 167, 168, 169, 170, 171, 173, 174, 175, 176, 177, 178, 179, 180, 181, 182, 183, 184
20:1	160, 165
20:1–3	160
20:1–5	160
20:2–3	160
20:4	161
20:4–5	160
20:4–44	160, 230
20:5	40, 162, 171
20:5–9	69
20:5–10	160
20:5–17	161
20:5–26	162
20:5–28	209
20:5–29	160, 161
20:6	23, 62, 84, 96, 97, 162
20:7	36, 40, 118
20:7–8	162
20:8	23, 36, 40, 69, 78, 118, 139, 304
20:8–9	22, 162, 170
20:9	23, 71, 83, 99, 105, 152, 153
20:10	23, 162
20:10–26	212
20:11	12, 14, 20, 101
20:11–12	171
20:11–13	162
20:11–17	160
20:11–24	177
20:12	15
20:13	12, 14, 15, 20, 23, 69, 78, 304
20:13–14	162, 170
20:14	23, 71, 83, 99, 105, 152, 153
20:15	62
20:16	15, 162
20:17	54, 55, 170
20:18–21	162
20:18–26	160, 161
20:20	15
20:21	12, 14, 15, 20, 23, 78, 304
20:21–22	162, 170
20:22	23, 55, 71, 83, 99, 105, 152, 153
20:23	12, 13, 23, 40, 54, 162, 210
20:24	15, 162
20:25	14, 15, 20, 139, 156, 162, 177
20:25–26	156, 174
20:26	116, 118, 120, 156, 163, 177, 180
20:27	104, 105
20:27–29	160, 161, 162
20:28	62, 121, 162
20:29	162, 174
20:30	26, 36, 40, 126, 143
20:30–31	118, 160
20:31	36, 42, 116, 118, 120, 163, 167, 180
20:32	26, 36, 41, 53, 165, 166, 167, 174, 204
20:32–38	160, 165, 166, 167
20:32–44	160, 167

Ezekiel (cont.)

20:32–49	165
20:33	29, 40, 54, 69, 78, 211
20:33–38	165, 166, 167
20:33–44	27, 71
20:34	13, 40, 54, 55, 69, 78, 105
20:35	99, 305
20:36	99
20:37	171
20:38	62, 167, 171
20:39	101, 105, 153, 161, 166, 167, 174, 175, 180
20:39–44	160, 166, 167
20:40	62, 99, 167, 168
20:40–44	146, 166, 167
20:41	13, 23, 40, 54, 55, 71, 83, 99, 105, 166
20:42	52, 62, 99
20:43	27, 149, 167
20:44	71, 153, 166, 168, 170, 179
20:49	53
21	114, 148
21:2	52, 94
21:3–4	176
21:5	191
21:7	52, 62, 94
21:8	52, 62, 94, 100, 148
21:8–9	8
21:9	148
21:10	55
21:12	101
21:14	52, 94, 97, 100, 302
21:14–19	297
21:16	52, 302
21:16–17	227
21:17	211
21:19	302
21:22	100, 101
21:24	211
21:26	99, 211
21:29	54, 227
21:29–32	227
21:30	211, 212, 227, 228
21:30–32	227, 228
21:32	228, 229
21:33	52, 94, 97, 100
21:35	55
21:36	52, 78
21:37	100, 101
22	14, 175
22:1–5	123
22:2	14, 161
22:3	4
22:4	204
22:4–5	14
22:6	4, 211
22:7	14, 15
22:7–8	15
22:7–12	14
22:8	15
22:9	11, 15
22:10	15, 54
22:10–11	12
22:11	15, 16, 20
22:12	16, 20
22:14	100, 101
22:14–15	14
22:15	12, 13, 40, 54
22:16	23, 52, 83, 99, 101, 104, 105
22:19–22	198
22:21	52, 99
22:22	69, 304
22:24	62, 102
22:25	211
22:26	12, 13, 15, 102
22:29	62, 102, 176
22:30	62, 176
22:31	52, 78, 99, 304
23	114, 123, 126, 153, 161, 169, 173, 209, 296, 305
23:2	162
23:2–21	210
23:3	139, 304
23:4	209
23:6	94, 97

Ezekiel (cont.)

Reference	Pages
23:8	139
23:10	54
23:12	52, 94, 97
23:14	44, 116, 118, 127
23:15	133
23:18	54
23:19	305
23:21	15
23:23	94, 97
23:24	73, 94, 101, 229
23:25	104, 304, 305
23:26	305
23:27	15
23:29	15, 54, 304, 305
23:30	204
23:31	304
23:34	100, 101
23:35	15
23:36	161
23:37	116, 118, 120
23:38	15, 84, 96, 97
23:39	84, 96, 97
23:42	102
23:44	15
23:45	305
23:46	94
23:47	94
23:48	15, 62
23:49	15
24	114, 153
24:1	189
24:2	211
24:3	26
24:3–14	123
24:4	102
24:5	102
24:6	304, 305
24:7	11, 305
24:8	11, 99
24:10	102
24:13	15
24:14	55, 100, 101
24:15–24	123
24:16	153
24:21	3, 104, 263
24:23	3, 7
24:24	101
24:26	84, 96, 97
24:27	84, 96, 97
25	191, 192
25–32	83, 182, 187, 188, 190, 191, 197, 198, 199, 202, 205, 206
25:1–7	188, 199
25:1–17	189, 190
25:1—26:6	193
25:1—28:23	191
25:2	52, 94, 304
25:3	54, 62, 200
25:4	198
25:5	202
25:6	62
25:7	54, 202
25:8	53, 154
25:8–11	188, 199
25:10	198, 201
25:11	202
25:12–14	188, 199
25:13	12, 18, 54, 95, 104
25:14	97, 101, 198, 202
25:15–17	188, 199
25:16	54
25:17	202
26	192, 193
26–27	296
26–28	294, 298
26–32	189
26:1	189
26:1–6	200
26:1–21	190
26:1—28:19	188
26:2	53, 95
26:3	52, 83, 94, 100
26:4–5	192
26:5	100, 101
26:6	202

Ezekiel (cont.)

26:7	94, 95, 97, 99, 103, 204, 211
26:7–13	192
26:8	94, 101
26:9	45
26:12	45
26:13	102, 295, 305
26:14	100, 101, 192, 295
26:15–18	191, 201
26:15–21	192
26:16	211, 305
26:16–18	297
26:19	95, 193, 305
26:20	95
26:21	191, 305
27	65, 191, 193
27:1–36	190, 191
27:3	52, 193
27:3–5	193
27:5	221
27:7	305
27:10	52, 65, 94
27:12	52, 65, 305
27:12–25	296
27:13	305
27:14	65, 94
27:15	55, 65
27:17	62, 305
27:18	305
27:21	211
27:22	305
27:22–23	65
27:26–36	193
27:27	95, 305
27:27–29	305
27:28–36	201
27:29–34	297
27:29–35	297
27:30	305
27:31	305
27:32	305
27:33	94, 95, 97, 99, 211, 305
27:33–35	305
27:34	95
27:35	101, 211
27:36	191
28	191, 193
28:1–10	190, 193, 200
28:2	53, 239
28:2–10	200
28:9	53
28:10	100, 101
28:11–19	190, 191, 193
28:12	211, 239
28:12–15	193
28:13	302, 305, 306
28:16–19	193
28:17	200
28:19	191, 201
28:20–23	188, 190, 194
28:21	52, 94
28:22	52, 94, 100, 102, 105, 155, 202, 203
28:23	18, 52, 56, 57, 99, 202
28:24	200
28:24–26	191, 194, 203, 204, 205
28:25	23, 54, 55, 60, 62, 69, 83, 97, 99, 105
28:25–26	xix, 11, 27, 60, 61, 63, 81, 90, 105
28:26	24, 60, 95, 96, 97, 101, 104, 105, 200, 203
29	56, 72, 191, 195
29–32	189, 194
29:1	189
29:1–16	190, 194, 201
29:1—32:32	188, 191
29:2	52, 53, 94, 211
29:3	52, 56, 94, 100, 211, 304
29:4	52, 56, 94
29:4–5	56
29:5	72, 96, 100
29:6	202
29:6–9	194, 200
29:8	12, 18

Ezekiel (cont.)

29:9	18, 53, 95, 202
29:9–12	200
29:9–16	194
29:10	18, 52, 94, 95, 100
29:12	12, 13, 18, 40, 54, 95
29:13	54, 55
29:13–16	194
29:14	55
29:15	201, 253
29:16	202, 203
29:17	189
29:17–21	189, 190, 194, 204
29:18	211
29:19	73, 96, 101, 102, 211
29:21	84, 96, 97
30	102
30:1–5	195, 204
30:1–9	195
30:1–19	191, 195
30:2	52, 94, 97, 100
30:3	195
30:4–5	94
30:5	94, 104, 195
30:6	104
30:6–9	195
30:7	95
30:8	202
30:9	25, 84, 94, 96, 97, 101, 195, 227
30:10	211
30:10–12	195
30:12	100, 101, 163
30:13	211
30:13–19	195
30:14	163
30:15	78, 304
30:17	104
30:18	25, 95, 97
30:19	202
30:20	189
30:20–26	191, 195
30:21	52, 211
30:22	100, 211
30:23	12, 13, 40, 54
30:24	211
30:25	54, 198, 202, 211
30:26	12, 13, 40, 54, 202
31	223
31–32	192
31:1	189
31:1–18	191, 196, 201, 232
31:2	102, 211
31:3	221
31:6	83
31:8	302
31:9	302
31:10	196, 221
31:11	196
31:14	221
31:15–16	221
31:18	102, 196
32	102, 189, 191
32:1	189
32:1–16	191, 197
32:2	197, 211
32:3	94, 95, 97, 99
32:7	95, 97, 303
32:7–8	197
32:9	94, 95, 97, 99
32:9–10	197
32:10	94, 95, 97, 99, 163, 211
32:11	211
32:11–16	197
32:12	104
32:15	18, 202
32:17	189
32:17–32	191, 197
32:20	104
32:22	102, 104
32:23	102, 104
32:23–30	201
32:24	104
32:25	102
32:26	65, 94, 100, 102
32:29	211
32:32	201

Ezekiel (cont.)

32:33	95
32:38	95
33	146, 168, 177
33–48	29
33:1	169
33:1–9	173
33:2	18, 62, 102
33:3	62
33:9	55
33:10	7, 21
33:11	26, 55
33:12	55
33:14	55, 229
33:15	14, 21, 55
33:16	229
33:18	55
33:19	55, 229
33:20	53, 105
33:21	54, 123, 189
33:23	52, 96
33:24	2, 52, 53, 62, 95, 99
33:25	45, 62
33:26	16, 20, 62
33:27	12, 19, 52, 57, 95, 96, 99, 104, 302, 303
33:28	18, 52, 62, 100, 102, 103
33:29	16, 18, 62
33:33	101
34	235, 240
34–37	294
34:1–6	25
34:1–10	235, 243
34:1–31	234
34:1—39:24	294
34:2	52, 94, 97, 100
34:2–6	218, 243
34:2–10	209
34:3	103
34:4	7, 11, 55, 105
34:5	54, 219
34:6	54
34:8	87
34:10	218, 244
34:11–16	27
34:12	54
34:13	13, 52, 55, 62, 95, 100, 103, 105
34:14	52, 95, 100, 103
34:16	105
34:17–22	147
34:21	54
34:22–24	xxiii, 234, 237
34:23	146, 210, 302, 303, 306
34:23–24	212, 226, 232, 234, 242
34:23–31	27, 236
34:24	100, 101, 210, 211, 235, 236
34:25	12, 13, 24, 25, 62, 96, 97, 101, 105, 171, 235
34:25–28	24, 25, 28
34:26	9, 24, 25, 55, 96
34:26–27	9
34:27	12, 24, 25, 62
34:28	12, 24, 25, 62, 95, 96, 97, 101, 105
34:28–29	204
34:29	26, 62, 105
34:30	104, 105
34:30–31	236
35	83, 188
35:2	52, 94
35:3	52, 54, 94, 95, 100
35:6	304
35:7	55, 102
35:8	99, 104
35:9	55
35:10	53, 62, 154
35:12	52, 95, 100, 103
36	61, 89, 155, 156, 179, 180, 182, 204
36:1	52, 61, 64, 65, 97, 100, 103
36:1–7	200
36:2	53, 105
36:3	52, 94, 97, 100
36:4	52, 61, 95, 100, 103

Ezekiel (cont.)

36:5	62, 97
36:5–6	52, 99
36:6	52, 62, 94, 95, 97, 99, 100, 105
36:7	105
36:8	52, 61, 94, 95, 97, 99, 100, 101, 103
36:8–15	27
36:9	13, 52, 94, 95, 97, 99, 100
36:10	95, 101
36:11	12
36:12	97, 101
36:12–15	18
36:15	94, 95, 97, 99
36:16	170, 179
36:16–23	179
36:17	62, 102, 105, 124
36:17–19	170
36:18	62, 78, 304, 305
36:19	12, 13, 40, 54, 179
36:20	22, 23, 101, 105, 153, 154, 179, 203
36:20–23	71
36:20–32	154
36:21	101, 105, 153
36:21–30	46
36:22	27, 94, 95, 97, 99, 101, 105, 124, 146, 152, 153, 154, 156, 170, 179
36:22–23	22
36:22–32	149
36:22–38	27
36:23	23, 52, 69, 97, 99, 101, 104, 105, 152, 153, 154, 155
36:23–38	55, 79, 89, 175
36:24	13, 55, 62
36:25	46, 152
36:26	152, 169
36:26–27	79, 146, 155, 156, 175, 178
36:27	25, 28, 152, 155, 177
36:28	62
36:30	24
36:31	27, 105, 149, 155
36:32	27, 146, 149, 153, 170, 179
36:33	101
36:34	18, 62, 101
36:35	62
36:36	97, 100, 101
37	xix, 27, 114, 129, 146, 159, 295, 300
37–48	xxv, 295, 296
37:1	105, 304
37:1–14	102
37:3	295, 303, 306
37:4	94, 97, 100
37:5	105, 304
37:6	105
37:8	105
37:9	52, 94, 97, 100, 105
37:10	97, 105, 304, 306
37:11	26, 146, 204
37:12	52, 62, 94, 97, 100, 102, 146
37:13	102, 146
37:13–14	29
37:14	62, 78, 79, 81, 100, 101, 105
37:15–24	235
37:15–28	114, 124, 146, 237
37:16–28	237
37:21	13, 62, 103
37:21–24	237
37:21–28	85, 237
37:22	52, 62, 95, 100, 103, 146, 209, 211, 237, 239
37:22–24	242
37:22–25	xxiii, 237
37:23	36, 40, 118, 237, 239
37:23–24	239
37:23–25	234
37:24	25, 146, 177, 210, 211, 226, 237, 239, 240
37:24–25	212, 232, 236

Ezekiel (cont.)

37:24–28	237
37:25	62, 210, 211, 226, 237, 239
37:26	13, 171, 297
37:26–28	146
37:27	234, 237, 297
37:28	52, 97, 101, 104
38	72, 84, 294, 297
38–39	xv, xix, 11, 50, 53, 62, 68, 93, 188, 282, 294, 295, 296, 297
38:1	94
38:1–6	63, 82, 84
38:1–39:10	295
38:2	52, 94, 211, 239, 306
38:2–3	58
38:2–4	71
38:2–6	65
38:3	52, 94, 211, 239
38:3–9	62
38:4	52, 55, 56, 62, 73, 94, 103, 304, 305, 306
38:4–5	57
38:5	52, 94
38:5–6	65
38:6	52, 58, 72, 94
38:7	95, 304, 306
38:7–8	71
38:7–13	66, 67
38:7–16	66, 68, 82
38:8	24, 52, 55, 60, 61, 64, 67, 84, 85, 95
38:8–9	66
38:9	52, 67, 95
38:9–10	73
38:10	67, 84, 96, 99, 102
38:10–12	53
38:11	24, 67, 96
38:11–13	85
38:12	52, 55, 65, 67, 96
38:12–13	67, 73
38:13	52, 57, 65, 96, 304, 306
38:14	24, 52, 84, 96, 97
38:15	58, 72, 94, 97, 304, 306
38:16	23, 65, 66, 83, 84, 95, 97
38:17	64, 80, 98
38:17—39:10	295
38:18	52, 62, 84, 96, 99
38:18–19	69
38:18–23	62, 63, 69, 70, 82
38:19	52, 62, 84, 96, 99, 303, 304
38:19–20	70
38:19–22	69
38:20	62, 70, 99
38:21	99
38:21–22	57
38:22	52, 56, 57, 62, 70, 99, 303, 304, 305, 306
38:23	23, 52, 57, 60, 69, 71, 83, 99, 152, 155, 203, 304
39	63, 71, 84, 294, 297
39:1	52, 94, 100, 211, 239
39:1–2	71
39:1–8	71, 73, 82
39:2	55, 58, 62, 72, 100
39:3	100
39:3–6	71, 72
39:4	52, 61, 72, 100, 295, 306
39:5	100
39:6	24, 57, 72, 101
39:7	52, 57, 97, 101, 153
39:7–8	84
39:8	101
39:9	57, 73, 101
39:9–10	62, 73
39:9–16	73, 82
39:10	101
39:11	74, 96, 102
39:11–16	62, 73, 74, 295
39:12	57, 102
39:13	102
39:14	57, 102
39:15	74, 102
39:16	102
39:17	52, 61, 103, 306

Ezekiel (cont.)

39:17–20	58, 62, 74, 75, 76, 82, 295
39:17–24	73
39:18	57, 103, 211, 306
39:19	103
39:20	103, 306
39:21	54, 90, 77, 104
39:21–29	72, 76, 82, 84, 85
39:22	57, 60, 62, 104
39:23	52, 54, 87, 104
39:24	104
39:25	60, 105, 153
39:25–29	294
39:26	24, 27, 60, 62, 105
39:27	23, 55, 60, 83, 105
39:28	54, 55, 57, 60, 62, 85, 105
39:29	78, 81, 105, 304
40–48	xix, xx, xxii, xxiii, 21, 52, 83, 114, 124, 125, 135, 139, 146, 212, 241, 288, 294, 295, 296, 299
40:1	54, 306
40:2	62, 129
40:3	132, 304
40:4	52, 94
40:5	304, 306
40:47	304
41:1	304
41:4	306
41:21	132
42:11	132, 229
42:16–18	306
42:16–19	304
43:2	129, 135, 302, 303, 304, 305, 306
43:3	129, 131, 135, 302
43:4	129
43:5	129, 306
43:7	101, 105, 211, 303
43:7–9	124, 209, 210
43:8	16, 101
43:9	115, 211, 303
43:10–11	149
43:11	135, 177
43:12	135
43:13	304
43:16	306
44	21
44:1	55
44:1–3	241
44:3	21, 211
44:4	129, 302
44:5	52, 94, 135
44:6	26, 230
44:7–8	21
44:9	297, 306
44:10–14	22
44:13	16, 149
44:15–16	22
44:18	22
44:20	12, 13, 21
44:22	11, 12, 13, 21
44:23	12, 13, 21
44:24	15, 177
44:25	12, 13, 21
45:1	62
45:1–8	297
45:2	306
45:4	62
45:7	211
45:7–9	241
45:8	62, 211, 212
45:8–9	218, 243
45:9	211
45:10	303
45:16	62, 102, 211
45:17	211
45:21–25	241
45:22	62, 96, 97, 102, 211
46:1–7	241
46:2	211
46:3	62
46:4	211
46:6	139
46:8	211
46:8–10	242

Ezekiel (cont.)

46:9	55, 62
46:10	211
46:12	211, 241, 242
46:16	211
46:17	55, 211, 242
46:18	54, 242
47:1	55, 307
47:6	55
47:7	55, 307
47:8	307
47:12	291, 297, 307
47:13	62
47:13—48:35	297
47:14	62
47:15	62
47:18	62
47:21	62
47:22	12, 13
48:12	62
48:14	62
48:20	306
48:21	211, 241
48:22	211
48:29	62
48:31–34	306
48:35	124, 297, 302, 306

Daniel

2:47	182
3:28–29	182
3:31–4:34	182
4:30–33	221
6:26–28	182
7–11	262
7–12	xxiv, 251, 263, 264, 265–66
7:20–21	265
7:26	265
8	262
8–10	264
8–12	264
8:7	263
8:7–8	264
8:9	263
8:17	263
8:22	264
8:23	264
8:23–24	263
8:25	264, 265
9:4–19	89
9:12–14	263
10:14	97
11–12	68
11:10–13	264
11:13	264
11:31	264
11:35	263
11:36–39	265
11:40	263
11:45	265
12:4	263

Hosea

1:1	208
1:5	96
1:6	105
2:18	96
2:23	96
3:5	88, 97, 235, 236
5:14	216
5:15	88
6:9	15
8:1	221
10:1	225

Joel

1:1–14	79
1:6	97
1:15	79
1:16–20	79
2:1–2	79
2:2–11	79
2:3	18

Joel (cont.)

2:11	79
2:12–27	79
2:16	68
2:20	18, 68, 94, 97, 100
2:25	68, 97
2:27	68, 94, 97, 100, 101
3:1—4:21	79
3:1–2	78, 79, 81, 105
4:11	101
4:17	74
4:18	96
4:19	18

Amos

1–2	188
1:1	208
1:4	72, 101
1:7	72, 101
1:10	72, 101
1:12	72, 101
2:2	72, 101
2:5	75, 101
2:7	71, 101, 105
2:10	23
3:12	219
4:10	18
7:1	64, 94, 97, 99, 100, 102, 298
8:9	96
9:7	182
9:11	235
9:11–12	231

Jonah

3	182

Micah

1:1	208
4:1	97
4:1–3	232
4:2	182
4:4	25, 105
5:5	241
5:9	96
6:4	23
6:6–7	178
7:13	18

Nahum

1:13	25
2:12	25, 105
2:12–13	216

Habakkuk

1:8	221
2	263
3:3	264

Zephaniah

1	xix, 81, 82, 84
1:2–3	69, 82
1:7–8	75, 103
1:11	96
1:18	69, 99, 260
2–3	188
2:15	24
3	63
3:3	105
3:4	15
3:8	69, 99
3:8–10	63
3:9–10	182
3:13	25

Haggai

1:8	102

Zechariah

1:6	98
3:8	231

Zechariah (cont.)

4:3	291
4:14	291
6:12	231
7:13	87
8:6	98
8:12	24
9	188
9:9–10	231, 241
10:5	68, 97
10:8	88
10:10	105
11:1	221
12:3	96
12:9	96
13:2	96
13:4	96
14:5	99
14:6	96
14:7	96
14:8	96
14:11	24
14:13	96, 99

Malachi

1	182
1:11	182
2:11	16
4	266

New Testament

Matthew

1:22	283
2:5	283
2:15	283
2:17	283
2:23	283
3:3	283
4:14	283
5:17	283
8:17	283
12:17	283
13:14	283
13:35	283
21:4	283
21:5	287
21:42	283
22:40	283
24:15	283
26:54	283
26:56	283
27:9	283

Mark

1:2	283
14:49	283

Luke

1:70	283
3:4	283
4:17	283
4:21	283
12:10	283
16:16	283
24:25	283
24:27	283
24:44	283

John

12:15	287
12:38	283
13:18	283
15:25	283
17:12	283
19:24	283
19:36	283

Acts

1:16	283

Romans

5:14	297
9:33	287
11:26	287

Philippians

2:12	169

Hebrews

12:22	287, 290

James

2:23	283

1 Peter

2:6	287
5:8	216

Revelation

1:1	291
1:7	286
1:9–20	296
1:10	302
1:13	302
1:15	302
1:17	302
2:4	302
2:7	302
2:9	288
2:14	289
2:16	286
2:17	291
2:20	289, 302
2:23	302
2:27	302
2:28	291
3:7	289
3:9	288
3:11	286
3:12	287, 288, 302
4–5	296, 297
4:1	302
4:1—5:1	296
4:2	298, 302
4:3	298, 302
4:5	302
4:6	302
4:7	302
4:8	302
4:9	302
4:10	302
4:11	298
5:1	302
5:5	286, 289
5:7	302
5:13	302
6:4	297, 302
6:6	303
6:8	294, 303
6:9	288
6:12	303
6:16	303
7:1	303
7:2	303
7:2–8	297
7:3	303
7:4	286
7:5	286
7:10	303
7:13	295, 303
7:14	303
7:15	288, 297, 303
7:17	303
8:3	288
8:4	297, 303
8:5	288, 303
8:7	303
8:12	303
8:13	297
9:4	303
9:11	289, 290
9:13	288
9:14	290

Revelation (cont.)

9:17	303
9:21	303
10	296
10:1	303
10:2	303
10:7	300
10:8	303
10:9	303
10:10	304
10:11	297, 304
11	286, 287, 300
11:1	288, 304
11:2	288
11:3	291
11:7	300
11:8	287, 290, 304
11:11	304
11:13	304
11:19	288
12	289
12–13	285
12:1–6	287
12:3	304
12:7	289
12:7–10	289
12:14	304
13	297
13:6	288
13:15	304
13:17–18	284
14:1	287, 290, 304
14:2	304
14:3	285
14:6–20	285
14:8	285, 290
14:10	304
14:15	288
14:17	288
14:18	288
15:1	285, 300
15:2–4	284
15:3	283, 285, 289
15:3–4	284
15:4	298
15:5	288
15:6	288, 304
15:8	288
16:1	288, 304
16:6	304
16:7	288
16:12–16	295
16:14	304
16:14–16	297
16:15	286, 304
16:16	290, 304
16:17	288, 304
16:17–21	299
16:17—19:10	281
16:18	304
16:18–21	299
16:19	287, 290, 304
17	296
17:1	304
17:1–3	297, 305
17:2	305
17:3	305
17:4	305
17:5	297, 305
17:6	305
17:16	305
17:17	300
18–22	xxv, 295
18:1	305
18:3	305
18:7	305
18:9	297, 305
18:9–19	296
18:10	287
18:11	305
18:12	305
18:13	305
18:15	305
18:16	287, 305
18:17	305
18:18	287, 305
18:19	287, 305

Revelation (cont.)

18:21	287, 295, 305
18:22	295, 305
18:23	295, 296
18:24	305
19:2	305
19:4	305
19:6	305
19:8	305
19:11	305
19:11–21	295
19:15	306
19:17	306
19:17–21	282, 294, 295, 297, 300
19:18	306
19:19	306
19:21	306
20	300
20:3	300
20:4	306
20:4–6	295
20:5	300, 306
20:7	300
20:7–10	282, 294, 295, 300
20:8	289, 296, 297, 306
20:10	306
20:11	298
20:11–15	295
20:12	306
21–22	288, 295, 296
21:3	288, 297
21:5	306
21:7	306
21:9—22:5	296
21:10	286, 290, 306
21:11	306
21:12	286, 306
21:13	306
21:15	306
21:16	306
21:17	306
21:19	306
21:19–20	298
21:22	288, 299, 306
21:24	297
21:26	297
21:27	306
22:1	307
22:2	291, 297, 307
22:4	307
22:7	286
22:10	293
22:11	307
22:12	286
22:16	289, 291
22:19	307
22:20	286

1 Maccabees

7:17	63

Sirach (Ben Sira)

7:11	233
48:17	64

Dead Sea Scrolls

1QIsa	250, 257
1Q20 (*1QGenesis Apocryphon*)	90
4Q22 (4Qpaleo-Exodm)	51
4Q27 (4QNumb)	64
4Q47 (4QJosha)	254
4Q70 (4Q Jera)	257
4Q73, 74 (4QEzeka-b)	257
4Q169 (4Q*Nahum Pesher*)	80
4Q174 (*4QFlorilegium*)	89
4Q177 (*4QCatenaa*)	89
4Q182 (*4QCatenab*)	89
4Q385b (*4QPseudo-Ezekiel*)	52, 66, 89, 266
11Q13 (*11QMelchizedek*)	61, 89
11Q19 (*11QTemple Scroll*)	50, 86, 87, 88, 89, 91

Dead Sea Scrolls (cont.)

Damascus Document   89
Jubilees   89
Pseudo-Jeremiah   89
Songs of the Sabbath Sacrifice   89

Greek Papyri

Papyrus967 (LXX)   55, 79, 175, 209, 237, 239

Philo

De vita Mosis 1.48–55   289

Josephus

Antiquities IV.126   289

Rabbinic Literature

Exodus Rabbah 3   285
Sifre Numbers 131, 157   289

Other Ancient Sources

Pindar, *Olympian Odes* 13.21   220
Plato, *Phaedus* 278   255

Author Index

Achenbach, R., 3, 32
Ackerman, S., 37, 38, 48
Ackroyd, P., 1, 30
Aejmelaeus, A., 253, 276
Ahroni, R., 59, 106
Albertz, R., 1, 30
Albright, W. F., 150, 158
Alexander, P., 90, 106
Allen, L., 4, 30, 159, 161, 166, 171, 172, 185
Alster, B., 119, 137
Amiet, P., 217, 244
Andersen, F. I., 187, 206
Anderson, G. W., 4, 32, 250, 268, 277

Bachmann, M., 287, 308
Baentsch, B., 2, 3, 30
Baker, J., 141, 156
Baltzer, D., 77, 106
Barnett, R. D., 216, 244
Barr, J., 127, 129, 137, 251, 252, 276
Bartelmus, R., 159, 160, 167, 185
Bauckham, R., 284, 308
Bauer, H., 262, 276
Baumgarten, A., 85, 106
Beale, G. K., 286, 292, 293, 294, 295, 296, 297, 298, 300, 308
Beck, A., 201, 207
Beentjes, P., 12, 30
Begg, C., 217, 244
Ben Zvi, E., 70, 106
Ben-Porat, Z., 59, 106
Berger, K., 281, 292, 308
Berges, U., 288, 308
Bergler, S., 78, 106

Berlin, A., 163, 186
Bernstein, M., 81, 84, 90, 91, 106
Berrin, S., 68, 106
Bertholet, A., 261, 276
Bettenzoli, G., 155, 156
Betz, O., 68, 106
Black, M., 155, 157
Blenkinsopp, J., 1, 2, 30, 31, 79, 106
Block, D., xvii, 4, 30, 53, 61, 65, 106, 191, 193, 195, 206, 217, 222, 228, 234, 235, 238, 240, 241, 244, 261, 276
Boadt, L., 190, 195, 196, 206
Bodi, D., 200, 206
Bøe, S., 64, 65, 106, 282, 294, 297, 300, 308
Bogaert, P.-M., 257, 262, 263, 264, 265, 276
Böhl, E., 280, 308
Borger, R., 221, 228, 244
Brenner, A., 153, 157
Brettler, M., 163, 186
Briggs, R. A., 288, 308
Brin, G., 86, 106
Brooke, G., 68, 83, 86, 89, 90, 106, 107, 109, 254, 277
Brueggemann, W., 150, 158, 202, 207
Buchanan, G., 84, 107
Burrows, M., 2, 3, 4, 5, 30
Busse, U., 286, 309

Calloway, P., 86, 107
Cambier, J., 292, 299, 308
Caquot, A., 229, 245
Carley, K., 39, 48, 113, 137

Carmignac, J., 89, 107
Carson, D. A., 90, 106
Causse, A., 144, 156
Chapman, S., 266, 276
Chazon, E. G., 80, 89, 107, 108
Childs, B., 151, 152, 156, 266, 267, 276
Clements, R., 113, 137
Clifford, R. J., 232, 245
Cogan, M., 254, 277
Coggins, R., 113, 137
Cohen, C., 43, 47, 48, 49
Cook, S., xvii, 53, 59, 107, 143, 156, 214, 246
Cooke, G. A., 2, 21, 30, 212, 245, 261, 276
Cornill, C., 256, 257, 261, 276
Corral, M., 195, 199, 206
Cortese, E., 34, 48
Cox, C., 252, 276
Crane, A. S., 212, 238, 245
Crawford, S., 91, 107
Cross, F. M., 64, 110

Daube, D., 68, 107
Davidson, A. B., 144, 157
Davis, E., xvi, xx, 113, 114, 137
Day, J., 121, 128, 137, 138, 139, 157, 210, 245
Day, P., 123, 137
Deiana, G., 281, 308
Deissler, A., 298, 308
Denaux, A., 238, 246
Dijkstra, M., 228, 245
Dimant, D., 52, 80, 107, 108
Dohmen, C., 291, 299, 308, 311
Donner, H., 118, 137
Dorman, M., 107
Doudna, G., 80, 107
Driver, S. R., 2, 5, 30, 53, 107
Du Rand, J. A., 284, 308
Duguid, I. M., 212, 239, 245
Duhm, B., 79, 107, 280
Durlesser, J., 191, 206

Eichrodt, W., 117, 137
Eliezer of Beaugency, 47, 48
Emerton, J. A., 229, 246
Evans, C., 92, 110, 280, 286, 308, 310

Fabry, H.-J., 5, 32
Feist, U., 280, 308
Fekkes, J., 283, 289, 291, 294, 297, 300, 308
Fenske, W., 284, 285, 309
Fischer, G., 284, 309
Fishbane, M., 1, 4, 13, 30, 32, 59, 68, 72, 81, 107, 174, 185, 229, 245, 263, 276
Fisk, B., 59, 107
Fitzpatrick, P., 51, 59, 107
Flint, P., 51, 107
Flusser, D., 68, 107
Fohrer, G., xvi, 151, 157, 287, 288, 298, 309
Fokkelman, J., 12, 30
Forbes, A. D., 187, 206
Ford, D., 150, 157
Fornberg, T., 282, 292, 309
Fox, M., ix, 253, 276
Frankemölle, H., 288, 309
Frey, J., 286, 290, 309
Friebel, K., 237, 245
Friedman, R., 33, 48
Frölich, I., 89, 107
Frymer-Kensky, T., 46, 48

Galambush, J., xvii, 123, 124, 125, 137
Galling, K., xvi
Gangemi, A., 281, 309
Ganzel, T., 35, 40, 41, 44, 45, 46, 48
García-Martínez, F., 266, 276
Garr, W. R., 132, 137
Garscha, J., 82, 107
Gehman, H. S., 108, 237, 245
Gerleman, G., 59, 107
Gese, H., 21, 30

Giesen, H., 285, 286, 289, 290, 309
Ginsberg, H., 72, 107
Goldman, Y., 250, 276
Goulder, M. D., 281, 282, 309
Gowan, D., 200, 206, 232, 245
Grabbe, L., 59, 109
Graf, K., 2, 3, 30
Greenberg, M., xvi, 4, 8, 9, 21, 26, 30, 34, 37, 48, 51, 53, 108, 130, 137, 159, 163, 166, 171, 185, 189, 193, 195, 196, 197, 199, 206, 234, 261, 276
Greene, T. M., 299, 309
Gross, W., 171, 185, 235
Gruenwald, I., 52, 107

Haak, R., 59, 109
Hahn, F., 287, 311
Halperin, D., xv
Hals, R., 52, 108, 206
Hanson, A. T., 282, 309
Haran, M., 21, 30, 40, 48
Hayes, J., 1, 31
Hays, R., 59, 108
Hellholm, D., 282, 292, 309
Hempel, J., 298, 309
Hengel, M., 286, 290, 309
Henze, M., 68, 89, 106, 107
Herbert, E., 61, 90, 106, 108
Hess, R., 234, 244
Hölscher, G., xv
Hoppe, L. J., 212, 246
Horgan, M., 68, 108
Horst, L., 2, 31, 79, 109
Hossfeld, F.-L., 52, 63, 74, 83, 108, 235, 245
Hübner, H., 282, 292, 309
Humbert, P., 40, 48
Hurvitz, A., 33, 48

Irwin, W. A., 148, 157
Iseminger, G., 59, 108
Jastram, N., 64, 108
Jauhiainen, M., 282, 309

Jenkins, F., 284, 289, 309
Jeremias, J., 129, 137
Johnson, A. C., 55, 108, 237, 245
Joosten, J., 6, 31
Jörns, K.-P., 285, 309
Joyce, P., xvii, 8, 26, 27, 31, 53, 108, 113, 137, 139, 145, 147, 151, 157, 169, 185, 201, 202, 206, 210, 230, 245
Jüngling, H.-W., 5, 32

Kaddari, M., 38, 44, 48
Kaminsky, J., 147, 157
Kamionkowski, S. T., 36, 48
Kase, E. H., Jr., 108, 237, 245
Kasher, R., 34, 37, 38, 43, 48, 128, 129, 137
Kaufman, S., 50, 58, 86, 108
Keck, L., xvi, 166, 186, 246
Keel, O., 216, 219, 245
Keil, C. F., 130, 137
Kelle, B., xxiv
Kilian, R., 2, 3, 5, 31
Kislev, I., 43, 48
Kister, M., 80, 108
Klausner, J., 84, 108
Klawans, J., 46, 48
Klostermann, A., 2, 5, 31
Knobloch, F., 253, 276
Knohl, I., 5, 31
Koch, K., 164, 185
Kowalski, B., xxv, 282, 309
Kraetzschmar, R., 261, 276
Kratz, R., 175, 185,
Krüger, T., 160, 166, 167, 171, 174, 175, 178, 185
Kugel, J., 85, 106
Kugler, R., 5, 31
Kutsch, E., 161, 185
Kutsko, J., 38, 48, 114, 115, 116, 122, 123, 126, 127, 128, 131, 133, 134, 137

Laato, A., 213, 214, 231, 245

Lancelotti, A., 280, 281, 310
Lang, B., 161, 185, 186, 217, 220, 226, 229, 245
Lapsley, J., 28, 31, 149, 150, 151, 157, 169, 185
Lauha, A., 65, 108
Leander, P., 262, 276
Lebram, J., 265, 276
Lee, P., 288, 310
Lemaire, A., xvii, 59, 107
Levenson, J., 21, 31, 121, 135, 137, 212, 245
Levey, S. H., 234, 240, 245
Levine, B., 5, 31, 44, 48,
Levinson, B., [AQ: no pages]
Levitt Kohn, R., 2, 3, 4, 5, 31, 34, 36, 37, 40, 41, 43, 44, 46, 48, 208, 245
Lim, T., 61, 108
Lindblom, J., 144, 157
Lipschits, O., 1, 31
Lohse. E., 287, 288, 309
Luckenbill, D. D., 220, 245
Lust, J., 89, 108, 160, 185, 190, 206, 229, 237, 238, 245, 250, 254, 257, 259, 262, 264, 265, 267, 276
Lutz, H.-M., 82, 108
Lutzky, H. C., 117, 138
Lyons, M., 2, 12, 13, 31, 208, 246

Maag, V., 298, 310
Maier, J., 68, 108
Mandel, P., 109
Marconcini, B., 281, 310
Marcos, N. F., 290, 310
Marquis, G., 252, 253, 254, 276
Masson, M., 261, 277
Matties, G., 150, 157, 174, 185
McDonald, L., 266, 278
McKenzie, S., 34, 49
McLay, R. T., 251, 277
Meer, Michaël N. van der, 250, 278

Mein, A., xvii, 27, 31, 38, 48, 147, 149, 157, 169, 185
Meinhold, A., 182, 185
Melugin, R., xx
Meyers, C., 46, 48, 187, 206
Middlemas, J., 1, 31, 116, 117, 118, 119, 120, 125, 128, 138
Milgrom, J., 5, 6, 7, 8, 11, 27, 31, 35, 40, 48, 223, 246
Miller, J., 1, 31, 127, 138
Miller, P., 199, 206
Moenikes, A., 241, 246
Montgomery, J., 91, 109
Moor, J. C. de, 53, 108, 228, 245
Moore, M., xxiv
Moran, W. L., 229, 246
Morgan, D., 143, 157
Moyise, S., 292, 297, 298, 299, 301, 310
Muilenburg, J., 155, 157
Myres, J., 59, 109

Nebes, N., 167, 185
Neusner, J., 5, 31
Newsom, C., 191, 207
Nicholson, E., 33, 48
Nicole, R., 282, 310
Nihan, C., 3, 5, 6, 32
Noth, M., 34, 40, 49

O'Connor, M., 46, 48, 187, 206, 262, 278
O'Rourke, J. J., 285, 310
Odell, M., xvii, 26, 28, 31, 32, 51, 65, 109, 115, 117, 118, 120, 121, 122, 125, 126, 137, 138, 149, 157, 168, 186, 215, 217, 223, 246
Ohnesorge, S., 160, 161, 185
Otto, E., 3, 5, 32, 288, 310

Parker, H. M., 281, 310
Parker, S. B., 228
Parpola, S., 232, 246

Paton, L. B., 2, 5, 32
Patte, D., 109
Patton, C., xvii, 34, 39, 49, 143, 156, 214, 246
Paul, S., 43, 49, 51, 65, 107, 109
Paulien, J., 292, 310
Payne Smith, J., 262, 277
Pfisterer Darr, K., xvi, 143, 156, 166, 186, 214, 217, 246, 280, 310
Pickett, W., 40, 49
Pili, F., 229, 246
Plett, H., 59, 109
Pohlmann, K.-F., xvii, 83, 109, 159, 161, 166, 167, 169, 172, 175, 179, 186
Porter, S. E., 280, 283, 310
Pulikottil, P., 250, 277

Raabe, P., 195, 201, 203, 207
Rabenau, K. von, 82, 109
Rad, Gerhard von, 128, 138
Raitt, T., 2, 32, 146, 157
Rappaport, U., 80, 108
Ratzinger, J., 298, 308
Regt, L. J. de, 12, 30
Rendtorff, R., 5, 31
Renz, T., 28, 29, 32, 116, 138, 167, 169, 186, 190, 207
Reventlow, H. G., 4, 32, 155, 157
Robinson, T. H., 79, 109
Rofé, A., 238, 246, 254, 277
Röllig, W., 118, 137
Roloff, J., 287, 310
Römer, T., 159, 186
Rosenthal, E. I. J., 262, 277
Rowley, H. H., 155, 157
Ruiten, J. T. A. G. M. van, 283, 311
Ruiz, J.-P., 281, 296, 299, 300, 311

Saebø, M., 59, 68, 107, 109, 298, 311
Sanders, J., 92, 110, 266, 267, 277, 278, 280, 310
Sanderson, J., 51, 109
Satterthwaite, P., 234, 244

Schaik, A. van, 284, 311
Schearing, L. S., 34, 49
Schenker, A., 89, 108, 238, 245, 250, 276, 277
Schiffman, L., 83, 106
Schimanowski, G., xxv
Schlier, H., 291, 311
Schmid, H. H., 298, 310
Schrade, H., 298, 311
Schroer, S., 132, 138
Schultz, R., 3, 4, 11, 32
Schunck, K.-D., 238, 246
Schüssler Fiorenza, E., 291, 300, 311
Schwagmeier, P., 159, 171, 175, 186
Schwartz, B., 26, 27, 32, 33, 41, 43, 49, 168, 180, 186
Sedlmeier, F., 160, 161, 186
Seebass, H., 65, 84, 109
Seeligmann, I. L., 4, 32, 68, 109, 268, 277
Sellin, E., 79, 109
Shields, M. E., 153, 157
Silbermann, L., 109
Simian-Yofre, H., 226, 246
Skehan, P., 250, 277
Smend, R., 2, 32, 261, 277
Smith-Christopher, D., 1, 32, 149, 157
Söding, T., 299, 308
Speiser, E. A., 239, 246
Stavrakopoulou, F., 120, 138
Steck, O., 298, 310
Stegemann, H., 86, 109
Stemberger, G., 291, 292, 311
Steudel, A., 65, 79, 109
Stevenson, G., 288, 311
Stevenson, K. R., 125, 138
Stiebert, J., 149, 157
Stone, M. E., 80, 89, 107, 108
Strong, J., xvii, 26, 28, 31, 32, 115, 137, 168, 186, 202, 207
Swanson, D., 86, 109
Sweeney, M., xvi, xvii, xx, xxi, xxii, xxiv, 59, 73, 109, 163, 186

Swete, H. B., 281, 290, 311

Talmon, S., 13, 32, 65, 92, 109, 110, 250, 256, 277
Taylor, J. G., 119, 121, 138
Thoma, C., 298, 311
Tigay, J. H., 254, 277
Tilborg, S. van, 291, 311
Tooman, W. A., 63, 109
Toorn, Karel van der, 119, 136, 137, 138
Torrey, C. C., xv
Tov, E., 55, 61, 89, 90, 106, 108, 110, 250, 251, 252, 253, 254, 256, 257, 260, 267, 277, 278
Trebolle Barrera, J., 254, 255, 278
Trible, P., 130, 138
Tuell, S. S., 21, 32, 212, 246

Ulrich, E., 64, 110, 257, 266, 267, 278

Van Dyke Parunak, H., 195, 207
Vanhoye, A., 281, 283, 284, 294, 296, 297, 311
Vawter, B., 212, 246
Vermes, G., 90, 110
Vervenne, M., 266, 276
Villiers, P. G. R. de, 287, 311
Vogelgesang, J. M., 281, 311

Waard, J. de, 12, 30
Waltke, B., 262, 278

Wellhausen, J., 3, 5, 32
Wenham, G., 234, 244
Westermann, C., 65, 110
Wevers, John W., 229, 246
Whitley, C. F., 141, 157
Wildberger, H., 84, 110, 261, 278
Williamson, H. G. M., 90, 106
Wills, L., 86, 110
Wilson, A., 86, 110
Winer, G., 261, 278
Winter, U., 231, 246
Winton Thomas, D., 141, 157
Wolff, H.-W., 78, 110
Wong, K., 4, 32
Woude, Adam S. van der, 91, 110
Wright, B., 252, 253, 278
Wright, D., 46, 49

Yadin, Y., 87, 110
Young, F., 150, 157

Zenger, E., 63, 108, 159, 186, 279, 311
Ziegler, J., 251, 278
Zimmerli, W., xvi, 3, 5, 21, 32, 52, 74, 110, 113, 138, 149, 150, 151, 157, 159, 171, 186, 202, 206, 207, 214, 246, 256, 257, 262, 278
Zippor, M., 253, 278
Zwickel, W., 161, 186

www.ingramcontent.com/pod-product-compliance
Lightning Source LLC
Chambersburg PA
CBHW071146300426
44113CB00009B/1106